PRELUDE TO THE FIRST WORLD WAR

THE BALKAN WARS
1912–1913

PRELUDE TO THE FIRST WORLD WAR

THE BALKAN WARS
1912–1913

E. R. HOOTON

FONTHILL

Fonthill Media Language Policy

Fonthill Media publishes in the international English language market. One language edition is published worldwide. As there are minor differences in spelling and presentation, especially with regard to American English and British English, a policy is necessary to define which form of English to use. The Fonthill Policy is to use the form of English native to the author. E. R. Hooton was born and educated in England and now lives in the United Kingdom; therefore British English has been adopted in this publication.

Fonthill Media Limited
Fonthill Media LLC
www.fonthillmedia.com
office@fonthillmedia.com

First published in the United Kingdom and the United States of America 2014

British Library Cataloguing in Publication Data:
A catalogue record for this book is available from the British Library

ISBN 978-1-78155-249-0

Typeset in 10pt on 13pt Minion Pro
Printed and bound in England

Contents

Acknowledgements

This book has been made possible thanks to the kindness and assistance of a number of people to whom I would like to express my thanks. These include Dr Piet Kamphuis, President of the International Commission for Military History in 2013, who provided numerous contacts, and Dr Nicholas Evans, a fellow member of the British Commission for Military History, together with Lieutenant Panagiotis Gerondas, Hellenic Navy History Department, and Admiral John Paloubis, Hellenic Maritime Museum, for their comprehensive information on Hellenic Navy operations. Professor William Philpott, of the Department of War Studies at King's College London provided valuable advice as Secretary General of the British Commission for Military History, while Ms Carmen Rijnoveanu provided vital information on Romanian operations and Dr Dmitar Tasic helped by answering questions on Serbian forces and operations. But, above all, I wish to thank Dr Efie Paschalidou, Director of the Hellenic Army History Directorate, who provided not only information but also contacts and was unstinting in her support, for which I am eternally grateful. All errors of fact or of interpretation are my responsibility.

Preface

On the centenary of the First World War one of the most pressing questions being asked is 'Why did Europe go to war after a century of peace?'

With the conclusion of the Napoleonic Wars the rivalries of the continent's major powers were renewed and made more intense because that conflict had unleashed nationalistic and social fervour. Yet after the Congress of Vienna, there seemed to be an understanding, rather than a formal arrangement, that while disputes between them might degenerate into local conflicts, these would not be allowed to engulf the continent. Consequently, when the rivalries of the Great Powers erupted like a string of firecrackers into a series of conflicts between 1854 and 1878 (the Crimean War, the Second Italian War of Independence, the Austro-Prussian War, the Franco-Prussian War and the Russo-Turkish War of 1877–78) the remaining neutral powers were able to persuade, or to coerce, the combatants to a diplomatic solution.

To strengthen their hand in maintaining the peace the Great Powers began to weave a web of alliances and agreements. They were usually intended to be preventive insurance policies to ensure that no Great Power would be isolated during a crisis. Yet ultimately they would bring all the Great Powers into conflict through an interlocking system of commitments, although conflict was not inevitable. The agreements and alliances did not automatically place the continent on a war footing, for ultimately everything depended upon the perception of national interest by government leaders.

The Balkan Wars demonstrated this quite clearly, for they brought to a head the long Austrian and Russian struggles for regional dominance. Their sabre-rattling alarmed all the Great Powers and especially their key allies, Germany and France respectively. Conflict was avoided when Berlin and Paris made it very clear that they would not honour their agreements over a dispute in the Balkans that was outside the terms of their alliance. This forced their allies back from the brink, but barely a year later pledging their unstinting support to the same allies had a disastrous effect. Ironically it was the Balkan Wars that were the catalyst for calamity, for they exploited the weakness in the Great Powers' diplomatic relations to bring them into direct conflict.

During the nineteenth century nationalist fervour within ethnic minorities grew steadily and nowhere was it more ardent than among the Christian subjects of the

Ottoman Empire. Just as a volcanic crack in the ground can create a mighty peak, so the Christians expanded in bursts of activity to create new nations that aspired to ever more of their former master's territory. Yet every paroxysm threatened to collapse the continental house of cards by aggravating relations between the Austrian and Russian Empires.

The former feared that the success of Slavic Christians would encourage the splintering of its empire along ethnic and nationalist lines. The latter encouraged its fellow Slavs to pave the way for its ultimate ambition of controlling access into the Black Sea. Despite these mutually exclusive policies, even here the two empires sought diplomatic solutions that would avoid potential conflict. The Great Powers in turn sought to restrict the Christians' aspirations, and these restrictions irked the regional leaders who grew increasingly restive at Great Power interference, although anxious to obtain their support.

Ultimately peace depended upon the quality of the leaders, especially in Vienna and St Petersburg but also among the young nations of the Balkans. This was underlined by Austria's annexation of Bosnia-Herzegovina in 1908, undertaken largely for reasons of domestic politics. The Russians connived at this in anticipation of support for one of St Petersburg's diplomatic flights of fancy which was quickly brought to earth. The other Great Powers reluctantly rubber-stamped Austria's actions, which increased Russian distrust of Vienna, and led the Balkans' Slavic leaders to manipulate the Great Powers into accepting new seizures of Ottoman territory. This narrowness of vision was personified by Bulgaria's Tsar Ferdinand whose demands for dynamic military action ignored the implications for his key ally, Russia. As a result, St Petersburg's support switched to Serbia in a desperate attempt to recover diplomatic prestige after a decade of humiliating foreign policy failures.

The Slavic states and Greece would enter into a secret agreement, the Balkan League, which snubbed the Great Powers who then saw the upstarts rapidly secure most of the Ottoman Empire's European territories and bring Austria and Russia to the verge of war. The ruinous expenditure of partial mobilisation led Austria's leaders to conclude war would be more cost-effective. The Austrian 'hawks' clamoured for an attack upon Serbia, and one of the loudest was the heir to the throne, Archduke Franz Ferdinand, although such action would be anathema to Russia. By the summer of 1914, Vienna and St Petersburg, desperate to recoup international prestige, were set to collide over Serbia.

The assassination of Franz Ferdinand was the excuse Vienna had been seeking, especially as there were clear links between the assassins and Serbian intelligence. In their obsession with settling accounts with Serbia, the Austrian military leaders dismissed Russian reactions even when they included threats to mobilise. The Russians believed they could not afford to abandon their Serbian allies and the only remaining obstacle to war was the wilful man-child Kaiser Wilhelm II of Germany. His failure to rein in his junior ally in the Triple Alliance quickly saw Europe's chess game move to checkmate and in 1918 saw him betrayed by the army he so adored.

The diplomatic, economic and social factors that led to the Balkan Wars are sketched out in this book but only to provide outline background. For a more detailed diplomatic, economic and social history of these events, readers may wish to consult many of the works in the Bibliography. One underlying factor in these events was military insecurity due to the rapid pace of technological change, and this receives more attention in this work, which is primarily intended to be a military history.

In dealing with the European military background the author must draw the reader's attention to the detailed works of Herrmann, Stevenson, and Stoker and Grant. The influence of the events they describe in the Balkan conflicts was considerable, which is why this work—the first detailed English-language history of this little known yet key conflict—has been strongly influenced by them, although all errors of fact or interpretation are mine alone.

As I have tried to show, the Balkan Wars were a watershed between the Napoleonic Wars and the First World War, and combined many of the elements of warfare that evolved between 1814 and 1914. Despite the development of ever more lethal weapons, the armies were deployed, led and operated in much the same way as in the Napoleonic Wars. But in the Balkan Wars the influence of modern weapons began to shape both offensive and defensive tactics on the battlefield. There were indications of what was to come not only on the battlefield but also above it, with the first military use of aeroplanes in Europe. The conflict also saw the first European example of electronic warfare, the ramifications of which now extend into computer hacking. The aeroplane would also make its first mark on naval warfare, and the First Balkan War also saw the first modern submarine attack.

The lessons of the Balkan Wars battlefields were barely recognised when the Great War broke out a year later, the former being a prelude to the latter but on a much smaller scale. Both the First Balkan War and the Great War began as conflicts of manoeuvre and ended as conflicts of positional warfare, although often as sieges. Why then were the lessons not learned?

The military events of the First World War have been, and will be, examined and re-examined during the centenary and many observers will dismiss the efforts of the generals and admirals. Military leaders are often accused of trying to fight the next conflict in the same way as the last one, but this crass observation ignores the fact that experience governs us all. In 1914, the military leaders faced a totally new situation for which their experience was inadequate because it involved a whole raft of technologies—most of which had appeared only during the previous three decades.

Reliable, accurate, rapid-firing weapons—both artillery and machine guns—began reaching the armies in large numbers only after the turn of the century. The new artillery in particular revolutionised the battlefield, of which it became both king and queen. The new guns made First World War battles artillery contests, with the infantry playing a secondary role, or as the French put it, 'artillery conquers the ground, infantry occupy it'. The generals were slow to recognise this because their experience was largely of inaccurate, slow-firing field artillery, and consequently they initially underestimated the value of heavier ordnance. The Balkan Wars provided the first indication of the new battlefield, and while the French certainly recognised the need for heavy artillery, they had little time to make the necessary preparations. The presence of older generation ordnance both here and during the Russo-Japanese War made it difficult for generals to recognise that the battlefield was changing rapidly.

The Balkan conflicts saw a continuation of the later Napoleonic Wars tradition in which infantry used field fortifications. The use of trenches—especially noticeable in the American Civil War—became more extensive, but the Balkan Wars saw the change from linear defence to defence in depth which would shape the later battles on the Western Front. However, the Balkan conflicts also appeared to show that the traditional tactic of storming these fortifications with the bayonet was still relevant. Careful study would have shown that the reliance upon all-arm co-ordination, the concentration of resources and the use of fire-and-movement tactics were the keys to battlefield success. But there was no time for armies to make such assessments; indeed, in contrast to the Russo-Japanese War, in which several European powers produced detailed official military histories, military information was largely available only from civilian sources.

Only with hindsight can the changes that led to the deadly battlefields of the First World War and especially those on the Western Front be detected. This account—the first detailed military history in the English language of the two Balkan conflicts—aims to describe not only what happened on the battlefields but also what they meant in terms of military development. The apparent paucity of sources proved an illusion; there were more than enough both printed and on the world wide web to provide a detailed picture of what happened, while specialised printed sources helped to fill the gaps.

A major problem lies with dates and names. Different dates are often given for the same battle, as many of the sources, especially from Eastern Europe but also Greece, used the Julian calendar. While Athens converted to the Gregorian calendar almost a century ago, the Hellenic Army official history used by the author retained the original Julian calendar dates. With most of the world now using the Gregorian calendar, I have used this for all dates in this work.

This is relatively straightforward compared with the massive task of providing common place names. The Ottoman Empire naturally renamed many places, but its Christian subjects often retained their own names and where ethnic communities overlapped the same place might have several names. This is further complicated by the attempt by contemporary authors to render the names into a readable form. Thus the last Greek victory before taking Salonika was at Giannitsa, which is also written as Janitsa, Jennitsa, Jenitsa, Yaannitsa, Yanitsa, Yenice Vardar or Yenidje Vardar. I have opted to use modern names where possible, based on modern atlases, but have retained the names of a few older localities that were renamed a decade or so after the conflict to help understand contemporary accounts. This will help the modern reader follow the text, although there may be some confusion with regard to a few key locations such as Bitola (also called Monastir), Edirne (commonly known as Adrianople but Odrin to the Bulgarians) and Shkoder for a town usually referred to in contemporary accounts as Scutari. The index includes the place names used in the text, and for the reader's convenience some alternative names and spellings. However, as I am writing in English for the English-speaking reader I have anglicised many of the major cities, so that Beograd becomes Belgrade and Thessalonika becomes Salonika.

CHAPTER 1

Gathering around the Sick Bed

During the second half of the nineteenth century and the first decade of the twentieth century, Europe's chancelleries were preoccupied with the Eastern Question: the future of the Ottoman Empire, which was also called 'the sick man of Europe'. Territorial greed attracted neighbours around the sickbed and, when mixed with nationalist ambition and base vengeance, led to Machiavellian intrigues and ultimately to two short but bloody Balkan Wars.[1]

At the beginning of the nineteenth century, the Ottoman Empire extended westwards across the Middle East from the Caspian Sea. It held the Caucasus, the Crimean Peninsula and most of the Black Sea, including its gateway of the Straits (the Bosphorus, Sea of Marmara and the Dardanelles), while its boundaries in the Balkans were defined by the Dniester, the Danube, the Carpathian Mountains and the Adriatic. Nominally the empire controlled the North African coast from the Nile to Algiers, although in practice Algiers, Tunisia, Libya and Egypt were autonomous. By 1900, the Crimea and much of the Caucasus had been lost, while in North Africa only Libya remained under Constantinople's direct rule, with Egypt a *de facto* protectorate of the British Empire. In the Balkans the Sublime Porte's[2] rule still extended to the Adriatic but was restricted to a contracting strip of land in the southern region.

Officially the Islamic state tolerated other religions and under the millet (nation) system provided them with a degree of local autonomy. In reality only Muslims were permitted to own land, which turned the millets into super-ghettos whose Christian inhabitants were treated as second-class subjects, acting both as beasts of burden and cows to be milked. This made the Balkans an extremely volatile region, with the bellicose Montenegrins securing autonomy for their mountain homes during the eighteenth century. From the end of that century, social and political unrest increased under the influence of the French Revolutionary and Napoleonic Wars as the millet system proved too fragile to contain nationalist pressures. There were successful Greek and Serbian uprisings, the former with the assistance of the Great Powers, and by the mid-1830s the Porte was forced to recognise Greek independence and Serbian autonomy, although the last Ottoman garrisons in Serbia were withdrawn only in 1867.[3]

Reform and the millet system were diametric opposites, but both blinkered the outlook of young nationalists whose aspirations were largely confined within their own ethnic group. Both in 1839 and 1856, as the Porte tried to modernise the empire, all the Ottoman Empire's subjects were declared theoretically equal, which further undermined the millet system. But potential Muslim leaders made no effort to develop the necessary multi-ethnic political framework required as the foundation of a modern empire and this created a vacuum filled by narrow nationalist passions.[4] The complex ethnic nature of the Balkans proved another major hurdle, for the tide of migration had swept back and forth across the region for more than a millennium, scattering human flotsam and jetsam who were further divided by religion.

During the 1870s, the Porte's grip on the Balkans (for the region in 1912 see Table 1) was steadily loosened by a combination of factors resembling the fob watches carried by most contemporary European leaders. The casing and the winding mechanism were provided by the Great Powers, with Balkan nationalities acting as the intricate internal mechanism. This sometimes moved autonomously, sometimes in alignment and sometimes interacting, but always it sought to turn the hands in the direction of total independence.

The industrialised Great Powers of Europe sought to expand their influence by controlling this nationalist mechanism. Most were traditional diplomatic rivals, such as the Austro-Hungarian Empire, France, Great Britain and Russia, with fluid relationships in which they united to resolve a specific crisis then returned to separate paths.[5] When St Petersburg made a new land-grab in the Balkans in 1853, it discovered that the 'sick man' had powerful friends not only in Austria, its traditional competitor for Ottoman territory, but also in London and Paris. Together they forced the Russians to withdraw an army from the Balkans; then the Franco-British-Turkish alliance destroyed the great naval base of Sevastopol in the Crimean War (1853–56).

This reflected international concern over control of the Straits which most of the Great Powers preferred to be controlled by the weak Porte rather than one of their own. The British were especially sensitive to any threat to their imperial communications through Egypt's Suez Canal which London came to control from 1875.[6] In addition, London had very substantial financial investments in the Porte, the City raising £180,259,836 in loans during the two decades from 1854, of which only £938,541 was ever repaid.[7] France, Europe's leading continental power until 1871, had maintained close and privileged trading relations with the Ottoman Empire since the sixteenth century in a relationship that would last until the establishment of the Turkish republic after the First World War. The Anglo-French view prevailed, and the Treaty of Paris (1856) saw the Great Powers pledge to respect the Porte's independence and territorial integrity, this consensus lasting until the emergence of the German Empire in 1871 caused the European map to be redrawn.

Russia was the traditional foe of both Austria and Turkey, and during the eighteenth and nineteenth centuries steadily expanded at the latter's expense by exploiting its position as temporal arm of the Orthodox Church to interfere with the Ottoman Empire's internal affairs. St Petersburg's ultimate ambition was to seize Constantinople and control the Straits for strategic advantage. In the first decade of the twentieth century, 45 per cent of the nation's exports sailed from the ice-free Black Sea ports past Constantinople, including 87 per cent of Russia's wheat exports.[8]

During the first half of the nineteenth century, the Russians nibbled at the Porte's northern borders. Tsar Nicholas I told the British ambassador in 1853:

We have a sick man on our hands, a man gravely ill; it will be a great misfortune if one of these days he slips through our hands, especially before the necessary arrangements are made.

However, it was not until May 1861, during the opening days of the American Civil War, that the phrase 'sick man of Europe' first entered the language in the pages of *The New York Times*.

Russia's traditional rival was Austria, for whom the Balkans was a major trading region, which assumed greater importance after defeat in the Austro-Prussian War of 1866 ended economic ambitions in Germany. Vienna increasingly focused upon the Balkans with hopes of further expansion into the region.[9] Specifically it wished to expand into Bosnia-Herzegovina to secure its Dalmatian coastal territory. But with an ethnic mix just as diverse as the Ottoman Empire, Vienna did not wish to see minorities such as the Hungarians, Czechs and Slovaks follow the pattern of the Porte's Christian subjects and seek independence. Austrian desire for Balkan territory brought it into direct conflict with Serbia, which also wanted Bosnia to help it join Montenegro and create a unified Slavic state. The conflicting aims also increased tension between Austria and Russia, which, in the aftermath of the Crimean War, regarded itself as the Balkan Slavs' protector.

Yet Austro-Russian rivalries were soon overshadowed and influenced by the new Great Power, the German Empire, which was proclaimed in 1871 at the Palace of Versailles to symbolise the overthrow of France's pre-eminent position in Europe. Germany was now Europe's most powerful state, but in order to avoid an alliance of powers which might strangle the infant empire, Chancellor Count Otto von Bismarck secured with Austria and Russia the League of the Three Emperors (Dreikaiserbund) in 1872. A result of the strategic earthquake was that France ceased to support the Treaty of Paris and Bismarck encouraged St Petersburg to tear up the treaty.

Although it had little interest in either the Balkans or the Middle East, Germany now created a fiscal earthquake that had the gravest effects upon the Ottoman Empire. Berlin's decision in 1873 to abandon the silver standard precipitated a worldwide financial crisis known as The Great Depression. One effect of this was to weaken Britain's world economic leadership, for London's economic stagnation lasted until 1897. The fundamental problem, as in 2008, was unbridled financial speculation in both the United States and Europe. Another factor was the opening of the Suez Canal, which rendered obsolete the huge fleets of sailing ships that traded between Europe and Asia. They could not transit the waterway under sail while the prevailing east–west winds made it difficult for them to cross the Mediterranean, and this disrupted trade.

The impact upon the Ottoman Empire was especially great, for after the Crimea War it became dependent upon foreign loans as its rickety finance system slowly began to collapse. The loans were originally to fund the modernisation of the empire and extended into law, finance, education and the armed forces. They also paid for new postal, telegraph and railway systems, with £70 million alone raised in 1870 for railways. But while the Porte acquired the trappings of the nineteenth century it remained hampered by a sixteenth-century political system in which policy was decided by the Court and its provincial legates; indeed, the Sultan closed the national assembly in 1876. The reforms were opposed by the conservatives and the Islamic clergy who ensured that much educational time was spent learning Arabic and studying the Koran. Unfettered by this traditionalism, Christians received a broader education which helped them to dominate the empire's commerce and provided further fuel to Muslim resentment.

Ottoman trade declined as import duties were slashed and export duties were raised, with loans now needed to pay interest on earlier debts. By 1875, nearly 44 per cent of the Porte's revenues were needed to service this debt, and it became increasingly difficult to acquire new loans. Desperate for revenue, the Porte increased taxation and seized produce when money was not available, the burden falling most heavily upon the Christians, and ultimately food seizures created a famine. But it was to no avail. In October 1875, the Ottoman Empire suspended payment of the debt and effectively declared itself bankrupt.[10]

In the past the myriad fractious Christian ghettos had hampered unified resistance. The Balkans was a bubbling pot of some dozen ethnic groups, many of whom opted to follow Islam, while even the Christians were divided, the Orthodox Church alone being split into Bulgarian, Greek, Serbian and Russian elements each with their own patriarch. Mutual suspicion and hatred were obstacles to unified resistance to the Porte, while tensions in Albania and Montenegro were further aggravated by an obsession with vendettas. The ethnic problem was enflamed further after the Crimean War when the Russians reoccupied the Crimea and parts of the Caucasus, which led to the flight of up to half a million Muslims. Many settled in Thrace, Bulgaria and Macedonia where they were allowed to drive Christians from their lands and take their revenge. This wrecked Constantinople's schemes to neutralise Bulgarian nationalism with reforms; thousands of Bulgars fled to Russia, with the remainder restive and ready to make common cause with other Slavs.[11]

Trouble in Bulgaria had serious financial implications because it accounted for 20 per cent of the Ottoman Empire's exports, mostly to former subjects Greece, Serbia and Rumania. The spark that ignited this highly combustible situation was the crop failure in Bosnia in the autumn of 1874, followed by a harsh winter exacerbated by the high-handed actions of the tax collectors. In 1875, both Christians and Muslims in Bosnia revolted, which led to the usual cycle of massacre and counter-massacre as the Porte's forces brutally sought to restore order.[12] The savagery was a regional characteristic, which sadly continues into modern times, for revolts against Ottoman rule were not just attempts at liberation but also a struggle for survival in which failure led to bloody reprisals. Rebels did not expect mercy from the Turks and saw no reason to be merciful either to their oppressors or to those they believed supported them.[13]

While public opinion within Austria, France, Britain and Russia largely ignored Christian massacres of Muslims, those of Bulgarians by Ottoman forces inflamed passions, especially in Russia. But Russian pan-Slavism did not automatically lead to intervention for it might isolate Russia from its Dreikaiserbund colleagues, so St Petersburg tried in vain to persuade the Porte to implement reforms. Eventually the Russians intervened by proxy and encouraged a Serbo-Montenegrin invasion of the Ottoman Empire in July 1876 led by a Russian general. The Serbs believed that, just as Piedmont spearheaded Italian reunification, they would unite the southern Slavic peoples.[14] Before the invasion and to avoid isolation,

St Petersburg signed the Reichstadt Agreement with Vienna, committing both to co-ordinating their Balkan policies. There was a pledge that if the Serbo-Montenegrin forces defeated the Ottoman army, Russia would receive part of Bessarabia on the Rumanian border while Austria would receive Bosnia. Both powers also reserved the right to sanction border adjustments in the Balkans. An autonomous Bulgaria would be created only if the Ottoman Empire collapsed; its size would be restricted and it would exclude Rumelia.[15]

But within two months the Ottoman forces had smashed the invasion, reigniting pan-Islamic sentiment within the empire. Only Russian pressure prevented an Ottoman counter-invasion and forced a return to the status quo in February 1877, while a disappointed St Petersburg transferred support from Serbia to Bulgaria.

There was growing international support for an autonomous Bulgaria among the Great Powers, who sought to calm the situation. This support was reflected when their ambassadors in Constantinople held a conference that demanded sweeping reforms, although these were rejected by the Porte. Even as the ambassadors met, a new Russian agreement with Austria—the Budapest Convention—saw Vienna agree to adopt a benevolent neutrality towards Russian military intervention against the Ottoman Empire. In return, Austria would be allowed to occupy Bosnia, and Russia would ensure the war did not lead to a large Slavic state in the region.[16] The Porte's intransigence gave St Petersburg the excuse to declare war on Constantinople in April 1877 and strike into the Balkans. By 1878, supported by Balkan troops, the Russian Army had severely defeated the Ottoman forces and was closing on Constantinople, halting only in the face of demands by the other Great Powers.[17]

During the war Russian success on the battlefield led St Petersburg to support a greater Bulgaria, which became a reality at the Treaty of San Stefano in March 1878. The treaty, which also gave Montenegro, Rumania and Serbia formal independence, created a large and autonomous Bulgaria that included much of ethnically diverse Macedonia.[18] Such a Slavic power bloc under Russian influence was widely regarded as the thin end of the wedge where Russian territorial ambitions were concerned. It would clearly give St Petersburg an excuse for further interference in the Ottoman Empire, whose powers had clearly been reduced. The agreement edged Europe to war because Austria felt betrayed and Britain feared the proposed Bulgaria would be a springboard for Russian ambitions in the Mediterranean. Within the Balkans, the prospect of a greater Bulgaria that incorporated Macedonian territory alarmed both Greece and Serbia, who also had aspirations in this region.

To preserve the peace, and to demonstrate the new German Empire's diplomatic status, Bismarck argued that he was an honest broker and that his country had no interests in the Balkans, and he convened a Congress at his Berlin palace to resolve the situation. However, he was partly driven by self-interest, for he recognised that pan-Slavism posed a serious threat to both the German and Austrian Empires, whose substantial Slavic minorities might follow the example of those in the Balkans and seek secession. The Congress also posed a threat to the Dreikaiserbund, as it forced Bismarck to support either Austria or Russia, although he was aided by Britain's traditional antipathy towards Russia. A week before the Congress of Berlin met, London and Constantinople concluded a secret agreement that allowed the British to secure the approaches to the Suez Canal by occupying Cyprus. The British also supported both the Turks and the Austrians, for Lord Salisbury declared the San Stefano Treaty was a flagrant contravention of the principle of nationalities. In doing so, he set the scene for a Russian humiliation.[19]

In June/July 1878, the month-long Congress of Berlin began to rewrite the Treaty of San Stefano to redress the balance of power, and the resulting Treaty of Berlin (like the Munich Agreement of 1938) was loudly acclaimed at the time. Although Montenegro, Rumania and Serbia again had their formal independence confirmed, the Congress provided the new Balkan nations only token consultation and they were humiliated by the treaty, while the Ottoman Empire regained Macedonia and Thrace. Although Bulgaria achieved *de facto* independence, nominally as an autonomous principality within the Ottoman Empire, it suffered most from the new agreement. The Macedonia decision deprived it of 70 per cent of its new territory and saw half the ethnic Bulgarian population returned to the Porte, some in Christian-ruled Eastern Rumelia. The loss of Macedonia was a particular blow, but even Russia agreed the region's ethnic diversity meant that no single Balkan country had a justified claim to the whole territory. Even Greece, which had not participated in the conflict, benefited, as vague references to adjusting boundaries in the Berlin Treaty would eventually lead to it receiving southern Thessaly and southern Epirus under the Treaty of Constantinople in 1881.[20]

Austria's 'neutrality' was rewarded in July 1878 when it sent four divisions under XIII Corps to occupy Bosnia and the spit of land between Serbia and Montenegro, called the Sanjak (district) of Novi Pazar, although the Ottoman Empire would maintain troops in both regions for thirty years. The Great Powers, including Britain, accepted this, but the action was bitterly resented by Serbia and Montenegro as well as by Christians and Muslims in the occupied territories. The region was on a Christian religious fault-line, with Roman Catholics in the west and the Eastern Orthodox in the east. Many Bosnian Muslims were the descendants of those who had fled from Hungary at the end of the seventeenth century and had been joined by Serbian Muslims who fled Christian uprisings.

Vienna's furious new Muslim subjects rebelled, demanding autonomy, and were joined by most of the Ottoman garrison. Vienna had to increase its garrison from 72,000 troops to 268,000 (a third of the Austrian Army) before the rebellion was suppressed by October, although low-level guerrilla warfare continued. Meanwhile, thousands of Austrian bureaucrats descended upon the province where the Serbs, as Eastern Orthodox subjects of a Roman Catholic-dominated state, remained second-class citizens still subject to oppressive Ottoman land laws, and attempts to improve the province's economy fell foul of opposition from Hungarian landowners.[21] The occupation also fuelled Serbian suspicions of their northern neighbour's ultimate goal.

The Berlin Treaty satisfied no one and humiliated not only Russia, which gained little territory and lost considerable prestige through its diplomatic failure, but also the Ottoman Empire, which lost much territory. Yet Germany was the ultimate loser, for it was forced into Austria's ever-tightening embrace, while Russia's withdrawal caused the collapse of the Dreikaiserbund. This was briefly revived in 1881, but the perennial problem of conflicting Austrian and Russian policies in the Balkans led to its final collapse in 1887.

While the Treaty of Berlin suited the Great Powers, it was unsatisfactory for the Balkan states. They were largely excluded from the Congress, perhaps because Bismarck recognised that meeting their mutually conflicting demands would have been a labour that even Hercules would have rejected. The Balkan Slavs regarded the agreement as a barrier to their national aspirations and one they would need to scale in the face of opposition from the Great Powers. Consequently the treaty was challenged in every succeeding decade by some new upheaval, while between times there was intense jockeying for power and influence sometimes sparked by internecine struggles. The Albanians, the Serbs and the Ottomans were all in conflict from 1878 to 1881, the Serbs entering Macedonia in 1879–80 only to be recalled under Ottoman pressure.[22]

These struggles were inevitable. Having achieved independence, the new governments wished to stamp the new nations firmly into a nationalist mould in terms of language, education and culture. But they were generally not viable economically or sociologically and soon they were seeking to expand to create an economic critical mass; Bulgaria wanted Eastern Rumelia and Macedonia, Serbia wanted Bosnia and the Ottoman territories to the south, Montenegro sought parts of Ottoman Albania, and the Albanians wanted some Montenegrin territory. Greek ambitions ranged from Macedonia, Crete and the Aegean Islands to the whole of Asia Minor, but to achieve this they required the support of the Great Powers, which was not forthcoming until the early twentieth century.[23]

The Bulgarians were especially bitter that they had been robbed of their 'birthright' and sought to regain the lost land of San Stefano; indeed, Sofia was selected as the capital because it lay at the heart of the Bulgaria envisaged by the treaty. As Bulgarian Premier Ivan Geshov would write in 1912, 'Was such injustice possible? Could such an injustice be reversed?'[24] Consequently, theirs was the first challenge to the Treaty of Berlin when a bloodless revolution in Eastern Rumelia provided Sofia with the excuse to annex the region in September 1885. The Great Powers' reaction was largely confined to protests, although Russia, which had opposed Sofia's actions, withdrew its officers who had led the Bulgarian Army.

The proclamation in July 1879 of a former officer in the German Army, Alexander of Battenberg, as the first Prince of Bulgaria alarmed Vienna because he was a nephew of Tsar Aleksandar II, whom he accompanied during the Russo-Turkish War. Austria responded by proxy and encouraged Serbia to challenge Bulgaria over Eastern Rumelia by demanding extra territory in return for recognition of the annexation, but the Serbs suffered a complete defeat in the three-week Serbo-Bulgarian War of November 1885.[25] Only Austrian pressure prevented a Bulgarian invasion, and Belgrade was forced to accept Sofia's actions in the March 1886 Treaty of Bucharest.

St Petersburg continued to retain an interest in Bulgaria, and in August 1886 encouraged army officers to stage a coup against Prince Alexander. He abdicated after he lost the decisive support of Bismarck and was succeeded in July 1887 by 'the Austrian candidate', Prince Ferdinand of Coburg, who was proclaimed in July 1887.[26] Ferdinand, a bisexual former officer in the Austrian Army, was unusual in having a wide range of hobbies including botany, entomology and philately, but he also had an inclination to authoritarian rule. In this he was opposed by Premier Stefan Stambolov, who sought to avoid reliance upon the Russians, and this led to an inevitable cooling of relations between Sofia and St Petersburg. This was reversed only after Stambolov's fall in May 1894, and his assassination fourteen months later, possibly at Ferdinand's instigation, laid the foundation for a *rapprochement* with Russia.[27]

During the last decade of the nineteenth century the next Balkan problem developed over the island of Crete, inhabited predominantly by Greek Christians who had frequently rebelled against their Muslim overlords. In 1878, a separate agreement, the Pact of Halepa, made the island an autonomous state within the Ottoman Empire, but the Porte revoked this in 1889. New rebellions broke out and Greek public opinion forced Athens to dispatch troops who quickly took control of the island, but this sparked the bloody and farcical thirty-day Greco-Turkish War in April 1897. In this conflict the Greek Army advanced into northern Thessaly and Epirus (the latter in support of an Albanian rebellion) only to be driven back in disorder.[28] The Great Powers swiftly intervened to stop further Ottoman advances, while the Greek garrison was forced out of Crete, to be replaced by foreign troops as the island was run by British, French, Italian and Russian admirals.

In August 1898, a Turkish mob in Crete massacred not only Cretan Greeks but also the British Consul and British troops. The Great Powers quickly forced the Porte to withdraw its troops from the island, which again became an autonomous state in December 1898 under a High Commissioner, Prince George of Greece. But the issue of union with Greece led to conflict with his Justice Minister, Eleftherios Venizelos, and despite the latter's resignation in 1901, his supporters staged a rebellion in March 1905 which led to a Cretan Assembly. This backed union with Greece in August 1905, but the Great Powers persuaded both sides to compromise. Prince George resigned and an election was held on a new constitution. Although the election went against Venizelos, Prince George quit the island and was replaced by former Greek Premier Alexandros Zaimis. Greek officers took over the Cretan gendarmerie as foreign troops withdrew, leaving the island under Greek control in all but name. In 1908, Cretan deputies again voted for union with Greece, but Athens, unwilling to provoke the inevitable reaction from the Great Powers, refused to recognise this until October 1912. The union was not formally recognised by the Great Powers until the following year, with Crete formally joining Greece on 1 December 1913.[29]

Even as the Cretan crisis began to cool, the twentieth century saw a new crisis whose sparks would ultimately ignite the whole powder trail. The Porte's decision in February 1870 to support a separate Bulgarian Orthodox Church independent of the Athens Patriarch helped to create a Macedonian consciousness.[30] This was anathema to Bulgaria, Greece and Serbia, all of whom regarded Macedonia as the natural region for their expansion. The ink on the Treaty of Berlin was barely dry before all three states were sending paramilitary bands across their borders into Macedonia to expand their influence. Initially the struggle focused upon winning 'hearts and minds' by founding hundreds of schools—each a platform for nationalist propaganda. The guerrilla-militia tradition was very strong among all these peoples and, long before Mao Tse-tung, they envisaged paramilitary control of areas whose occupation could then be secured by conventional forces. But the paramilitaries were no match for the Ottoman Army and were quickly crushed, and in Macedonia they quickly dissolved into banditry.[31]

In 1893, a revolutionary organisation was founded to liberate the Macedonian and Edirne (Adrianople) regions of the empire from Ottoman rule. It was known by several names: initially the Macedonian Revolutionary Organization (MRO), unofficially from *circa* 1896 to 1902 as the Bulgarian Macedonian-Adrianople Revolutionary Committees (BMARC), and then as the Secret Macedonian-Adrianople Revolutionary Organization (SMARO). In 1905, it was named the Internal Macedonian-Adrianople Revolutionary Organization (IMARO), although it is often referred to by an even later name as the Internal Macedonian Revolutionary Organization (IMRO). Whatever the name, the leaders wished to create revolutionary ferment to reduce the region to chaos and to encourage pressure from the Great Powers upon the Porte to concede administrative and electoral reforms and ultimately self-government. However, the majority of IMRO's leaders came from, or were associated with, the Bulgarian Men's High School in Edirne and because of this, IMRO became increasingly associated with Bulgaria.[32]

In 1896, IMRO went to what would later be described in revolutionary wars as 'armed struggle' (guerrilla warfare), establishing local administrations in sanctuaries and then indulging in internecine warfare against those who crossed the border from Serbia and Greece. A new organisation of exiles, the Bulgarian Supreme Committee, was then created in Sofia and persuaded IMRO to launch a full-scale rebellion in 1903. Like many insurgents (including the Greek Communists after the Second World War) they opted for conventional warfare and the rebellion was crushed by October 1903 through the deployment of 175,000 Ottoman troops in the usual welter of slaughter, rapine and looting. Most of the IMRO leadership were killed or captured and the organisation was wrecked.[33]

The Macedonian uprising did attract the attention of two of the Great Powers, Austria and Russia signing the Muerzsteg Agreement on 30 September 1903, which demanded the reorganisation of the Ottoman gendarmerie (Jardana) under foreign control. Constantinople accepted this on 25 November, but the agreement changed nothing within Macedonia and confirmed that neither Russia nor Austria wished to fight over the Balkans. The agreement also allowed for adjustments of administrative boundaries for ethnic reasons, which Macedonia's neighbours, in the power vacuum created by the destruction of IMRO, interpreted as *carte blanche* to increase their cross-border activities.[34]

In the aftermath, the IMRO survivors inevitably split into an eastern faction seeking a multi-ethnic Socialist federation, and a western one favouring unification with Bulgaria. A ferocious low-level struggle developed between the Bulgarian factions and Serbian and Greek bands, as well as the Ottoman Army. Meanwhile, the Russians and Austrians made common cause to establish administrative boards to help administer Macedonia—a policy the Porte was forced to accept but which it sought to undermine.

Despite European tensions, the successive Balkan crises would not ignite a major European conflict until 1914, and during the nineteenth century this owed almost everything to that supreme diplomatic juggler, Bismarck. He managed to preserve Germany's hold on the balance of power by playing off the rival powers, also easing tensions between France and Germany on the one hand as well as Austria and Russia. But with the collapse of the Dreikaiserbund, Germany and Austria were increasingly dependent upon each other and this was formalised with the signing of the Dual Alliance in 1879.

Encouraged by Bismarck to join the 'Scramble for Africa', France extended its possessions eastwards from Algeria to acquire another part of the Ottoman Empire, semi-autonomous Tunisia, although recently unified Italy had a greater claim to Tunisia through substantial commercial interests. When France made the country a protectorate in 1881, Rome's protests to the other Great Powers fell on deaf ears. Mortified and isolated, Italy listened to Bismarck's siren song and overlooked its traditional rivalry with its former Austrian overlords to join the Dual Alliance, which consequently became the Triple Alliance in 1881. At a stroke this neutralised Rome's potential threat to Austria, which could then concentrate upon the Russian front, while Rome perceived the agreement as a means of shielding itself from French attack. The agreement also provided powerful diplomatic allies for Italy's hopes of expanding across the Adriatic into Albania as the Queen of Italy was the Montenegrin ruler's daughter. However, as insurance Italy continued to seek covert diplomatic support from France, and when it joined the Triple Alliance it was on the understanding that there was no threat to Britain. The alliance was further strengthened in 1883 when Rumania became a member, although the term Triple Alliance was retained, but this made Bismarck's position with Austria and Russia even more delicate.

Europe's kaleidoscopic patchwork of alliances was largely defensive in concept, to provide mutual support against potential enemies, and was often augmented by agreements on both territory and trade. As they were usually subject to renewal, they did not create automatic diplomatic support, or even the foundations of a common foreign policy; indeed, the partners often squabbled. Within the Triple Alliance, Bismarck warned Vienna both in 1887 and 1895 that he did not feel that the Balkans and Near East were worth the risk of a major European war. More importantly, as Italy showed, the alliances did not create a corporate loyalty.[35] There also still existed the principle established by the Concert of Europe after the Napoleonic Wars by which the Great Powers sought diplomatic rather than military solutions to tensions. Fortunately, most international crises occurred outside Europe, which avoided direct confrontation.

Bismarck's objective with the Dual Alliance was to restrain Russia, and after the Serbo-Bulgarian War he sought to insure against an Austro-Russian war sparked by growing tensions in the Balkans. To this end, and to maintain France's isolation in Europe, he and the Russians signed the secret Reinsurance Treaty in 1887, which would last three years. The agreement guaranteed each partner would remain neutral if attacked by a third party, excluding Austria and France, while Germany would remain neutral if Russia seized the Straits. But after Bismarck's dismissal by Kaiser Wilhelm II and the establishment of a more assertive German foreign policy, the prospect of a coalition that might challenge Germany became a grim reality.

Russia wished to renew the secret Reinsurance Treaty, but Kaiser Wilhelm refused for fear it would undermine his efforts to strengthen ties with London, which was interesting in making common cause on several issues. He assumed that the Russians would remain isolated, but this ignored the effects of the resurgent French economy on Eastern Europe.

The economy had been revitalised after the Franco-Prussian War, and from 1888, French financiers began major investments in Russia to strengthen its industry and communications. This led to closer diplomatic relations and, surprisingly, the autocratic Russian monarchy and the French republic began to negotiate an alliance aimed as much against Britain as Germany. This was signed in 1894, and promised that if either partner faced mobilisation by one of the Triple Alliance powers then both would attack Germany, and in this lay the foundation for the long-feared European war two decades later. In 1896, the press revealed details of the Reinsurance Treaty, which led to an international outcry and increased distrust between the Great Powers, especially Britain, which feared German naval expansion.

French funds also flooded into the Balkans, often for military-related expenditure in a region where arms sales brought political influence. France's Schneider-Creusot squeezed out the region's traditional supplier, Germany's Krupp, aided by the excellent financial packages available on the Paris capital market.[36] By 1913, the French were heavily committed financially to both the Balkans and the Ottoman Empire and Paris held 80 per cent of Serbian foreign debt, one billion francs. A similar amount had been loaned to Greece, while Paris also held 60 per cent of Bulgaria's foreign debt. In addition, France held 63 per cent of the total loans granted to the Ottoman Empire, a total of some three billion gold francs (equivalent to £120 million in 1913 or £11.7 billion a century later) and in return controlled the tobacco market and many utilities in major cities.[37]

Given the close links between Paris and St Petersburg, this alliance should have strengthened Russia's position in the Balkans but after the Treaty of Berlin the Russians turned eastwards to acquire resources-rich territories from the ailing Chinese Empire. To secure its European territories, Russia rejoined the Dreikaiserbund in 1881, but suspicions of Austria after the Serbo-Bulgarian War made Russia prefer a direct agreement with Germany, which led to the Reinsurance Treaty. St Petersburg continued to support the status quo in the Balkans and formally co-ordinated this policy with Vienna in the Goluchowski-Murayev Agreement in May 1897.

Then the dynamic young Japanese Empire slammed the door on Russian expansion when it emerged as the surprising victor in the Russo-Japanese War of 1904–05, and this reawakened St Petersburg's interest in the Balkans. However, the Japanese victory undermined Russian prestige in the region, while Russia was hamstrung by the need to rebuild its armed forces, especially the navy, in the aftermath of the conflict. It was not until the end of the decade that Russia was in a position to take a more active role in support of Bulgaria and Serbia, whom it urged to form an alliance.

Austria's interest in the Balkans was based upon ethnic nationalism and commercial considerations. The Austrian Empire was actually an alliance between the kingdoms of Austria and Hungary which had separate governments and armies, and ethnic rivalry slowed policy decisions. The Hungarians increasingly challenged their partners and dragged their feet when it came to funding the army. The ramshackle structure was pinned together by some joint institutions and headed by Emperor Franz Joseph, who opposed any action that might lead to war. Vienna was also determined to restrict the expansion of the new Balkan states for fear it might encourage secession among the Slavic subjects on the Austrian Empire's periphery.

There were also strong commercial reasons for keeping the Balkans peaceful because they provided the Austrian Empire with up to 60 per cent of its imports and accounted for 75 per cent of its exports. Vienna wished to strengthen those commercial interests by expanding into the western Balkans using Bosnia as the springboard. Serbia was its greatest obstacle and Vienna eventually concluded this could be overcome either by political and economic control of the Slavic kingdom or by annexation. At the turn of the century the problem was less pressing because Serbia was ruled by the pro-Austrian Obrenovic dynasty. Vienna also sought to contain Serbia through alliances of its neighbours, but this seed fell on stony ground. Bulgaria was usually pro-Russian, and the only other significant Balkan military power, Rumania, sought Dobrogea, the Rumanian-populated and Bulgarian-ruled territory around the Danube estuary. But Bucharest had no intention of taking any action that would bring it into conflict with Russia. The Austrians succeeded in containing Serbia and Montenegro, which sought a port on the Adriatic, through a treaty with Italy in which both powers pledged to prevent any other country occupying the Ottoman-controlled Albanian coastline.[38]

Germany was determined to keep Rumania within the Triple Alliance for strategic reasons but was also anxious to preserve the status quo as it too sought new markets in the region. The new Kaiser Wilhelm had a personal interest in the Ottoman Empire and sought to strengthen ties between Berlin and Constantinople by funding rail links into the eastern part of the Ottoman Empire.[39]

The first threat to this house of cards occurred in Serbia during 1903. The Serbian Army was radicalised by reforms after its defeat by Bulgaria, its officers believing that their loyalty was both to the army and the Serbian state rather than to the monarchy.[40] When the last of the pro-Austrian Obrenovics, King Aleksandar, tried to establish an absolute monarchy, army officers murdered him and his unpopular wife but were later pardoned and elevated to the status of national heroes. One of those at the heart of the plot, Dragutin Dimitrijevic or 'Apis', would become the *éminence grise* in Serbian politics.[41] The assassination heightened Austrian concerns and undermined Vienna's hopes of maintaining the status quo.

The new king, Petar Karadjordjevic, regarded the Austrian occupation of Bosnia and the Sanjak as a significant threat to his country and sought allies. With Russia still absorbed in Asia, Belgrade looked towards Sofia and negotiated a series of agreements between April 1904 and June 1905, which included plans for a customs union, mutual military support and aid for Montenegro's Albanian ambitions. The agreements quickly became dead letters as endemic rivalries caused relations to deteriorate rapidly, and in 1907 Bulgaria sought a *rapprochement* with Austria.

Austria now decided to establish economic dominance over Serbia by means of a trade embargo on Belgrade's agricultural exports. The so-called Pig War of March 1906-June 1909 was driven largely by Hungarian landowners who regarded Serbian imports as competition to their agricultural dominance within the empire. The dispute extended into a competition to re-equip Serbia's field artillery batteries, with Austria demanding that the order be placed with Skoda because the Bohemian company was in financial difficulties. Instead Serbia ordered superior French Schneider-Creusot guns partly because Belgrade, whose debt to France was 300 million francs (£12 million in contemporary exchange rates) had been offered a 95 million franc loan (£3.8 million) by Paris in return. The Pig War continued, but Austrian attempts at economic domination were thwarted as Serbian farmers found new markets.[42]

Bulgaria was now in a stronger position, Ferdinand having steered a course closer to Russia as the nineteenth century ebbed. He began in February 1896, when his son and heir, Boris, converted from Roman Catholicism to Eastern Orthodoxy, a move that deeply offended Franz Joseph but brought Ferdinand closer to the Romanovs. In 1902, Russia and Bulgaria concluded a secret military alliance, but St Petersburg remained unwilling to support Bulgarian ambitions in Macedonia for fear it would cause an international crisis.[43]

While Europe's diplomatic minuet continued, the Ottomans pondered the humiliation of 1877–78. For many western-educated Turks, including the brightest minds of military and naval cadets at Prussian-run military schools, this was more than the Will of God. Within a decade of the Berlin Treaty they began to develop plans to reform and modernise the empire based upon a vision of what would now be described as a secular and multi-cultural identity. The movement got off to a hesitant beginning but gradually the reformers, the Young Turks (*Genc Turkler*), began to expand and followed the example of IMRO to create a cell-like structure for security.

Their plans were plagued by ethnic disputes which undermined their overall goal, but there emerged in 1906 under Bahaeddin Sakir the Committee of Union and Progress (Ittihat ve Terakki Cemiyeti or CUP), an umbrella organisation for reformers that quickly established branches in seventy-five Ottoman cities and towns, the majority in Europe. Much activity was abroad, away from the Porte's security apparatus, and the reformers held conferences in Paris in 1902 and in 1907, the latter advocating what would be described later in the century as 'armed struggle'.

In September 1907, bureaucrats and officers in Salonika led by postal officer Mehmed Talat established the Ottoman Freedom Society (Osmanlı Hürriyet Cemiyeti) and actively recruited in the Salonika-based III Corps, including Captain Mustafa Kemal. The Society merged with the CUP a year later, rapidly taking control of the latter organisation. Army support for the Young Turks was generated not only by a desire among young officers for reform but also because Sultan Abdul Hamid, 'Abdul the Damned', distrusted the army and navy. He starved both services of resources so that pay was in arrears and supplies arrived slowly, if at all, while the navy rusted at its moorings. There were numerous minor mutinies in every corps area and especially after the poor harvest of 1907.[44]

A year later, a meeting in the Baltic sent a wave of revolution through the Ottoman Empire. In the aftermath of the Boer War, which had demonstrated its diplomatic isolation, Britain began *rapprochements* with traditional rivals France and Russia. Britain began with France because both countries wished to avoid becoming embroiled in the Russo-Japanese War on the side of their respective allies. Relations were strengthened by the joint Anglo-French response to the German-inspired First Moroccan Crisis of 1905–06, and this in turn led increasingly to joint consultation and responses to crises. The joint policy extended to the Ottoman Empire, both London and St Petersburg being concerned by growing German interest in the Balkans.[45]

In June 1907, King Edward VII and Tsar Nicholas met in Reval (modern Tallinn) and decided to increase their countries' influence within Macedonia. Rumour inflated this move into a division of Macedonia at a time when the Ottoman Emperor's secret police seemed about to roll up the CUP. On 3 July 1908, part of III Corps, including Enver Bey, mutinied and demanded restoration of the 1876 Constitution. Troops sent to crush the mutiny instead joined the rebels. Then, on 7 July, the CUP assassinated Shemshi Pasha, who was investigating the organisation, and five days later III Corps began to march upon Constantinople.[46] With the revolt spreading rapidly and little attempt by the army to combat it, the Sultan was forced to restore the Constitution on 24 July and then to abdicate. He was soon replaced by Sultan Mehmed V, and went to live in Salonika.

Surprisingly, the elections for the new national assembly saw the CUP gain only sixty of the 275 seats, with the main opposition being the Liberty and Entente party, commonly called the Liberal Union, which gradually absorbed the ethnically based parties such as the Armenians. After the election, the CUP slowly evolved into a political party, gaining ground to secure 184 seats in the 1912 election. The Young Turks' view of the empire's future called for greater centralisation and tighter control, while their strident nationalism meant they had little sympathy for other ethnic groups or Christians, insisting that all teaching in schools throughout the empire was in Turkish.

Initially the empire's Christian subjects, including the rump of the IMRO, were willing to work with their new Ottoman masters. But the latter's intransigence, partly due to fear of further territorial losses especially in Macedonia, soon alienated this support. In July 1909, the Young Turks banned all political parties representing the minorities and by August 1912 the Macedonian guerrillas had returned to the hills.[47]

The Young Turks' revolution actually spurred Austria into new threats against the Porte's European territories. Late in 1906, concern over Hungarian support for the empire saw Archduke Franz Ferdinand, Foreign Minister Alois von Aehrenthal and General Franz Conrad von Hoetzendorf (Conrad), the new Chief of the General Staff, form an *ad hoc* political coalition. Budapest administered Croat and Slovene territories north of Bosnia in a nominal partnership similar to that between the Germans and Hungarians. To expand the territory under Hungarian control and to strengthen its support for the empire, Aehrenthal, who believed that the Balkan status quo was no longer feasible, proposed the annexation of Bosnia, which would be ruled from Budapest. He believed this would also undermine support for Serbia among its neighbours and expose it to dismemberment and occupation like Poland in the eighteenth century.

The sabre-rattling Conrad had joined the army after the Prussian defeat and been a member of the initial occupation force in Bosnia and the Sanjak. He was obsessed with a pre-emptive war against Serbia which, he believed, could be sparked by the annexation of Bosnia. However, Franz Ferdinand was more cautious and determined to avoid a war that might involve Russia and Germany. He was uncertain of German military intentions because conversations between the two prime Triple Alliance general staffs ceased after the appointment of General Alfred von Schlieffen as German Chief of the General Staff in 1896 until 1909.[48] Certainly, from 1905 the need to modernise meant that both the Austrian and

Russian armies temporarily lacked confidence in their own capabilities, so their governments were less inclined to rattle sabres, which noticeably eased tensions between them.[49]

The annexation became more urgent for Austria after the Young Turks convened a national assembly that included representatives from Bosnia. Austria feared they might demand the withdrawal of Vienna's troops from the provinces and the province's restoration to the Porte, and planning for the annexation accelerated but needed Russian agreement. Aehrenthal met his Russian counterpart, Alexander Izvolsky, in July 1908 and proposed changes in the Berlin Treaty to allow Vienna to favour Russian interests in the Straits in exchange for support in annexing both Bosnia and the Sanjak. In September, Izvolsky, a vain and stupid man, travelled to Moravia for a meeting at Buchlau Castle, which led to a formal agreement, the Buchlau Bargain, although the terms were subsequently disputed. Russia confirmed it had no objection to Bosnia's annexation but sought support in renegotiating those terms of the Berlin Treaty that related to the passage of warships in the Straits. The bone of contention would be the fate of the Sanjak, and Izvolsky later claimed its evacuation by Austrian troops was the price for annexation.

The Buchlau Bargain set the stage for the annexation on 6 June, but with the duplicity that was such a feature of Balkans diplomacy, St Petersburg tried to strengthen its position in the Balkans and leaked the Austrian intentions to Bulgaria. With all the Great Powers likely to be preoccupied by a new crisis there could be no threat to Bulgaria's formal independence from the Ottoman Empire, which Ferdinand announced on 5 June, and later he would anger Tsar Nicholas by giving himself the title of tsar.

The following day, Vienna formally annexed Bosnia and then, on 7 June, as Serbia mobilised, announced the evacuation the Sanjak and its restoration to the Ottoman Empire.[50] Russia had no time to generate any support among the Great Powers for its position on the Straits, which was doomed by Austria's flagrant violations of the Berlin Treaty which created a storm of diplomatic protest. Constantinople naturally protested not only at Sofia's defiance, which was not initially recognised by the Great Powers, but also at the annexation, before mobilising three corps (164,000 men) with the empty threat of restoring Ottoman sovereignty in Bosnia at bayonet point. But even the Young Turks could do nothing, apart from organising a commercial boycott of Austria, as Bulgaria formally negotiated its independence with the Porte with Russian aid and the Porte was bought off with compensation of £2.2 million.

Like powder smoke after a firework display, the threat of war hung in the air for six months as Germany sabotaged efforts to renegotiate the Treaty of Berlin. Italy, which supported its Triple Alliance ally's action in the hope of receiving coastal territory, was especially indignant when it received nothing and began to edge away from the alliance. The Berlin Treaty powers were forced to accept the *fait accompli* and agree that the treaty could now be amended after mutual consultation. But London remained opposed to any threat to Ottoman control of the Straits which dashed any hopes of Austrian support for Russia and this infuriated Izvolsky, who blamed Aehrenthal.

The Russians now supported Belgrade's demands for either a reversal of the annexation or compensation in territory, which raised Serb hopes of acquiring Bosnia both to expand its territory and gain access to the sea. But the Austrians blackmailed St Petersburg, threatening to publish all the previous decades' correspondence between them about co-operation in the Balkans, including the Buchlau Bargain. Under German pressure, Russia capitulated in March 1909 and formally accepted the annexation. Austria then twisted the Serbs' arms, forcing them first to keep their sabres in their scabbards and then to bow to *force majeure*. However, the replacement of Austrian by Ottoman garrisons in the Sanjak did open the way for the future establishment of a land bridge to Montenegro. Faced with accepting either the *fait accompli* or seeing an Austrian attack upon Serbia that might provoke a European war, both Britain and France agreed in April 1909 to amend the Berlin Treaty, giving formal recognition of the Austrian action. Serbian Foreign Minister Milovan Milovanovic observed to friends, 'Europe wants quiet, nothing but quiet. We are told we are in the right but that being in the right is of no use to us.'[51] In the aftermath, a humiliated Russia began to revamp its plans to speed up mobilisation, which would have a significant impact upon the early days of the First World War. These plans ensured that Russians would launch an offensive long before Austria and Germany anticipated it, while an acceleration of the army's modernisation programme would improve its capabilities.[52]

Forced to accept the *fait accompli*, the Serbs bided their time and prepared their revenge, although their impulsive Montenegrin allies desired active opposition to the annexation. Within Serbia the annexation spurred the creation of both National Defence (Narodna Odbrana) to promote Serbian interests in the annexed provinces and Unification or Death (Ujedinjenje ili Smrt), the latter organised by 'Apis' to force policy changes. Serbia was compelled to reduce National Defence to a cultural organisation, but its founding members, who included the 1903 regicides, then formed the Black Hand (Crna Ruka) secret society to help create a Greater Serbia including Macedonia, Bosnia and Croatia. It was covertly supported by many people high in Serbian ruling circles including Crown Prince Aleksandar. When the Balkan War broke out, many Bosnians tried to join the Serbian Army and some came into contact with the Black Hand which supplied them with weapons and bombs. One was the Bosnian Gavrilo Princip, who would meet Franz Ferdinand in Sarajevo with fatal consequences.[53] The annexation also confirmed the feeling among the small Balkan nations that they could not count upon the support of the Great Powers to meet their aspirations. Such was the isolation felt by Serbia that in October 1908 it discussed an alliance with the Ottoman Empire—a move quickly quashed by the Great Powers.

Austria's land-grab tore up the Goluchowski-Murayev Agreement, and its failure to keep its part of the Buchlau Bargain marked a diplomatic watershed for the Russians, who began to develop a more assertive Balkans policy.[54] Diplomatically humiliated, St Petersburg was determined to thwart Vienna's Balkan ambitions aided by the fact that it was now well on the way to military recovery following defeat at the hands of the Japanese. Russian policy in the Balkans now aimed both to create a military counterpoint to the Austrian Empire and to restore its position as patron and protector of the Balkan Slavs. Encouraged by the brief Serbo-Bulgarian *rapprochement*, the new Russian Foreign Minister, Sergei Sazonov, ordered his ambassadors in Belgrade and Sofia, Nicholas Hartwig and Anatol Nekliudov, to encourage closer relations between the two countries. This policy faced hurdles of dynastic, ethnic and national rivalries, especially over Macedonia, yet despite their mutual suspicions and antagonisms the smaller Balkan Christian states did begin to make common cause in an atmosphere of growing nationalist fervour.

This common cause was further encouraged by events among the Albanians at the western extremity of the Ottoman Empire. Although they included Christian tribes, many of them Roman Catholic, the majority were Muslim and shared Ottoman culture.[55] The Albanian Muslims had supported the Young Turks' revolution in the hope of gaining autonomy, but the centralisation policies dashed these hopes and fuelled fears that the Porte would seek tighter control of this remote region. The Catholic minority was the first to revolt, but by the spring of 1910 open defiance had extended throughout the Albanian lands. In May 1911, a meeting at Vlore demanded the creation of an autonomous Albania from the surrounding Ottoman provinces which extended as far east as the River Vardar.[56]

The initial revolt was crushed and Sultan Mohammed visited Kosovo in June 1911. Two months later, Constantinople made concessions which included the restoration of local schools and permission for men to carry arms, but this failed to cool the embers. The conflict was quickly renewed and forced the empire to reinforce the garrison in a vain effort to restore the Porte's rule, although many soldiers who were opposed to fighting their co-religionists joined the rebels. The Serbs and Montenegrins, seeing the Albanian revolt as an opportunity to expand southwards, smuggled weapons to rebels in Kosovo and also staged border incidents against Ottoman forces.

The Albanian insurgency in the Kosovo area challenged both the province's Serbian population and Serbian hopes of gaining access to the sea, yet fear of Austrian intervention made Belgrade act with great caution. The revolt also challenged Greek goals in the Epirus region on the north-western frontier, but concerns over a premature war with the Porte stayed Athens' hand. Only Montenegro took a direct role in aiding the rebels, its ruler Prince Nikola Petrovich Njegosh exploiting his dynastic links (he was father-in-law to the Italian and Serbian kings and two Russian grand dukes) to further his ambitions, which culminated in his assuming the crown as king on 28 August 1910. The Albanian revolt saw Serbia, Greece and Montenegro make common cause to prevent an autonomous Albania, and naturally they sought Bulgarian assistance.

In March 1909, Milovanovic attempted a new *rapprochement* during a visit to Sofia, but this foundered within four months on the usual issues, especially Macedonia. But while passing through Belgrade, Tsar Ferdinand met King Petar and their personal relationship heralded warmer national relations aided by a personal slight suffered by the Tsar during an official visit to Germany. While in the Potsdam Palace he was invited by the Kaiser to look at some flowers outside the window; when he did so, Germany's ruler, who had a juvenile sense of humour, slapped him on the bottom. Although he swiftly received an apology, Ferdinand did not turn the other cheek and later awarded France's Schneider-Creusot rather than Krupp a substantial contract to modernise his field artillery.[57] Meanwhile, Russia's new ambassador to Belgrade, Hartwig, fostered more cordial relations with St Petersburg while his colleague Nekliudov gently pushed for an alliance between Sofia and Belgrade. The pro-Russian Bulgarian government, led by Premier Ivan Geshov, and the President of Parliament, Stojan Danev, were receptive but Macedonia remained the insurmountable hurdle, for regaining the region had become a Bulgarian obsession.

It was Italy that would create the right atmosphere for a Balkan alliance due to its ill fortune in the 'Scramble for Africa'. France had thwarted Italy in Tunisia, while an attempt to seize Abyssinia with Anglo-German support failed catastrophically in 1896, leaving only Libya (the Ottoman provinces of Tripolitania, Fezzan and Cyrenaica, known as Trablusgarp in Turkish) within its grasp. In 1902, Paris secretly supported Italian ambitions in the region, but there was little information about its economic potential and it had few attractions. By 1910, when reports circulated in Rome of mineral and potential agricultural wealth, Italy decided to annex the region in the belief it would have the support of the Arab population.

In September 1911, Rome presented an ultimatum to the Porte, demanding control of the region. The CUP government was conciliatory and offered transfer of *de facto* control while it nominally remained part of the Ottoman Empire, like neighbouring Egypt, but even this was not enough and Rome declared war on 29 September. The Italian Navy neutralised the Ottoman Navy in the Adriatic, the eastern Mediterranean, North Africa and the Red Sea before seizing most of the Dodecanese Islands in the eastern Aegean between 24 April and 20 May. It also seized the port of Tripoli in October, but when the army arrived to project Italian power inland it was fiercely opposed by both the Turks and local Arabs led by Mustafa Kemal, who defeated the invaders at Tobruk in December. By the end of the year, Italy barely controlled the coastal strip and faced a prolonged guerrilla war. Fighting formally ended only with the Treaty of Ouchy (also called the First Treaty of Lausanne) on 18 October 1912, by which the Ottoman Empire conceded Libya in exchange for the return of most of the Dodecanese. But the outbreak of the Balkan War gave Italy the excuse to retain the islands until after the Second World War.[58]

The Italian invasion of Libya led to the dissolution of the Turkish Parliament and the re-election of the Liberal Union Party, but agitation by army officers saw the resignation of the War Minister Mahmud Shevket Pasha on 9 July 1912. He was followed on 16 July by the Grand Vizier (Sadrazam) Sait Pasha, Shevket Pasha being replaced by Nazim Pasha and Sait Pasha by Gazi Ahmed Muhtar Pasha on 21 July. The new Grand Vizier appointed three of his predecessors to the Cabinet, ended martial law, and in October 1912 attempted to introduce laws that banned military interference and participation in politics. But with the Balkan War breaking out, the government had to sign a peace treaty with Italy and this so angered the army that it forced him out and replaced him with the elderly Kamil Pasha. This Old Turks government, more openly intransigent than its predecessor, refused to provide autonomy for either Albania or Macedonia, as Sofia demanded on 14 August 1912. It also refused to institute reforms to protect non-Muslim subjects of the Porte, but the government also opposed the CUP or Young Turks agenda espoused by many army leaders, which caused serious friction with the army.[59]

The failure of the Ottoman forces to hold Libya provided encouragement to many ethnic groups within the Balkans who knew that thousands of Turkish troops had been withdrawn to shield southern Anatolia from the threat of Italian invasion. The Ottoman Empire's weakness was all too apparent, and Bulgaria saw an opportunity to seize Macedonia at bayonet point although recognising this would require allies. On 29 September 1911, as Italy declared war on Turkey, Russian ambassador Nekliudov advised Foreign Minister Teodor Teodorov that the new conflict would provide an excellent opportunity to reach an agreement with the Serbs. Ferdinand and Geshov were holidaying in France, so it was left to Teodorov and the ambassador to Italy, writer Dimitar Rizov who was in Sofia on leave, to approach Milovanovic who was now Serbian Premier. He had independently come to the same conclusion and replied favourably three days later. Rizov went to Belgrade in October, and this led to a three-hour secret meeting between Geshov and Milovanovic on the Belgrade–Nis night train during which it was agreed to discuss the possibility of a military alliance based upon Macedonian autonomy and a preliminary outline of spheres of influence.[60]

Belgrade dispatched Doctor Miroslav Spalajkovic as its ambassador to Bulgaria in December and negotiations began in earnest.[61] Despite the clandestine nature of these talks, key political leaders as well as both monarchs were consulted, while Nekliudov and his staff acted as intermediaries. The territorial elements were the most difficult to arrange, and the first draft, produced by the Serbs on 3 November, was rejected by Sofia. But both sides persevered and a treaty was hammered out which recognised that Thrace should be in Bulgaria's sphere of interest while Kosovo, the Sanjak and Albania would be within Serbia's. They would seek autonomy for Macedonia, which the Bulgarians regarded as the first step towards its integration, following the precedent established with East Rumelia in 1885.

With these terms the Treaty of Friendship and Alliance (generally referred to as the Balkan League) was signed by Geshov and Milovanovich on 13 March. It was, nominally a defensive alliance against Austria, Rumania and Turkey, which included provision for concerted action if any of the Great Powers attempted either to annex or to occupy any part of the Ottoman Empire in the Balkans. But a secret annexe signed the following day provided for war against the Ottomans if the empire's internal or external troubles endangered either state's national interests, and this also confirmed the division of the anticipated spoils. There was one important provision clearly defined in Article 2, which stated that if it proved impossible to organise Macedonia as an autonomous region then there would be a line of demarcation between the Rhodope Mountains and Lake Ohrid. Kriva Palanka and Ohrid would remain in Bulgarian hands and Serbia would have the territory north of the line and would not seek any Bulgarian territory south of the line. A decision on any adjustments to this line would ultimately rest with the Russian Tsar. The Bulgarians were content because they believed their army would take most of the contested territory from the Ottomans, arrogantly assuming that if this was not the case, the Tsar's arbitration would favour them.

Serbian support for this part of the agreement was lukewarm, and while people like the army chief-of-staff, General Radomir Putnik, appreciated the military support against the hated Austrians, they were unhappy about abandoning Macedonian areas which they regarded as Serbian. On 1 July 1912, Milovanovic, who was willing to surrender much of Macedonia, died and was replaced six weeks later by Nikola Pasic, who had been his predecessor as Premier. Despite a stutter and close associations with Bulgaria, where he had relatives, Pasic was the Radical party leader of Parliament and an ardent nationalist who favoured securing as much of Macedonia as possible.[62]

Detailed military planning did not begin until 29 April, and the day Milovanovic died the chiefs-of-staff, Putnik and General Ivan Fichev, began producing a detailed plan based upon the treaty. On 12 May, they signed a military convention in Varna in which Fichev pledged 200,000 men against the Turk, while Putnik promised 150,000. If Rumania attacked Bulgaria, Serbia would provide 100,000 troops and if Austria attacked Serbia, it would be reinforced by 200,000 Bulgarian troops.

While these military talks continued, the Serbs and Bulgarians were briefing the Russians—first Danev at the beginning of May, then Pasic the following month—each with copies of the treaty for St Petersburg's consent. They were surprised to discover that although Russia supported the treaty's anti-Austrian element, it opposed military action against the Ottomans that ran contrary to its own interests. Danev was informed that Russia did not wish Thrace to be within the Bulgarian sphere of interest as this clashed with Russian ambitions, although Pasic was delighted to hear that the St Petersburg would not allow Austria to strike into Serbia or the Sanjak.

The Russian attitude meant that the Serbs and Bulgarians made their military preparations in even greater secrecy. Putnik and Fichev met at Euxinograd, near Varna, from 29 June to 3 July to confirm the outline of the military convention. They were split over the amount of support that Bulgaria would provide for the Thracian and Macedonian campaigns, the impasse being broken only when the Bulgarians agreed to provide stronger forces in Macedonia. It was envisaged that two Serbian armies would advance from the north-west upon Kumanovo-Kratovo and Skopje with seven infantry and one cavalry divisions, while a Bulgarian army of three divisions would advance towards Kyustendil-Skopje on the Serbian left. Together they would envelop the Ottoman Vardar Army, and afterwards the Bulgarians would be allowed, if they wished, to switch troops to Thrace.[63]

After signing the Varna Agreement, Fichev went to Belgrade to discuss further details, which led to Serb agreement to send either one division or the whole of the 2nd Army to Thrace once the Ottoman forces in Macedonia had been defeated. In turn, Bulgaria would station a small division in Macedonia, although Putnik and his deputy, Colonel Zivojin Misic, questioned the necessity of this decision and may have realised it was scheduled to hold Salonika.[64]

As political tensions in the Balkans rose at the end of August, Bulgaria urged both general staffs to complete planning in readiness for war at a moment's notice. Fichev's confidence in the ability of his forces to defeat the Ottoman forces in Thrace had been eroded and now he sought to reinforce them, even if it compromised the earlier agreement. This began a process of dilution which would create further bones of contention between the two sides in the following months. On 5 September, Fichev met Misic at Belgrade and again brought up the question of Bulgaria's contribution to the Macedonian campaign. He asked the Serbs to release their allies from their agreement to provide three divisions, but Misic refused. However, as Athens joined the conspiracy it was clear that the Ottoman forces in Macedonia would be overwhelmed and the Serbs reluctantly conceded that

Sofia could now dispatch only one division to Macedonia. The proviso was that it would be under Serbian operational control, but there was no immediate response from Sofia which was determined to cut adrift its Macedonian military commitment.

On 13 September, the Bulgarian military leaders sent a message through the Serbian military attaché, Major Danilo Kalafatovic, that they wished to concentrate all their forces in Thrace apart from garrisons holding fortifications at Dupnitsa and the Struma Pass. The Serbs reluctantly accepted this on 28 September (two days before mobilisation) because they were anxious to begin hostilities before Albania achieved autonomy, but they made a condition. One Bulgarian division would operate with the Serbs in Macedonia until Ottoman forces were pushed south of the Skopje-Veles-Stip line when it could be transferred to Thrace. Sofia reluctantly accepted this condition because the Serbs agreed to send troops to Thrace and also because the division in Macedonia would be well placed to take Salonika.

Sofia was also anxious to bring Athens into the anti-Ottoman alliance, although both had their sights firmly set upon the great Macedonian port of Salonika. Nationalist Greek Army officers had formed an organisation similar to that in the Serbian Army and in August 1909 rebelled, demanding reforms within the services and government. This led to the dismissal of their commander-in-chief, the heir to the throne Prince Constantine, and his brothers, who were then restored after Venizelos came to power following elections in August and November 1910 because he was determined to mend fences with the monarchy in order to push through his reform programme.[65] The nationalist Venizelos, unlike so many of his Balkan contemporaries, was also a realist who recognised that Crete could not join Greece without the support of the Great Powers. He adopted a conciliatory policy to the Porte, which foolishly reacted by increasing a boycott of Greek commerce in Salonika while massacres of Christians in Macedonia further enflamed political passions. Consequently, Venizelos was forced to seek another path.

In April 1911, he privately proposed to Fichev the joint defence of Macedonian Christians with the ultimate objective of a defensive alliance against the Ottoman Empire but received no reply. A new attempt was made six months later when the Greek ambassador to Sofia, Demetrios Panas, informed Geshov that his country would fight alongside Bulgaria if it was attacked by the Ottoman Empire. The Bulgarians were less than enthusiastic, having an understandably low opinion of the Greek Army after their 1897 defeat, but the Balkan League partners recognised that in any struggle against the Ottoman Empire, Athens could not be neutral. The Bulgarians also recognised that their own prospects in Thrace would be enhanced if the Greek fleet could prevent the Ottoman troops from crossing the Aegean.

Negotiations began during the last week of February 1912, directed by Venizelos and Geshov with Panas acting as intermediary. The Greeks would not accept an autonomous Macedonian region, while the Bulgarians refused to define spheres of interest. Fatally confident that their army would be the ultimate arbiter in such a contest, they had agreed no division of Ottoman territory when the treaty was signed in Sofia on 29 May 1912, by which Bulgaria pledged to mobilise 300,000 men while Greece would commit 120,000. Mutual aid was promised if the Turks attacked them or if the Greeks and Bulgars in the Ottoman Empire did not receive their rights under international law and internal agreements.[66] The Greeks had territorial ambitions not only in Macedonia but also in the Greco-Albanian-inhabited Epirus, Thrace and islands in the eastern Aegean, the last compromised by the Italian occupation of the Dodecanese. In negotiations for the military convention, signed on 5 October, Athens made a last-minute attempt to initiate talks on Macedonia and Thrace but was rebuffed by the Bulgarians.

Immediately afterwards, the Bulgarians and the Serbs separately began to reel in bellicose Montenegro, which had advocated war since 1911 but had been rebuffed by both Belgrade and Sofia. The Montenegrins were not made aware of the discussions between Serbia, Bulgaria and Greece, but an official visit by Montenegro's King Nikola to Vienna in mid-April 1912 provided an opportunity for the Montenegrin Premier and Defence Minister Mitar Martinovic to meet Teodorov, Rizov and Danev in the Habsburg capital. This meeting led to understandings rather than to a formal alliance, although Bulgaria did agree in August 1912 to provide Montenegro with financial assistance, while a 'gentleman's agreement' with Greece was reached shortly afterwards.

Dynastic suspicions delayed an agreement between Montenegro and the Serbs, but Martinovic, finally aware of the alliances, began negotiating in September with the Bulgarians in Lausanne, Switzerland. This led to a draft treaty, with the Serbs as co-signatories, the agreements being formally signed on 27 September. Serbia now lacked only an agreement with Greece, which quickly led to another 'gentlemen's agreement'. The Greeks did produce a draft alliance on 22 October, with proposals on dividing territory, but the war broke out before it could be discussed and left Athens with no firm commitment from its allies. What was grandly referred to as the Balkan League was actually a patchwork of *ad hoc* agreements stitched together with no thought to the strategic implications. It satisfied few and offered too many hostages to fortune.

Austrian intelligence informed new Foreign Minister Count Leopold Berchtold in July of the Serbo-Bulgarian treaty and the Russians were officially informed shortly afterwards, but while Vienna tried to prevent an attack upon the Ottoman Empire neither St Petersburg nor Rome provided much support. When the other Great Powers learned of the Balkan League they were appalled, recognising that it was a major threat to a European peace. Russian delight in assisting this diplomatic coup dissipated when French Premier Raymond Poincaré was informed by St Petersburg about the Serbo-Bulgarian alliance during his visit on 9–11 August. He expressed the common view held in the chancelleries of the Great Powers when he said, 'This is an agreement for war' and warned his hosts that France would not support Russia in a Balkan War unless Germany was drawn into the conflict. Such a prospect was growing steadily, for European tensions had risen after the second Moroccan (Agadir) Crisis in 1911, which increased suspicion among the Great Powers and led to further expansion and modernisation of their armies and navies.[67]

Consequently, from September 1912, the Russians and Austrians tried desperately to rein in the Balkan states and to prevent an attack upon the Ottoman Empire. On 26 September, on behalf of the Great Powers, Russia warned them that neither St Petersburg nor Vienna would tolerate any change in territorial arrangements within the Balkans. They demanded an end to pressure upon the Porte, as the Great Powers tried to persuade him to introduce reforms. But the Turks regarded this as interference in their empire's internal affairs, while the Balkan states were indifferent to these promises and wanted Macedonia and Albania for themselves.

Even as the diplomats shuttled from capital to capital, Ottoman control over its Balkan possessions steadily weakened, especially in Albania and Macedonia where guerrilla warfare led to the usual retaliatory massacres by the Turks while Macedonian terrorism stoked the fires. In what seemed an omen of impending disaster, a massive earthquake around Gallipoli in August killed more than 1,100 people, made 100,000 homeless and destroyed 10,000 homes.[68] The summer had already seen significant Albanian gains with the rebels taking Skopje in May before advancing upon Bitola to control large areas. On 18 August, Constantinople bowed to the inevitable and informally accepted the Albanian rebels' terms, with the Porte's acceptance on 4 September bringing a formal end to the Albanian revolt.

The Serbs were now desperate to act against the Ottoman Empire before Albanian autonomy became a reality, while the Bulgarians were equally determined to acquire Macedonia. They forced their Serbian allies to surrender more of Macedonia in exchange for a free hand in Kosovo and northern Albania in order to pave the way for expansion to the Adriatic. With the land-grab now agreed, the Balkan states began to mobilise and issued an ultimatum on 2 October which demanded reforms in Macedonia, with the dye cast ten days later when the Porte rejected calls by the Great Powers for Macedonian reform.

With numerous incidents along its northern borders, especially Montenegro, as guerrilla bands sought to cross the frontier or engage border guards, the Porte made heavy-handed efforts to restrain the Balkan states. The Ottoman navy and coastguard blockaded fifty-eight Greek steamers, a fifth of the merchant fleet, either in Ottoman-controlled ports or in the Straits.[69] Athens stationed a merchantman off the Straits in the Black Sea to warn off ships sailing for the Straits, but this vessel had to race for Varna when a torpedo boat was sent to detain it.[70] In the hope that Athens would remain neutral, the Porte opted for a gesture of good faith and released all these vessels on 13 October, but three days later, when it became clear this gesture had been futile, seventeen Greek steamers (18,088 grt) and twenty-five tugs and ferries in Ottoman ports were seized. This represented nearly 6 per cent of the Greek steamer fleet, while other vessels would be trapped in the Black Sea.[71] The Ottoman authorities also struck at Serbia and in mid-September seized eighteen rail wagons of Serbian military equipment that had been unloaded at Salonika.[72] Although there are reports that this equipment, including Schneider 75-mm field guns, was sent east, most appears to have remained on the dock at Salonika where it was found by the Greeks who forwarded it to the original owners.

Despite pressure from the Great Powers, Bulgaria and Serbia began to mobilise on 30 September, the Ottoman Empire soon following. The French desperately tried to defuse the situation and, on 4 October, persuaded most of the Great Powers to oppose territorial changes to the Ottoman Empire. Two days later, Austria and Russia, again acting in concert over the Balkans on behalf of the other Great Powers, warned the Balkan League against attacking the Porte.

However, faced with the prospect of an autonomous Albania, Montenegro had begun mobilisation in mid-September. Sporadic fighting broke out on the Montenegrin-Ottoman border near Tuzi in July and steadily escalated in early September. The Tuzi garrison was reinforced by a battalion which sailed across Lake Shkoder to end Montenegrin attacks on 20 September. The following day, and again on 28 September, Montenegro informed Sofia that it was waiting for the Bulgarians to set the date for the grand offensive, but the Bulgarians did not respond so King Nikola decided to start the war to display his Slavic patriotism and fighting spirit. They had little regard for the Serbian Army or Serbian paramilitaries, although the latter had been conducting cross-border operations into the Sanjak and been bested in most clashes. On his own initiative, and in a desperate effort to seize Albanian territory, Nikola launched a new assault upon Tuzi during the night of 8/9 October after his youngest son, Prince Petar, fired a ceremonial shot across the frontier to open the war formally.[73]

Its allies' and friends' envoys in Constantinople quickly delivered a list of demands which they knew the Porte would reject. On 14 October, Venizelos welcomed Cretan delegates to the Greek Parliament and ignored an Ottoman demand for their withdrawal. Three days later, the Ottoman Empire declared war upon Bulgaria and Serbia, and the same day the Greeks, who had demanded the release of all their ships on 15 October, withdrew their envoys from Constantinople. They also announced both the annexation of Crete and a declaration of war upon the Ottoman Empire as the Porte hastily signed the Treaty of Ouchy.

Table 1   Balkans Statistics 1912

Country	Area (sq km)	Population
Turkey (European)	169,300	6,130,000
Bulgaria	96,300	4,329,000
Greece	64,600	2,632,000
Serbia	48,300	2,912,000
Montenegro	9,000	250,000
Rumania	131,350	7,070,000

Source: Schurman p. 31

CHAPTER 2

Bayonets and Battleships

Until the great conflagration of 1914–18, popular culture presented war as both exciting and romantic. The images in paintings, prints and drawings showed massed ranks of men under national and regimental banners charging foes who gave way in the face of self-justified national will. The dead and dying lay in decorous poses, while the mortally injured were portrayed almost as if they were suffering severe bouts of migraine or indigestion. Vaguely aware of the risks, men usually went joyously to war, which they saw as a brief period of adventure in contrast to the endless drudgery of their daily lives and one in which they also helped to shape great events.

However, the generals and admirals were uncertain, for prolonged and profound technological change had altered almost everything on the battlefield. The impact was felt throughout what the Germans and Russians called the tactical (army corps), operational (army and army group) and strategic (multiple army group) levels, although in the Balkan Wars the tactical level was divisional operations, the operational was corps and the strategic was army. Yet the minds of many military leaders remained influenced by the Napoleonic Wars as the centenary of the Battle of Waterloo approached.

The later Napoleonic Wars saw campaigns that involved armies of up to half a million strong, with greater emphasis at the tactical level upon massed cannon. Wise generals shielded their infantry in earthworks, usually strongpoints or redoubts, although the Duke of Wellington preferred to use reverse slopes. Infantry assaults led by a screen of skirmishers were conducted in columns or in lines to provide the maximum firepower from the short-range, smooth-bore, flintlock muskets and ended in mêlées involving cold steel. Cavalry could pin down infantry, but rarely broke into or through infantry formations and were also used for scouting before the battle and afterwards, either for harassing the defeated or covering a retreat.

Even a century later, troops still deployed shoulder to shoulder with fixed bayonets led by sword-wielding officers beneath regimental and national banners, sometimes with bands playing rousing music. Artillery continued to engage the enemy with direct (line-of-sight) fire, the field guns deployed almost within rifle shot of their foes, while Russian infantry were still firing by volley as late as 1905. In the summer of 1914, General Louis Franchet d'Espèrey (who would later command Allied forces at Salonika facing the Bulgarians) rode with his staff and watched lines of blue-coated troops with red kepis and trousers advance upon the German lines with colours flying and bands playing the 'Marseillaise'. He turned to General Philippe Pétain, a corps commander and former War Academy lecturer (Professeur à l'École de Guerre), and proudly asked, 'Well, Professor, what do you think of this movement?'[1] Ironically, Pétain was one of the very few generals to appreciate the realities of modern war, and for his pains had almost been driven out of the French Army.[2]

Between the Napoleonic Wars and the First World War an industrial revolution had spread across Europe in waves of technological change, especially in the fields of metallurgy, chemistry and mechanical and electrical engineering.[3] While avid consumers of the products, the army leaderships were often drawn from landowners who remained on the periphery of industrial society, whereas navies required men with greater technologically proficiency. For European armed forces, each of the five decades before the Great War saw the appearance of at least one major product with a significant impact upon the battlefield. This undermined the confidence of military leaders and made them reluctant to rush to battle for fear their enemies would reveal some new war-winning technology. This caution among the armed forces acted as a safety catch on relations between the Great Powers throughout this period despite frequent sabre rattling. Generals like d'Espèrey might recognise the impact of one or two items of new technology, but they rarely comprehended the significance of the accumulated effects of a technological revolution which accelerated in the two decades leading up to the First World War.[4]

The flintlock musket was converted to take a percussion cap which was more reliable in all weathers but retained the separate propellant charge and bullet to reduce firing rates to three rounds a minute and accurate ranges of only 100 metres. Rifling of the musket provided a longer range and greater accuracy, while production became cheaper as it incorporated American ideas of identical and massed produced components to assemble complete weapons.[5] However, improved rates of fire emerged only with the development of unitary cartridges in which the igniter, propellant and bullet were combined in a brass-bound unit. This led to breech-loaded weapons which were faster to reload, and this munitions technology would later be extended to field artillery.

Artillery saw even greater changes from the Napoleonic Wars when they had been smooth-bore weapons of iron and bronze fired by powder in the vent, or flintlock mechanisms later replaced by percussion-cap ignition. They too were muzzle loaded with bags of propellant and then either solid shot or shrapnel, canisters of musket balls designed to explode over the heads of the enemy. Shells were increasingly used by heavier guns both for siege warfare and coast defence, but crude fuses made them unreliable.[6]

During the nineteenth century, smooth-bores were augmented and then replaced by rifled cannon, both muzzle- and breech-loading, firing shells with greater range and accuracy.[7] The unreliability of earlier breech-loading weapons was overcome by using high-quality steels, yet the recoil of all cannon meant that once a gun was fired it had to be laboriously hauled back into position (re-laid) and re-aimed. This reduced rates of fire to two or three rounds per minute, while gunpowder propellant restricted field artillery ranges to about 5 km against targets within their line-of-sight.

Gunpowder was vulnerable to damp, decomposed quickly and created dense clouds of sulphurous smoke every time the weapon was discharged. Because it burned very inefficiently, it left thick residues in the barrel which had to be cleaned regularly to prevent blockages. In 1884, the great French chemist Paul Vieille produced a nitrocellulose explosive propellant (Poudre B) that produced virtually no smoke and left very little residue in barrels, and this entered service two years later. Other nations quickly developed similar propellants and soon rifle cartridges throughout Europe were being filled with the new compositions. The new unitary cartridges were about half the size of their predecessors, down from 10.2–15.4 mm to 6.5–8 mm, were more reliable and produced higher energy levels with greater lethality. The new small arms ammunition was accurate up to a kilometre and because the rounds were smaller, rifles could be designed to take a magazine containing up to half a dozen, while bolt-action mechanisms gave firing rates of up to ten rounds per minute.

The new cartridges helped in the development of efficient self-loading (automatic) weapons with even higher rates of fire. Automatic weapons had emerged during the 1860s based upon the Gatling multi-barrelled, hand-cranked mechanism in which each barrel was automatically loaded separately then rotated into the firing position. These Gatling-type weapons were also used by navies, but with gunpowder rounds they were prone to jamming and had to be cleaned frequently. The expended energy of the new cartridges operated mechanisms that automatically ejected the spent cartridges, loaded new rounds into the breech and fired them. Hiram Maxim was the first, in 1884, to produce a weapon capable of operating for long periods, firing at rates of around 600 rounds per minute.[8]

Chemical engineers also exploited nitrocellulose solutions to improve artillery propellants, and mixtures based upon picric acid were developed from 1887 for artillery as melinite (French), lyddite (British) and ecrasite (Austrian). However, they could prove extremely sensitive, which was why the Germans opted from 1902 for the less powerful, but safer, trinitrotoluene (TNT). The British and French would follow suit with amatol and schneiderite respectively, with the Balkan armies using most of these compositions. All of these propellants were up to 300 per cent more powerful than gunpowder, hence the term 'high explosive'. French De Bange field guns used the new propellants in the traditional way as charges in calico bags, but Krupp introduced unitary shells in which the propellant and projectile were contained, like rifles, in a brass cartridge case. In a test between the two in Chile in 1890, Krupp guns fired 3–10 times faster than the De Banges, which had to be re-laid each time they were fired.[9]

The new propellants intensified the gun's recoil and while naval weapons could counter this with hydraulic cylinders, these were too bulky for most army cannon. For armies the initial solution was to absorb recoil with rubber rings and springs, but while this doubled firing rates, the mechanisms required frequent maintenance and were still unreliable. The problem was overcome by a French Army team led by Lieutenant Colonel Albert Deport, assisted by Captains Henri Étienne Sainte-Claire Deville and Émile Rimailho, who developed a hydro-pneumatic recoil-reduction mechanism with a long hydraulic cylinder and piston attached to the barrel. The combination of fluid and air pressure absorbed the recoil of the gun and produced only minute gun movements throughout the firing cycle, making it unnecessary to re-lay it every time it fired.[10]

Adopted in the famous 75-mm Modèle 1897 field gun, this weapon, with unitary rounds, had a range of 8.5 km and a firing rate of fifteen rounds per minute, although a very experienced crew could double this for short periods, and these type of weapons were aptly named Quick Firers.[11] Deville also developed an automatic fuse setter to select bursting distances for shrapnel shells. The gun was first publicly displayed in 1899, and armaments works throughout Europe were soon producing their own Quick Firers, although the French weapon is usually regarded as the best.[12]

It proved more difficult to adapt recoil mechanisms to howitzers, whose barrels were elevated to fire heavier shells. Gun makers Ehrhardt and Krupp found two solutions, the former with a graduated recoil system that shortened recoil in proportion to the barrel's angle (this system also being adopted by Schneider). The latter moved the cradle trunnions under the breech so that the barrel's elevation did not affect clearance in what became a combined gun and howitzer. However, both solutions had weaknesses, leading Schneider and Krupp to adopt either composite systems or controlled recoil and rear trunnions.[13]

Given that Europe's last conflicts before the First World War were in the gunpowder age, it is perhaps not surprising that European tactics were slow to respond to the new technologies, although there was a consensus that they accelerated the decline of cavalry. Firepower doomed cavalry's shock role on the battlefield and restricted their ability to exploit victory, reducing their roles to secondary tasks to act as scouts, screen infantry movements or act as mobile infantry. Another response to the greater range and lethality of warfare was to reduce the visibility of men to the enemy at longer ranges by abandoning the brightly coloured traditional uniforms for ones of a dowdier hue.[14]

Growing infantry firepower enhanced the importance of defensive operations, and the Napoleonic trend of building battlefield redoubts (strongpoints) continued during the nineteenth century, armies increasingly digging rifle pits (foxholes) which they soon extended into trench systems.[15] Armies had also used wooden obstacles in an attempt to restrict assaults upon these earthworks, but the development of barbed wire provided engineers with a medium which was easy to erect and a significant impediment to movement.[16] Even when armed with muzzle-loaded rifles, Confederate infantry calculated one man in a trench or rifle pit could stop ten in the open, a ratio that increased steadily with the new generation of rifles and automatic weapons. In the last major action of the Russo-Japanese war, the Battle of Mukden (now Shenyang) in February-March 1905, the Japanese suffered 22 per cent casualties in assaulting Russian defences.

At the tactical level battlefield movement remained linear, although at operational and strategic levels troops approached the battlefield in columns. Battalions still moved in two-deep waves on the battlefield, but in the face of increased firepower they advance in a single, loose skirmish line which might exploit natural cover in fire-and-movement tactics and was reinforced once contact was made with the enemy.[17] The skirmishers would seek to dominate the enemy with their firepower and/or outflank them until the point when the enemy was perceived to be wavering. Then the main body of troops would deliver a bayonet charge at either the weakest point in the enemy line or in the flank. However, it was noticeable that the skirmisher firefight tended to consume battlefield reserves, which made it difficult to deliver a decisive blow.

The problem of taking increasingly stronger defences divided infantry leaders, with most relying upon numerical superiority to overwhelm the enemy rather than trying to manoeuvre them out of their positions. The more thoughtful, such as Pétain, believed that firepower, including heavy artillery, should be used thoroughly to suppress the defences before such an infantry assault was launched. Fire-and-movement was time-consuming, and the desire for a more dynamic means of achieving victory led many to agree with France's Colonel Louis de Grandmaison, who was 51 years old when the Balkan Wars broke out. Grandmaison and others in the French staff looked at successful attacks upon defences from the American Civil War onwards and were especially influenced by the recent Russo-Japanese War in which Japanese mass assaults delivered with suicidal bravery had often broken through Russian lines or into fortifications.[18]

They conceived the concept of all-out attack (*attaque à outrance*) in which the side with the strongest will, the greatest courage and the greatest dash (*élan*) would overcome the enemy defences, with the emphasis upon bayonets rather than firepower to rout the enemy. Consequently, assaults during the Balkan Wars upon defences would be delivered by waves of bayonet-wielding infantry, one Bulgarian general casually speaking of losing 10,000 men against Turkish fortifications just as the Japanese had at Port Arthur.

It was not appreciated that frontal assaults upon field fortifications had succeeded in the past because the defenders had been stretched to breaking point, and this was certainly true during the latter stages of the American Civil War. The generals also tended to ignore the impact of growing firepower as well the expansion of the battlefield over dozens of kilometres, which made for difficult battlefield communication. This still relied upon written messages carried by couriers on horseback or runners, all exposed to enemy fire.[19] Frontal attacks based essentially upon blind faith would prove extremely costly and, during the First World War, largely ineffective, but they reflected the contemporary belief in 'manliness' based upon courage and dedication.[20]

The advances in artillery also discouraged the generals from seeking new infantry tactics. Quick Firer field guns were now capable of smothering trench systems with a blanket of high explosive and shrapnel shells, and they were sure this would destroy the defences and kill the occupants. Gunners no longer had to be deployed within sight of the target (exposed to small arms fire) because they had developed new methods which allowed them to conduct indirect fire with the aid of forward observers using telephones, telegraphs or signal flags. Moreover, the guns were now so accurate and their ammunition so reliable that they could fire over the attacking infantry until the latter were almost on top of the enemy. Although the Russo-Japanese war had limited influence upon the Balkan states, it did provide insights into tactics and the Bulgarians learned the importance of indirect fire before an infantry assault. In the aftermath of this war gunnery experts agreed that no amount of ammunition expenditure would allow field guns to destroy enemy field guns, so by 1910 counter-battery work focused upon neutralising them by killing their crews and horses.[21]

The Russo-Japanese War also demonstrated the value of heavy artillery. Both sides used 120-mm guns on the battlefield, while during the Battle of Mukden the Japanese used 11-inch (279.5-mm) former naval guns to bombard the Russian positions. But these weapons were heavy and slow, with the French in particular regarding them as an impediment to their freedom of manoeuvre. In 1909, the general staff representative told the Chamber of Deputies' Budget Commission, 'You talk to us of heavy artillery. Thank God we have none. The strength of the French Army is in the lightness of its guns.' But within two years the French Army had reversed its position and sought more heavy artillery. This was in response to the increase in German heavy artillery, and other armies increasingly wished to deploy their own heavy artillery in the field.[22]

Soon generals would recognise that heavy artillery was far more effective at breaking enemy defences than Quick Firer field artillery, yet no matter how heavy the bombardment there would always be sufficient defenders to stop an infantry assault. Field artillery remained a vital tool in assaulting enemy defences, even in 1918, when Quick Firer field guns were the foundation for the rolling (or creeping) barrage that preceded all infantry attacks. This would follow a short but intense multi-hour 'hurricane' bombardment by every calibre of gun, designed to neutralise rather than destroy the defender by stunning him or forcing him to take cover. Artillery would become the arbiter of the battlefield during the First World War, inflicting more than 60 per cent of all casualties and leading the French to coin the phrase 'Artillery conquers the ground and the infantry occupy it.'

Automatic weapons made defence easier because a few weapons distributed across the battlefield could dominate a large area and were too difficult for the gunners to detect. Initially they were regarded as a form of field artillery mounted on horse-drawn carriages, the Japanese using theirs to lay down concentrated fire over the heads of the assaulting infantry.[23] During the Edwardian period, most armies came to regard machine guns as infantry support weapons, and the Japanese moved theirs up to the infantry firing line despite this exposing the crews to rifle fire. Machine guns in the Balkan Wars operated in detachments with divisions or brigades, their prime role being to provide defensive fire support.

At the operational and strategic levels the technologies of the Industrial Age were more wholeheartedly embraced, with command and control conducted occasionally by wireless telegraphy (radio). Normally communication was by telegraph, augmented by the unreliable telephone whose calls over long distance were plagued by poor reception so that officers often had to shout down them.[24] Strategic transport in the Balkan Wars was mostly by rail but augmented by ship because the region had few rail lines. The largest concentration of railways was in the Eastern or Thracian theatre, while in the Western theatre they were mostly concentrated in the Vardar valley.

The region's most important rail line ran north-west to south-east and was used by the world-famous Orient Express. It ran from Belgrade through Sofia, Plovdiv, Drama and Eridne to Constantinople, with a secondary branch line at Nis running down the Vardar valley to Salonika, which was itself connected by rail to Sofia. There were also two narrow-gauge lines: one in the Sanjak of Novi Pazar between Skopje and Kosovska Mitrovica, and the second from Salonika to Bitola. Occupation of this rail network should have given the Ottomans the advantage of interior lines, but at the outset of war many non-Muslim rail employees were dismissed and their Muslim replacements lacked either the experience or the training to work the lines efficiently. In addition to this rickety rail system, the Greeks had lines from Athens to the frontier at Larisa and Trikala, while Montenegro had a narrow-gauge line that wound its way through the mountains between the Adriatic at Bar and the western shore of Lake Shkoder. These limited land communications made maritime traffic vital, and here the Allies would have the tremendous advantage of the Greek merchant fleet, while the Hellenic Royal Navy denied the Porte the opportunity of bringing in troops from the Middle East.

Operational- and tactical-level transport was by road—rarely paved and usually rutted earth tracks that turned into a swamp when it rained.[25] Motor transport was in its infancy, with unreliable vehicles whose fragile axles or suspension systems easily broke on the uneven roads; Serbia had only 150 vehicles and the Ottoman Empire barely twice that number, while the Bulgarians would mobilise only forty-eight including thirty-six motor cars.

The prime means of transport for most of the armies consisted of unsprung wooden wagons or carts drawn by at least one pair of grey oxen, and their progress was inevitably slow. The rural economies of the Balkans had always been short of horses and oxen, which meant severely reduced transport for all the armies at the tactical- operational level. On both sides the authorities tried to requisition pack and draught animals together with wagons and carts, the Ottoman Empire having to buy 48,000 horses and oxen for its army. However, the cunning peasantry had long been adept at palming off the poorer animals and vehicles while retaining the best for their own use. The Bulgarians would mobilise 28,000 carts, but their 1st Army had only 10,960 oxen for 8,650 vehicles, while the 3rd Army had only 3,060 bullocks for 7,375 vehicles.

Horses were used to pull guns as well as carts which carried smaller loads, no more than six shells, but on the deeply mired and often flooded roads they moved just as slowly as the oxen.[26] The Serbian Army requisitioned 50,000 horses, 42,000 oxen and 21,000 carts, but many military districts had to 'borrow' animals and carts, while some units had to replace oxen with cows. The Timoska II Division was short of 350 horses, leaving gun teams with four rather than six, while Dunavska II Division was short of 60 carts.[27] In the mountains, pack mules were used and where they were not available able-bodied men as well as women were used as porters.[28]

The armies who fought in the bloody Balkan Wars were all drawn from rural rather than industrial societies, their ranks filled by the peasantry who were stoic, hard-working, unquestioning, religious, nationalistic and largely illiterate men.[29] Rural societies place less emphasis upon education than industrial ones, which made it difficult to lead the massed ranks, the task falling to professional, semi-literate, non-commissioned officers. Most of their junior officers were literate professionals such as teachers, senior management from commercial enterprises and lawyers augmented by shopkeepers and the like, many from urban backgrounds. Indeed, in the Bulgarian army only 22 per cent of the officers had rural backgrounds.[30] The Ottoman Army before the war dismissed nearly 14,000 older, often illiterate, officers who had started in the ranks (ayals), but was unable to replace them.[31]

Professional officers led at regimental level and above, although few showed any profound understanding of the new battlefields because the only requirement for an officer was to display bravery under fire. They were rarely concerned with the welfare of their men in terms of food, shelter or basic hygiene, and this would cause major problems during the campaigns. No army paid much attention to field hygiene, the peasant soldiers relieving themselves wherever and whenever they felt, as in peacetime, and every army would be plagued by cholera epidemics exacerbated by a lack of medical staff and facilities. The shortage of leaders meant a high ratio of officers to men: one officer to twenty men in the Bulgarian army, 1:27 in the Ottoman and 1:44 in the Serbian. The Bulgarian army, for example, had only 7,102 officers (4,150 reserve) but needed 11,673, so was 39 per cent under establishment, and junior officers in the active army were promoted to make up the numbers.[32] Consequently, the armies were organised into cumbersome formations, the smallest division in the Bulgarian army having 23,692 men, while the largest had 37,335; Serbian Ban I divisions had 35,000 men and Ban II divisions had 20,000. Command and control of these massive formations was difficult, and initiative evaporated if there were high losses among the officers.[33]

There were also severe shortages of technically trained personnel to work the new technologies; indeed, the 500,500-strong Bulgarian Army needed 4,215 telegraphists but had only 1,269.[34] None of the armies was self-sufficient in arms and ammunition, and all suffered severe shortages of equipment (20 per cent of Ottoman troops were unarmed) with active formations getting the lion's share of modern rifles, uniforms, great coats, boots, webbing, blankets, tents and tarpaulins.[35] What was left filtered down to the reserve units who often had civilian footwear, as did some Serbian active troops, while some marched barefoot.

The men were organised into infantry companies, usually of 150–250 men, with four companies to a battalion and three battalions to a regiment. Cavalry were organised into squadrons of about 100 men, with four squadrons to a regiment. In most armies the divisions were 'triangular', i.e. organised into three infantry regiments, but Bulgarian divisions were 'square' formations with four infantry regiments, and Montenegrin divisions were organised into two or three brigades with a varying number of battalions. Divisions were usually grouped into army corps, which the Bulgarians and Serbs designated 'armies', while Ottoman army corps (formed in 1908) were grouped into armies. The pre-war Greek Army had three army corps (Alpha, Beta, Gamma) but the shortage of staff officers meant that on 28 September all the divisions were placed directly under two army headquarters, although during the campaign *ad hoc* corps groups known as Army Sections (*Tmima Stratias*) were created, with divisions placed under the operational control of one divisional commander.

The Ottoman Army had taken great care to get the best men, and its peacetime strength was nearly 336,750 men, most of whom were conscripts. It was organised into active

(*Nizamiye*) and local reserve (*Redif*) formations, with regional army inspectorates in the Balkans, Thrace, the Caucasus, Syria and Mesopotamia, each with a *Redif* inspectorate. The army's mobilised strength, when the regular units were filled out with the army reserve (*Ihtiad*) and when *Redif* formations joined the colours, was nominally 700,000, but this was never achieved and the quality was clearly diluted.[36] Substantial forces were needed elsewhere in the empire, which eventually mobilised in the Balkans some 337,000 men from whom a field army of some 293,200 was created, the remainder being fortress or lines-of-communication forces. The regular (*Nizam*) troops wore the brown-khaki (other ranks) or grey-green (officers) uniform introduced in 1909, while many of the *Redif* retained the dark blue 1893 uniform with red fez.

Regimental instruction was poor, with little field training, and the men were generally neither well fed nor healthy. This meant that they found long marches exhausting, and the problem was exacerbated by poor administrative work at regimental headquarters that often left the men without food or water. This was in contrast to the advice of German military missions, whose most distinguished member was general staff officer and military writer Major Wilhelm Freiherr von der Goltz.[37]

The mission consisted of officers on government or private contracts with the Ottoman Army, and the Porte, supported by Berlin, rejected their attempts to volunteer for active service when war broke out. Despite this, a few attached themselves to units, notably Hauptmann Gustav von Hoachwaechter, who joined Mahmud Muktar Pasha in III Corps. Goltz would have liked to join them, but as a designated army commander in the German Army he was forbidden from leaving the country and during the Balkan Wars he was restricted to writing advisory letters to his Ottoman friends. However, when Colonel Pertev Bey visited Germany in March 1913 to buy heavy artillery, Goltz did try to help him.[38]

The Germans made little progress in modernising the Ottoman Army, and in the summer of 1912 the Porte informed Berlin that it would not renew the contracts of field-grade officers attached to 'model regiments'. Early in October, the German military attaché in Constantinople, Major Walter von Strempel, informed his superiors that it was highly likely the Ottoman forces would be defeated in Thrace and that the Greeks would enter Macedonia.

The Germans did influence the reorganisation of forty-three *Nizam* divisions in 1911, from 'square' to 'triangular' organisation, and for the first time they acquired organic artillery and also began to reorganise the 54 *Redif* divisions.[39] The need to defend the Caucasus front tied down seven *Nizam* and eight *Redif* divisions, while to hold the Porte's Middle East subjects in check required twelve *Nizam* and eleven *Redif* divisions. This left twenty-five *Nizam* and twenty-seven *Redif* divisions for the Balkans, which could be augmented by adding further *Redif* formations and creating new *Nizam* formations from independent units.

There were 713,400 rifles, ranging from 280,000 of the excellent 7.65-mm Mauser M.1890 and M.1903 to 300,000 11.4-mm Martini-Henry M.1874 and 9.65-mm Mauser M.1887, and even 14.7-mm British Snider-Enfields.[40] These were augmented by 388

German Maxim M.1909 or Maxim Nordenfelt 1892 automatic weapons. The artillery, supplied exclusively by Krupp, consisted of 736 75-mm field guns (M.1904 and eighty-eight M.1910) augmented by 80-mm and 90-mm field guns as well as 70-mm mountain guns, either without recoil mechanisms or with obsolete mechanisms. But there was little mobile heavy artillery, although Krupp had sold eighteen 105-mm guns, eighteen 150-mm howitzers and thirty-six 120-mm howitzers.[41]

Their prime enemy was the Bulgarian Army, which prided itself as being the Prussia of the Balkans and had a peacetime strength of nearly 62,000.[42] By 1905, a third of the Bulgarian budget was going to the army, whose officers had the highest pay rates in the country and included many intellectuals as well as the sons of small businessmen.[43] Upon mobilisation the authorities were swamped with conscripts and volunteers, 79.5 per cent of the male population flocking to the colours to create an army of almost 500,500 men. Sofia could put 376,300 into the field, organised into six regular and three reserve infantry divisions, each with a pair of artillery regiments, one with thirty-six Quick Firers and the other with thirty-six older guns. There was also a cavalry division and four machine-gun detachments with sixteen weapons. The troops usually wore a uniform described as 'tobacco-brown', although officers had a grey-green uniform, while many men used some of the older dark green uniforms.

The army had a conventional structure, with the active army consisting of a professional core augmented by recruits, which would be reinforced upon mobilisation by reserve army men aged up to 40. It tried to synthesise the influences of the German, Italian and Russian armies and was widely regarded as well trained, with an unusual emphasis upon night operations.

At the outbreak of war, the Bulgarians had 343,428 rifles, the majority Austrian 8-mm Mannlicher M.1888, M.1890 and M.1895, with single-shot, bolt-action 10.66-mm Berdan II (M.1871) rifles later augmented by 75,000 rifles from Russia, 50,000 7.62-mm Mosin-Nagant M.1891s and another 25,000 Berdan IIs. Some reservist troops had a breech-loading version of the Snider as the single-shot 15.2-mm M.1869 Krnka which they had bought from Bulgarian military surplus. These were augmented by 232 Maxim M.1908 machine guns.

The artillery park had 1,000 pieces, including 324 Schneider 75-mm Mle 1904 field guns, 306 Krupp 87-mm M.1886 and seventy-eight 75-mm M.1886 field guns, augmented by ninety-two Krupp (fifty-six 75-mm M.1904 Quick Firers and thirty-six 75-mm M.1886s) and fifty-four Schneider (thirty-six 75-mm Mle 1907 QFs and eighteen Mle 1897) mountain guns. They were well equipped with heavy artillery from French sources, with eighteen heavy howitzer batteries equipped with thirty-six Schneider Mle 1909 120-mm QF field howitzers and thirty Krupp M.1891 120-mm field howitzers, while the fortress/siege artillery park had twenty-four 120-mm Schneider L/28 Mle 1907 guns and twenty-four 150-mm Schneider L/12 Mle 1897 howitzers as well as twelve Krupp 120-mm L/30 guns, fourteen Krupp 150-mm L/30 guns and six Krupp L/25 120-mm guns.

The Serbian Army learned the lessons from its defeat in 1885, and from 1906 underwent a modernisation programme, although its staff were not as good as the Bulgarians.[44] It had a peacetime strength of 168,700 which was split into three levels (Bans) aged 21–31 (I Ban), 32–38 (II Ban) and 39–45 (III Ban), the last essentially almost a militia, and formation designations reflected this, with the Dunavska I and II Divisions being I and II Ban units respectively. Upon mobilisation, strength rose to almost 336,350 in ten infantry divisions, half formed from II and III Ban men, and a cavalry division, so that Belgrade could put 319,000 into the field. The men themselves had a reputation for both toughness and endurance, while their junior leaders showed considerable tactical skill. The I Ban troops wore the M.1908 standard khaki uniform, the II Ban troops retaining the older dark blue M.1896 uniforms with red trousers, while III Ban troops rarely received uniforms and retained their civilian clothing with the occasional item of uniform.

The Serbs had 288,000 rifles, I Ban troops receiving 100,000 7-mm Mauser M.1910 rifles augmented by M.1899s and M.1899/07s, while II Ban men had 45,000 10.15-mm Mauser-Koka M.1880 (a locally made derivative of the Mauser M.1871/84) single-shot rifles converted into magazine weapons as M.1880/07s, as well as Berdan II (M.1887) rifles, single-shot Mauser-Koka M.1884 carbines also being used. The III Ban troops had 10.6-mm Berdan IIs and 10.2-mm Mauser M.1871 single-shot, bolt-action rifles, while the infantry regiments had 230 Maxim M.1910 machine guns distributed among them to augment their rifles.

Serbian field artillery was the usual mixture of old and new: 324 Schneider-Creusot Mle 1907/1907A 75-mm QFs and 264 De Bange 80 mm Mle 1885 field guns, augmented by 36 Schneider-Creusot Mle 1907 and eight Schneider-Danglis 75-mm QF and thirty De Bange 80-mm Mle 1885 mountain guns. There was also a large heavy artillery train, including forty modern Schneider-Creusot weapons (of which twenty-three were Mle 1910 120-mm howitzers and eight were Mle 1910 150-mm howitzers, the remainder being 120mm guns) and forty older Schneider-Canet weapons (twenty-two Mle 1897 120-mm howitzers, twelve Mle 1897 120-mm guns and six Mle 1897 150-mm mortars). During the war, Serbia also acquired from Schneider-Canet thirty-two Mle 1910 120-mm guns and eight Mle 1910 150-mm howitzers.

The Greek Army, widely regarded as the weakest in the Balkans following its disastrous performance in 1897, had begun a radical reorganisation after the arrival of a French military mission in 1911, but the following year it still lacked clear war plans.[45] The active army in peacetime had a strength of some 22,680, conscripts remaining with the colours for two years before spending twenty-one years in the First Reserve and eight in the Second Reserve.

In the aftermath of Greek independence, the army had been quite small and was essentially an internal security force because the Great Powers guaranteed national borders, and it expanded only after Bulgaria's annexation of Eastern Rumelia. For much of the nineteenth century, Athens relied upon guerrilla warfare to project Greek power by stimulating uprisings in enemy territory which the army would ultimately aid, a concept reminiscent of twentieth-century wars of 'national liberation'.[46] The 1897 war made it all too aware of its shortcomings: lack of both a general staff and a supply organisation, as well as an incompetent bureaucracy due to patronage.

Reforms began under Crown Prince Constantine, who was also *de facto* army commander, but these created unrest and led to his brief dismissal. Reinstated as the first Inspector General of the Army in 1911, he began to modernise the army aided by the arrival of French General Joseph Eydoux's military mission. The French modernised the mobilisation system and then reorganised the divisions on the 'triangular' pattern, using surplus regiments to create new divisions. This enabled Athens to mobilise 125,000 men, augmented by an 80,000-strong National Guard for second-line duties such as guarding rail lines, and to create a field army of seven divisions with 110,000 men, twice the size anticipated by foreign observers. Most of the infantry wore the olive-khaki M.1908 uniform, although the Evzone light infantry had the distinctive highlander folk costume with pleated kilt (*fustanella*). Some reservists wore the old dark blue M.1896 tunic with grey trousers.

The army had some 190,000 rifles, the first-line units having 115,000 6.5-mm Mannlicher-Schoenauer M.1903 and M.1907 bolt-action rifles, while reserve units had the 11-mm Gras M.1874 rifle augmented by eighty-four Schwarzlose M.1907 machine guns. There was a shortage of artillery but most of it was modern, including 168 Schneider-Creusot Mle 1906 75-mm QFs and ninety-eight Schneider-Danglis Mle 1906 and 1912 75-mm QF mountain guns. There were reportedly seventy-two heavy guns, including Krupp 105-mm howitzers, 100-mm and 150-mm guns together with Schneider-Canet 120-mm guns.

The smallest army facing the Turks was that of Montenegro, whose population was famed for its bellicosity and whose guerrilla fighting and bandit traditions made them experts at small-unit operations.[47] The army was organised on territorial and tribal lines, with nine brigades formed in 1880 and a tenth added in 1910, while there were three active battalions. The brigades varied in size from three to eight battalions for a total of fifty-eight battalions, each of four or five clan-based companies, with strengths varying from 407 to 1,059.

Young men aged 18 or 19 receiving a year's basic training before joining a first-line reserve until they were 53, when they were transferred to the second-line reserve. The Montenegrin army lacked supply and medical organisations but its most serious deficiency was in leadership which often devolved onto clan chiefs. Some officers had been trained abroad, but there were fewer than thirty-five technically trained officers and only one staff officer. Most officers were selected by King Nikola for political reasons and displayed no interest in modern ideas, opposing the promotion of the few foreign-trained officers. Of the brigade commanders only three had completed military school, the remainder having either received short courses or merely a little local training, while only two of the four division commanders had trained in an Italian military school. The monarch was supreme commander, although he lacked any staff apart from orderlies and was little more than a warlord.[48]

Upon mobilisation the army had some 45,000 men, of whom 35,600 were in the field organised into four divisions augmented by a Serbian volunteer brigade of four battalions. The regular troops had the khaki M.1910 uniform, but the vast majority of men wore the colourful traditional dress. The army suffered from a serious shortage of heavy weapons, but had received substantial supplies from Russia: 10,000 rifles and fifty-five guns in 1909 alone. By the outbreak of war there were 40,000 Mosin-Nagant 7.62-mm M.1891 rifles augmented by 20,000 Werndl M.1870/1873 and 11-mm Gras M.1874 rifles, while the reservists had some 30,000 Berdan II (M.1870) rifles. There were only twelve Maxim MG 08 machine guns and half a dozen Nordenfelt Gatlings, although another fifty Maxims were acquired during the war.

The field army had twenty-six batteries with 106 guns, including eight Russian 76.2-mm M.1902 QFs and six Krupp 80-mm, fourteen Italian 90-mm M.1876 and six Krupp M.1887 75-mm field guns as well as six 76-mm M.1902 QFs, nine 75-mm Krupp M.1886, twelve 75-mm Italian and four 70-mm Krupp mountain guns. The heavy artillery consisted of eleven 120-mm M.1875 guns, six 210-mm howitzers, eight 150-mm mortars, a couple of 105-mm Russian M.1875 guns and six 120-mm Armstrong M.1860 guns, the last being used for coastal defence.

Neutral in the First Balkan War and decisive in the Second was the Rumanian Army, the largest in the Balkans with a peacetime strength of 100,300, but it had seen no combat since 1878, apart from suppressing a peasant revolt in 1907.[49] It was divided into the active army (*Armata Activa*) with men aged 21–23, the reserve army (*Reserva Armatei*) whose men were 29–40, and the militia (*Militii*) with men aged 41–46. Upon mobilisation the army could expand to nearly 507,000 men in 247 infantry battalions, ninety-three cavalry squadrons and 181 batteries organised into five corps, with ten active and five reserve infantry divisions augmented by two cavalry divisions and three reserve brigades. The active troops had the new grey-green uniform issued in 1912, but many reservists retained the old blue uniform, gunners wearing a brown uniform. The quality of the officer corps is impossible to determine, but they would not be stretched by their short campaign which saw the army encounter no major problems.

The Rumanians had 6.5-mm Mannlicher M.1893/1892 rifles and carbines, and during 1912 imported 50,000 Steyr M.1912 rifles together with 60,000 8-mm Mannlicher M.1890/1895s, although some reserve troops were still equipped with the Austrian OEWG-built Peabody-Martini M.1879. About 130 Maxim and Schwarzlose machine guns had also been imported from Austria and Germany. The artillery park had 564 75-mm Krupp M.1904 QF field guns, sixteen 75-mm Schneider QFs, and forty-two 87-mm Krupp and twelve 63.5-mm Armstrong mountain guns. There were twenty-five heavy batteries with sixty 105-mm Krupp M.1910 QF howitzers, thirty-two 120-mm Krupp howitzers and eight 150-mm Schneider QF howitzers.

All armies had a regular militia component recruited from the youngest and oldest men, often augmented by a gendarmerie, but around the armies there was also a plague of paramilitaries. The majority were militias or bandit-guerrilla bands organised on a religious or tribal basis and made up of poorly equipped men with a collection of weapons and often in colourful traditional dress.[50] While they might harass isolated groups of troops or supply trains, they were primarily interested in the traditional Balkan pastimes of ethnic cleansing, murder, rape and pillage. It was not always clear which side they supported. Christians fought under the Crescent and Muslims under the Cross, but their objective was always to preserve their ethnic grouping from outside domination or annihilation. Macedonia also saw ethnically based guerrilla forces, often loosely organised into groups (*chetas*) of from one to four dozen men. There were some forty-four Bulgarian *chetas* as well as Serbian National Defence and Greek Macedonia fighters, all of whom sought to secure Macedonia for their country.

Some paramilitaries were attached directly to armies as scouts, the Greek Army of Epirus having nine companies with 1,800 Macedonian scouts as well as platoons with nearly 450 Epirot scouts, while some 6,000 Albanian Catholics (*Malisori*) joined the Montenegrin Army. The Ottoman paramilitaries included the *Bashi Bazouks*, mercenaries who were notorious for their lack of discipline and brutality and had once been organised by the Ottoman Army. Now they were usually created by locals to support the army and receive payment in loot. Small groups of Muslim volunteers would join Turkish corps in the Catalca Line from November 1912.

There were also two major autonomous groupings of irregulars. To support the Bulgarians, the Macedonian-Thracian Legion (Macedono-Odrinsko Opalchenie Division) was formed on 23 September 1912 from nearly 13,900 Orthodox Christians together with some 500 foreign volunteers and 275 Armenians.[51] It was equipped by the Bulgarian Army with Berdan rifles and did not disband until October 1913. Thousands of Cretans also fought alongside the Greek Army, both in formations and as platoon-size scouting units, some seventy-seven being formed with an establishment of nearly 3,560, usually in uniform but sometimes in traditional dress.

On Goltz's advice, the Ottoman Army had begun to redraft its war plans in 1909, integrating them with the mobilisation plans of the active and reserve formation.[52] By the eve of war, the Ottoman general staff had a dozen plans to meet every contingency, the most detailed, which incorporated suggestions from the relevant armies, being Plan 5 against the Balkan Pact and Greece. Ottoman operations were also influenced by Plan 1, against Bulgaria in Thrace, and Plan 4 against Bulgaria, Serbia and Montenegro, but priority was given to the defence of Macedonia and Epirus. Plan 5 anticipated attacks by up to 556 infantry battalions (including 288 Bulgarian, 140 Serbian and 72 Greek) and envisaged 385 Ottoman battalions in Thrace and 273 in Macedonia. Like the other plans, it envisaged remaining on the defensive at strategic level and aimed to thwart the Bulgarians, whom the Ottoman general staff recognised were the primary threat. Once they were neutralised, the Porte's generals were confident that their troops could defeat other enemies in detail. However, the general staff were uncertain whether or not the main Bulgarian blow would fall in Thrace or Macedonia, and had prepared for either eventuality, but army and corps commanders were encouraged to use their forces aggressively at the tactical-operational level and to exploit major fortified centres.

The weakness of Ottoman plans was that they failed to anticipate a co-ordinated offensive by their enemies from all sides, which compromised all hopes that the army would preserve the empire's Balkan territories. The army was expected to hold key population centres together with fortified centres, but this exposed it to defeat in detail, while the paucity of rail communications denied it the advantage of interior lines. There were also concerns that the mobilisation schedules were impractical, for it was optimistically calculated that the active forces could be ready within a week and the reserve forces a week later. However, a meeting of the Supreme Military Council on 25 June calculated that a twenty-five-day preparation period was inadequate and informed the War Ministry that it would take twice this time before the army was ready to give battle.

The mobilisation plans had also been disrupted by a continued rebellion in Yemen and the war with Italy. Five 1st Army divisions scheduled to defend Thrace—the 2nd, 6th, 7th, 8th and 9th—had to dispatch a total of twelve battalions to Yemen and Syria. The 1st Division was scattered from Thessaly to Constantinople, with its 3rd Infantry in Albania together with the 2nd Division's 4th Infantry and a battalion each from the 4th and 9th Divisions. Drafts also had to be sent to flesh out the 6th Division to defend Anatolia in case the Italians landed there.

If the Christian armies were to overcome the Porte it was obvious that they would need to co-ordinate their efforts, and this work was led by Bulgaria and Serbia.[53] The foundation was laid by the military co-operation agreement of 29 April 1912, which was nominally designed to provide mutual assistance in response to an attack upon Bulgaria by either Rumania or the Ottomans, or an attack upon Serbia by Austria.

Fichev was the driving force behind Bulgarian war planning and had played a key role in the negotiations. When Head of Operations in 1903, he drafted a strategy based upon an active defence to thwart an Ottoman advance north of Edirne along the River Meric. It involved two divisions facing Macedonia and three facing Thrace, but was amended the following year to create a defence force on the southern frontier, the Rodop (Rhodope) Detachment. By 1908, the Bulgarians had switched to an offensive strategy based upon speed and initiative in the Grandmaison style, in which two new corps-sized armies (2nd and 3rd) would punch south-east into Thrace while a new detachment advanced southwards to the Aegean and a third army pinned down the Turks in Macedonia. To support it, a major intelligence operation was launched to collect information about the Thracian terrain, supported by extensive training and studies of foreign experience.

When he became chief-of-staff in 1911, Fichev committed almost the whole Bulgarian Army into Thrace. It would bypass Edirne and head directly to the Ottoman capital via Tekirdag, and this plan would be the foundation of allied strategy, although it required Serbian support. For their part, the Serbs, under Putnik, were more concerned about taking Macedonia, which was why they had requested 100,000 Bulgarians to help ensure victory in the Vardar valley. The Bulgarian presence would certainly help Bulgaria achieve its aim of securing Macedonian territory, but it placed Fichev in a dilemma. He could achieve his military objective of destroying the main Ottoman force in Thrace only by abandoning Bulgaria's political ambitions in Macedonia. He grasped the nettle and decided to concentrate almost all his troops in Thrace, even though this would allow his allies to grab much of the disputed territory. Despite his previous agreements with the Serbs, he would now send only a token force to Macedonia but would rub salt in the wound by seeking Serbian troops for his Thracian campaign.

In August, Fichev persuaded Putnik to agree that most of the Bulgarian forces would be deployed in Thrace because it was the decisive theatre. He also persuaded him to supply up to three divisions to help invest Edirne, although Putnik was reluctant to supply cannon-fodder for this role. Fichev's agreement to use the corps-sized Rodop Detachment to cover the Serbian left proved little compensation. On 14 September, the Serbs revealed their revised plans in which eight divisions (1st and 3rd Armies) would split Macedonia in two by advancing upon Pristina and Kumanovo, while each side would contribute a division for a third army under Serbian command (2nd) on the right of the Rodop Detachment. This was accepted by Fichev on 28 September after he received confirmation that following the Serb victory in Macedonia, they would support the siege of Edirne. The Bulgarians were confident that they could mobilise within ten days like the Serbs, although their active forces and cavalry would be ready in half that time. For Serbia's Montenegrin allies the objectives were to secure the fortified town of Shkoder and northern Albania, and they planned to mobilise within eight days.

With fewer staff officers, the Greeks were slower to make formal military arrangements. They would assemble 100,000 men in Thessaly for an advance into Macedonia to take Salonika, while another 20,000 in Epirus would take Ioannina. They believed they could mobilise four divisions in six days and another three in eight, not seeking to integrate their operations with their allies until early October. It was on 5 October that a statement of intentions was signed in Sofia, the signatories including Captain Ioannis Metaxas, who would be Greece's dictator in the late 1930s. This agreement guaranteed the commitment of the Hellenic Navy, which would prevent the Ottoman Empire moving troops by sea. The Hellenic Navy was Athens' greatest contribution to the Balkan League, and when Panas claimed to the incredulous Bulgarians that his country could contribute 600,000 men to the war effort, he explained that 200,000 were Greek troops and the remainder were Ottoman troops who could not be transported to Macedonia and Thrace.[54]

Navies remained strongly influenced by the golden age of sail, although sailing vessels were now largely confined to coastal trade and warships outwardly bore no resemblance to the Hearts of Oak that clashed at Trafalgar. Oak was replaced first by iron and then by steel, while coal-powered steam engines augmented sails until triple-expansion engines made sails obsolete. By 1880, the iron and bronze, muzzle-loaded, smooth-bore cannon were replaced with steel, rifled, breech-loaded guns firing conical projectiles that made armour plate essential for protection. The new generation of ordnance, with hydraulic cylinders to absorb recoil, extended engagement ranges from one nautical mile up to 3.5 nautical miles, with accuracy and rates of fire undreamt of by any of Nelson's officers.[55]

This had a fundamental impact upon tactics, and a 1,500-year tradition of taking enemy warships was gradually replaced by a new aim—to sink them. In Napoleonic times cannon fire disabled the enemy by destroying either the rigging or the crew, the ship then being boarded and taken. Indeed, few wooden warships were directly sunk by cannon fire. At Trafalgar, for example, only one of thirty-three Franco-Spanish ships of the line was sunk, while twenty-one were taken, although a third of the latter were lost in the post-battle tempest and two were scuttled.

Even in Napoleonic times shells were feared for their ability to set ships ablaze, and this remained a threat because steel-hulled warships had timber decks and fittings as well as coal bunkers. Now shells could crack open hulls, although at Tsushima, the final naval battle of the Russo-Japanese War, while most of the eighteen major Russian surface combatants (battleships and cruisers) were sunk, seven struck their colours and were boarded, two promptly being scuttled. Weapons technology now made it impossible for boarding parties to sweep onto warship decks, the boarding party being largely restricted to investigating merchantmen, although major navies continued cutlass drill until after the Great War.

Another feature of Napoleonic naval warfare to become a casualty of the new technology was the close blockade in which ships patrolled close to ports. The new generation of coastal defence artillery together with the latest underwater weapons, the mine (once known as the torpedo) and the (self-propelled) torpedo, compelled even the mightiest navies to blockade beyond range of these weapons and often beyond sight of the coast. The torpedo also played a part in naval battles, being a major threat, as the Japanese demonstrated on several occasions, and allowing small navies to threaten even the mightiest navy's largest battleship.

Yet the age of sail continued to influence naval design, for while the main armament might be either in turrets or shielded mountings fore and aft, major warships retained the main gun deck of their predecessors, as may be appreciated by visits to HMS *Victory* and *Warrior* in Portsmouth, the USS *Olympia* in Philadelphia, the RHS *Averoff* in Greece and the HIJMS *Mikasa* in Japan. Some Ottoman warships used in the Balkan Wars were designed with broadside armaments, although most had been modernised before the conflict with pintle-mounted guns and armoured shields. Even if fleet actions were no longer exchanges of broadsides at pistol range, they were fought at relatively close range with lines of battle sailing parallel as each ship selected a target and tried to smother it with shell fire.

The battleship and the line of battle remained at the heart of naval actions, and the design of steel-armoured pre-dreadnought battleships was standardised from the 1880s. Their main armament was either in open-topped barbettes, in which the guns were raised to fire and lowered to reload, or more usually in armoured turrets fore and aft of the superstructure. This armament consisted of slow-firing, breech-loaded, rifled guns (10–13 inch or 254–330 mm), which matured during the 1890s and was designed specifically to penetrate the strongest armour. Yet armour development was not static and from the mid-1890s Krupp produced armour plate that was thinner, and lighter, than its rivals but also much stronger, with a 133-mm layer giving protection equivalent to 305 mm of earlier belts of armour.

But every development in armour was quickly matched by an advance in gunnery. Navies quickly adopted the propellants developed for armies, although they retained bags of propellant and separate projectiles in larger guns for ease of handling and to adjust ranges. Improvements in metallurgy exploited the new propellants and would see the British 12-inch (305-mm) 35-calibre gun, introduced in 1895 with a muzzle velocity of

737 m/s, being replaced a decade later by a 45-calibre weapon with a muzzle velocity of 830 m/s.

Battleships also carried a secondary battery usually of 6–9.2 inches (150–230 mm), although some had 10-inch (250-mm) weapons, breech-loaded Quick Firers similar to field artillery. They were to inflict secondary damage on other battleships and also to help protect the battleship from smaller surface combatants. These weapons, in turrets, hull casements or even in open positions protected by a simple anti-splinter gun shield, were usually mounted on the gun deck. They were augmented by smaller 3 or 4-inch (75–100 mm) or less Quick Firers, machine guns and electrically powered Gatlings, to both rake the decks of enemy battleships and protect the battleships from torpedo boat attack.

The battleships were supported by cruisers, which replaced the sailing frigate and corvette and were designed for long-range, autonomous patrols. Until the introduction of the triple-expansion engine, many cruisers, including those of the Ottoman Navy, augmented their engines with sail and had broadside armament, but the Porte's ships were later rebuilt along more modern lines. The Great Powers used cruisers to execute imperial policies, but in naval warfare they were used for reconnaissance, to impose blockades and to raid enemy commerce.

Cruiser main armament was generally 5.5–9.2 inches (140–230 mm), and the ships were designed for high speeds to evade more heavily armed opponents. But as armoured warships and naval Quick Firers became more common, a degree of armour protection was essential. The solution was to introduce an armoured deck to prevent plunging fire penetrating the boiler and engine rooms, which, together with main magazines, were below the waterline, while the propulsion compartments were further sheltered by coal bunkers. Limited armour protection was later installed in hulls, but from the mid-1870s there emerged cruisers with armour protection similar to that of battleships, which they closely resembled. These armoured cruisers were designed to support battleships by engaging and sinking anything smaller and were often popularly included with battleships under the generic term 'ironclad'. France's Admiral François Ernest Fournier proposed in his highly influential work of 1896 *La flotte nécessaire* fleets based entirely upon the armoured cruiser and torpedo boat.

The torpedo boat was a nineteenth-century development, although the torpedo was found in a variety of ships including battleships and cruisers. The term 'torpedo' originally meant a static underwater explosive charge, but this was later renamed the mine after Robert Whitehead developed the self-propelled torpedo. This replaced spar torpedoes, which were explosive charges at the end of a timber beam, but both required fast, highly manoeuvrable vessels.[56] Whitehead's weapon was steadily improved so that by 1912 it had a range of about 3 nautical miles (5.5 km) and a speed of 30 knots at a pre-set depth, although the older weapons used by the Hellenic and Bulgarian Navies could make only 7 knots and had a range of about half a nautical mile (600 metres).

The torpedo boats were supposed to operate *en masse* to overwhelm larger warships, but having to approach close to the target to deliver their weapons exposed them to enemy fire, while their low freeboard meant that they could not operate in high seas. The Russo-Japanese War, in which some 300 torpedoes were expended, had begun with a surprise night attack by torpedo boats upon the Russian fleet, and many navies hoped to emulate this feat.[57] To keep these naval hornets at bay, navies developed larger and more seaworthy torpedo boats with 3 or 4-inch guns as torpedo boat destroyers, or destroyers, both to screen the ironclads and to act as torpedo platforms in their own right during fleet actions.

The development of more powerful guns and the torpedo meant that battles were fought at greater ranges. This was reflected in the two decades preceding the Balkan War, with fleet actions fought at ranges of 1.5 nautical miles (2.7 km) during the Battle of the Yalu River in 1894, and subsequently at distances ranging from 2.7 nautical miles (5 km) to 4 nautical miles (7 km). At Santiago Bay in 1898, the US ships came within 0.85 nautical miles (1.6 km) of the enemy, while in one clash the Russian fleet in the Pacific opened fire upon the Japanese at 8 nautical miles (15 km). Most contemporary optical rangefinders were effective only to 3.25 nautical miles (6 km) and were used only for the largest guns, leaving the gun crews to aim the smaller ones by sight. Consequently, targets were rapidly obscured by shells of all calibres either straddling or striking the ship, and this made fire control extremely difficult.

Six years before the Balkan Wars, radical designs from British shipyards would revolutionise naval warfare. The new dreadnought battleships rationalised their main armament to a single calibre while retaining some smaller-calibre weapons for self-defence, and a similar principle was adopted for the new armoured cruisers which had capital ship main armament and were designated battlecruisers. With their steam turbines, rather than triple-expansion steam engines, and 10–12 inch big-gun armaments, the new generation of capital ships rendered obsolete the ironclads, which could neither outrun nor outgun them. However, this emphasis upon larger-calibre weapons would cause naval engagements to be conducted at longer ranges in the next four years, ranging from 6 to 9.7 nautical miles (11 to 18 km).

The new science of wireless telegraphy widely introduced in the decade before the Balkan Wars provided more efficient command and control at operational and strategic levels, allowing fleets to cover wider areas, but the vulnerability of radio transmitters to shock when the guns fired (a reason for dedicated command ships replacing battleships during amphibious operations in the Second World War) meant that tactical-level communication was still by flag. However, in fast-moving battles over smoke-shrouded seas this could be extremely unreliable, as demonstrated during the battlecruiser clash at Jutland. Commanders still tended to lead from exposed bridges, even when the larger ships provided the security of armoured conning towers, most admirals ignoring them because they gave too narrow a view of the action.

The latest development was the submarine torpedo boat. Submarines were developed from the 1880s, but all suffered inherent propulsion problems and while Nordenfelt produced steam-powered vessels which were sold in 1888 to both Greece and Turkey by the notorious arms dealer Basil Zaharoff, they never became operational! It was left to Irish-American inventor John P. Holland to create an efficient and effective design which used an internal combustion engine to sail on the surface and to power the electric batteries that provided underwater propulsion. The US Navy purchased the first Holland boat in 1900, and four years later the French submarine *Aigrette* was the first to be fitted with a diesel engine.

Most of the world's naval powers would have a role in the Balkan Wars, if only in safeguarding their citizens, as was the case with the Royal Netherlands Navy. The fleets in the Mediterranean had only pre-dreadnoughts and armoured cruisers, although dreadnoughts were on the stocks or fitting out in several fleets. Despite the Royal Navy remaining predominant in those waters, to safeguard the approaches to the Suez Canal its strategic-level focus had switched to the North Sea, aided by the *Entente Cordiale* which saw its French ally provide the keel of Allied defence in the warmer waters. Nevertheless, the Admiralty did deploy one of its battlecruisers to this theatre in order to face down any potential challenger in the diplomatic crises.

Greece and Turkey were the region's prime maritime powers, but at the turn of the century their navies were suffering serious neglect through a lack of maintenance and capital investment.[58] Economic problems meant that Athens gave fiscal priority to other areas, while in Constantinople royal suspicions of the navy's political reliability starved it of funds. In 1903, the Royal Navy rated the Ottoman Navy as 'non-existent', with only one gunboat able to raise steam in a crisis.[59] The Porte was also notorious for delaying payment—in 1897, Krupp was owed vast sums for delivering artillery—and although the Young Turks established a fundraising organisation in 1910 to buy new ships, this had achieved little by 1912.[60]

In 1912, the Ottoman Navy was the region's largest, consisting of five ironclads, two protected cruisers, ten destroyers, ten torpedo boats and more than twenty gunboats. It nominally possessed the advantage of being able to operate on two fronts, the Black Sea and the Aegean, which would allow it to destroy its enemies in detail. The fleet appeared to have made significant improvements in the decade before the First Balkan War, but was plagued by infighting between vested interests and the bureaucracy. Many officers were too old and lacked basic naval education, while maintenance was poor because, even on the eve of the Great War, up to 95 per cent of Ottoman seamen were illiterate.

Rear Admiral Sir Douglas Gamble, who assumed command of the seventy-two-strong British naval mission to the Ottomans in September 1908, secured some improvements, notably in junior officer training, but the problems of dealing with nine naval ministers eroded his influence and scuttled his plans to reduce the officer corps, although in 1909 he did organise the first fleet exercise in twenty years. In May 1910, he was dismissed following a dispute over the naval construction plan, and the work of his successor, Vice Admiral Hugh Williams, was compromised by navy ministers who were trained in Germany and thus were naturally Germanophile.[61]

The Porte had already recognised the need to update the fleet, and in 1903 acquired from British and American yards a couple of protected cruisers, *Abdul Hamid* (later *Hamidieh*) and *Medjidieh*, with speeds of 21–23 knots. It had also purchased a dozen destroyers and torpedo boats (and two torpedo gunboats) from German, French and Italian yards from 1906 onwards, while three of the older ironclads were rebuilt and modernised between 1903 and 1907.[62] After the Young Turk revolution, Berlin gained political kudos by the transfer of a miniature fleet of warships, including two Brandenburg class pre-dreadnoughts, renamed *Hayreddin Barbarossa* and *Torgud Reis*, and four S.165-class destroyers which Schichau had been building for the German Navy.[63]

The Ottomans had actually wanted an armoured cruiser to match the new Greek warship *Averoff*, their gaze having fallen on the newly built SMS *Blücher*. She was built as a 'super armoured cruiser' in response to London's battlecruiser but before Berlin had learned details of the British ships, so she lacked a 'big-gun' armament and was obsolete when completed.[64] The Germans hastily built their own proper battlecruisers, SMS *Goeben* and *Moltke*, the latter also being offered to the Ottoman Empire, until the German Navy vetoed both this plan and the earlier one to sell the *Blücher*.

The Ottomans selected the SMS *Kurfürst Friedrich Wilhelm* and *Weissenburg* because they had Krupp nickel steel, unlike the other two Brandenburgs which had compound armour. Both had been reboilered and upgraded in 1902–04, but were beset with condenser problems which reduced their speed to 8–10 knots and took some time to prepare operationally.[65] Before their arrival, the Ottoman battle line could move only at a sedate 12 knots, but the new ships were nominally faster at 16.5–17 knots, although their condenser problems continued to plague them.

This substantial improvement was offset by the loss of the 42-year-old casement corvette *Avnillah* (an ironclad acting as a guardship or floating coastal defence battery), three torpedo boats (one of which was scuttled but later raised) as well as six gunboats, including the whole Red Sea Squadron during the Italo-Turkish War.[66] In April 1912, in response to a raid by the Italian armoured cruisers *Giuseppe Garibaldi* and *Varese* which shelled the Dardanelles forts, the Porte laid a minefield and closed the Straits, much to the irritation of the Great Powers. Their pressure led Italy in May to lift its blockade of Constantinople, while the Ottoman Navy cleared the mines at the cost of a tug acting as a minesweeper. In July 1912, five Italian torpedo boats made a night-time reconnaissance of the Dardanelles before being driven back by gunfire from the extensive fortifications on both sides.[67]

This war, and the general inefficiency of the Ottoman government, meant that in October 1912 the Ottoman Navy was short of both coal and munitions, all of which had to be imported through Rumania. The shortage of engineers, and the navy ministry's failure to appreciate the need for maintenance, meant that many ships suffered engine and boiler problems which either reduced their performance or left them out of action. The problems were underlined by the state of the Brandenburgs in 1912. Despite being purchased barely two years earlier, they were suffering from corroded piping, the breakdown of the telephone system and faulty watertight doors. Worse still, both ships' rangefinders and ammunition hoists were removed.[68]

Across the Aegean the Hellenic Royal Navy began the century with three recently upgraded Hydra-class coastal defence battleships built in French yards a decade earlier, with two of the three main turrets abeam near the bridge.[69] Supporting these ironclads were eight torpedo boats, a training cruiser and ten gunboats, but as Constantinople expanded its fleet Athens followed suit, with eight British- and German-built destroyers ordered and launched from 1906. In response to the acquisition of the Brandenburgs, Athens tried in vain to buy two French pre-dreadnoughts, but it benefited from the 1899 will of shipping millionaire Georgios Averoff who left £300,000 (the equivalent of £3.3 million in the twenty-first century) to strengthen the Hellenic Navy. This money was used to acquire a new Italian-built high-speed armoured cruiser which would bear his name and play a major role in the conflict.[70] She was armed with four 9-inch (228-mm) and eight Armstrong 7.5-inch (190-mm) guns, although one of the latter had been damaged in the boring process but was still operational. The cruiser's acquisition led the Ottoman Empire to fear it would be used to spearhead a Greek landing on the Gallipoli Peninsula, so Constantinople strengthened the garrison.

Just as important as new ships was the arrival of a British naval advisory mission in April 1911 under signalling specialist Rear Admiral Lionel Tufnell, who remained in Greece for two years and was very highly regarded.[71] The Admiralty's half-hearted support for the mission was reflected in the fact that Tufnell was on half-pay at the time of his assignment, while his eight-man team had to resign their commissions. However, a Commander Cardale was seconded to the Hellenic Navy just before the war to help the Greeks improve destroyer operations.[72]

Tufnell thoroughly reformed the navy by improving education and training, drafting a signal book and taking it on two six-month cruises to practise manoeuvres, gunnery and amphibious operations. He emphasised gunnery training against mobile targets and introduced smokeless propellants which increased firing rates. He also introduced modern tactics which were constantly practised, even when it led to accidents, and honed the Hellenic Navy into a deadly weapon. The British also helped in other aspects, with a Lieutenant Waring devising a new fuse for the Whitehead Model 1870 torpedoes which would make their name in Salonika, while Engineer-Commander Watson would help the Greeks keep their ships operational during the blockade. As a result of the training programme, the Hellenic Navy's stores, coal and ammunition were limited at the outbreak of war, although this did not significantly restrict operations.[73]

At the very last minute, Athens expanded its fleet with six destroyers. The first four were being built by Cammell Laird in Britain for Argentina when they were acquired for £592,000 (the equivalent of £57.8 million in 2014 values). As international tension grew, they were commissioned into the Hellenic Navy on 19 September and departed with foreign crews to rendezvous off Algeria on 12 October with the SS *Ionia* which carried their Greek crews. However, the *Aetos* suffered engine failure and had to be towed to the rendezvous by a sister ship.[74] After a day's familiarisation, the crews sailed these ships to Greece where they arrived just as war broke out and became the Aetos class, although the *Aetos* herself, towed to her new berth, needed urgent repairs to her engines and missed the first five weeks of the conflict.[75]

Also acquired at the last minute were two German V1-class destroyers, paid for by Greeks living in the United States, and which became the Keravnos class. These ships sailed down the Bay of Biscay coast in late October, although the *Keravanos* had to put in to Brest for repairs and departed only in early November.[76] Because all six destroyers, classified as Scouts (*Anichneftiká*), were acquired at the last minute, the *Aetos*'s 21-inch (530-mm) and the *Keravanos*'s 19.7-inch (500-mm) torpedoes were not delivered due to British and German neutrality during the conflict. Their guns also had limited stocks of ammunition.

The other regional powers were in the Black Sea and had only a token naval capability. The Bulgarians had six torpedo boats, a torpedo gunboat, two patrol boats and a torpedo/ gunnery school ship in what was essentially a coastal defence force rather than a navy, its primary role being to prevent an Ottoman blockade of the sea lanes to Russia.[77] To support the ships, the coastal defences included two 240-mm, four 100-mm, two 65-mm, one 57-mm and fourteen 47-mm guns augmented by twenty torpedoes covering minefields with 353 mines in stock. The Rumanian Navy, with a protected cruiser and three sea-going torpedo boats plus a riverine force of seven torpedo boats and six gunboats, was also a purely defensive force which would play no significant role in the conflict.[78]

Despite a growing worldwide interest in submarines, by 1912 the Ottoman Navy had ordered none, while Greece had ordered two from France in September 1910, these having a submerged displacement of 460 tons and an underwater speed of 8 knots. Two years later, Lieutenant Commander Stefanos Paparrigopoulos took the commissioning crew for the first, RHS *Delfin*, to Toulon, and they were still working up when the international situation led Athens to order the boat to join the fleet. Despite the difficulties, Paparrigopoulos and his men sailed 1,100 nautical miles (more than 2,000 km) to reach Corfu on 4 October and soon joined the new Submarine Command.

While Britain still dominated the sea lanes with 37,000 ships, including 10,750,000 grt of steamers and 270,000 grt of sailing vessels, both Greece and Turkey had substantial merchant fleets which would be important during the conflict. The Ottoman Empire had 143 steamers (69,833 grt) and 900 sailing vessels (180,000 grt) which were a vital part of its strategy for defending the empire's European territory. Constantinople's war plans envisaged the transport of troops from Syria and Palestine across the Aegean to reinforce the southern approaches to Salonika.[79] However, this plan was thwarted by the establishment of a Greek naval blockade in the waters of the Aegean, but in compensation the Ottoman Navy commandeered twenty-four Greek steamers (46,872 grt) on 16 October 1912 in order to transport troops along the Black Sea coast and across the Sea of Marmara.[80]

At the beginning of the century the Greek merchant fleet had 107 steamers (144,975 grt) and 925 sailing vessels (145,361 grt) but the demand for shipping as well as domestic financial incentives meant that by 1912 it had grown to 287 steamers (304,430 grt) and 1,035 sailing ships (145,000 grt). The importance was reflected by the growth of activity in Piraeus. In 1901, of 2,018 ships (2,187,939 grt) entering the port, 674 (650,940 rt), of which 33 per cent of hulls and 29.75 per cent of tonnage, were Greek. By 1905, the figures were 2,451 (2,845,045 grt) and 959 (868,519 grt), or 39 per cent of hulls and 30.5 per cent of tonnage, and by 1911 these had risen to 2,709 (3,695,644 grt) and 1,300 (1,200,000 grt) or nearly 48 per cent of hulls and 32 per cent of tonnage.[81]

Despite the loss of nearly six per cent of the Greek steamer fleet in mid-October due to Ottoman activity, Athens met its transport and supply requirements by chartering some ninety-five Greek-registered steamers (a third of the fleet). It was also able to maintain trading links with the rest of the world as well as providing auxiliaries, including half a dozen armed merchant cruisers and two hospital ships.[82]

The Balkan Wars would not only mark the first use of the modern submarine but also the European debut of the other great military technology of the twentieth century, heavier-than-air aviation.[83] Tethered observation balloons were used in the French Revolutionary Wars, while from the American Civil War onwards they became a feature of all major armies for reconnaissance, augmented around the turn of the century by powered balloons or dirigibles.

A successful heavier-than-air machine, the aeroplane, flew just before Christmas in 1903, and within a few years similar machines were developed in Europe. They were extremely unreliable, little more than toys, but in 1909 their military potential became apparent through two events. In July, Louis Blériot flew across the English Channel, and the following month the Reims air meeting allowed the Wright Brothers to demonstrate their superior technology, influencing the construction of more efficient and more capable aircraft.

The public clamour for states to buy aeroplanes led most European armies, and some navies, to create what ultimately became their air forces, although service chiefs were initially extremely reluctant to accept this new technology. However, they changed their minds when exercises showed the aeroplane to be a useful reconnaissance tool. While experiments were conducted in bombing, aerial photography and artillery fire direction, the aeroplane's prime role remained that of reconnaissance, although many armies still preferred the balloon.

The Balkan air arms emerged through public pressure, and as French aircraft had the best reputation in Europe, Blériot, Deperdussin, Nieuport and Robert Esnault-Pelterie (REP) monoplanes were bought as well as Henri Farman and Maurice Farman pusher biplanes. Until local pilots were trained, they were often flown by mercenaries and adventurers.[84] The Ottoman Army, which had ordered German-made Harlan monoplanes as bombers together with projectiles, had two operational at the beginning of the war together with a Blériot, two Deperdussins and a REP. Of their enemies, the Bulgarians had five Blériots and Farmans, the Serbs had three Blériots, and the Greeks had four Maurice Farmans, and when Rumania entered the war it had four Blériots and four Henri Farmans.

These were the forces that went to war with the Turks, fighting on a multitude of fronts. The fighting was concentrated in two very different theatres: the Eastern—dominated by the Bulgarian Army, and the Western—dominated by the Serbs and Greeks with the assistance of the Bulgarians and Montenegrins.

CHAPTER 3

The Eastern Theatre—
The Hollow Triumph

The war's most dramatic events took place in the Thracian plain, the cockpit of the Balkans, where the Bulgarians isolated Edirne, routed the Ottoman Army and then advanced almost to the gates of Constantinople and on to the Gallipoli Peninsula. The Ottoman forces then rallied at Catalca to inflict a resounding defeat upon their enemies and also held the peninsula.

The rolling Thracian plain is bounded in the west by the Rhodope Mountains which rise up to 2,191 metres, and extends north of the River Arda almost to Edirne, being bisected by the River Meric which runs almost north-south down to the Aegean at Enez. To the east is the broad watershed of the River Ergene bounded by the rugged and forested Strandzha Mountains which approach the Bulgarian border, while westward it extends to Catalca. The main railway ran from Plovdiv across the border to Edirne and then down the Meric, which it crossed south of Kuleli, 50 km south of Edirne, to run through the Ergene valley and Catalca to Constantinople. A branch line ran south of Kuleli, and near the port of Dedeagac it met the coastal line leading west to Salonika. Another branch line from the Constantinople railway ran from near Mandira, on the River Ergene, north through Babaeski to Kirkkilisse.

Edirne, the region's communications centre, was only 24 km from the Bulgarian border, lying at the confluence of the Meric and the Arda, whose headwaters were in the Rhodope Mountains. The railway to Constantinople ran along its western edges, while the main road from Bulgaria ran into the city from the north-west, with another running up the Arda valley to Orkateui and from there to Demotika, south of Kuleli, on the Meric. A third major road ran from Edirne to Constantinople along the northern part of the Ergene valley through the fortified town of Kirkkilisse, 55 km east of the city, and eventually ran alongside the railway to Catalca.

The region was strategically vital to the Ottoman Empire, both to secure communications with the western theatre in Macedonia and to shield Constantinople. The Porte's military leaders recognised this importance and had wished to create a quadrilateral of great fortress bases in order to secure their position, but Sultan Abdul permitted work only on Edirne to anchor western Thrace, while in eastern Thrace the Porte's commanders could rely only upon the older defences of Kirkkilisse, which had two forts, one with a mere four guns.

To hold the Ottoman Empire's European domains the general staff created the Western and Eastern Armies on 2 October, the latter army under Lieutenant General Ferik Abdullah Pasha who was selected on the basis of his success in the 1910 manoeuvres.[1] He had four regular and three provisional (reservist) army corps, but decided to strengthen the field army by removing a division from IV Corps at Edirne to form IV Provisional Corps with one active and one or two reserve divisions, the original IV Corps then being renamed the Edirne Fortified Area.

Abdullah Pasha kept the bulk of these forces as a field army under his direct command together with the Edirne Fortified Area and a detachment assembled around Kircaali. It was planned to create a separate reserve army around Constantinople with three provisional corps.[2] Correctly anticipating that the Bulgarians would advance upon the Ottoman capital, but believing that they would not be ready for a month, he decided to follow the general staff's war plan and adopt a strategic-level defence. But Abdullah Pasha also opted for an offensive at the operational level and use Edirne as a breakwater against the Bulgarian waves. Once the Bulgarians bypassed the fortress, their exposed flanks would be enveloped by his field army, largely concentrated around Kirkkilisse. The reservist Kircaali Detachment, with some regular army stiffening, would deploy north of the Arda to shield the vital Salonika–Constantinople railway, a slender reed for so important a task.

The Ottoman staff had mistakenly assumed that their forces would take thirty days to complete mobilisation because many reserves would have to be railed in from Anatolia. Their forces in the Balkans had also been weakened, with the equivalent of two divisions siphoned off from regular units and sent to Yemen. This left the field army with a nominal eight

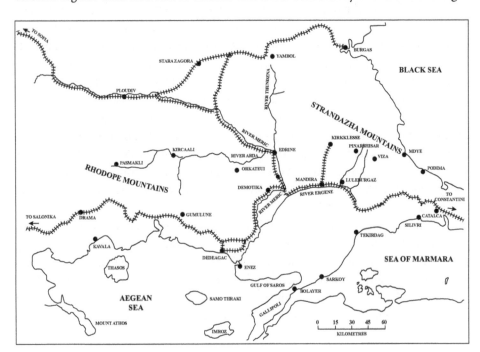

regular and eight reserve divisions together with a cavalry division cobbled from brigades. The Edirne Fortified Area had two regular and three reserve divisions, while the Kircaali Detachment would have two reserve divisions. Mobilisation began on 23 September, but it was only from 1 October that it picked up pace, and it was in fact never completed because the rail system was strained to breaking point. Many foreign experts working on the rail system fled the war zone, while local railmen and maintenance staff, often drawn from the Christian minorities and with little sympathy for the empire, were dismissed.

A plethora of mechanical problems meant many locomotives broke down, disrupting the whole mobilisation process. By 20 October, the Eastern Army had received only 132 of its scheduled 247 trains, while the Hellenic naval blockade prevented Ottoman troops being brought in from Anatolia and Syria.[3] This especially hit the movement of reserve forces, and plans to bring in XVI Provisional Corps (three reserve divisions) from Anatolia were abandoned and the corps disbanded. Moreover, fears of a Greek amphibious operation led to the diversion of XV Provisional Corps (three reserve divisions) to the defence of the Gallipoli Peninsula. Consequently, the Eastern Army, whose planned wartime strength was 478,850 but had only 115,000 men, was deprived of the advantage of interior lines by an overstretched rail system, while many units were assembled from troops of different formations.[4] At a stroke Abdullah Pasha's planned forces had been halved and each regular corps had to be filled out with a reserve division. Worse still, he suffered a severe shortage of draft livestock, cavalry regiments being 300 horses under establishment.[5]

Undaunted, by 7 October the Ottoman general staff judged their forces ready for battle and on the same day created the reserve army around Constantinople, ordering the European armies onto the offensive to disrupt enemy mobilisation. Abdullah Pasha stated that he would be ready to begin by the evening of 20 October, although the loss of 11th Division to Major-General Mehmet Shukru Pasha's Edirne Fortified Area meant that IV Provisional Corps needed another ten days to assemble. His field army had its right anchored on Kirkkilisse by Brigadier General Mahmut Muhtar Pasha's III Corps (38,000 men) while the left with Major-General Ahmet Abuk Pasha's IV Provisional Corps (20,000 men) was at Haskoy. Facing north-west between them were II Corps (14,000 men) in the north and I Corps (20,000) in the south under Major-Generals Shevket Turgut Pasha and Omer Yaver Pasha respectively. The cavalry covered the field army's left to the Meric, while at Edirne was Shukru Pasha (50,000 men) with Brigadier General Mehmet Yaver Pasha's Kircaali Detachment to the west. On 21 October, Abdullah Pasha ordered the bulk of the field army to hold the Bulgarians while Muhtar Pasha's III Corps, in association with Shukru Pasha's Edirne Fortified Area, would envelop the enemy, influenced like many European armies by studies of Hannibal's victory at Cannae in the Punic Wars.

Brimming with confidence, War Minister Nazim Pasha, who had graduated from France's St Cyr military academy, told officers as they set out for Thrace, 'Don't forget to take your full-dress uniforms with you because you will need them for entry into Sofia two months from now.'[6] At the front the leaders were less optimistic, with many of Abdullah Pasha's units, especially the poorly trained reservist formations, under strength and short of weapons. Discipline was weak even among the regular troops, while morale was fragile at best, and Abdullah Pasha knew that even in the active units 60 per cent of the infantry were poorly trained. Worse still, Ottoman intelligence failed to provide much information on the enemy's intentions.

Ottoman planning had always followed the logical assumption that since Bulgaria's territorial ambitions were focused upon Macedonia, it would deploy most of its troops in that region. The general staff assumed the enemy would commit only three infantry divisions and some cavalry east of Edirne, and this did reflect Fichev's original plans when he became army chief-of-staff in 1910. However, he then radically redrafted those plans, partly in recognition of Ottoman military weaknesses shown in the Italo-Turkish War.

Fichev sought to smash the Porte's forces in a rapid campaign before large reinforcements arrived from Anatolia and, also influenced by Cannae, he too planned to envelop the enemy by exploiting his local numerical superiority. The field army headquarters, nominally under Tsar Ferdinand with Lieutenant General Mikhail Savov as his deputy but with Fichev in actual command, was established at Stara Zagora.[7] He retained control of Major-General Atanas Nazlamov's Cavalry Division and 11th Division forming at Plovdiv, but created three corps-sized armies with eight divisions: Lieutenant General Vasil Kutinchev's 1st (fifty-five battalions, thirty-seven batteries), Lieutenant General Nikola Ivanov's 2nd (fifty-six battalions, forty-two batteries) and the 3rd (sixty-four battalions, forty-eight batteries) under Lieutenant General Radko Dimitriev. In Macedonia was Major-General Georgi Todorov's reinforced 7th 'Rilska' Division (thirty battalions, twenty-four batteries) with nearly 48,470 men and 108 guns as part of the 2nd Serbian Army, and the Rodop Detachment (eighteen battalions, seventeen batteries) under Major-General Stiliyan Kovachev's reinforced 2nd 'Trakiyska' Division with some 33,160 men and seventy-four guns augmented by 16,000 paramilitaries.

Many of the Bulgarian commanders, all of whom were in their early 50s, had served in both the Russo-Turkish and the Serbo-Bulgarian Wars. Fichev, aged 52, had graduated from the Italian Military Academy in 1898 and become chief-of-staff in 1910, but Ferdinand felt he was too cautious and openly distrusted him. He therefore appointed as his assistant the controversial 55-year-old Savov who had served in Stambolov's government as War Minister, fallen out with his master and been cashiered. His commission was restored through Ferdinand's influence in 1897, and for five years from 1903 he was again War Minister, resigning his commission over a corruption scandal. Yet he shared the Tsar's views on the army, and with war imminent he received the new position as a mark of imperial favour and the two would combine to undermine Fichev.[8]

Kutinchev and Dimitriev, both 53, would work as a team. Kutinchev was the more cautious but capable officer and became army chief-of-staff in 1914, but had been *de facto* commander of the 1st Army since 1908. Dimitriev, 'Our Radko', was more controversial, and since the Russo-Turkish War had maintained close links with the Russian Army, acting for them as a translator. He was exiled after being involved in the coup against Prince Alexander and served ten years in the Russian Army before returning to Bulgaria where he was army chief-of-staff between 1904 and 1907. He compensated for his short stature with a restless and aggressive nature, his charisma replacing any serious thought about the changing battlefield. Returning to the Russian Army for the Great War, he led two armies to ruin through his carelessness or incompetence, which possibly contributed to his execution by the Bolsheviks in 1918.[9] Ivanov was the youngest, at 51, and had played a role in the annexation of Eastern Rumelia, later being War Minister for fourteen months from November 1896, and was given the 2nd Army in 1907.[10]

With 122,750 men, Ivanov was to advance down the western bank of the River Meric and screen Edirne. Kutinchev's 88,470-strong 1st Army with 180 guns on the eastern bank of the river was to sweep southwards across the plain as bait for the unwary Turks, while Dimitriev's 95,325-man 3rd Army, supported by 220 guns, would drive across the rugged and easily defendable Strandzha Mountains. But Dimitriev, whose short stature reminded many of Napoleon, was a fire-eater and Fichev was justifiably confident 'Our Radko' would drive his men onward irrespective of obstacles to envelop the Ottoman Eastern Army. Fichev did not realise he had numerical superiority, thinking that the enemy had up to 250,000 men. He believed that his campaign would need to rely upon surprise to achieve victory, although he was very conscious that if his gamble failed, his allies would be defeated in detail.

The Bulgarian rail system, with 212 locomotives and 5,040 items of rolling stock, was capable of moving 63,335 tons and was totally committed to the mobilisation, which was completed by 17 October. The following day, Bulgaria declared war and its troops immediately crossed the border after a short bombardment.[11] However, the mobilisation was not without problems, for Fichev's decision to reinforce the Thrace theatre meant some Bulgarian division commanders were uncertain as to which armies they had been assigned, while the incomplete rail system in eastern Bulgaria meant several of Dimitriev's divisions had to march to their assembly points.[12]

As they entered the Ottoman Empire under sunny skies, the Bulgarians, like most of their allies, indulged in what would later be called 'ethnic cleansing'. They drove Muslims from villages and farms, often burning the buildings after the barns had been emptied of grain from the good summer harvest to feed the conquerors.[13] Here, as elsewhere, some Turkish men fought back as guerrillas, but they could do nothing to prevent the flood of enemy troops who engulfed their homes, and those captured were rapidly hanged.[14] Little news of this ill treatment reached the outside world, and the Bulgarian advance was also conducted behind a screen of disinformation. Savov told journalists the objective was Edirne and that, like the Japanese at Port Arthur seven years earlier, he was willing to sacrifice 100,000 men. But, as the famed German military leader Field Marshal Helmuth Graf von Moltke (Moltke the Elder) observed, 'No plan of operations extends with certainty beyond the first encounter with the enemy's main force.' Bulgaria had confidently believed that the enemy would not be able to concentrate 200,000–250,000 men until 9 November, but now found that within three days of its declaration of war its troops were encountering an enemy advance.

The Bulgarians were also handicapped by divisions within the leadership. Rather like Gamal Abdel Nasser in 1967, the Bulgarian government had regarded the threat of war as a tool to seek a diplomatic solution. The politicians had no stomach for a conflict and

Geshov's government informed Ferdinand and the military leadership that they wanted
to seek the intervention of the Great Powers in order to end the war. In a triumph of
hope over experience, the politicians believed the Great and the Good of Europe would
impose a solution on Macedonia to pave the way for Bulgarian annexation. The Tsar and
the army were determined to impose a solution upon Constantinople at bayonet point,
and on 22 October he telegraphed:

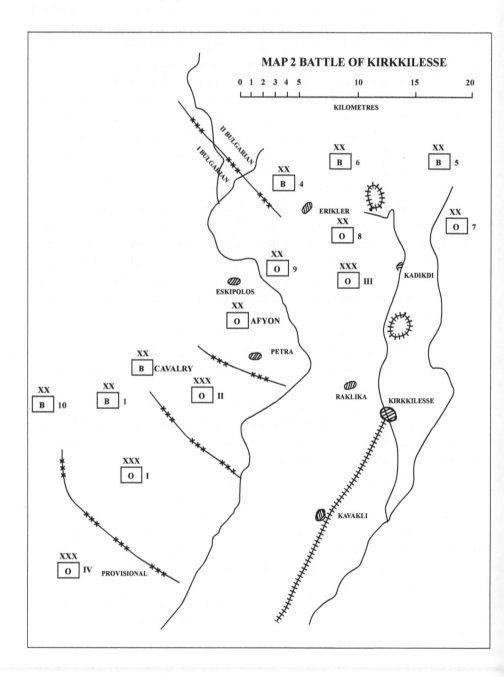

The proposition of the President of the government is very strange, since up to this minute our arms everywhere confirm my hopes and since the spirit of the army is excellent and is directed toward decisive battles with the centuries old enemy.

The situation remained in limbo until the Bulgarians succeeded on the battlefield, but it showed an ominous lack of unity in strategy.

As the Tsar sent his telegram the first major clash began as each side sought to envelop the other around Kirkkilisse.[15] Kirkkilisse lay where the high road from Edirne to Constantinople met the main road through the Strandzha Mountains, and with spurs from the mountains coming down to the plain nearby it made an excellent defensive position. The Ottomans had planned an extensive fortification system of ten positions around the town, but when war broke out only two old-fashioned open redoubts existed. One was at Raklica, north-west of the town, which had only four of its planned dozen 120-mm Krupp guns, and the other was at Skopo, on the bank of the Ergene, which had none of its planned ten Krupp 87-mm guns. Had they arrived, Goltz's pre-war claim that the defences could hold off the German Army for three months might have been feasible. The positions were no more than 2 km from the town, which was well within enemy artillery range, but were augmented by some trenches and battery positions.[16]

Deprived of this anchor in the east, Abdullah Pasha would have preferred a more cautious strategy, but late on 20 October, Constantinople demanded a counter-offensive in which Yaver Pasha's I Corps, Turgut Pasha's II Corps and Abuk Pasha's IV Provisional Corps would pin down the enemy, allowing Muhtar Pasha's III Corps and Shukru Pasha's Edirne garrison (now Edirne Provisional Corps) to envelop them. As the orders arrived it began to rain heavily and within four days most of the roads were marshes, while mists rose to impede reconnaissance.

Meanwhile, Ivanov quickly seized the Mustafa Pasha bridge, the sole crossing point over the Meric north of Edirne, the defenders having attempted unsuccessfully to demolish it. Kutinchev's 1st Army then advanced into the plain, its 3rd 'Balkanska' Division on the right, temporarily under the operational control of Ivanov's 2nd Army but with Kutinchev able to call on one or more brigades if necessary, and Nazlamov's Cavalry Division on its left extending patrols to the western foothills of the Strandzha Mountains. Between them, west to east, were the 10th 'Sborna' and 1st 'Sofiyska' Divisions, but the weather hampered the advance and the only information about the Ottomans came from Christian refugees and deserters.

At first Dimitriev's 3rd Army was held back because Fichev wished first to ensure that Ivanov's 2nd Army was securely masking the Edirne garrison as Kutinchev pushed forward along the only two metalled roads in northern Thrace. With the defences at Kirkkilisse an unknown quantity, it was decided to leave Kutinchev on a loose rein ready to help Ivanov mask Edirne and, when that was achieved, to help Dimitriev assault the Kirkkilisse defences. Dimitriev did not start to cross the border until late on 21 October, his divisions advancing in mutually supporting columns, with 4th 'Preslavska' Division on the right, 6th 'Bdinska' Division in centre and 5th 'Dunavska' Division on the left. By the first evening he was in the northern foothills of the Strandzha Mountains, but there was only one usable route and most of the army had to travel through an 8-km-long defile.

The following day, 22 October, as the rain briefly eased, the mutually surprised two armies collided. The Bulgarians had not anticipated that the Ottoman forces would move forward, while the Turks were surprised by the speed of the enemy advance which had averaged 15 km a day despite the poor road conditions.

Kutinchev's 1st Army found itself in contact with three of Abdullah Pasha's corps, but the most alarming threat came from Shukru Pasha in Edirne whose two active divisions sortied from mid-morning. Aided by fortress heavy artillery, they pushed back the Bulgarian right by the late afternoon and continued to advance after dusk in the belief that the enemy was retreating. But just before midnight the Ottoman divisions were counter-attacked by a brigade each of the 1st 'Sofiyska' and 3rd 'Balkanska' Divisions, which inflicted heavy losses and drove Shukru Pasha back 2 km. Another Ottoman probe from Edirne to the west was driven back in disorder by Ivanov's 2nd Army which advanced cautiously, stopping every few kilometres to dig in and secure its gains.

To the east the bulk of Abdullah's field army (west to east), Abuk Pasha's IV Provisional Corps and Yaver Pasha's I Corps with five divisions, encountered the three remaining brigades of the 10th 'Sborna' and 1st 'Sofiyska' Divisions, while Turgut Pasha's II Corps with four divisions faced Nazlamov's Cavalry Division to give the Ottomans numerical superiority on the plain itself. Earlier in the day, Nazlamov had taken Yaver Pasha's baggage train but now Turgut Pasha pushed him back until he was stopped when part of the 'Sofiyska' Division came up. Although stretched to the limit, the Bulgarians were able to hold their own, greatly aided by machine-gun and shell fire, especially shrapnel, which eroded Turkish morale. This was further undermined by frequent bayonet charges by infantry, who advanced screaming 'Stab 'em' ('*Na Nozh*', literally 'By knife') and '*Hurra*', skilfully supported by field artillery.[17] Both Turgut Pasha and Yaver Pasha were stopped, while one of Abuk Pasha's two reserve units, Izmit Division, suffered heavy losses. During the night of 22/23 October, Bulgarian counter-attacks struck I Corps, shaking even its regular divisions, especially 3rd Division, which fell back in near panic, abandoning several batteries in the confusion.

However, the decisive action was taking place on the Turkish right in the north where the highly regarded and aggressive Muhtar Pasha's III Corps was fighting on his home ground with full, regular, divisions. He ordered the advance to begin in the early hours of 22 October, but darkness and mist delayed movement until dawn, by which time rain was again turning the roads into quagmires which slowed artillery and transport especially on the right.

Anticipating contact with weak Bulgarian forces, Muhtar Pasha's troops soon ran into Dimitriev's right flank division, Major-General Kliment Boyadzhiev's three-brigade 4th 'Preslavska' Division and also the 5th 'Dunavska' Division, which together totalled 66,000 men. Shortly before noon the Turks stumbled upon Dimitriev's divisions and attempted to drive them back, but their attacks usually collapsed under heavy artillery fire while they received little support from their own batteries. The Ottoman III Corps was now deployed in a line south-east of Erikler, in the open with Muhtar Pasha's flanks anchored on crossroads, the right on the heights near Kadikoi (held by the 7th Division) and the left at Petra (Afyon Division). He lacked reserves and faced forty-eight enemy battalions with a force less than half that in a fluid tactical situation to which he responded by hastily creating a regimental-size tactical reserve.

Confused by a stream of conflicting reports, Abdullah Pasha decided late on 22 October to go onto the defensive. He ordered III Corps to hold their positions north-west of Kirkkilisse while the other corps withdrew to a new defensive line some 8 km to the east. This withdrawal was under way during the morning of 23 October when the Bulgarians attacked. Boyadzhiev's 'Preslavska' Division of Dimitriev's 3rd Army approached unchallenged to within 200 metres of Muhtar Pasha's reserve Afyon Division near Eskipolos, which they then struck with bayonet charges. The reservists collapsed, abandoning Petra, although Muhtar Pasha himself tried to rally them, while the two regular divisions on his right were under heavy pressure.

Muhtar Pasha retreated to a new line by the late morning, but during the early afternoon he faced a renewed threat to his right, again with powerful artillery support. Both flanks began to collapse under this pressure, Muhtar Pasha ordering a retreat covered by his centre division (the 9th), and this allowed Dimitriev to push III Corps into Kirkkilisse by dusk at the cost of 1,000 men. There was a fierce duel for Kirkkilisse between Dimitriev and Muhtar Pasha the following day, before the latter was ordered to abandon the town during the night. Bulgarian scouts failed to discover their departure until the following morning when the Ottoman guns did not respond to the enemy bombardment. At Kirkkilisse station Bulgarians captured five locomotives and 200 wagons plus stocks of coal, while nearby depots provided a large amount of food, fodder and ammunition.[18]

The other Ottoman corps also came under sustained attack during 23 October, and even when they were able to repel bayonet attacks the men suffered mounting losses from heavy artillery fire. Undaunted, Abuk Pasha's IV Provisional Corps staged a counter-attack during the afternoon spearheaded by its battered reserve division, and this pushed back part of Kutinchev's 'Sofiyska' Division. Turgut Pasha's II Corps had the easiest time of the day, for he finally realised he faced only Nazlamov's Cavalry Division and during the late afternoon advanced 2 km, but this was Abdullah Pasha's only good news. By dusk Abuk Pasha was reporting that his forces had taken heavy losses, Kutinchev's 1st Army had recovered and was pushing back I Corps, while III Corps appeared to be in a critical condition. Renewed attacks by the Edirne Provisional Corps were cut down by heavy artillery fire, although Shukru Pasha was able to thwart Bulgarian probes towards the city, but with the deteriorating situation during the afternoon in the east Abdullah Pasha felt his only option was to order another retreat. As Shukru Pasha's forces fell back steadily into the fortifications, the rest of the field army withdrew eastwards.

Dawn on 24 October saw the Bulgarians renew their attacks, and as the four Ottoman corps struggled to contain them they received Abdullah Pasha's orders to retreat, which put them in even greater danger. They now had to disengage from the enemy and then retreat some 30 km to more easily defended positions on the eastern edge of the plain along the River Karaagac between Pinarhisar and Luleburgaz. Luckily the Bulgarians were exhausted and their scouts were lax, so it proved surprisingly easy for the Ottomans to break contact. The muddy roads and shortage of draft animals made retreat difficult, causing confusion and panic as well as the loss of much matériel including two aeroplanes and fifty-eight guns (fifty-five of which were from III Corps), while in the confusion some 2,000 men deserted.

While the bulk of Abdullah Pasha's forces escaped and were reinforced by six battalions and nine batteries from XVI Provisional Corps, they had been soundly defeated due to poor intelligence compounded by even poorer decision-making, often in ignorance of the situation. Casualties amounted to some 4,500 men, including up to 3,000 prisoners, and Muhtar Pasha later estimated that the Turks lost a third of their war matériel. On 25 October, a demoralised Abdullah Pasha asked Muhtar Pasha, the son of a Grand Vizier and former Naval Minister, 'In order not to fall into a worse situation, I beg you to ask the Council of Ministers, of which you are a member, to settle the question by diplomacy.'[19]

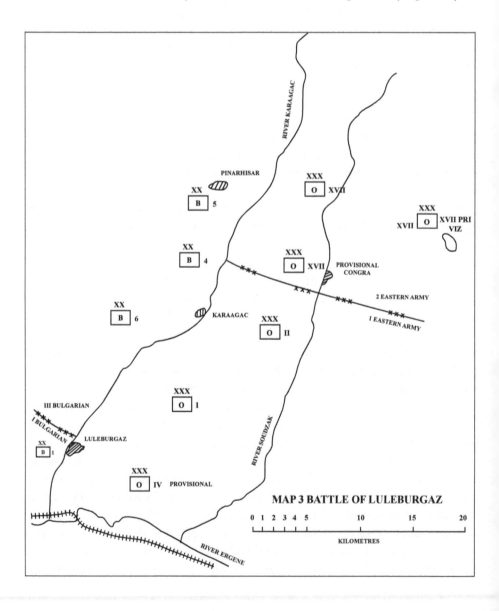

MAP 3 BATTLE OF LULEBURGAZ

By contrast, Bulgarian planning had produced a strategic triumph within six days of the outbreak of war, boosting morale. The victory might have been even greater had the 1st and 3rd Armies co-ordinated their operations more effectively. The scale of the defeat completely demoralised the Ottoman forces, but Sofia's butcher's bill totalled 5,700, including 1,700 dead and missing. Bulgarian prestige soared and French War Minister Alexandre Millerand would claim that its army was the best in Europe and that he would prefer 100,000 of their soldiers as allies than any other European army.

The terrain between Pinarhisar and Luleburgaz was easier to defend. The River Karaagac was in flood, running in a south-westerly direction from the Strandzha Mountains to the deep and steeply banked River Soudzak, and to the east the terrain was dominated by a line of steep, scrub-topped hills with average heights of 300–400 feet (90–120 metres). The new Ottoman positions in these hills were approached across open fields cut by numerous small rivers and streams running south into the Ergene. Two roads ran through the hills from Kirkkilisse via Pinarhisar to Viza and between Luleburgaz and the Ergene. The railway to Constantinople ran along the northern bank of the river, which it crossed just south of the hill line.[20]

The situation was so serious that War Minister Nazim Pasha assumed overall command and established a forward headquarters on 25 October, while three days later Abdullah Pasha split his command for better command and control. The IV Provisional Corps commander, Abuk Pasha, was given the First Eastern Army, with his old corps joined by I and II Corps, a total of ten divisions (half active, one composite) to cover the southern route. The Second Eastern Army, with eleven divisions (three active), was placed under the XVIII Provisional Corps commander Hamdi Pasha, with his old corps, Muhtar Pasha's III Corps and XVII Provisional Corps, to cover the northern part of the line. Total strength had risen to 129,500 men, supported by 342 guns, but both army commanders had to rely upon the same small corps staffs to meet their greater responsibilities, and the reorganisation was still under way when the Bulgarians arrived.

Hamdi Pasha further simplified his own command arrangements by making Muhtar Pasha semi-autonomous, while he himself controlled the six less reliable reserve divisions. The men had finally rallied and their discipline was restored, partly because on 26 October Abdullah Pasha stationed men behind them with drawn revolvers and orders to shoot any who fled. Retreat was permitted only on written order from the corps commander.[21] The Ottoman forces began to dig shallow trenches in order to strengthen the naturally strong defensive terrain while regiments deployed a picket screen west of the Karaagac to slow the anticipated Bulgarian advance.

The Bulgarian leadership had failed to press home their advantage following the victory at Kirkkilisse as Fichev rested the whole army, including the cavalry, for up to three days. The fire-eating Dimitriev, given tactical command of the two armies on the grounds of seniority, urged his superiors to pursue the enemy, but Savov and Fichev were reluctant to rush forward to face what they still assumed was a numerically superior Ottoman army.[22] They reorganised their forces and intended to use Dimitriev's 3rd Army to march upon Pinarhisar from Kirkkilisse in order to pin down the enemy while Kutinchev's 1st Army enveloped them from Luleburgaz. Dimitriev retained his three divisions, 4th 'Preslavska', 5th 'Dunavska' and 6th 'Bdinska', a total of eight brigades (one in reserve), while Kutinchev lost one division which had to shield his communications from sorties by the Edirne garrison. He had reorganised his forces around Babaeski and now had only the 1st 'Sofiyska' and 10th 'Sborna' Divisions with four reduced brigades, so the divisions had sixteen rather than twenty-four battalions, giving the Bulgarians an overall strength of 110,000 with 360 guns.

The advance was resumed only on 27 October as the weather briefly cleared. The impetuous Dimitriev, supported by Nazlamov's Cavalry Division, pushed his spearheads forward as fast as possible across the plain east of Kirkkilisse, although the main body was slowed by muddy roads which were the usual flooded cart tracks. The following day, they encountered the Ottoman outposts and a surprised Abdullah Pasha, whose departure for the front was so hasty that he left behind his baggage and did not don fresh clothes for two days.[23] Meanwhile, Dimitriev's rapid advance meant that he lost contact with the more cautious Kutinchev who was a day behind, further slowed by retreating Ottoman pickets, although Pinarhisar fell to a 2,000-strong band of Bulgarian paramilitaries. Savov was also unable to keep up with Dimitriev, now two days' hard ride away, leaving him responsible for operational-level activity while Dimitriev was responsible for the tactical level.

Dimitriev's forces were spread thin: his 'Dunavska' Division faced the whole of Hamdi Pasha's Second Eastern Army, which had Muhtar Pasha's III Corps on the right across the northern (Pinarhisar) road and XVIII Provisional Corps south of the road, with the XVII Provisional Corps' three reserve divisions around Viza ready to plug any gaps. Dimitriev's other two divisions faced Abuk Pasha's First Eastern Army, which had Turgut Pasha's II Corps on its right, the IV Provisional Corps on its left, across the southern road, and Yaver Pasha's I Corps in the centre. The 'Preslavska' Division faced Turgut Pasha while the 'Bdinska' Division faced IV Provisional Corps, which would soon also face Kutinchev's two divisions.

The two armies lined up along the Karaagac and during the night of 28/29 October suffered under a sharp frost, a timely reminder that winter was rapidly approaching. Around dawn, Dimitriev began his attack without waiting for his colleague and sent Major-General Pavel Hristov's 'Dunavska' Division south of the Pinarhisar road to the village of Congra, which lay some 10 km east of the Karaagac at a major local crossroads between the two rivers. Simultaneously, III Corps began its advance to take the wooded high ground on the western bank of the Karaagac. Until the early afternoon the two armies probed each other, Hristov's mid-afternoon attempt to break the deadlock by crossing the Soudzak with four of his six infantry regiments being broken up by Turkish artillery fire. Muhtar Pasha's counter-attacks completed Hristov's discomfiture, although he retained a bridgehead, as Dimitriev told his men 'Die where you stand but do not give way.'[24] Artillery had now assumed a vital role on the battlefield; as the Ottoman forces had fewer Quick Firers, the numerous modern Bulgarian guns poured heavy and accurate indirect fire upon the enemy positions while the defenders' response was inaccurate and light.

Hritsov's southern neighbour, Boyadzhiev, decided to break through Turgut Pasha's corps with a mass attack on a narrow front around Karaagac village supported by all twelve of his batteries. The guns were drawn up wheel to wheel while Nazlamov's squadrons formed up behind him ready to exploit the success. Turgut Pasha himself had two divisions in shallow trenches supported by his own reserve division and could also call upon Yaver Pasha's 3rd Division and a reserve division from IV Provisional Corps. The Bulgarian guns pounded the enemy artillery into submission, and as the Ottoman fire faded away at about noon, Boyadzhiev's infantry charged across the river and into the hills. After ninety minutes of hand-to-hand combat, Turgut Pasha's men gave way, two regular divisions collapsing into groups of fleeing survivors. The rout was halted only after two reserve divisions counter-attacked, but the Bulgarians still held a bridgehead east of Karaagac village although at terrible cost. Dimitriev had come close to breaking through the Ottoman line and might have achieved more if he had co-ordinated his assaults. But he was more interested in testing his mettle at the front and was often close to the front ranks, being lucky to escape injury from shells.

While Dimitriev engaged the enemy right and centre, Kutinchev's forces advanced upon Luleburgaz. He attempted to envelop the Ottoman left, but IV Provisional Corps, with one understrength active division and a reserve division, proved more than a match for him. Kutinchev's 'Sofiyska' Division, supported by Dimitriev's 'Bdinska' Division, was to strike the Ottoman positions just north of Luleburgaz while the 'Sborna' Division took the village railway station from dismounted cavalry. The assault on the Turkish positions lasted all day, but the defenders' fire (the whole Turkish line had a total of ninety-six machine guns), and the fact that the 'Bdinska' brigades struck on diverting axes, saw the Bulgarians driven back in the late afternoon. A Bulgarian counter-attack that resulted in the recapture of Luleburgaz was little compensation, although it recovered four railway locomotives and sixty items of rolling stock.

The chaos of the battlefield was reflected in Ottoman leadership. Muhtar Pasha's energy, competence and political connections led Nazim Pasha to bypass the ineffectual Hamdi Pasha to communicate directly with him, while Abdullah Pasha increasingly usurped Abuk Pasha's authority. During the night of 29/30 October, Nazim Pasha and Abdullah Pasha, who believed the enemy was on the verge of a retreat, ordered a general offensive the following morning, with Hamdi Pasha's Second Eastern Army ordered to envelop the Bulgarian left. Dimitriev's forces had been weakened by heavy casualties, but he learned that he would receive two divisions from the Edirne siege force once they were relieved by the Serbs, and he pressed Fichev to resume the attack the following day. He and Kutinchev planned a general offensive from dawn, although Nazlamov's Cavalry Division had now been sent across the Ergene to screen the Bulgarian right.

During the morning of 30 October, Dimitriev's 'Bdinska' Division drove back a reserve division of Yaver Pasha's I Corps and, with bands playing, moved forward in the face of heavy rifle and machine-gun fire to threaten Turgut Pasha's left. Turgut Pasha and Boyadzhiev each aimed to advance, but the Ottoman moved first, using Yaver Pasha's 3rd Division and a reserve division. They managed to take the enemy positions, but their heavy losses prevented them from exploiting the success. Boyadzhiev then launched his delayed attack to drive Turgut Pasha back across the river and rout a reserve division, although the effort cost one of his regiments half its men. Dimitriev increased the frequency of night attacks, sometimes illuminated with searchlights, as ferocious bayonet charges remained the prime Bulgarian tactic.

By contrast, the Second Eastern Army attack upon the 'Dunavska' Division, spearheaded by III Corps supported by the two reserve corps, was extremely successful. Despite Hristov desperately and unsuccessfully launching bayonet charges to retrieve the situation, by dusk he had lost his bridgehead. There was bad news too for the Bulgarians on the opposite flank, where Kutinchev's forces had great difficulty reorganising after the previous day's action. They attacked sequentially and without co-ordination, led by the 'Sborna' Division, but were held by heavy rifle fire. Although the 'Sofiskya' Division was able to fight its way from Luleburgaz, it was driven out by counter-attacks, while an Ottoman reserve division repulsed a bayonet charge just after dusk.

Nazim Pasha was concerned about his left, which he reinforced with the equivalent of a division from newly arrived reserve units. Abdullah Pasha, who spent the day watching the battle from a hilltop, had grown more concerned about the situation on the whole front, which had by now been penetrated in several places. Artillery ammunition was running short through high consumption, while the supply system collapsed because of the poor roads aggravated by the Ottomans' usual poor organisational skills. Not even Abdullah Pasha was exempt from the problem, and his first substantial meal was courtesy of war correspondent Ellis Ashmead-Bartlett sharing his personal rations.[25]

Bulgarian gunners now focused upon the enemy infantry positions and they virtually abandoned counter-battery work in near contempt of the enemy gunners. While Abdullah Pasha recognised that Muhter Pasha might be able to envelop the enemy, he concluded the crisis could be resolved only by another retreat. The Bulgarians were more optimistic, despite their own setbacks, boosted by news that a brigade of the 3rd 'Balkanska' Division would reach them by the following day having made a forced march of some 95 km in forty-eight hours. Dimitriev ordered Hristov's 'Dunavska' Division to hold out and, with Kutinchev, agreed to launch a general offensive the following dawn.

As cold winds swept the battlefield on 31 October, the attack began just as Abdullah Pasha started to withdraw. The 'Bdinska' attack shattered I Corps while the 'Preslavska' completed the destruction of II Corps. On the Turkish left, Kutinchev's attack was supported by Nazlamov's Cavalry Division, which crossed the river to cut the rail line and complete the demoralisation of IV Provisional Corps. Abuk Pasha's First Eastern Army was routed, some of its divisions being reduced to 1,000 men and a battery, and it was forced to retreat 5 km, although this compromised Muhtar Pasha's attack. Despite the Second Eastern Army's attack being launched piecemeal, it was fighting well until news began to filter in about Abuk Pasha's defeat, forcing Hamdi Pasha to swing back his left to contain the break-through.

The Bulgarians were again exhausted by their exertions of the past three days; even Dimitriev ordered his divisions to consolidate and reorganise. Some unit commanders, such as Major-General Pravoslav Tenev of the 'Bdinska' and Boyadzhiev of the 'Preslavska', pushed forward on their own initiative, but even they stopped upon encountering resistance. The Ottoman retreat eastward was eased by the fact that it was along paved roads, while the pursuing Bulgarians were still plagued by swampy routes.

This second Ottoman defeat, the bloodiest battle of the war and the largest fought in

Europe between 1870 and 1914, cost the Bulgarians 20,160 men, including almost 2,535 dead, while the Turks lost 22,000, including 2,800 prisoners, and forty-five guns. It was again decided by the lack of coherent command among the Ottoman forces and the superiority of the Bulgarian artillery. Yet a lesson missed by the numerous observers was that to overcome a trench-based defence system required the concentration of overwhelming force on a narrow front, as Boyadzhiev had demonstrated. The defenders did not lack spirit but were often too ready to counter-attack without adequate artillery support, which exposed them to murderous Bulgarian artillery fire. Throughout the battle the Edirne garrison did nothing, although even a demonstration against the Bulgarian right would have forced them to divert troops.

Thrace was clearly lost and the way to Constantinople was now open, but, contrary to modern claims that the Turks conducted a well-executed retreat in good order, contemporary reports by correspondents with military experience suggested that it verged on a rout.[26] Civilians mixed with the troops and all were short of both food and water, the soldiers having only raw mealie-cobs for ten days and anything else they could find. With water in short supply and contaminated by thousands of humans and animals, the men were weak and vulnerable to digestive disorders including enteric fever, dysentery and cholera. The last quickly ravaged the army and vaccines were in short supply, the bacillus having been discovered only the previous year, while it was impossible to rehydrate the unfortunate victims. The dread disease was carried eastward by the army and, with hundreds dying on the road, it soon began to claim Bulgarians as well.[27]

The victory had left the Bulgarians bemused, for while their military leaders hoped to annihilate the enemy they had failed to prepare a contingency plan for pursuing a defeated Ottoman army. Their two victories over Abdullah Pasha convinced them of the superiority of their troops and led them to underestimate their enemies, with terrible consequences. Yet there were good reasons to rest; the men were exhausted, the roads appalling and even the Bulgarian supply system was being strained by the pace of warfare and the growing distance from the supply depots. Nor was there any support from the railway because this ran under the guns of Edirne, which blocked all movement. The fruits of victory were abandoned as the Bulgarians rested and for five days licked their wounds, the advance being resumed only on 6 November, while the cavalry's failure even to harass the retreating enemy threw away any hope of a complete Ottoman collapse.

Catalca

For Ferdinand the victories brought the tantalising prospect of a conqueror's entry into Constantinople. All that stood between him and this glittering prize was the Catalca Line some 30 km west of the metropolis and 7 km east of the village and rail station of Catalca, where the weary Ottoman troops began to rally.[28]

The line ran for 35 km along terrain which has been described as of 'tremendous natural strength'.[29] Anchored on the Black Sea coast by the 8-km Terkos Bay it ran along a high ridge ranging from 62 metres beside the lake to 198 metres at its southern end where it overlooked an 8-km inlet of the Sea of Marmara, Buyuk Cekmece Bay. The ridge, whose 209-metre highest point is a few kilometres south of Terkos Bay, consists of open grassland giving magnificent views westward over the valley through which two small rivers, the Karasu and Sazli, empty into the inlet. The swampy ground around the lake and inlet not only made the position impossible to outflank but also reduced the front to 25 km, with positions up to 7 km behind.[30]

The defences were originally earthwork redoubts designed by a German engineer called von Blum (Blum Pasha), who also laid out Edirne's defences during the Russo-Turkish War to protect Constantinople from land attack. Only twenty-one of Blum's thirty-seven planned redoubts were built on the crests and forward slopes of the hills, but in response to improved artillery the Catalca Line was strengthened by upgrading existing positions and building eight new redoubts. Belgium's famed fortress engineer General Henri Brialmont proposed building seven strong forts in the line, although only three were completed, but on German advice the Turks created ten open-topped and concrete-walled revetments, some with fixed guns, along the western base of the ridge, the guns normally being stored in nearby sheds.[31]

By November 1912, the Catalca Line consisted of twenty-seven positions overlooking the Karasu, some held by two rifle companies and some with up to four heavy guns, while eight positions covered each bay. All were linked by telephone and telegraph, whose wires were buried to protect them from shell fire, and they were supported by well-placed magazines. By 1912, the Catalca Fortified Area under Brigadier General Ali Riza Pasha, with Colonel Cevat Bey as chief-of-staff, had some 180 fixed and mobile pieces of ordnance.[32] But following the 1908 coup, when the Ottoman Army opted for forward defence in western Thrace, the Catalca Line field artillery was sent westwards and many positions were decommissioned. This process accelerated when the Balkan League declared war, with men and equipment sent to reinforce Edirne.

From 2 November, the Ottoman forces frantically tried both to restore and to improve the defences, just as Hitler would rebuild the West Wall in 1944. Trench systems were dug up to 7 km in front of the strongpoints, with barbed-wire entanglements laid out before them, while machine guns covered the anticipated prime axes of advance. Munitions were brought in from the east, a transport and medical infrastructure was created and civilians (especially Greeks and Bulgarians) were evacuated from villages. Nazim Pasha made it clear that the position was to be held at all costs and is reported to have had fifty-two officers shot for dereliction of duty on 3 November.[33] The Ottoman Army was now on the defensive at all levels, its objectives throughout the Balkans now being simply to retain the major urban centres and keep open communications.

The ordnance stripped from the defences was hastily replaced by guns taken from reserve divisions, the coastal defences of the Straits and even schools to create an artillery reserve directly under Riza Pasha, while the navy pledged ironclads to provide fire support.[34] By 17 November, the Fortified Area had eighty-one batteries with 316 guns, but most were deployed some 2 km behind the line of redoubts because the existing positions were too exposed, although a few remained in front to provide direct fire support. The batteries were in groups of three to seven, with two groups (thirty-three batteries) on the right under Lieutenant Colonel Sadik Sabri, two (twenty-nine batteries) in the centre under Major Ali Seydi, and nineteen batteries supporting the left under Major Ali Ihsan. In this arrangement was the beginning of centralised battlefield fire control, which would prove so important in the later European war.

On 5 November, Nazim Pasha held a conference for army commanders to outline his plans for the forthcoming battle at the village of Hadimkoy, which lay alongside the railway line within the Catalca defences. The army was reorganised, all the provisional corps and reserve divisions being disbanded, and a new command created: the Catalca Army comprised, from north to south, III Corps (Muhtar Pasha), II Corps (Hamdi Pasha) and I Corps (Yaver Pasha). The swampy areas on either flank would be covered by regimental-size detachments. Nazim Pasha recognised that the new army had to hold enemy assaults but he also realised that it would need reinforcement. Troops were already being rushed in from the east, including two regular divisions from the Caucasus, and eight reserve divisions from Constantinople and Anatolia, most of them deployed in three provisional reserve corps. The I (Abuk Pasha) and II (Curuksulu Mahmut Pasha) were deployed on the boundaries of the active corps to counter-attack enemy penetrations of the defences, while the III Provisional Reserve Corps (Izzet Fuat Pasha) acted as operational-level reserve behind them.

This was a defence-in-depth concept which the Germans would separately develop with great effectiveness during the winter of 1916/17. Nazim Pasha picked members of his own staff for the key roles in the new campaign, but a Bavarian staff officer, Major Otto von Lossow, joined him as commander of the III Corps' Northern Wing Detachment. Altogether Nizam had 140,570 men supported by sixty-two machine guns, and a mood of grim determination was created with the realisation by the Ottoman forces that if these defences were lost then so were both the capital and the war.

The Bulgarian armies squelched along the roads, although their spearheads still managed to make 15 km a day for nearly a week, and with their supply lines now strained to breaking point, the exhausted men faced a new threat from cholera. Following their reorganisation, Kutinchev now had six infantry brigades of the 1st 'Sofiyska', 6th 'Bdinska' and 10th 'Sborna' Divisions plus the Cavalry Division, while Dimitriev had eleven infantry brigades of the 3rd 'Balkanska', 4th 'Preslavska', 5th 'Dunavska' and 9th 'Plevenska' Divisions, the 'Balkanska' and 'Plevenska' Divisions being fresh. Dimitriev was in overall command of the field army and the military leadership were extremely confident, indeed over-confident, about the prospects of success, although they were 210 km from their rail heads. The Bulgarian advance guard began to reach the Catalca Line from 9 November, although Kutinchev and Dimitriev's troops did not arrive in strength until 14 November, the 3rd Army in the north and the 1st Army in the south. Surprisingly, Bulgarian intelligence had little information about the defences because the army had never anticipated reaching Constantinople. The best information was six years old and came from a staff officer who had inspected the defences on his own initiative.

The government in Sofia, now alarmed at the course of the war, was reluctant so see an assault at Catalca, fearing that a repulse would undermine Bulgaria's recent strategic and political successes but aware that victory would adversely effect relations with St Petersburg. The Russians seethed with resentment that their young client was on the verge of achieving St Petersburg's age-old objective of taking Constantinople, although the other Great Powers seemed more relaxed about the prospect. As Bulgarian troops reached the Catalca Line, on 12 November the Ottoman Empire requested an armistice through the Russian ambassador to Sofia, Anatol Nekliudov. This was forwarded to the Bulgarian headquarters at Yambol but irritated Ferdinand who pondered the matter until 14 November. He then forbade the government, on the grounds of national honour, from informing its allies about the armistice request until he had consulted his military leaders.[35]

Ferdinand sought to buy time for total victory and immediately demanded that his generals should storm the Catalca Line. Fichev and even Savov demurred, arguing that their troops were still arriving and that they were in no position to conduct an assault off the march, but Savov did reluctantly agree to visit the front and to confer with Kutinchev and Dimitriev. When he arrived on 15 November he discovered that while, on paper, his troops had overwhelming superiority, totalling 176,360 men, cholera was sweeping through the ranks and had swamped the medical services. More than 29,700 men (nearly 17 per cent) would fall victim to the scourge, of whom 4,600 died, while typhoid was also endemic among the ranks.[36] Even Dimitriev was unenthusiastic about a new offensive and wanted to await the end of the siege of Edirne, which would release both troops and heavy artillery with which to strike the line. Yet both men recognised this would give the Ottoman forces time to recover, so they felt that they had crossed the Rubicon and had no alternative but to attack. Perhaps both also hoped that their previous near-miraculous successes would be repeated. Savov recommended an attack when he met the Tsar the following day, and the order was promptly issued. Talking up the prospects, Savov informed journalists, 'Gentlemen, we shall be in Constantinople in eight days.'[37]

Dimitriev's plans were based on the assumption that the Ottoman troops would break, as they had at Kirkkilisse and Luleburgaz, provided he maintained continuous pressure upon them. In fact he had no other options given the strength of the Ottoman position, but he did learn the lesson of Luleburgaz and ordered the infantry to be echeloned in depth. His army, 109,360 men with 306 guns, would use the fresh 'Balkanska' and 'Plevenska' Divisions to break into the defences, with the other two divisions following close behind to exploit their success. Kutinchev, with nearly 67,000 men and 156 guns, had the 'Sofiyska' and 'Bdinska' Divisions as the assault force, with the remaining division in reserve. Dimitriev also hoped his artillery superiority would wreck the defences and allow him to exploit his perceived numerical superiority. The decision anticipated the mistakes of the early battles on the Western Front during the next three or four years and repeated those of Pickett's Charge at Gettysburg forty-nine years earlier.[38]

A short but intense bombardment opened the Bulgarian attack at 5 a.m. on a foggy 17 November. The vapours, exacerbated by battlefield smoke and heavy rain, made communication and co-ordination difficult so that the troops advanced into a dark murk. After the bombardment, forty-two Bulgarian battalions charged across what would later be called no-man's land and came under intense rifle and machine-gun fire from forty-seven Ottoman battalions. For once their supporting artillery cowed the Bulgarian guns by deluging them with a mixture of shrapnel and high explosive before they rained shrapnel down on the Bulgarian infantry. Within four hours the assault had been stopped along the whole line, the Bulgarians having failed to penetrate the enemy positions after coming under fire from Ottoman ironclads while trapped before them in the early afternoon. Their heavy shells tore bloody holes in the Bulgarian ranks and were especially demoralising; indeed, similar naval gunfire support would demonstrate its effectiveness on numerous occasions during the Second World War. The only success came when a regiment of Major-General Ivan Sarafov's 'Balkanska' exploited their expertise in night assaults. They advanced half a kilometre to establish a bridgehead in Muhtar Pasha's line south of Lazarkoy with a surprise bayonet charge and seemed poised to roll up the Ottoman line.

They were thwarted literally by the fog of war, which prevented them signalling their success to Dimitriev. As Sarafov's men awaited reinforcements, Ottoman staff officers rode up, discovered the bridgehead and galloped away to raise the alarm. Soon every available Ottoman gun was turned upon the bridgehead until the 9th Division could launch a counter-attack that drove out the intruders by midday. But Muhtar Pasha was seriously injured in the fighting and was replaced by Abuk Pasha, the I Provisional Corps commander, whom he briefed before being evacuated to Constantinople by train. Even as the battle raged around Sarafov's bridgehead, Dimitriev renewed his infantry assault after a new bombardment that began at dawn on 18 November, but there was no time to bring up fresh units. Sarafov was the first off the mark, but the other divisions did not jump off until an hour later and achieved nothing. Kutinchev's 'Sofiyska' on the right, south of the Sazli, had great difficulty even reaching the enemy wire and was unable to penetrate it, while the neighbouring 'Bdinska' north of the Sazli was stopped by fierce fire by II Corps. Dimitriev called off the attacks in the early afternoon, having suffered nearly 15,900 casualties, including 2,900 killed and 1,390 missing, most of whom were blown to bits by heavy guns while another 1,600 fell out of the ranks with cholera. The losses were especially serious, as fourteen infantry regiments were decimated, which was another reason why Dimitriev abandoned further attacks. He withdrew his men to the other side of the valley where they dug in, watched by the Turks, who had suffered only 5,000 casualties.

Bulgaria's first defeat and the circumstances surrounding it would prove all too familiar over the next four years. They had tried to bulldoze the defences with inadequate artillery support, especially of heavy guns. Their numerically superior field guns could neither put down an adequate weight of fire nor strike the defensive system throughout its depth (there were some 'friendly fire' incidents), while counter-battery operations were almost impossible. A long, precarious supply line left the men tired, hungry and ill and limited the number of rounds in the limbers, while the attackers were also plagued by accurate heavy and very heavy naval artillery fire. It also underlined the adage first coined in the American Civil War, and confirmed by the Ottoman defenders of Plevna in 1877, that one man in a trench is worth ten in the open. But the lessons of this battle and its predecessors were not learned. As Hall observed, 'The shadows of the First World War rapidly obscured these battles and their lessons.'[39]

For the Porte this was a morale-boosting victory, the first major success over a European army in some 200 years, and reflected the restoration of discipline and improved confidence in men who had lost much equipment. Yet it was a defensive victory only, and only a successful offensive could restore the empire's fortunes. But for this the Ottoman Army lacked the matériel and capability. The Bavarian von Lossow staged a brief but unsuccessful attempt to clear Terkos Bay but was back to his start line by 19 November, while two feeble Turkish attacks on 22 and 23 November were easily held. Nevertheless, with Ottoman confidence restored, Constantinople deeply offended the German officers at the front when it requested that they leave.[40]

The defeat had a major impact upon Bulgarian strategy. Dimitriev's troops were withering on the vine and by 22 November he was down to 85,600 battle-ready troops. He could neither advance nor withdraw, so a stalemate settled on the Catalca Line while Ferdinand's dismissal of the Ottoman armistice request threw away a unique political opportunity to end the war on favourable terms to Sofia. Dimitriev's armies were unable to regain the initiative because they had lost too many experienced men, both non-commissioned officers and junior officers, which left it less effective, like the German Army after Verdun and the First Battle of the Somme. Moreover, with so many troops pinned down in the east, Sofia could do little to restrain the ambitions of its allies in Macedonia, the area at the heart of its territorial aspirations.

In the aftermath of the battle both sides concentrated upon digging in and dealing with cholera. As the battle raged, 4,600 Bulgarians and more than 6,170 Turks were taken to hospital with the disease, of whom 630 and nearly 600 respectively died. Indeed, by 1 December, up to 20,000 Turks were affected.[41] The remaining troops strengthened their positions or watched occasional artillery duels.

On 21 November, Constantinople again sought an armistice, which was quickly accepted by the Bulgarians, Serbians and Montenegrins but not the Greeks, and this went into effect on the evening of 3 December. Yet both sides along the Karasu continued to strengthen their positions and improve training as the Ottoman forces established winter quarters. An uneasy truce lasted for two months, during which the murder of Nazim Pasha saw the appointment of Ahmet Abuk Pasha as commander of the Catalca Army, whose strength rose to 166,700 men, with 357 guns. However, only the regular corps had a reasonable ratio of officers to other ranks with an average 1:32, while the reserve corps had an average ratio of 1:42. As the armistice began to dissolve, the new Ottoman government was determined to restore its fortunes by an offensive around the Gallipoli Peninsula, and on 6 February Abuk Pasha ordered I Corps to make a supporting attack that evening at Buyuk Cekmece Bay backed up by seven batteries, while III Corps would stage a feint.

The attack began on 8 February as volunteers were landed from two torpedo boats behind the enemy lines in a diversionary operation that cost them half their number. Simultaneously, surprise attacks by I Corps took the bridge across the bay's entrance as well as a hill 3 km to the east to threaten the flank of the 10th 'Sborna' Division. The following day, every division of Catalca Army joined in the offensive, although each deployed only one or two battalions as pressure mounted upon 'Preslavska'. The Ottoman forces overran almost all the Bulgarian forward positions, a 'Sborna' regiment narrowly escaping envelopment. Fortunately, Dimitriev had anticipated the problem and developed positions 15–20 km to the west in easily defendable terrain to which the defenders withdrew by 12 February before raining fire upon the exposed Ottoman infantry. The Ottoman forces quickly recognised the futility of trying to storm these defences and by 15 February the front was again stabilised. This allowed Dimitriev to relieve 'Preslavska' and 'Sborna' with 1st 'Sofiyska' and 9th 'Plevenska' Divisions and then transfer the 3rd 'Balkanska' followed by the battered 'Preslavska' to Edirne.

In mid-March, the Catalca Army staged small-scale attacks to improve its positions, and III and II Corps were some 10 km west of the Catalca Line by 19 March. With an advance of 20 km to create a vulnerable salient, I Corps on the left had the greatest success, but like most of the captured terrain this was difficult to hold. Abuk Pasha was unhappy with orders demanding that he continue the attack, even though this might leave his divisions exposed. Instead he held the new forward positions with regimental-size formations organised loosely into a series of outposts with company strongpoints about a kilometre behind, while the Catalca Line redoubts remained firmly in divisional control. This too anticipated the German defence-in-depth tactics developed by Major Max Bauer and Hauptmann Hermann Geyer and introduced in December 1916.

Dimitriev, unhappy about the loss of terrain, was delighted to receive Savov's orders on 20 March to regain ground as part of a diversionary operation to cover the assault upon Edirne. The attack upon the I Corps salient began at dawn on 25 March and used 'Sofiyska' and a brigade of 'Bdinska' covered by a cavalry brigade while the 3rd Army struck the Ottoman II and III Corps with 'Plevenska' supported by 'Dunavska'. Like their enemies, the Bulgarians deliberately used only part of their infantry. The attackers found they were pushing at an open door; the defenders' outposts gave ground easily, but their resistance stiffened around the company strongpoints. On the Ottoman left I Corps was pushed back about 5 km, the defence rallying on two hills west of Buyuk Cekmece Bay and south of Catalca, with the Turks determined to hold their bridgehead around the inlet.

By now X Provisional Corps, led by Major-General Hursit Pasha, had reinforced the Catalca Army and Abuk Pasha decided to use it for a counter-offensive. It would support I and II Corps, between which was inserted Izzet Fuat Pasha's III Provisional Corps, with two divisions (active and reserve). On 26 March, the Bulgarians continued to probe with little success while Hursit Pasha's corps was brought forward and he was given overall tactical command around Buyuk Cekmece Bay, the Ottoman Navy providing fire support. The Bulgarians continued to push the Turks westward throughout that day and the following one, although they faced mounting counter-attacks.

These encouraged Hursit Pasha to order a major attack for 30 March, and with naval fire support this broke through the Bulgarian lines and pushed them back 1.5 km. But the defenders easily contained a larger attack the following day, and despite some skirmishing until 3 April, the front stabilised, each side having lost some 3,000 men. A new armistice on 15 April ended the war on this front, just as the Ottoman Army was beginning to demonstrate its ability to fight successfully in the field against the Bulgarians.

This offensive reawakened Russia's fears that its Balkan ally would achieve its own goal of taking Constantinople and consequently St Petersburg promised Sofia full support

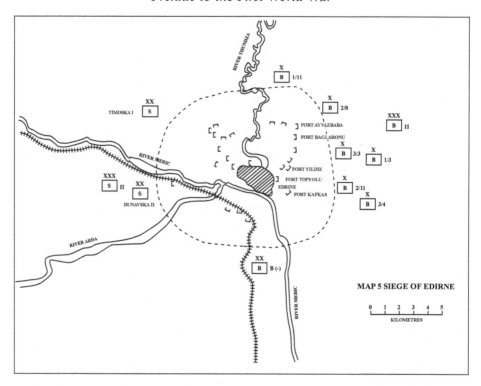

MAP 5 SIEGE OF EDIRNE

in peace negotiations. The Bulgarians took this to mean backing for their Macedonian claims in the 'disputed territories' as well as in negotiations with Rumania and Greece. The Russian promises came as Bulgaria considered renewing attacks upon the Catalca Line, but in a spate of optimism these plans were now abandoned.

As for the Ottomans, the failure of their offensives and the subsequent fall of Edirne left them exhausted and they proposed another armistice on 7 April. This was concluded at Catalca by Generals Stefan Toshev and Ziya Pasha on 15 April, but involved only those two countries, although it was maintained until the Treaty of London was signed in April 1915. It left a substantial part of the Bulgarian Army in eastern Thrace and unable to exert pressure in Macedonia as relations between Sofia and its allies deteriorated.

During the Catalca Line campaigns Edirne remained a foot on the Bulgarian windpipe, for the Sofia–Constantinople railway ran within the city's fortified ring. Success or failure on the Catalca Line depended upon a rapid end to the siege, yet its capture had originally been a secondary Bulgarian objective.[42]

Edirne was the capital of Thrace and one of the Ottoman Empire's three largest cities, with 87,000 people, more than half of whom were Turks (47,000), with large groups of Armenians, Greeks and Jews but relatively few Bulgarians, although a significant number lived in the surrounding countryside.[43] The city was surrounded by low hills and lay just east of the confluence of the Meric and the Arda, the former running along its southern suburbs before turning south, and the winding River Tundzha bisected the city from the north. Low hills to the east and west were surrounded by rolling open plains, while the terrain immediately south of the city was marshy.

As a communications hub Edirne had a key role in Ottoman operational plans. Yet the city's importance as a fortress was recognised only after its loss during the Russo-Turkish War when its four forts proved totally inadequate. When the city was regained, Blum Pasha began to lay out a defensive circle of twenty-four forts and redoubts up to 5 km from the city centre.[44] Polygonal in shape, they were up to 5 metres high, surrounded by a ditch and originally had heavy artillery, but by 1912 were defended only by infantry and Gatling guns.

From the 1880s, the Ottomans followed German advice and began to create a new web of defences based upon nine small but mutually supporting positions up to 4 km from the city centre. Built of brick and stone (later concrete) and augmented by earth, their walls were 6–7 metres thick and 3–3.5 metres high, with field artillery embrasures. They were surrounded by ditches 4–5 metres wide and 4 metres deep, augmented by barbed-wire entanglements. The Porte purchased twenty-nine heavy guns from Germany, and when the forts were completed in February 1910 each had three or four supplemented by machine guns.

Even as they were completed, Goltz recommended a new system of strongpoints up to 8 km from the centre. The following year, the city was stripped of some artillery, including heavy guns, to reinforce the Dardanelles' defences, while some of the original positions were decommissioned. Even in this state they would remain a vital part of the defence, like similar positions around Verdun in 1916, especially in the north-east.

In 1911, Edirne became the base of the new IV Corps under Ahmet Abuk Pasha who was extremely interested in Goltz's suggestions, and by April 1912 work had begun on the new line of defence based upon eighteen strongpoints. However, this was not scheduled to be completed until 1916, and when war broke out only three forts (Yildiz in the east, Karaagac in the south, and Ayvazbaba in the north-east) were complete (one west of the Meric and the others east of the river). As war with the Balkan League seemed imminent, his men dug trench systems to link the strongpoints, the trenches being only 80 centimetres deep with wooden shelters covered by corrugated iron. But 100 metres in front of them were barbed-wire entanglements about 8 metres deep, the wire held in place by iron stakes, while in the north-western sector the entanglements were twice as far away and twice as deep.

At the outbreak of war the defences had a circumference of 37 km and were divided into north-western, western, southern and eastern sectors. The north-western sector was the strongest because it straddled the most likely axis of attack. It had thirteen positions, two decommissioned, but many were exposed to artillery fire, while the eastern sector had fifteen positions of which two had been decommissioned. The southern sector was more difficult to assault because of open ground and had only one decommissioned and four active positions, but relied extensively on field fortifications. The western sector had only field fortifications based upon a 100-metre plateau above swampy ground. A telephone network with buried wires linked the forts and the headquarters in the city centre, while paved roads ensured that reinforcements and supplies could reach them in all weathers.

Between the forts and the city were heavy artillery emplacements ready to cover the approaches with fire. Apart from Buyuk Tasocagi, which anchored the north-eastern corner, all the forts lost their artillery which was used to form sixty-eight fixed flanking batteries in earth or concrete positions with six 210-mm mortars, nineteen 150-mm mortars, eighty-four 150-mm guns, forty-nine 120-mm guns, thirty-two 105-mm guns and 208 87-mm guns. There were also twenty-three mobile batteries with eighteen 150-mm howitzers, four 150-mm mortars, eighteen 120-mm guns and howitzers, thirty-six 105-mm guns and howitzers and forty-six 75-mm guns. The fortress also had two anti-balloon guns as well as an observation balloon to direct the heavy artillery, but without hydrogen gas facilities it was never inflated.

As women and children were evacuated from the city, Abuk Pasha departed to command the new IV Provisional Corps on 10 October, leaving much of his original command under the French-trained and white-bearded Mehmet Shukru Pasha, with 51,575 troops including the 11th Division and three reserve divisions. Abdullah Pasha informed him that he was to act as a magnet to attract enemy forces and also to threaten them to undermine a Bulgarian advance, but the elderly Shukru Pasha lacked knowledge of his own forces and knew even less about the Bulgarians.

For their part, the Bulgarian general staff lacked detailed information about both the defences and the size of the garrison. Yet their intelligence organisation had been probing Edirne's secrets for years, an undercover staff officer having been assigned to the consulate in 1909. The reports were studied in 1911 and the general staff concluded that Edirne should be attacked immediately. An exercise based upon this plan held the following year convinced Ivanov that it was practical. But Fichev needed every man to thrash the Ottoman armies, and he knew that assaulting Edirne, whose strength was unknown, would compromise this strategy, so he opted simply to screen the city. He was also aware that its capture might alienate the Russians, who regarded it as within their sphere of influence. Immediately before war was declared, the Russian military attaché, Colonel Georgii Romanovski, specifically warned Fichev not to attack Edirne on these very grounds. This suggests that St Petersburg desired a Bulgarian victory but not an overwhelming one, and the Russophile Bulgarians reluctantly concurred in order to ensure diplomatic and material assistance.

But the Russians changed tack after Luleburgaz and, with the Bulgarians close to Constantinople, Ambassador Nekliudov, informed Sofia on 4 November that his government no longer objected to the taking of Edirne. By bending to the wind the Russians may have hoped to persuade their client to be more accommodating to their interests in the Straits. Sofia had just accepted St Petersburg's offer to act as arbitrator on the division of Macedonia, and since they might lose part of this prize the Bulgarians felt Edirne might provide some compensation. Perhaps the Russians were also cynically hoping that the siege would drain Bulgarian resources and prevent them from taking Constantinople.

Ivanov crossed the frontier on 18 October and reached the River Arda within three days before moving south to cut the Constantinople railway on 28 October. Assisted by Kutinchev's 3rd 'Balkanska' Division, he threw a screen in an arc across the north of Edirne, although the city retained an open road link to the south-east. Ivanov's mission changed as the Bulgarian forces grimly fought for Luleburgaz, and fears grew that the Edirne garrison would sortie to assist their comrades. On 29 October, Fichev and Savov bit the bullet and ordered a full siege for which Ivanov had already received three heavy (120-mm) batteries, an observation balloon unit and some aeroplanes. The orders reached Ivanov the following day, together with the welcome news that reinforcements were on the way.

This followed the Serbian victory at Kumanovo on 25 October, which allowed Belgrade to honour its pre-war pledge to aid its fellow Slavs at Edirne, the order being received by General Stepa Stepanovic of the 2nd Serbian Army two days later. His Timoska I and Dunavska II Divisions began to depart their railheads on 30 October with 47,275 men, seventy-two guns including heavy pieces, 4,142 horses and 3,946 carts, and they arrived as Ivanov completed the investment. The Serbs, whom Ivanov once described in an order of the day as 'dear and loving guests', took almost half of the 47-km circumference siege line from 5 November. The Timoska Division relieved the 2nd Brigade/9th 'Plevenska' Division, and although Ivanov lost 'Plevenska' to the field army, it was replaced by the recently formed 11th Division.

Ivanov completed the encirclement on 9 November, having already suffered more than 3,800 casualties, and deployed a brigade each of 8th 'Tundzhanska' and 11th Divisions opposite the eastern sector. The 'Tundzhanska' Division (minus one brigade) faced the southern sector, while Dunavska II and Timoska I faced the western and northern sectors respectively, the latter augmented by the Bulgarian 55th Infantry. The early days of the siege saw some probing, but from 10 November the allies began a heavy bombardment directed by balloon, and possibly by aircraft. This intensified from 14 November but inflicted little damage and the Bulgarian generals realised that while it would help demoralise the defenders, it would not make them capitulate.

The armistice that had been agreed on the Catalca front was accepted at Edirne on 8 December, although Ferdinand demanded an infantry assault upon the city in order to gain more favourable peace terms. The general staff pointed out this would contravene the armistice terms, and there was little enthusiasm for military action after the defeat in the Catalca Line. Shukru Pasha strengthened his defences, adding half a metre of earth to the tops of his forts, digging deeper, laying land mines, improving his radio communications and increasing training for reservists as well as rationing food. For their part, the besiegers also strengthened their positions and the Bulgarians brought back five batteries of 120-mm guns from Catalca.

Despite the siege not being actively prosecuted, it still had an effect upon the inhabitants. Edirne's water supply was cut on 4 November, leaving the inhabitants to rely upon the river and wells, while food from outside gradually dried up, and although shortages of food, sugar and salt were something with which the besieged learned to live, the men constantly craved tobacco. With the armistice the besieged hoped in vain that the Bulgarians would allow supplies of food to enter the city, but the besiegers would permit only two rail wagons of medicine to cross the siege lines in return for permission to run some trains under the guns of the fortresses. An Ottoman observer later claimed that the enemy ran 180 wagon-loads of food for the Bulgarian Army in Thrace together with Russian and Czech volunteers.[45]

From mid-December, Shukru Pasha began to ration food and requested a relief operation on 26 January after the CUP coup. This had been an objective of the Young Turks' coup, the new Foreign Minister Gabriel Effendi Noradounghian stating, 'If Edirne continues to resist, we shall fight to relieve her. If Edirne falls, we shall fight to retake her.' Yet the only response at the end of January was first to promote Shukru Pasha to the rank of lieutenant general and then to inform him that the armistice would cease on the evening of 3 February. He was not informed of plans for an offensive in Gallipoli. An hour after the armistice ended, Bulgarian heavy guns, two-dozen 120-mm and 150-mm howitzers, began to shell the city.

The bombardment seemed to be targeted on civilian parts of the city, especially those where foreign consulates were located, to bring political pressure upon Shukru Pasha, and it continued day and night, causing casualties and damage. To boost morale, Shukru Pasha launched a seven-battalion sortie at dawn on 9 February against a concentration of Bulgarian artillery north-east of the city. However, the attack failed despite support from two field artillery regiments and heavy guns, the attackers being channelled by wire entanglements into a killing ground. Within two hours they retreated, having suffered some 600 casualties, including nearly 140 dead and missing. It heralded a series of bloody but inconclusive skirmishes while the bombardment continued and was strengthened by the arrival on 13 February of seventeen Serbian batteries with fifty-eight guns, including eight 150-mm and twenty 120-mm howitzers and ten 120-mm guns, most of the howitzers having recently landed in Salonika. The besiegers' artillery received aerial support, usually from observation balloons which also took photographs, although aeroplanes occasionally flew overhead to seek details of the defences. On 15 November, a Bulgarian aeroplane dropped leaflets demanding the surrender of the city, and this was repeated on 6 February. Shortly afterwards the aeroplane, for the first time in Europe, played a more direct role by dropping hand grenades but without any effect.

By 5 March, the garrison was running seriously short of food, having killed half their draft animals and slashed the bread ration. Indeed, they soon released their Bulgarian prisoners to reduce the number of mouths in the city. To further isolate the city, the Bulgarians conducted the first of what would later be called electronic counter-measures. They tried to jam radio communications between Edirne and Constantinople by sending a signal on the same wavelength, although this was only partly successful. Shukru Pasha was informed of a new round of armistice negotiations and was asked to hold out until 2 April, but he was well aware that the garrison's morale was collapsing. Lack of food was not one of the besiegers' concerns, but they too suffered hardship because the Thracian plain offered little protection from the hard winter, while the trenches were sometimes 2 metres deep in snow. The nearest trees were 15 km from the city, so the men lacked timber for shelters and firewood, all of which had to be imported together with food. Blizzards during February aggravated the situation, and with the men huddling together for warmth, lice brought typhus, while the lack of drinking water led to outbreaks of cholera which further eroded morale.

The Bulgarians had lost their enthusiasm for the war, realising that the Young Turks' coup meant there would be no capitulation and only Edirne offered any prospect of ending the war triumphantly. Yet it was a formidable fortress and as Fichev observed, 'If we attack

Adrianople, we can fail and sustain great losses; if we do not attack, the war will continue.' Following the Catalca Line battles, Ivanov recognised a frontal assault upon Edirne would be risky and bloody. He hoped the harsh winter and starvation would bring the defenders to their knees, but reluctantly recognised that this would not be sufficient. Savov requested more Serbian men and heavy artillery on 9 February, but the response underlined the growing tensions between the Balkan League allies. Belgrade agreed to provide artillery but reserved the right to claim compensation in terms of land and money, Sofia offering only financial restitution. With Bulgaria already in dispute with Greece over Salonika, and the Serbs controlling much of Macedonia, it was essential that the Bulgarian Army complete its victory in Thrace ready to reinforce the country's claims on Macedonia.

Bulgarian–Serbian tension increased when the armistice with the Ottoman Army expired. Less than a month later, on 22 February, Pasic sought a revision of the March 1912 treaty, claiming that Belgrade had exceeded its formal commitments in the agreement. He sought more Macedonian territory to indemnify Serbia for the loss of an Adriatic port and argued that Bulgarian territorial gains in Thrace would compensate them for the loss of Macedonian territory. Sofia made no official response, for it needed Serbian support at Edirne and still counted upon Russian diplomatic support over Macedonia.

The new Serbian artillery expanded the number of besiegers to 149,225, of whom 120,000 were combatants (32,000 Serb). With the Greek success at Ioannina, there was growing pressure for an assault upon Edirne, with Ivanov and Ferdinand the most strident advocates, and even the Russian general staff through Romanovski joining the chorus. Their stridency was balanced by a more cautious approach from Fichev and Danev, while Premier Geshov told Savov that the government feared heavy casualties and did not wish him to attack. Yet the increasingly pressing issue of Macedonia saw the government make common cause with the 'hawks' to end the Edirne dilemma. Fichev later claimed that the fall of the city was inevitable due to the lack of food and the Ottoman inability to relieve it, but Savov recognised he had to break the deadlock quickly in order to save Bulgarian national and army morale.

The weather plagued preparations, the thaw in early March causing floods, and trench foot added to the soldiers' suffering. The Bulgarians' 6,000 wagons were fully committed in moving men and matériel, but conditions were so bad that carts took up to eight days to make a round trip. The movement of heavy guns alone took fifteen days and each required a team of at least six oxen. Savov sent the battle-hardened 3rd 'Balkanska' and 4th 'Preslavska' Divisions from Catalca, but there were disputes over where to deliver the main blow. Ivanov's staff had been planning the assault for some time and wished to strike the eastern sector. They recognised that the defenders were so confident they could hold the strongest part of the shield that they would not expect an attack upon it. Savov was doubtful, but after a personal reconnaissance he agreed, and on 20 March he directed Ivanov to storm the city while Dimitriev launched a diversionary offensive on the Catalca front.

Just before midnight on 23/24 March, Ivanov issued orders for an assault on the boundary of the eastern and northern sectors the following night using the 'Balkanska', 'Preslavska' and 11th Divisions together with a brigade of 'Tundzhanska'. To exploit Ottoman concern about the weak southern sector, he decided upon a diversionary bombardment here and

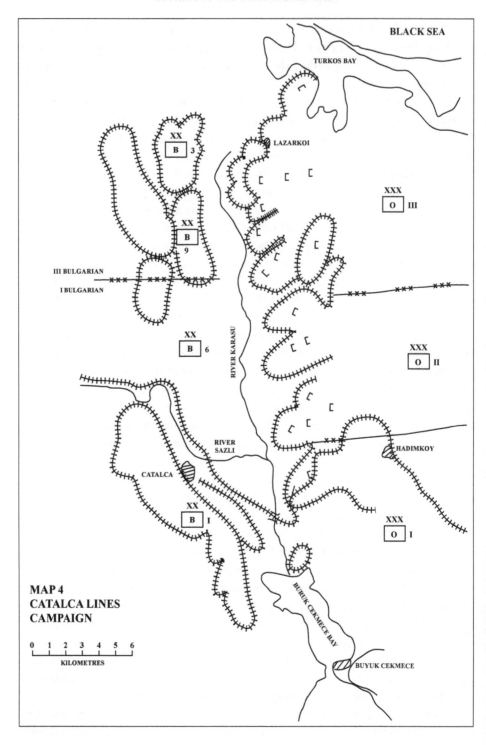

BLACK SEA

TURKOS BAY

LAZARKOI

XXX
O   III

III BULGARIAN
I BULGARIAN

XX
B   3

XX
B
9

XX
B   6

RIVER KARASU

XXX
O   II

RIVER
SAZLI

CATALCA

HADIMKOY

XX
B   I

XXX
O   I

BURUK CEKMECE BAY

BUYUK CEKMECE

MAP 4
CATALCA LINES
CAMPAIGN

0   1   2   3   4   5   6
KILOMETRES

also upon the western and north-western sectors. These would also be attacked by the rest of 'Tundzhanska' in the south and by the Serbs in the west to draw off reserves. The assault troops were issued with wire-cutters and Bangalore torpedoes to blast through wire entanglements, and to achieve surprise the Bulgarians covered their bright buttons with cloth or tissue paper and sacking was wrapped around horses' hooves to reduce noise.

During the early afternoon of 24 March, the allies began a bombardment that used only part of their artillery in order to deceive the enemy and conserve ammunition. The shelling lasting into the early evening and then ceased almost everywhere except on the north-western defences where it continued until midnight. Shortly afterwards, in the first minutes of 25 March, the bombardment was renewed for two hours and then, as the moon rose, the 'Tundzhanska' and Serbs launched their diversionary attacks against the 11th Active and Gumulcine Reserve Divisions. More than half of the Ottoman battalions were in reserve north of the Meric but a fierce day-long battle sucked in these reserves across a single bridge and they were ultimately able to contain the attack.

Meanwhile, the Bulgarians began their main assault in the east supported by 226 guns, the infantry reinforced by assault engineers and bombing parties. They faced a line of seven forts starting with the new Ayvazbaba and in a line to the south Baglaronu, Cevizlik, Kestanelik, Yildiz, Topyolu and Kafkas. The assault force began to move forward quietly just after midnight and formed up at the wire some four hours later. They cut the entanglements where possible, or covered them either with straw-filled sacks or their greatcoats, then stormed forward to close with an *ad hoc* division of ten active and reserve battalions. Within fifty minutes the Ottoman trenches were full of men stabbing at each other with bayonets. The 'Tundzhanska' brigade took Baglaronu followed by Ayvazbaba, repulsed counter-attacks and drove 3 km into the Ottoman lines to begin rolling up the defences. Cevizlik fell and by morning 'Balkanska' had taken the southern-section forts of Yildiz, Topyolu and Kafkas, the demoralised defenders often surrendering after token resistance or even welcoming their enemies.

By morning the Ottoman position was becoming desperate and the garrisons in the south and west were ordered back into their fortresses, both to stabilise the defence and to create reserves. But morale was collapsing and a Bulgarian cavalry regiment managed to ride into the city centre to capture Shukru Pasha. He had already opened surrender negotiations with Ivanov, the terms being discussed in French, and they were completed in the early afternoon.[46] The assault had cost the Bulgarians some 8,000 casualties, including 1,700 dead and missing, to bring their total casualties to 18,300. Of the 61,250-man garrison, some 13,000 had been killed and 48,000 captured, but only 28,500 survived captivity due to Bulgarian neglect. The Serbs suffered some 1,500 casualties, including 450 dead and missing. The booty was immense, the Bulgarians capturing more than 12,200 rifles, mostly modern Mausers, with about a thousand rounds each, twenty-four machine guns and six Nordenfelt Gatlings, eighty-two guns (including thirty-six heavy and two anti-aircraft) and 15,500 shells.

The storming of Edirne added to Bulgarian army prestige, for this was the first European city to be stormed in the twentieth century, a testament to the bravery and *élan* of the Bulgarian infantry. Bulgarian sources suggest their guns staged a creeping (or rolling) barrage to sweep ahead of their troops while some field guns moved forward with the infantry to provide direct fire support. But as Hall observed, the death of so many men was simply to satisfy the military leadership's prestige and to inflate the national pride of Ferdinand and some Bulgarian politicians.[47] Strategically it was counter-productive, for it diverted forces away from Macedonia, Sofia's prime political objective, and squandered them upon a city of limited strategic and economic value. Foreign observers paid little attention to the siege, or the success of night assaults, and even less to the ominous failure of heavy artillery against modern forts which would be repeated only three years later at Verdun.

Relations between the Bulgarian and Serbian commanders Ivanov and Stepanovic were good, and when Ivanov received the latter's congratulations the Bulgarian graciously acknowledged the debt owed to their allies. But the capture of Shukru Pasha became a symbol of the deteriorating relations between the allies as press campaigns became increasingly strident. Bulgarian cavalry had captured him in the western (Serbian) sector and the Serbs therefore claimed that he should be their prisoner, although he had surrendered to Ivanov. When the Bulgarians ordered the Serbian troops to leave on 27 March, they were miserly with rolling stock so the Dunavska II did not entrain until 31 March, but eventually Stepanovic's men rejoined the Serbian Army by 17 April.

Western Thrace and the Rhodopes

The Bulgarians also had success in western Thrace.[48] The main force was Kovachev's 2nd 'Trakiyska' Division with Haskovo and Rodop Detachments, a total of 33,160 men with 74 guns. They faced Kircaali Detachment under Mehmet Yaver Pasha with a division each of reservists and home guards (*Mustahfiz*) stiffened by 36th Infantry of 12th Division, some 17,550 men, of whom 6,820 were home guard and 3,600 were regulars. They were to shield the Salonika–Constantinople railway which at one point lay only 40 km from the Bulgarian border. The line could be approached through two north–south passes from the Arda valley through the Rhodope Mountains at Kircaali in the east, held by the reserve division, and at Pasmakli in the west, held by the home guards.

The reserve division was hit first. Its flanks were turned on 21 October, and it retreated 25 km to new positions from which it launched fierce counter-attacks to recover Kircaali. By the evening of 14 November, the division was within 4 km of the town, but the Bulgarian Haskovo Detachment (renamed the Kardzhali Detachment) was reinforced and the Ottomans fell back to their start line. The home guard also staged a dynamic defence, but first retreated 5 km on 26 October to avoid encirclement and then staged counter-attacks to regain much of the lost ground by 1 November. Renewed Bulgarian attacks carried them back to the mouth of the pass, yet the outnumbered and third-rate Ottoman forces had made a significant achievement that helped to stabilise both fronts by mid-November.

Yaver Pasha's plans were undermined by events in the east, where victory by the Bulgarian Rodop Detachment over the Western Army's (Kato) Nevrekop Detachment on 16 November saw them quickly take the town of Drama. This cut the railway to end Yaver

Pasha's mission and threaten him with double envelopment. The Rodop Detachment now made a three-pronged attack over difficult mountainous terrain with rapid progress against negligible resistance from either the Ottoman Army or the local Pomaks (Bulgarian-speaking Muslims) to take the whole Rhodope region by 30 October.

From 17 November, Yaver Pasha faced attacks along most of his front and despite his best efforts, he was finally surrounded and forced to seek terms ten days later. He surrendered the following day, with 9,120 men and eight guns, while 1,000 more men were captured during mopping up. Many others deserted to join their families, but some 1,500 under a Major Nasuhi struck eastwards, fought their way across the Meric and reached Ottoman lines in Gallipoli on 30 November. Meanwhile, the Kardzhali Detachment had advanced to the Aegean, taking Gumulcine on 22 November and reaching the port of Dedeagac four days later, the port having been in friendly hands since 19 November when it had fallen to the Macedonian-Thracian Legion. The port, which had 4,000 inhabitants, was the only significant harbour east of Salonika with direct access to the railway, whose line ran onto a small pier. But there was no protected harbour, the water inshore was shallow and cargoes had to be transferred by barge to ships lying some 800 metres off shore.[49]

The port was used to strengthen the Bulgarian grip on eastern Thrace thanks to the Greek merchant fleet. On 21 November, the 1st Brigade of Todorov's 7th 'Rilska' Division embarked at Salonika and disembarked five days later near Dedeagac to absorb the Kardzhali Detachment before it marched eastwards to enter the port with the rest of 'Rilska' on 27 November.

Gallipoli

Major Nasuhi's break-out and the Dedeagac landing highlighted the growing importance of the Gallipoli Peninsula.[50] The peninsula and the Dardanelles were heavily fortified against naval incursions, but growing fears of a Greek amphibious landing led to the assignment of XV Provisional Corps with two reserve divisions and a regular infantry regiment to the peninsula. They were joined by the Palestine-based 27th Division and some independent reserve regiments, 40,000 men in total, to form Fahri Pasha's Canakkale Fortified Zone. However, a new threat emerged in November as Bulgarian light forces began to fan out to the Sea of Marmara to secure the Catalca front flank, and on 24 November they took Silivri.

Fahri Pasha threw a screen to the north, but his land defence was half-way down the peninsula along a ridge south of Bolayir at its narrowest point, where there was a position originally constructed by the British and French during the Crimean War. The 7-km-long position ran from the Gulf of Saros to the Sea of Marmara, consisting of a parapet with some redoubts, and was armed with some field guns. Further Ottoman fears of a Greek landing to support the main Bulgarian advance led Constantinople to reinforce the Gallipoli garrison from 27 November with two reserve divisions and 15,000 men.[51] Fahri Pasha sent the Canakkale Division to the south of the peninsula and placed the 27th

Division in the Bolayir defences. The newly arrived Edremit Reserve Division was sent to cover potential landing sites in the west, including Suvla Bay and what later became Anzac Cove, while the Afyon Division was in reserve. On the Asian side of the Dardanelles a provisional corps headquarters was established with three reserve divisions.

Meanwhile, Todorov's 'Rilska' began to march towards the peninsula, picking up detachments from the forces on the Catalca Line as it did so. In early December, Todorov approached the Sea of Marmara, but the Porte offered to extend the Catalca Line armistice to the peninsula and this was accepted on 9 December. However, there was a squabble over Sarkoy on 11/12 December and as a result the armistice did not take full effect until 15 December. Todorov occupied the town a week later, but it was no prize, having been completely wrecked by the August earthquake in which 2,800 of its inhabitants were killed. He kept his troops north of the Bolayir defences for the greatest flexible tactical response.

Ottoman concern about a landing was justified, for Sofia had advocated just such an operation to Athens whose General HQ and fleet considered that it might help the navy to reach Constantinople.[52] The commander of the Greek Army, Crown Prince Constantine, had originally proposed establishing advanced bases at Kavala and Dedeagac to join a march upon Constantinople. Then Venizelos said it would be better to use a spare division to take the Gallipoli Peninsula and to free the passage of the Hellenic fleet to Constantinople, one of Athens' key demands in exchange for an armistice. On 1 December, Constantine's chief-of-staff, Major-General Panagiotis Danglis, said that Constantinople should be the Greek Army's prime objective and produced a new plan which underestimated the garrison at 30,000. While the Bulgarians increased pressure around Bolayir, there would be a landing on the south-western peninsula by I, IV and VII Divisions, Konstantinos Konstantinopoulos's Evzoni Detachment and the 3rd Cavalry, some 25,300 men and 48 guns, mostly short-range mountain artillery.

The greatest hurdle to Athens' ambitions was the shortage of troops, who were fully committed in Macedonia and Epirus, and it gave the capture of Ioannina the higher priority. Danglis later proposed a landing by II Division with nine batteries, 32,300 men and twenty-eight guns, but the need to strengthen the Epirus front, and the navy's growing doubts about the prospects for a successful landing, saw the plans shelved. By then Bulgarian interest had also evaporated due to growing tension with Greece over Macedonia.

Meanwhile, a coup by the CUP and the death of Nazim Pasha saw the Gallipoli front flare up again. The Ottoman command was reorganised and Chief of the General Staff Lieutenant General Ahmet Izzet Pasha, who had just returned from directing a counter-insurgency campaign in Yemen, became War Minister. He inherited a plan to seize the initiative at the operational-strategic level through an amphibious assault from the Sea of Marmara supported by attacks from Gallipoli and the Catalca Line.

To execute this operation the general staff assembled three divisions (one reserve), a cavalry division and nine batteries under Brigadier General Hursit Pasha's new X Provisional Corps, with Lieutenant Colonel Enver Pasha as his chief-of-staff.[53] Hursit Pasha would be landed at Sarkoy and drive westwards, while Fahri Pasha's forces, now organised into two provisional corps, would strike from the Bolayir Line to encircle the Bulgarian forces and the Catalca Army pinned down the enemy. This plan was almost complete as the armistice dissolved in February 1913 and Izzet Pasha seized the opportunity to strike.

The Bulgarians had also reinforced their forces facing Gallipoli and assigned them to the new 4th Army led by Kovachev on 28 December, which had his old 2nd 'Trakiyska' Division, the 7th 'Rilska' Division and the Macedonian-Thracian Legion, each with three brigades, as well as the Cavalry Division, with most of his 92,300 men some 10 km north of the Bolayir Line. With the collapse of the armistice on the evening of 7 February, Kovachev, as a precaution, sent 'Rilska' to the Bolayir Line where it would prove to be a barrier between Hursit's planned beachhead and Fahri Pasha's troops.

Fahri Pasha's attack would be made by the 27th Division on the right and a Provisional Division on the left, with the Afyon Division ready to exploit any success, but he anticipated further reinforcement with the arrival of the 30th Division from the Caucasus by 10 February. The Ottoman advance on the morning of 8 February was supported by only thirty-six guns and the cruiser *Medjidieh*. In a thick mist the leading provisional division was able to approach within 30 metres of the 1st Brigade/'Rilska' Division's trenches. The defenders, supported by seventy-eight guns, were driven back in confusion some 20 km into secondary positions where the attack was held by midday. The attackers had now advanced beyond their artillery support, and with no counter-battery fire the Bulgarian guns inflicted heavy casualties. Bulgarian counter-attacks during the afternoon broke the morale of the attackers who were back on their start line by dusk, having lost about half their 15,000 men, while Bulgarian casualties, officially 530, were probably about 1,000.[54] Of greater concern to Kovachev was Hursit Pasha's landing.

Hursit Pasha had begun planning on 7 January and had been assigned twenty-two steamers of which half would carry the assault wave of 31st and 32nd Divisions supported by half the Mamuretulaziz Reserve Division together with 500 tons of supplies. The planners displayed great attention to detail, and load-planning exercises showed the need not only for more freighters ships to carry cargo but also ferries which could easily roll vehicles off the deck and onto the beachhead.[55] However, it was assumed that most of the troops would disembark onto Sarkoy's piers.

As preparations neared completion they received two setbacks: first it was learned that the Bulgarians had strengthen their forces; then cholera broke out in the reserve division. Undaunted, the Ottoman troops began to embark on 1 February, only for storms to disrupt the assembly of ships and leave many men severely seasick. This forced their commanders to postpone the operation and then disembark the troops when the weather improved, by which time they had consumed most of their combat rations.

The task force, with nearly 19,860 men and forty-eight guns, re-embarked on the night of 5/6 February and departed the following evening in the knowledge that the Catalca Army and Fahri Pasha's troops would launch supporting attacks. Despite everything, morale was high and the task force arrived off Sarkoy the following morning in choppy but navigable waters, only to discover that the naval gunfire support group was absent. It did not appear until two hours later and as it began shelling coastal positions, pontoons carrying three battalions made for the pebbled beach a kilometre west of Sarkoy. They grounded just before midday and within thirty minutes had established a kilometre-deep bridgehead which was steadily expanded during the day. The defenders, two Macedonian-Thracian Legion battalions, were too weak to hold the enemy, but they did beat off an Ottoman evening assault upon Sarkoy despite naval gunfire support. Denied Sarkoy and its pier, the Ottoman forces found it difficult to ship artillery or supplies ashore despite a 30-metre-long temporary pier built by their engineers in the beachhead.

This eased the Ottoman supply problem from the morning of 9 April as the Turks renewed their assault upon Sarkoy. The defenders had been reinforced by a Bulgarian battalion, but by midday they had been driven out, although not before they destroyed the town's little pier. For Hursit Pasha this was good news, but reports that X Corps headquarters and both infantry divisions had completed their landing were offset by word that Fahri Pasha's attack had been smashed. Hursit Pasha's bridgehead had now been expanded a kilometre to the east and two more kilometres north but still lacked field artillery, which remained in the ships.

Recognising that if the Ottomans established a major beachhead it would be a potential threat to the forces opposite the Catalca Line, Kovachev was determined to crush the enemy foothold. He assembled the Macedonian-Thracian Legion on the eastern side of the beachhead and the 'Trakiyska' in the west, while 'Rilska' sent four battalions and three batteries to the north, and immediately began to probe the defences from the night of 9/10 February, aided by air reconnaissance which determined the best place for a counter-attack.

The arrival of enemy reinforcements increased the fears of Hursit Pasha and Fahri Pasha, who both pressed Constantinople for authority to evacuate the beachhead and transfer the troops to the Gallipoli Peninsula for fear of a renewed assault upon the Bolayir Line. Just after noon on 10 February, as Hursit Pasha's artillery was finally being unloaded, Izzet Pasha reluctantly authorised the evacuation. Although Enver Pasha had wished the operation to continue, he organised a skilful withdrawal and in the early morning of 11 February the evacuation was complete, Enver being one of the last men to leave. The corps reinforced Gallipoli and Hursit Pasha assumed command of the newly established Gallipoli General Forces, while Fahri Pasha became commander of the Provisional Forces Command and the coastal defences. The decision was the result of a power struggle between the staffs of Fahri Pasha and Hursit Pasha, to whom Major Mustafa Kemal was soon attached.

The Ottoman troops had certainly regained their fighting spirit, but the well-planned operation was frustrated by bad weather and prevented them from exploiting the enemy's operational-level weakness. By moving their forces up to the Bolayir defences the Bulgarians had accidentally pulled the offensive's fangs, the Gallipoli troops being left to storm strong defences that had powerful artillery support. This exposed the amphibious operation, whose total losses were only forty men, including eight dead, but it seems that Hursit Pasha took counsel of his fears rather than risking what could well have been a successful defence of his beachhead. The landing highlighted the problems of twentieth-century amphibious warfare, which were repeated in the same theatre two years later.

It also demonstrated the difficulty of taking ports rapidly, a point underlined thirty years later at Dieppe. Bulgarian success in Gallipoli and Catalca proved to be their most successful defensive battles of the Balkan Wars and, more importantly, they retained the initiative, which allowed them to take Edirne unchallenged the following month.

In the aftermath of the Sarkoy failure the Ottoman general staff decided to reinforce Gallipoli from the Catalca Army which on 11 February was ordered to send II Provisional Reserve Corps with the 30th Active and Samsun Reserve Divisions to Gallipoli. However, the move was delayed because all available ships were still carrying Hursit Pasha's corps to Gallipoli. The Gallipoli forces were reorganised, Fahri Pasha's forces at Bolayir being redesigned the Bolayir Corps, while the coastal defences now came under a new Maydos Corps (Brigadier General Mehmet Ali Pasha). Fahri Pasha was relieved and Mustafa Kemal became the Bolayir Corps chief-of-staff, gaining experience that would serve him well in his defence of the Gallipoli Peninsula against Franco-British forces. The decision to renew offensive operations on the Catalca front meant that X Corps and the 31st Division were transferred northwards at the end of February. With the second armistice, the Bulgarians began transferring forces from Gallipoli to the west: the 'Rilska' and Legion in April with Kovachev's combat-proven 4th Army headquarters and 'Trakiyska' in June, followed by the Cavalry Division in July.

CHAPTER 4

The Western Theatre— The Ebb and Flow of Ambition

The western theatre saw the Ottoman forces involved in a desperate and ultimately futile struggle to hold imperial territory against all four allies.

It was potentially ideal terrain for defensive operations, being largely mountainous with heights of 1,500–2,000 metres divided by narrow river valleys cutting through the precipitous slopes. This should have eased the task, especially in the winter when cold winds from the north lash southern Albania and north-western Greece to create a bone-chilling cold and leave mountain communities snowbound for weeks. There are only a few broad arable valleys, such as that around Lake Shkoder north-west of Shkoder (Iskodra), and a few narrow and often marshy coastal plains. Communications were further hampered by lakes such as Ohrid and Prespa on the Greek border, which shielded the western approaches to Bitola.

But there were few railways, and even fewer good roads, especially in the wild western and north-western parts of the region where communications were usually based upon paths trodden across the slopes. The prime communications centre was Skopje for both the road and rail networks, the latter based on a few single-track lines. One ran northwards past Pristina to Kosovska Mitrovica, another north-east up the Morava valley past Kumanovo to Nis, and a third west along the upper Vardar valley through Tetovo to Gostivar. In addition, there was a branch line running south-west from Skopje through Prilep to Bitola before eventually turning east to enter Salonika. The main line ran south through the Ovce Polje plain east of Skopje and then down through Veles along the lower Vardar valley to Salonika. Another key town was Shkoder, which controlled Albanian territory down to the northern River Drin, whose upper course was divided between the northern White Drin (Drina Beli) and the southern Black Drin (Drina Zi) which leads to Lake Ohrid. Montenegro wanted Shkoder because it was the administrative capital of a rich region whose possession would end the kingdom's dependence upon foreign finance, but it was also the capital of the eleventh-century principality of Zeta.

Western Army commander Lieutenant General Ali Riza Pasha faced an impossible task for he was tasked to retain as much territory as possible, but as Frederick the Great once observed, 'He who tries to hold everything holds nothing.' On paper Riza Pasha had 276 infantry battalions, split almost evenly between active and reserve, but many were weak because there had been a large Ottoman demobilisation in August and the remainder had been stripped to meet counter-insurgency requirements. Against an establishment of 418,900 men he had only 188,000 scattered along the frontier, where they were exposed to defeat in detail by forces with a combined strength of 610,000.[1] Ottoman mobilisation was slow, and of 274 trains of men and matériel allocated to Riza Pasha only 188 arrived, while, as usual, it was difficult to find horses and oxen to pull the guns and wagons.[2]

To meet the prime threat from Serbia he created Lieutenant General Halepli Zeki Pasha's Vardar Army, which was deployed on a narrow front but in great depth, with its rear echelon at Bitola some 300 km from the Serbian border. The Iskodra Provisional Corps and Ipek Detachment faced Montenegro, contact with the Vardar Army being the responsibility of the Taslica and Pristine Detachments. Yanya Corps in Epirus and the Thessaly-based VIII Provisional Corps faced the Greeks, while in eastern Macedonia the Ustruma Corps with Nevrekop Detachment watched the Bulgarians. On the defensive at both the strategic and operational levels, Riza Pasha hoped to hold the passes against the Christian hordes. Until Nazim Pasha became War Minister, the Ottoman plan had envisaged meeting the enemy at Ovce Polje, but Nazim Pasha, influenced by Grandmaison, switched to an offensive strategy and ordered the Vardar Army to advance, destroy the Serbs in a surprise attack and then defeat the Bulgarians in detail.[3]

The subsequent operations were fought on four distinct fronts which will be dealt with in sequence: the northern (the Sanjak of Novi Pazar and Kosovo), the eastern (eastern Macedonia), the southern (Greek) and western (Albanian).

THE NORTHERN FRONT

The exposed Sanjak of Novi Pazar, with Kosovo to the south, had been defended by reserve forces since the Austrians withdrew in 1908. The defenders were the divisional-size Taslica Detachment in the Sanjak and the brigade-size Pristine Detachment in Kosovo, while the threat from Montenegro to the Sanjak led to the creation of the brigade-size Ipek Detachment with active troops.[4] The 30,000 Ottoman troops faced more than 122,000 men, a steam-hammer to crack a nut, in terrain dominated by steep, wooded slopes where the weather during the later stages of the campaign was dominated by frost and snow. While Putnik would be criticised after the war for committing so many men to what many regarded as a secondary front, its seizure was a key element of Serbian policy.[5]

The main threat to the Ottomans was the Serbian Army led by the craggy-featured 65-year-old Putnik. The heavy smoking general came from a family originating in Kosovo and received a basic education from his teacher father. Putnik joined the army in 1863 and distinguished himself in wars with the Ottoman Empire, but was regarded as an ascetic and an introvert. He clashed with King Milan when he refused to commission one of the monarch's friends after he failed the officer's entrance examination, but Putnik was rehabilitated under King Petar's rule during which he became War Minister on three occasions. He was a detailed planner but also very authoritarian and extremely reluctant to delegate initiative to his army commanders.[6]

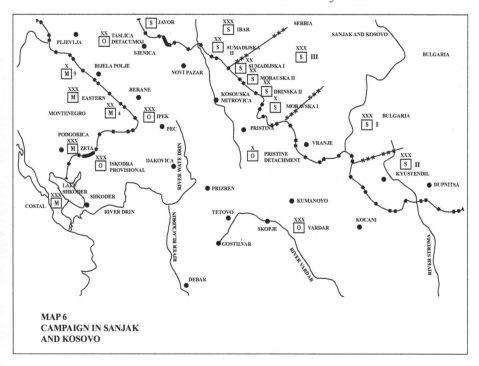

MAP 6
CAMPAIGN IN SANJAK
AND KOSOVO

It was this planning which ensured that by commandeering the whole rail network the army was mobilised on schedule by 18 October.[7] Serbian strategy envisaged the three armies, with some 281,350 men and 400 guns, converging to force the Turkish Vardar Army into a decisive battle around Ovce Polje. A frontal attack would be made by the 1st Army, with 131,900 men and 154 guns, while the 2nd and 3rd Armies (a combined strength of 156,400 men with 252 guns) enveloped the enemy.

In the meantime, General Mihailo Zivkovic's Ibar Army and Lieutenant Colonel Milovoje Andelkovic's Javor Brigade (37,400 men with forty-four guns) would take the Sanjak to create a land bridge between Serbia and Montenegro before advancing into Kosovo province.[8] The town of Kosovo, once the heart of medieval Serbia, would be taken by General Bozidar Jankovic's 3rd Army, with 77,800 men and ninety-six guns, during its envelopment of the Vardar Army, but this would also help Zivkovic and Andelkovic to secure the centre of the province. East of the Sanjak, Brigadier General Janko Vukotic's Montenegrin Eastern Corps, with 12,000 men and thirty-two guns, would advance first into the western Sanjak and then western Kosovo, and King Nikola hoped that the capture of Prizren, the provincial capital, would make it capital of a Serbo-Montenegrin kingdom.

On 18 October, Vukotic struck eastwards with a division and two brigades, including the Serbian volunteer 'Donjovasojevicka'. The 9th 'Durmitorska' Brigade had the most delicate mission, for it had to advance from northern Montenegro into the Sanjak in parallel with the Austrian border and then pause to await Vienna's reaction. While the Austrians disapproved of the move, they made no physical attempt to restrain the

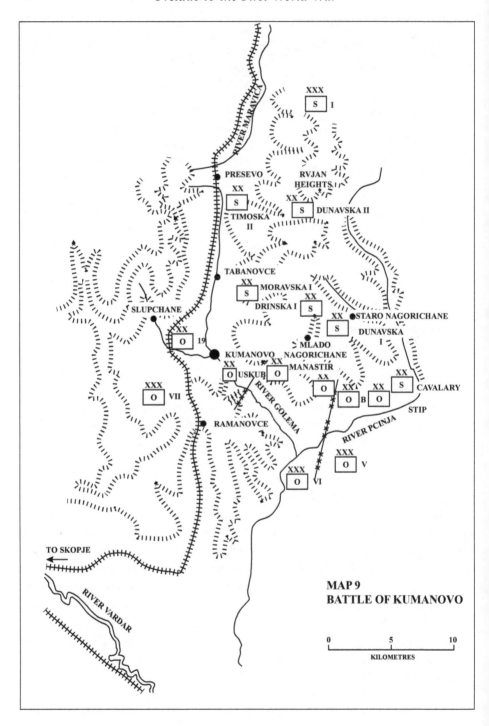

MAP 9
BATTLE OF KUMANOVO

0   5   10
KILOMETRES

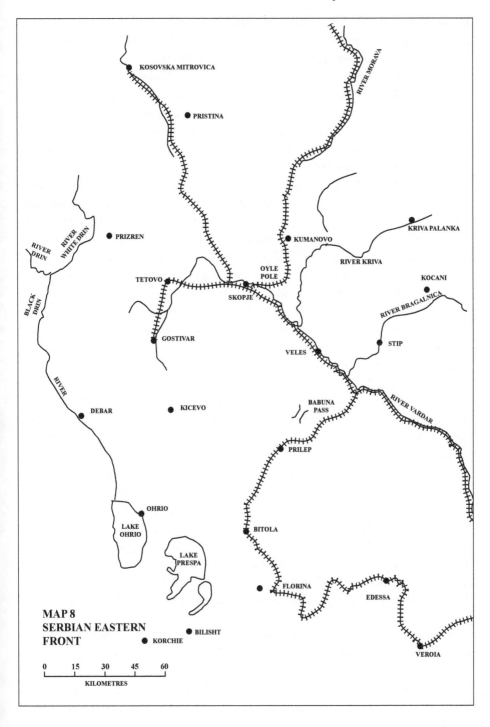

MAP 8
SERBIAN EASTERN
FRONT

0   15   30   45   60
KILOMETRES

Montenegrins and, when he realised this, King Nikola ordered the brigade to resume its advance. Together with the Serbian Javor Brigade, it took Pljevlja on 10 November and drove the surviving defenders into Austrian-occupied Bosnia.

In the south the two brigades of the 4th 'Niksicka' Division struck from central Montenegro. The northern one took the crossroads at Bijelo Polje on 24 October before advancing south-east to take Berane on 29 October and secure the south-west of the district. The southern brigade encountered fierce resistance from Ipek Detachment, which was defeated only on 21 October and linked with the Ibar Army, the joint force taking Pec on 2 November and Dakovica two days later.

Zivkovic's Ibar Army had entered the Sanjak on 18 October, but also paused while Belgrade awaited Austrian reactions. Indeed, Andelkovic's brigade was ordered to remain on the border and enter the region only if Vienna remained passive.[9] In the absence of any overt Austrian military moves, the Serbs resumed their advance westwards to take the capital, Sjenica, after a two-day battle on 22 October, as the main force surrounded Novi Pazar which fell the following day. Part of the Sumadijska Division then moved south to support Jankovic's advance upon Kosovska Mitrovica, which fell to the Ibar Army on 28 October.

It was Jankovic who actually opened the Balkan War for the Serbian Army on the night of 15/16 October, twenty-four hours after learning that Belgrade intended to declare war. He had earlier received pleas for help from Serbian paramilitaries inside the Ottoman border who had been driven back by Pristine Detachment and Albanian paramilitaries at a cost of nearly 950 casualties. The Albanian paramilitaries pushed them across the border, but Jankovic still refused to intervene because his country was not officially at war with the Ottoman Empire. Only when war was imminent did he order Colonel Milovan Nedic's Moravska II Division to help the paramilitaries, and together they drove the Albanians back across the border on the morning of 17 October.

Jankovic's troops followed them into Kosovo, and he exploited his overwhelming numerical superiority to push back the defenders by repeatedly turning their flanks. The Ottoman forces tried to hold Pristina, a largely Albanian town that had been the site of an epic fourteenth-century battle between the Turks and a Serb-led alliance, but in the face of envelopment the defenders abandoned it on 23 October. Jankovic paused to celebrate this morale-boosting victory but the following day the 3rd Army commander was forcefully reminded by a furious Putnik of his role in the grand design.[10] Even then he sent only part of his force along the railway towards Skopje, as the bulk of the 3rd Army remained around Pristina.

On his own initiative, Nedic pursued the Ottoman forces along the upper Vardar towards Tetovo, a decision later rubber-stamped by Jankovic, while Moravska II remained in the upper Vardar until late November when it was transferred to the 1st Army. By now the remnants of the Ipek and Pristine Detachments had retreated to Prizren, in the lower White Drin valley on the roads to both Shkoder and eastern Albania. This prize fell to Jankovic on 5 November to open the door to the Adriatic, but his men were exhausted, hungry and cold, lacking either adequate clothing or tents. Meanwhile, the Ottoman forces were reorganised at the end of October as the Montenegrin Border General Forces under Major-General Mahmud Hayret Pasha, who moved his headquarters (and 21st Division) down the Black Drin valley to Debar, half-way to Lake Ohrid.

The Serbian occupation of Kosovo did not bring peace, although many Albanian Muslim paramilitaries abandoned the fight and went home. The Serbs were initially conciliatory, especially Zivkovic's Sumadijska II Division, despite being advised to treat the Albanians severely, but officers such as Nedic took a harder line. This drove many Albanian Muslims to take arms against their new masters, who had to transfer to the province a reserve intended to meet a potential threat of Austrian intervention for a low-intensity, counter-insurgency operation.

Putnik's planning had never incorporated Serb dreams of access to the sea, and he did not reconsider until 2 November, when Pasic urged him to order a rapid advance to the Adriatic.[11] By now the Vardar Army was clearly on the ropes (see below) so Putnik raised no objections. Two days later, he ordered 64-year-old Jankovic, whose headquarters had now entered Prizren, to advance into Albania and secure the Adriatic between Lezhe and Durres. Jankovic protested that his men were in no condition to achieve this mission but was overruled.

He assigned the mission to the Drinska II and Sumadijska II Divisions under the former's commander, Colonel Pavle Paunovic, and in late November they became the Coastal Detachment. Jankovic's instructions to Paunovic were uncompromising: 'If you meet resistance act without mercy.' Paunovic moved rapidly across the mountains and within nine days reached Lezhe where Drinska II joined the Montengerins to take the port on 18 November. The advance encountered fierce guerrilla resistance, especially units which tried to disarm the gun-toting Albanians, although many Albanian Catholics fought alongside the Serbs and were especially helpful to the conciliatory Sumadijska II. Having reached the coast, Paunovic turned south on 24 November and pushed back two weak regiments of the 21st Division to take the Albanian capital Tirane on 28 November, followed by Durres two days later. Meanwhile, on 23 November, Nedic had been ordered to clear the Black Drin valley, which he did within three days after a display of his usual ruthless efficiency, and was then ordered into central Albania, taking Elbasan on 4 December.

Despite great hardships, the Serb troops had occupied most of northern and central Albania, but the region provided barely sufficient food for the inhabitants, whether man or beast, and there was little to spare for the invaders. The Albanians were naturally reluctant to sell food and starve themselves, while any attempt to requisition or seize food or fodder met resistance. The march was along narrow mountain paths with metre-deep snow and ice, many sliding to their deaths. Snow and mud sucked worn-out boots and shoes off men of the Sumadijska Division, while Drinska II had to use whole battalions to haul their guns. There was little shelter from the icy blasts, the men having to camp in the open even in snowstorms. Packhorses carried supplies, but the narrow paths meant that the beasts could be loaded only on one side, often with only seven or eight loaves, which left the men near starvation. Only when they reached the coast and Greek ships brought in food did the situation improve.

Yet Belgrade had achieved its territorial ambitions and controlled most of Albania to the River Shkumbin. This made the Serbs willing to accept an armistice on 6 December, but the Serbian arrival on the Adriatic had rung alarm bells in Vienna and Rome. Not only were Serbia and Montenegro now physically linked to create a large new Slavic state on Austria's southern border but there were also fears that Belgrade might allow one of the newly occupied ports to become a Russian naval base.

THE EASTERN FRONT

Putnik and King Petar established army headquarters at Nis on 18 October, anticipating that the Ottoman forces would concentrate in the Vardar valley and then await reinforcements from Anatolia. Intelligence mistakenly believed that there were 40,000 Ottoman troops at Ovce Polje which exposed them to a planned double envelopment in which a key role would be played by Crown Prince Aleksandar's 1st Army.[12]

The 25-year-old was the second son of King Petar and his *pince-nez* gave him the appearance of a teacher. He had spent most of his childhood in Montenegro where his father lived in exile and was educated in Geneva and St Petersburg. His brother's mental problems led to Aleksandar becoming Crown Prince in 1909, but almost immediately he contracted typhus which left him with permanent stomach problems.[13]

His five divisions were to advance up the Morava valley and cross the mountains into the Vardar valley, which was part of Macedonia's 'contested regions'. On his right, Jankovic's 3rd Army, after taking Kosovo, would sweep down the Vardar valley through Pristina to Skopje to turn the Ottoman left. On his left, in the upper Struma valley between Kyustendil and Dupnitsa, was 56-year-old gunner Stepa Stepanovic's multi-national 2nd Army. With 74,000 men (28,600 of whom were Serbs) of the Serbian Timoska I and Bulgarian 7th 'Rilska' Divisions, it was to march down the rivers Kriva and Bregalnica. Once the enemy was enveloped, the Bulgarians would drive down the Struma and ultimately take Salonika. Putnik's alleged obsession with enveloping the enemy at Ovce Polje and his failure to co-ordinate the enveloping arms was later criticised. He was said to have underestimated the time needed by the 3rd Army to move down the Vardar valley, and to have made Stepanovic's 2nd Army too weak.[14]

In the central Vardar, Zeki Pasha's Vardar Army was ordered to hold the frontier with the active 19th Infantry Division of Major-General Fethi Pasha's Skopje-based VII Corps. This corps had only 19,000 men, although two reserve divisions were marching up to support it. To surprise the Serbs, Zeki Pasha ordered V (Salonika) and VI (Bitola) Corps, each with a nominal four divisions and 32,000 men, to assemble around Kumanovo, 50 km north of Ovce Polje. With few trains available, this meant punishing forced marches of up to 150 km for the unfortunate troops of the two corps. Zeki Pasha had anticipated receiving reinforcements from Anatolia, and to shield their passage into Macedonia Major-General Ali Nadir Pasha's autonomous Ustruma Corps held the Bregalnica and Struma valleys with two divisions, while the divisional-size Nevrekop Detachment held the town of Kato Nevrekop.

Stepanovic quickly pushed into eastern Macedonia to isolate Zeki Pasha and then struck Nadir Pasha who held naturally strong defensive positions east of Kocani. Despite being shackled by poor communications, Stepanovic attacked on the afternoon of 22 October, but Nadir Pasha held him in a two-day battle until the Ottomans withdrew on the evening of the 23rd after pressure on their flank from a Rodop Detachment brigade upon Nevrekop Detachment. Nadir Pasha planned to join Brigadier General Hasan Tahsin Pasha's VIII Provisional Corps in Salonika, and his active 14th Division boarded trains on 28 October to take them south. That same day, the Bulgarian Rodop Detachment drove Nevrekop Detachment out of Kato Nevrekop towards Serres.

At this crucial point the Bulgarians threw two spanners into the works. On 26 October, the Bulgarian division commander Todorov suddenly informed Stepanovic he had been ordered by Sofia to move south towards Serres and ultimately Salonika. Tactfully, Todorov did not tell his Serbian commander that the instructions were to 'arrive at Salonika as soon as possible to prevent the Serbs from getting there first'.[15]

Stepanovic could do nothing yet, although left with only the Timoska I Division he still managed to occupy the Bregalnica valley to take Stip on 27 October. At this point the Bulgarians created another hurdle for him when Putnik received a request from Sofia for two Serbian divisions to help besiege Edirne. Although the Vardar Army remained a threat, Putnik loyally agreed and pulled Timoska I out of the line on 28 October before adding Aleksandar's Dunavska II Division three days later to create a new 2nd Army, still under Stepanovic. As he did so, Todorov marched down the Struma to destroy Ustruma Corps' reserve division near Serres, which he occupied on 5 November and then continued to his anticipated triumphal entry into Salonika.

Meanwhile, Putnik's 'anvil', Aleksandar's 1st Army, had crossed the frontier on 19 October and marched south, his left covered by his cavalry division under his brother Prince Arsen and Serbian paramilitaries. His spearhead, Moravska I Division, suffered a day's delay at the hands of Fethi Pasha's 19th Division but, without support, the Ottoman troops were outflanked and Aleksandar continued his march. This march was in echelon through the narrow valleys in the wooded mountains, along the Kriva and into the Pcinja valley in the east and the Moravica valley in the west. Colonel Ilija Gojkovic's Moravska I, followed by Colonel Dragutin Milutinovic's Timoska II, marched down the Moravica while Colonel Pavle Jurisich Sturm's Drinska I and Colonel Milos Bozanovic's Dunavska I marched along the Pcinja, followed by Colonel Michailo Rachic's Dunavska II. All assumed that they were pursuing demoralised troops.

Supply was a major problem because only twelve trains a day could run along Serbia's sole standard-gauge railway from Belgrade to Skopje, while poor roads caused the supply trains to make glacial progress. Food shortages were also due to the enlistment of so many men from bakeries and mills which consequently could not provide flour and bread. The Ban II and III units suffered especially badly, with Milutinovic's Timoska II regarded as the worse-supplied division.[16] Aleksandar's staff had failed to produce transport schedules, decisions having been left to junior officers who had to make last-minute decisions and lacked the authority to impose discipline. Reservist units were notoriously bad at observing these, and the massive traffic jams created in the rear further exacerbated the supply situation. Rachic's Dunavska II was unable to move for twelve hours, while

Milutinovic's Timoska II slowly dropped behind Gojkovic.

Meanwhile, a desperate Zeki Pasha opted for a forward defence north of Skopje in the hope of first giving Aleksandar a bloody nose and then defeating the other armies in detail. Fethi Pasha's VII Corps was ordered to fall back on Kumanovo, where it established sketchy defences to the north, while Major-General Cavit Pasha's VI Corps and Major-General Kara Sait Pasha's V Corps marched up from the south and arrived from 22 October. Four of the ten Ottoman divisions had to cover the Vardar Army's flanks and communications, which left only 57,000 men, less than half the enemy strength, and 164 guns, but an over-confident Zeki Pasha believed he faced only 60,000 Serbs. Fethi Pasha's VII Corps held the left with the 19th and Uskub Divisions, Cavit Pasha's VI Corps was in the centre with the 17th and Manastir Divisions, while Sait Pasha's V Corps on the right had the 13th and Istip Divisions supported by the Cavalry Division west of the railway running down the Moravica valley.[17] During the night of 22/23 October, the Vardar Army was ordered to dig in, but, in the belief that Nadir Pasha had pinned down Stepanovic on his right, Zeki Pasha gambled upon enveloping Aleksandar's Army with a co-ordinated assault the following day.

On 22 October, the Serbian spearheads pushed ahead through rain, mist and fog, unaware of either Ottoman intentions or strength even when they began to make contact with them towards the end of the day. During the evening Aleksandar halted some 10 km north of Kumanovo after Putnik ordered him to mark time in order to give the enveloping arms time to move into position. But the 1st Army commander decided to continue probing, having heard nothing from Prince Arsen's cavalry and the paramilitaries in the Pcinja valley. The Serbs held the lower slopes of the 875-metre Rujan Heights between the Moravica and the Pcinja, while the Ottoman forces held most of a 650-metre height around Mlado Nagorichane. This dominated the confluence of the rivers Golema and Pcinja and also faced Bozanovic, who had anchored himself on a newly captured ridge. Neither Sturm's Drinska I nor Gojkovic's Moravska I co-ordinated their operations while Bozanovic's Dunavska I on the left was exposed. Gojkovic, who had one regiment on the western bank of the Moravica, failed to carry out any reconnaissance, and a combination of complacency and exhaustion meant that the Serbs had scraped only shallow trenches. When the mists briefly cleared, Bozanovic and Sturm noticed enemy activity but failed to realise that these were preparations for an attack.

Zeki Pasha's plans for a co-ordinated assault were dashed soon after midnight on 22/23 October by the aggressive Fethi Pasha, a former ambassador to Belgrade. He decided to strike on his own initiative and simply invited his neighbours to join him. Just after dawn on a cold and rainy 23 October, Bozanovic saw the 17th Division's batteries on the move, assumed they were withdrawing, and sent Prince Asen's cavalry to attack them. The cavalry quickly discovered they had kicked over a hornet's nest and were rapidly driven back. This led Zeki Pasha to assume that the enemy was about to retreat and, now aware that his left was on the move, at 10.30 a.m. he gave his centre and right thirty minutes to strike the enemy while his Cavalry Division crossed the Moravica to get behind them.

The V Corps' attack, spearheaded by 13th Division, pushed back Bozanovic and inflicted heavy casualties, but Sait Pasha, having committed all his men, then had to pause during the early afternoon to bring up the Istip Division and this gave Dunavska I time to recover. Yet Bozanovic still did not think it necessary to inform his neighbour that he faced a major attack, and while Sturm in Drinska I did hear artillery fire on his left he assumed this was to support the Cavalry Division's advance. Only as the intensity of fire increased did he realise that his neighbour was under attack, but then Cavit Pasha struck his lines from 11 a.m. Here, as elsewhere along the 16-km front, the field batteries blasted gaps in the Ottoman ranks despite the increasingly muddy conditions which absorbed the high-explosive shells before they detonated. For the first time on a European battlefield, Quick Firer batteries became the backbone of the defence and prepared for their coronation as 'queen of the battlefield' in two years' time. By late afternoon the Serb centre and left had stopped the enemy, yet despite the noise of battle, Rachic of Dunavska II remained in camp almost like a visiting tourist.

Milutinovic of Timoska II showed more initiative as Fethi Pasha's 19th Division, supported by ten batteries, struck Gojkovic's Moravska I on the Serbian right at about noon. By now the Serbs were alert and while the Ottoman forces gained a little ground, they had lost surprise and in the face of Serb artillery fire were contained in a two-hour pitched battle. A Serbian counter-attack then drove them and the Cavalry Division back to their start line. Milutinovic began to feed men into the battle, but Aleksandar ignored his pleas to commit the whole division.

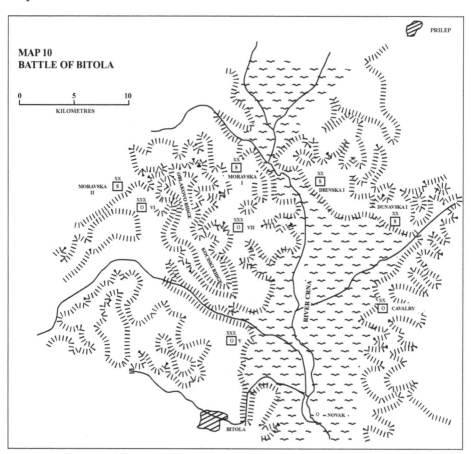

MAP 10
BATTLE OF BITOLA

Towards dusk the battlefield fell quiet yet despite a day of fierce fighting, Aleksandar still did not recognise the scale of the threat because his first echelon commanders failed to inform him. Still believing that he faced only covering forces which he would overcome the following day, he did not bring forward his second echelon forces and army artillery for fear they would clog the roads. His chief-of-staff, Colonel Petar Bojovic, went forward during the late afternoon and met Gojkovic, who was unable to convince him that he faced a major attack, Bojovic obstinately insisting that the Ottoman forces were weak and in retreat.

Bojovic changed his mind only after midnight on 23/24 October when he received an alarming report from Bozanovic that his division had suffered heavy losses and needed ammunition. Bojovic immediately roused the second echelon from their bivouacs and ordered them to march through the foggy night to the battlefield, which they reached from about 9.30 a.m. He ordered his centre and left to counter-attack, but Bozanovic said his division was too tired and remained on the defensive. By contrast, Zeki Pasha believed that the Serbian left was exhausted and was determined to finish off the enemy. He resumed his attack there at 5.30 a.m. on 24 October, with Cavit Pasha and Sait Pasha ordered to drive northwards to act as the anvil while the hammer, Fethi Pasha, enveloped the Serb right.

However, morning saw the Serb gunners back in action, supported by well-placed observers, to neutralise the enemy guns, including eighteen heavy pieces brought up from Skopje. The Ottoman batteries tended to fight private wars and were unable to conduct indirect fire due to a lack of forward observers. A captured Ottoman colonel later told the Serbs, 'You cannot imagine the hell-fire pouring from invisible Serbian guns. It caused at least 30 per cent of our casualties.'[18]

Cavit Pasha made frontal assaults to tie down Bozanovic while his reserve division tried to outflank the enemy together with Sait Pasha's reserve division. Instead they drove a salient into the Serb lines between Sturm and Bozanovic which exposed them to the full fury of the defenders' small arms, machine guns and artillery. Bozanovic's men resisted desperately for more than four hours, backed by their field artillery, before Dunavska II began to come up and by noon helped to stabilise the Serbian left, aided by the Cavalry Division.

On the opposite flank VII Corps struck alongside Cavit Pasha, but large-scale desertions from his reserve division following the loss of Pristina compromised the attack which then ran short of ammunition. Within thirty minutes, a counter-attack by Gojkovic's Moravska I, supported by Milutinovic, caused Fethi Pasha's demoralised reserve division to give way. By 2 p.m. it was streaming southwards, and this allowed Gojkovic to enter Kumanovo an hour later.

Cavit Pasha was also facing pressure from Drinska I and Dunavska II which came into the line on his left, but they did not co-ordinate their operations. This led to heavy losses until Sturm, with strong artillery support, hit the reserve Manastir Division from two sides and caused it to give way in the late morning. Cavit Pasha committed a rifle regiment, which stabilised the situation for a couple of hours, but this was decimated by artillery fire and Sturm's renewed attack in the early afternoon broke Ottoman morale. Some batteries were overrun as the infantry fled, and with the fall of Kumanovo most Ottoman batteries withdrew. Serbian artillery fire intensified thirty minutes later as Sturm began to strike the 17th Division on Cavit Pasha's right and it too began to withdraw, while the commitment of Dunavska I completed the rout as the Ottoman troops gave way.

Zeki Pasha, who would blame the disaster on the failure of his reserve units, ordered the Vardar Army to retreat. To cover them as best he could, he left behind detachments and even committed some war academy students, but the retreat soon dissolved into chaos. This cost the Vardar Army eighty-one guns, half its artillery including the eighteen heavy pieces, while a disgruntled Ottoman soldier tried to kill Zeki Pasha as he passed through Skopje. Fethi Pasha's VII Corps was virtually destroyed, while Cavit Pasha's VI Corps was decimated and lost all its artillery. The Turks later admitted that they had suffered 4,500 casualties, including 1,200 killed and nearly 330 taken prisoner, while the Serbs admitted losing a similar number (4,600) including 1,280 dead and missing (3.5 per cent of their troops), although one historian suggests each side lost 7,000.[19]

The Ottoman forces broke contact because the Serbs were too exhausted to pursue, while their Cavalry Division was typically useless. The battle was characterised by a total failure of intelligence on both sides, the Serbs being hamstrung by the obstinate belief that Ovce Polje would prove the decisive battleground. These factors prevented the Serbs exploiting their victory and afterwards Aleksandar advanced cautiously because neither he nor Putnik had any idea where the enemy was located. Consequently, Skopje was not encircled and occupied until the late morning of 26 October, when the Serbs took thirty howitzers left at the railway station.

It had been a hard-won victory, which earned Putnik promotion to marshal (vojvoda), but it was won more by the bravery and determination of the Serbian rank and file than the skill of their senior officers, who displayed a woeful lack of initiative and a tendency to follow personal agendas. Zeki Pasha's vain attempt to seek the operational-level initiative wrecked the Vardar Army and gave Belgrade control of much of the 'disputed zone' which they would prove very reluctant to relinquish.

Riza Pasha was in Salonika when he learned of the disaster, and on 25 October he ordered the Vardar Army to hold the key communications hub of Veles while the Ustruma Corps fell back on Salonika.[20] Recognising that the growing Greek and Bulgarian threat to the port made it essential to find a more central headquarters, he departed by train for Bitola the following evening. He arrived on 28 October, and ordered fifteen locomotives with 300 wagons to bring him supplies.[21]

Zeki Pasha's men were too demoralised to hold Veles, which fell on 27 October, and he divided his army. Fethi Pasha's VII Corps, reinforced by some 150-mm howitzers, retreated westwards following the railway along the upper Vardar through Tetovo and Gostivar, and over the mountains towards Kicevo which controlled entry into central Albania. He shielded Zeki Pasha's left flank as the remainder of the Vardar Army—V Corps and VI Corps—retreated south-west towards Prilep. By controlling this town and Bitola, Zeki Pasha would have the advantage of interior lines based upon the single-line railway running from the Vardar valley to Salonika and Edessa. With Fethi Pasha at Kicevo, the Ottoman forces now dominated western Macedonia's communications. Zeki Pasha established his headquarters in Prilep, where he joined Sait Pasha, who now had 13th, 15th and Istip Divisions, and was ordered to fight a delaying action. Cavit Pasha, who received 2,500 reinforcements while passing through Prilep on 28 October, was to strengthen the defences of Bitola. This now faced a threat from the Greeks to the south, and Zeki Pasha dispatched the newly arrived 16th Division in order to meet this threat.

With the Vardar Army's retreat westwards and Stepanovic's reorganised 2nd Army *en route* to Edirne, Putnik was forced on 29 October to redraft his plans. Jankovic's 3rd Army was now to advance west to the Adriatic while Aleksandar's 1st Army completed the destruction of the Vardar Army on its own. Aleksandar now advanced upon Prilep, having left one division to secure the eastern Vardar valley for Serbia. Pasic also advised Putnik to send troops to Salonika and get there before the Bulgarians and Greeks.[22] But the destruction of the Vardar Army remained Putnik's priority, which he did not wish to undermine by diverting troops to a secondary objective. With greater perspicacity than Pasic, he also recognised that if he joined in the race for Salonika with the Greeks and

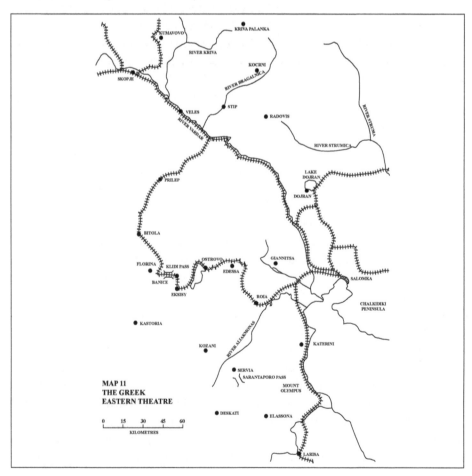

MAP 11
THE GREEK
EASTERN THEATRE

0 15 30 45 60
KILOMETRES

Bulgarians he would add another potential source of friction between the allies.

On 31 October, Aleksandar received detailed information from Macedonian paramilitaries about Ottoman defences north of Prilep. The town lay on the far side of the Babuna Mountains and was approached along a railway and road that followed the winding River Rajec through the Babuna Pass some 10 km to the north. The road was poor and at the southern entrance to the pass it turned sharply at Prisad before it ran down to Prilep. At the southern entrance, both road and railway were dominated by a 1,200–1,458-metre ridge running north to south on the west and a 1,534-metre ridge which arcs east of the road, the two arms seeming to reach to embrace the road.

Heavy rain hampered Aleksandar's advance. He fell ill and remained at his headquarters at Veles, trying to control events over an unreliable telephone line. Terrain and weather forced an advance in echelon with only a few batteries in support, and on 3 November spearheads of Gojkovic's Moravaska I, leading Sturm's Drinska I, encountered the enemy dug in on both heights. Gojkovic was advancing up the Rajec with one regiment while a second pushed through the mountains on his left.

His initial attacks were driven off, but he brought up his remaining two regiments which began to threaten the Ottoman left. The following day, they were reinforced by half of Sturm's division, the other half probing the Ottoman right. However, with little artillery, their attacks were costly. It was Sturm's troops in the west who finally turned the Ottoman flank, and without reserves Sait Pasha, who had only eight mountain guns, fell back to secondary positions south of Prilep on 5 November. He held them for a day before a Serbian frontal assault used bayonets and grenades to clear the trenches and drive V Corps across the swollen River Crna. The delaying action had been a success and cost Aleksandar some 2,000 casualties, while Sait Pasha lost 1,200, including 300 dead, with another 150 captured. Aleksandar was further delayed by heavy rain and snow, and Putnik had no choice but to grant his request for a pause to allow supplies to catch up.

Meanwhile, Nedic's Moravska II pushed along the railway to take Tetovo on 29 October and Gostivar two days later. Fethi Pasha had now been ordered to reinforce Bitola and left the 19th Division to delay Nedic around Kicevo. It inflicted 250 dead in a two-day action before it withdrew to Bitola to rejoin VII Corps which was holding the north-western approaches to the city.

The Ottoman Empire's last hope of retaining Macedonia was for Riza Pasha and Zeki Pasha to hold Bitola.[23] On paper the prospects were good, for the heavy rains had swollen the River Crna east of the city and turned much of the valley into a swamp up to 10 km wide and 4 metres deep. This natural obstacle, and V Corps, secured the city's north-eastern approaches from Prilep. The north-western approaches, held by Fethi Pasha, consisted of the steep-sloped Oblakovo Ridge which ranges from 1,150 to 1,493 metres and runs north-east to south-west, together with the 1,200-metre Kociski Ridge which runs south-eastwards towards the Crna. Cavit Pasha's VI Corps held the southern approaches against a potential Greek threat, with his headquarters at Florina. But while Zeki Pasha nominally had eight divisions, they totalled only 48,000 demoralised men with 100 guns who were short of ammunition and stretched to breaking point along a 40-km

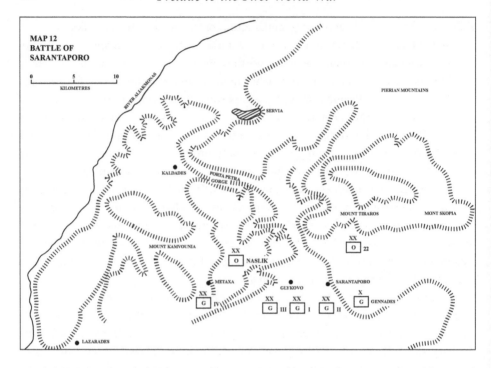

front.

Bitola was in the Bulgarian sphere of interest under the March agreement and it had never been one of Belgrade's objectives, yet it fell into its hand through good fortune. The catalyst was the unexpected Greek military success in the south, which left Athens well placed to take both Bitola and Salonika. The Greeks had indeed planned a march upon Bitola to help destroy the Vardar Army and, after his victory at Sarantaporo (see below), this was Constantine's objective, only for the government to order him instead to take Salonika. It was a move Constantine bitterly opposed, but to retain credibility with the Serbs in early November he sent a division north to Florina ostensibly to cover the advance upon Salonika. Sofia was unaware that Salonika was Constantine's objective and, with no troops available to secure its interests, it assumed that the Greek objective was Bitola. To forestall them, Geshov gambled that he could trust his fellow Slavs and sanctioned a Serbian occupation of Bitola with which Belgrade was more than happy to comply. For the Serbs, the Bulgarian request would not only remove the diplomatic hurdle to eliminating the Ottoman military but would also help tighten control of western Macedonia.

Meanwhile, Aleksandar's men, now nearly 108,550 strong, were awaited their supplies but requisitioned food and fodder locally where possible. On 8 November, Putnik ordered him to advance upon Bitola and Aleksandar split his forces to approach the city from the north-west and the north-east. Moravaska I joined Moravska II west of the Crna, while Drinska I was joined by Dunavska I and the Cavalry Division east of the river. Progress was slow, not only because of the rain and the awful roads but also because the Turks had wrecked the railway between Veles and Bitola, so supplies and artillery came forward slowly. Aleksandar did not reach the Ottoman positions until 14 November, by which time the weather had improved, so he decided to wait another three days of mild, dry, weather before beginning his attack.

The Serbs' slow approach allowed the Ottomans to strengthen their defences, but while few were optimistic about the prospects Zeki Pasha was determined not to await his fate like a sheep before a feast. On 13 November, having finally recognised that the Greek threat was weak, he ordered VI Corps, with 16th and 18th Divisions and a brigade-size Provisional Division, to move north to take the western slopes of Oblakovo Ridge, and left 17th and Manastir Divisions south of the city. Fethi Pasha was in the centre, based on Kociski Ridge, with 19th and Istip Divisions, while V Corps held a bridgehead across the Crna with 13th and 15th Divisions on either side of the Prilep road. Zeki Pasha intended to pin down Aleksandar using VII and V Corps and then envelop the Serbian right with VI Corps.

During the afternoon of 15 November, the vanguard of Aleksandar's left probed Sait Pasha and to prepare for his counter-offensive Zeki Pasha sent an *ad hoc* division from V Corps, together with a cavalry brigade, to reinforce Cavit Pasha. With only one supply channel, a hamstrung Aleksandar launched a frontal assault after a token reconnaissance. He planned to pin down the enemy centre with Moravska I and Drinska I, with Timoska II in reserve, and use his outer wings (Moravska II and Dunavska I) to turn the enemy flanks while the Cavalry Division pushed crossed the Crna at the Novak bridge. But on the night of 15/16 November, the impetuous Nedic struck Height 1,150, on the western side of the Oblakovo Ridge, in a battle which lasted through the morning and well into the afternoon. He was successful but at heavy cost, while the rest of the army remained relatively idle.

Aware of the potential threat to his counter-offensive, Zeki Pasha completed his preparations on 16 November. He set Cavit Pasha in motion during the morning of the 17th as the weather turned cold and a light rain fell. Cavit Pasha struck four of Nedic's battalions and drove both them and Gojkovic off the crests by mid-morning. But Nedic struck back, retook the crests and drove the Ottoman troops back into the valley. Simultaneously, Aleksandar began his main attack, which included Gojkovic, although he still faced a threat to his right, but Fethi Pasha held on in a mêlée of fierce attacks and counter-attacks. However, on the eastern bank of the Crna, Sturm and Bozanovic struck Sait Pasha hard and threatened his flank to force the Ottoman troops back across the river.

Undaunted neither by this setback nor news that Salonika had fallen, Zeki Pasha was determined to continue his attack, but during the morning of 18 November Sturm got across the main bridge over the Crna. Together with Gojkovic he pushed back the Istip and 15th Divisions on the VI and V Corps boundary while Nedic steadily drove Cavit Pasha down the slopes to block the road west to Ohrid. Serbian artillery support played a major role in these attacks, although the mud hampered the movement of both ammunition and guns. The well-established Ottoman guns also acquitted themselves well, and it was only the arrival later that day of Serbian heavy artillery in the counter-battery role which turned the tide and killed numerous teams of horses. Serbian artillery fire then inflicted heavy casualties upon the defenders, especially machine-gun crews, and as morale among the surviving infantry crumpled, the Serbs secured Oblakovo Ridge and pushed on towards Bitola.

Fethi Pasha tried many times to rally his men until he was killed by a rifle bullet, to become the most senior officer to die in the war.[24] By late afternoon even V Corps was crumbling, and it began to retreat in the early evening, taking with it the whole Vardar Army. It suffered 3,000 casualties, a third of them dead, with 5,600 captured, while some 5,000 reservists deserted to bring total losses to a third of its strength. The Vardar Army had been destroyed in all but name. It began to withdraw south-west towards southern Albania, disintegrating with every step, while Aleksandar's supply problems were eased when huge stocks of food were discovered with the fall of Bitola on 19 November.

Putnik had finally achieved his objective of destroying the enemy field army, but it had cost Aleksandar some 3,000 casualties, including almost 870 dead and missing, and he was allowed to recuperate at Bitola. However, the Cavalry Division went eastwards to take Ohrid on 22 November, the town having been the seat of an autonomous Bulgarian church authority until 1767. Elements of the Cavalry Division and Moravska II had gone south to take Florina on 21 November and to link up with the Greeks to complete the end of five centuries of Turkish occupation and all hopes of further Ottoman resistance in Macedonia.

THE SOUTHERN FRONT

Preparations

Given their experience some fifteen years earlier, the Ottoman generals were confident that they could contain the Greek threat which had to follow two axes divided by the Pindos and Gramos Mountains. The Pindos range, often called the spine of Greece, is some 160 km long and its highest point is Mount Smolikas (2,637 metres), while the Gramos range is part of the northern Pindos and reaches up to 2,520 metres, both ranges being formidable barriers.

In Epirus, southern Albania, the port of Vlore was a prize, but there was no direct route to it through mountains which are up to 1,000 metres high. Two roads followed the north-west to south-east courses of the southern River Drin and the River Vjosa and ultimately led to Berat. A slightly easier route ran north from the fortified town of Ioannina to Korce along the western bank of Lake Ohrid, either north to Debar or west to the sea. Ioannina was at the crossroads from which ran one of the few paved routes in Albania south along the River Louros to Arta. To defend the region the Ottoman Army had the Yanya Corps under Brigadier General Esat Pasha, former commander of the 23rd Division, but by 19 October it had fewer than 22,600 men.[25]

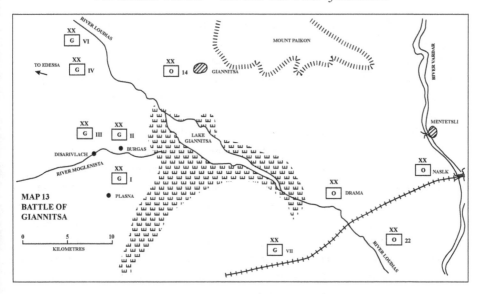

MAP 13
BATTLE OF
GIANNITSA

To the east, Thessaly has a number of broad river valleys running between the 1,000- and 2,000-metre mountain ranges, while the region's main railway ran along the coast from Athens and entered Salonika across the marshy estuary of the Vardar just west of Salonika. There was also a single-track line from Bitola through Edessa to the main line. The Ottoman general staff were confident that the VIII Provisional Corps under Brigadier General Hasan Tahsin Pasha, the former commander of the Ioannina garrison, could defend Epirus, for although he had only 29,300 men with thirty-six guns, he did control the region's road network. They ran across the mountains from Ioannina to Trikala and from Larisa up to Bitola via Florina, with another west to Korce. The shortest, and best, route from Thessaly to Salonika started on the 1912 border at the 610-metre Meluna Pass linking Larisa, in Greece, and Elassona, then in the empire. A contemporary account described it as a fair road, and some 20 km to the west was a cart track up the winding River Xerias that ran parallel to the pass.[26]

Led by the headstrong Constantine, the Greek Army had conceived the campaign in purely military terms. While they planned to advance from Larisa to Bitola to help their allies destroy Ottoman forces in southern Macedonia the politicians' eyes were on Salonika. Constantine, aged 44, was a professional soldier trained in Germany, his anglophile wife was Kaiser Wilhelm's sister, and like many military leaders he had no love for politicians. He had been military commander during the disastrous war with Turkey in 1897, and recognised his failures had contributed to the defeat.[27] He studied hard to overcome his shortcomings and even created his own military library, but a dozen years later he and his brothers were forced to resign their commissions only to be reinstated by Venizelos.[28] However, the Premier was determined to keep Constantine on a tight rein through his chief-of-staff, the very capable 59-year-old gunner Danglis, who was noted for organisational skills.[29]

Together they led the main Greek strike force, the Army of Thessaly, which had 100,000 men and ninety-six field, twenty-four mountain and fifty-four heavy guns as well as four aeroplanes, and during the first fortnight in October they concentrated around Larisa ready to strike through the Meluna Pass and along the Xerias routes. The sixty-three battalions and thirty-two batteries were organised into seven divisions, a cavalry brigade and two Evzone (light infantry) detachments under engineer officers Colonel Stephanos Gennades and Lieutenant Colonel Konstantinos Konstantinopoulos, the latter initially attached to I Division.

While there was no agreed strategy between army and government over Thessaly, there was a consensus over Epirus. Athens desired the region's economic capital, Ioannina, most of whose inhabitants were Greek, although the countryside was overwhelmingly Albanian. However, this was a secondary objective and the divisional-size Army of Epirus under Lieutenant General Constantine Sapountzakis had only eight infantry battalions and 10,500 men supported by twelve field, twelve mountain and eighteen heavy guns as well as 1,000 paramilitaries, and was supposed to have only a defensive mission.[30]

In Thessaly, Tahsin Pasha knew the Greeks were massing around Larisa, and to prevent them from breaking out he decided to fortify both the Meluna Pass in the west and Mount Olympus in the east. But on the frontier he had only Colonel Husamettin's active 22nd Division, a slender reed which was only 75 per cent of established strength, and he pinned his hopes on the arrival of two reserve divisions to hold back the Greeks.[31]

However, on the morning of 18 October, Constantine crossed the border and within hours Major-General Emmanuel Manousogiannakis's I Division (with Konstantinopoulos's column) was attacking Elassona. It was held by a single regiment, which had little chance against a full division and even less when Major-General Konstantinos Kallares's II Division arrived, but the defenders resisted stubbornly. Only under the threat of envelopment by Major-General Konstantinos Damianos's III Division did they withdraw during the night, Elassona falling on the morning of 19 October. Simultaneously, Gennades, supported by paramilitaries, struck in the west and advanced from Trikala to the border town of Deskati, 40 km miles west of Elassona, where he threatened to envelop VIII Provisional Corps. Tahsin Pasha withdrew Husamettin north to new defences in the Sarantaporo Pass 16 km south-west of Servia, where he was joined by Colonel Ismail Hakki's reserve Naslic Division.

The pass with the main road winds its way through the Pierian Mountains to the east and the 1,615-metre Mount Kamvounia in the west, reaching the valley of the River Aliakmonas near Servia, which lies just east of the northern entrance. A secondary road from Deskati ran down the Aliakmonas valley along the western slopes between Lazarades and Kaldades to meet the main route just beyond the narrowest part of the pass, the Porta Petra Gorge. On the eastern side of the pass was Mount Skopia, some 5 km north-east of Sarantaporo, with Mount Tiraros immediately north of the village.

Tahsin Pasha deployed Husamettin with twelve guns on the eastern side of the pass, and five of Hakki's battalions with ten guns on the western part, while his extreme right was covered by single battalion and in reserve were four battalions. The Ottoman defences were based upon positions near the southern entrance around key villages, notably Sarantaporo in the east and Glykovo on a south-facing spur in the west, with anchoring positions on Mount Tiraros and in Metaxas west of Glykovo.

Constantine had sent VII Division to Katerini, but the Ottoman forces still faced six Greek divisions which made contact on 21 October. That evening Constantine decided to keep Colonel Konstantinos Meliotes Komnenos's VI Division in reserve and to make a frontal attack up the pass with three divisions: I Division would be in the centre on the road, with II Division and the Evzones on its right and III Division on its left, the last striking Glykovo. Major-General Konstantinos Moschopoulos's IV Division would outflank the enemy right by driving through Metaxas and then following a narrow path along the western slope of Mount Kamvounia to reach Kaldades. Meanwhile, Colonel Demetrios Matthaiopoulos's V Division and Major-General Alexandros Soutsos's Cavalry Brigade would make a wider sweep to the west and roll down the Aliakmonas valley.

The attack began in fog, mist and drizzle soon after dawn on 22 October as the main force advanced across open terrain under intense fire. It suffered heavy losses to artillery as the men vainly tried to take stubbornly held defences in rugged terrain. Greek casualties might have been higher, but the Ottoman shell fuses were either unreliable or poorly fitted, while the soft ground in the lower ground absorbed shells before they detonated. Even after he committed VI Division on the right, Constantine was unable to break the bloody deadlock at the mouth of the pass due to lack of artillery support. The poor roads, little more than tracks, made it difficult to bring up the guns and it was not until the early afternoon that the Greeks finally received adequate artillery support.[32] Unfortunately, this was confined to the centre near the road, so the few men who forced their way into the Turkish trenches were usually driven out, although they did establish toeholds in the Ottoman main line of resistance.

The drizzle turned into torrential rain and V Division's progress was slow, allegedly due to fierce Ottoman resistance but more probably as a result of the terrain and the weather, while Soutsos's cavalry were described as moving 'in a leisurely manner'.[33] The best news came from the west where IV Division exploited its overwhelming numerical superiority to fight its way up the cloud-wrapped slopes and take Metaxas in the late afternoon. It pressed on to Kaldakes by the end of the day to earn the nickname 'The Winged Division' and threaten Tahsin Pasha's communications.

Hakki's counter-attacks kept these communications open, but Tahsin Pasha lost his nerve. He failed to commit his reserve and opted to retreat, but poor communications between him and the divisional headquarters caused confusion which led to panic. In the ensuing chaos much matériel was abandoned, including twenty-one of his thirty-six guns, but fortunately darkness and rain concealed the withdrawal. Ottoman casualties totalled 2,100, including 500 dead, while 700 were captured, the Greeks suffering 1,177 casualties, including 182 dead. Constantine did not discover the enemy's departure until the following morning, and his pursuit was 'leisurely' due to the usual problems of troop exhaustion and supply problems. The V Division did not receive orders to pursue the enemy and when Matthaiopoulos sought permission to isolate the Ottoman forces at Servia, he was ignored.

As he rested most of his troops, Constantine sent VI Division to pursue a reserve regiment over the northern slopes of Mount Olympus and cut the coastal railway. Meanwhile, part of Colonel Kleomenes' VII Division advanced along the railway towards the port of Katerini with half his men while the rest sailed along the coast. On 28 October, Kleomenes reached the town, drove out the garrison and pushed them along the railway.

Constantine's plan was to drive northwards through Kozani to Bitola, but Venizelos, with the support of both the government and King George, demanded that Macedonia's capital, Salonika, be taken first to forestall the Bulgarians. There was a heated exchange of telegrams in which Constantine concluded, 'My duty calls me to Monastir [Bitola], unless you forbid me.' Venizelos, who was also War Minister, tersely replied, 'I forbid you.' Constantine reluctantly obeyed but it soured his relationship with the Premier, who would engineer his abdication in 1917.[34]

Constantine had already dispatched V Division and the Cavalry Brigade to Kozani, which the latter took on 24 October to establish a Greek foothold in south-western Macedonia. The diversion of the cavalry meant that Constantine lost contact with the retreating Ottoman forces and assumed they were either behind the Vardar or south of Lake Giannitsa. It was decided that VII Division would block any threat from the latter while the rest of the army advanced through Giannitsa towards Salonika. The five divisions pursued the retreating enemy across the broad fertile plain, making 10 km a day in the rain and mud. On 29 October, the vanguard, with the Evzoni columns on the hilly flanks, cut the Bitola–Salonika railway at Veroia as Tahsin Pasha began to rally along the River Aliakmonas south of Giannitsa.

Constantine's supplies depended largely upon 23,000 pack animals, although the Greek Army mobilised some 100 motor vehicles including sixty trucks and vans. But there were few mechanics and during the advance to Salonika, barely half of these vehicles were used, the motor cars being restricted to carrying post and despatches.[35] The coastal advance benefited from both the railway line, augmented by two Ottoman trains hijacked by Greek railway staff, and coastal shipping. Supplies landed in the little harbour of Eleutherochori, 23 km north of Katerini, proved vital to Constantine, whose men had been on short rations for a week.

Tahsin Pasha's last opportunity to stop Constantine lay 25 km west of Salonika. There an enemy advance would be channelled between Mount Paikon to the north and the swamp-bounded Lake Giannitsa, more than 3 km long and 1.5 km wide, which lay astride the course of the River Loudias.[36] The enemy could approach either north of the waterway along the Edessa–Salonika road or along the coastal plain to the south where the railway to Salonika ran alongside the road to cross the Vardar over a steel bridge at Kavakli.[37]

The demoralised men of VIII Provisional Corps reached the lake on 28 October, and Tahsin Pasha deployed the newly arrived reserve Drama Division (Lieutenant Colonel Mustafa Hamdi) across the Edessa–Salonika road on his right while Husamettin's 22nd Infantry Division south of the waterway along the River Loudias blocked the coastal route. Hakki's Naslic Division, with an *ad hoc* reserve regiment, was held in reserve, but Tahsin Pasha then received further reinforcements. On 31 October, the Ustruma Corps' 14th Division (Brigadier General Galip Pasha) arrived in Salonika and was promptly dispatched to Giannitsa to relieve the Drama Division, which joined Husamettin on the Loudias. Tahsin Pasha was grateful for the five batteries the reinforcements brought, although he demanded another seven from Salonika. He had a strong 24-km-long position but only 25,000 men, and his back was to the unfordable 275-metre-wide Vardar.

It was Kleomenes' VII Division and Konstantinopoulos's Evzones south of the lake who first made contact with the enemy on 31 October as most of Constantine's army marched towards the Edessa–Salonika road from the south-west. Their progress was monitored by Turkish aeroplanes, which helped Tahsin Pasha conclude that Constantine planned to envelop his right with a diversionary attack on his left.[38] To meet the threat he switched the roles of the Drama and Naslic Divisions, breaking up Husamettin's division to give the latter four of his battalions and another five to Hamdi's Drama Division. The reinforced Naslic Division was now to hold the Loudias south of the lake while Mustafa Hamdi, further reinforced by a reserve regiment, was assembled as a counter-attack force which would strike in the north at the appropriate moment.

Far from planning to envelop Tahsin Pasha, Constantine had no idea that the Ottoman forces would make a stand. Still seething over Venizelos's interference, he was more concerned about an advance upon Bitola than reaching Salonika, and although ignorant of enemy dispositions, he did not anticipate any serious opposition. Indeed, as Kleomenes encountered the enemy, Constantine planned to make Giannitsa his headquarters the following day. During the afternoon of 31 October, the Greek vanguards crossed the River Moglenista and encountered stronger resistance from Ottoman outposts, making them finally realise that the enemy intended to make a stand. Kallares's II Division managed to establish a 2.5-km bridgehead at Burgas, which expanded when Damianos's III Division took Disari Vlach alongside it.

During the night, Venizelos informed Constantine of the Bulgarian victory at Luleburgaz and urged him to hurry to Salonika. Constantine loyally responded by ordering Kallares and Damianos to strike directly at Giannitsa on the following morning while I Division at Plasna covered their flank. Meanwhile, IV Division would come down the Edessa–Salonika road and seek to outflank the enemy right. On the other flank, VII Division would try to cross the Loudias and then take the bridge over the Vardar at Mentetsli in order to isolate Ottoman forces from Salonika, and VI Division was to take Mount Paikon to outflank the defenders from the north.

The attack began on the late morning of 1 November in heavy rain. Kallares, Damianos and Manousogiannakis made slow but steady progress, although I and II Divisions suffered badly, especially from Galip Pasha's artillery which had excellent fields of fire. Simultaneously, Moschopoulos drove down the Edessa–Salonika road and penetrated the Ottoman line until stopped in a counter-attack by one of Galip Pasha's regiments. Another regiment stopped VI Division just as its success on the lower slopes of Mount Paikon threatened Galip Pasha's batteries. They were quickly withdrawn but abandoned much ammunition.

By the end of the day, the Greeks had a bridgehead across the Loudias but were still outside Giannitsa, and Tahsin Pasha was confident that he could hold the line. During the evening he ordered Hamdi's Drama Division north to Giannitsa, the reservists marching through the night in a violent thunderstorm with hail and sleet. By now, Constantine appreciated the strength of the defence and hastily reorganised his forces for a co-ordinated assault upon the Ottoman lines at dawn. Supported by heavy artillery fire, the battered II, III and IV Divisions renewed their attacks, together with VI Division, and exploited their numerical advantage to overwhelm the defenders as Greek artillery began to dominate the battlefield.

Galip Pasha held out for two hours while Hamdi tried desperately to reach him, but by 9 a.m., with the Drama Division still several kilometres away, Kallares and Damianos had pushed back the 14th Division left, and within an hour the whole division followed. Kallares and Moschopoulos took Giannitsa at 11 a.m. at a cost of 975 casualties, including 188 dead, while the defenders suffered some 1,300 casualties. Worse still for the defenders, VII Division exploited the weakened defences south of the lake to establish a small bridgehead over the Loudias. The defenders succeeded in blowing up a wooden road bridge at Mentetsli, but paramilitary forces thwarted an attempt to demolish the steel rail bridge at Kavakli which allowed Kleomenes to cross and establish a bridgehead.

Salonika's western shield had been broken and left the way open to Constantine, who was no doubt greatly relieved that the 'diversion' would soon end. The battle had cost the Ottomans 1,950 men, including 200 prisoners and eleven guns, while the Greeks suffered 990 casualties, including 207 dead. Afterwards the Greeks would claim that in this battle and at Sarantaporo they had taken 37,000 prisoners, 106 guns and 75,000 rifles, while suffering 3,752 dead and 9,452 wounded.[39]

Although bombarded with telegrams from Athens urging him on to Salonika, Constantine had first to regroup his forces while the rail bridge captured by Kleomenes was repaired. It was not until the evening of 5 November that I Division crossed that bridge, while further up the river the next day other divisions used existing bridges or those they had built themselves to expand their bridgeheads.

Salonika

Retreating Ottoman troops now poured into Salonika; the remnants of Ustruma Corps and Nevrekop Detachment from the east and VIII Provisional Corps from the west. They and the local reserve division were placed under Tahsin Pasha's command on 3 November. The Greeks and Bulgarians were now racing for Salonika, but it was a reluctant Constantine who took the prize as his men exploited the rail bridge over the Vardar.[40]

Lying on a crescent of low hills, Salonika was both the largest city in Macedonia and the region's port at the centre of an important agricultural area. It had a cosmopolitan population of 120,000, among whom were 80,000 Sephardic Jews, the remainder including Bulgarians, Greeks and Turks.[41] The former Sultan, Abdul Hamid II, was a resident but the German gunboat SMS *Loreley* sailed in on 30 October and took him back to Constantinople.[42]

Nominally, Tahsin Pasha had six divisions but in reality he had only 26,000 men and seventy guns to hold the city, although he was well supplied as the city was a major base. But, as with Singapore thirty years later, the Ottomans never anticipated a serious land threat and the northern approaches were defended by only a couple of small obsolete forts and an unmanned battery. The biggest perceived threat was from the sea, and two coast defence batteries were built in 1897 with four 240-mm Krupp guns and six old-style 87 mm guns.[43] These were augmented by four 150-mm, four 75-mm and four 57-mm guns removed from the old ironclad *Feth-i Bulend* before she was sunk in the harbour by a Greek torpedo boat on the night of 31 October/1 November, further demoralising the garrison.

Fearful of the destruction a battle might inflict upon the city, the consuls of the Great Powers visited Tahsin Pasha on 7 November and persuaded him to open negotiations for a bloodless occupation. He might have gained time if he had played off Greek and Bulgarian rivalries, but he clearly believed a rapid surrender was best for his men.[44] He was right, because even as he met the consuls Constantine ordered a full-scale assault the following morning to pre-empt the Bulgarians. This was cancelled five hours before it was scheduled to start, when the Greeks learned of Tahsin Pasha's decision. That evening a relieved Constantine agreed generous terms in return for handing the city to the Greeks.

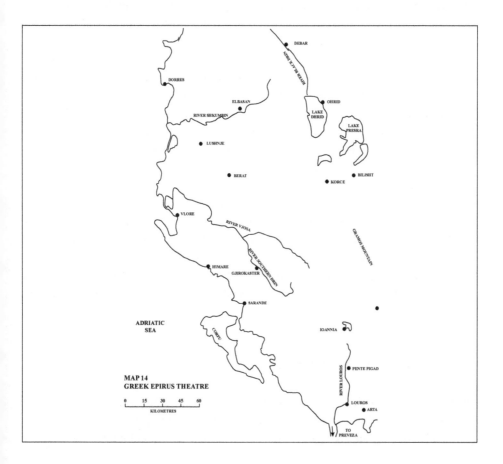

MAP 14
GREEK EPIRUS THEATRE

Ottoman troops were allowed to remain on parole, while the police and gendarmerie maintained law and order.

The surrender went smoothly, with the defenders cleaning their rifles before handing them over to the victors. At noon on the following day, Kleomenes' VII Division was the first to enter ,while Manousogiannakis's arrival consolidated Greek control and ensured that they benefited from the booty, which included seventy guns, thirty machine guns, 70,000 rifles, 1,200 horses and oxen. Constantine established a 25,000-man garrison in the city while other troops took up commanding positions in the hills to the north and north-west overlooking the Struma valley. Meanwhile, the Hellenic Navy occupied the Chalkidiki Peninsula which reaches like a hand into the Aegean. Control of the city was reinforced with the arrival of 300 Cretan gendarmes, part of a 1,450-man, Italian-trained force with a reputation for reliability.[45]

There was considerable Bulgarian chagrin at the Greek coup because Todorov's 7th 'Rilska' Division was almost within sight of the city when it encountered Kallares's II Division north of Salonika on the morning of 8 November. Kallares asked Todorov to stop shelling the retreating Ottoman troops who were about to surrender. Sofia had little information about events in Salonika, while Constantine's staff were unsure about the location of the Bulgarians, and this caused much confusion on both sides. But when Constantine met Kleomenes at Salonika railway station he told him to take his division through the city to block the Bulgarian advance.

Kleomenes obeyed and informed Todorov that only a staff officer would be allowed to enter the city. After tense negotiations, Constantine allowed Todorov to send a token force into the city and also established an uneasy joint urban administration. On 9 November, accompanied by both Crown Prince Boris and the Tsar's second son Prince Kyril, the Bulgarians finally entered the city and Todorov optimistically telegraphed the Tsar, 'From today Salonika is under the sceptre of Your Majesty.' The Tsar had told his son, 'How I envy you, my dear son, for your historic entry into the city of St Paul.'[46]

Barely four months later, Athens' triumph became tragedy. The Danish-born King George had arrived at Salonika in triumph and enjoyed a giddy social round of celebration. He had endeared himself to his subjects by his informality and would regularly walk among them like a private citizen. He was doing this on the evening of 17 March, accompanied only by an equerry, when a Greek anarchist gunned him down. The German battlecruiser *Goeben*, which he had been due to visit the following day, now had the doleful duty of escorting the royal yacht *Amphitrite* with his body to Athens, where they arrived on 27 March.[47]

Operations in Western Macedonia

With the fall of Salonika the Greek Army's attention increasingly swung westwards into Albania as Constantine tried to complete his disrupted pre-war plans.

His first step, ostensibly to shield his left, was to send Matthaiopoulos's V Division to Kozani, which it took on 24 October.[48] Four days later, Foreign Minister Lambros Koromilas requested Constantine's advance on Bitola once Salonika had fallen, and the following day the Crown Prince gave Matthaiopoulos permission, on his own judgement, to advance northwards as far as Bitola.

Most of the inhabitants around Kozani were Muslim and Matthaiopoulos had to secure his communications, which left him with only 7,000 men for the advance. Believing that there were few Ottoman troops between him and Bitola, he marched north to reach the Bitola–Edessa railway and take Banitsa on 1 November. He then turned east to seize the vital communications centre of Florina, which gave access to south-eastern Albania and controlled the southern approaches to Bitola.

He was unaware that Cavit Pasha had established VI Corps' headquarters in Florina on 31 October with Colonel Husnu Bey's 18th Infantry Division augmented by 2,000 elderly Albanian paramilitaries from Debar. Cavit Pasha planned a counter-offensive, and to assist it two active divisions were railed down to the town. Husnu Bey opted for an active defence, but decided to conduct guerrilla attacks with the paramilitaries to slow the Greek advance. He then ambushed Matthaiopoulos in the Klidi Pass on 3 November, routed him and inflicted 374 casualties, including 168 killed and ten prisoners who would be freed by the Serbs at Bitola. Husnu Bey's success was mirrored by Cavit Pasha's 16th and 17th Divisions, which retook Banitsa on the same day to secure the southern approaches of Bitola.

News of the disaster reached Constantine just as he was about to cross the Vardar. As his forces were fully committed, he could only order Matthaiopoulos to hold his positions, but Constantine did organise logistic support while the Army Ministry ordered a 2,000-man Larisa-based task force (a battalion and three batteries) to Kozani. But as V Division faced further pressure, Venizelos was forced to ask Belgrade to push harder at Bitola to divert the enemy.

The Ottoman troops, guided by a local peasant, outflanked V Division on the night of 5/6 November and hit its rear, causing panic in an engineer company and then taking nine guns, seven of which were later recovered. The dawn attack of the main Ottoman force completed the rout as the Greeks fled towards Kozani, held only by 300 garrison troops and gendarmerie augmented by 400 armed civilians. Luckily the Ottoman generals were more concerned about the Serbian threat to Bitola and soon sent their regiments north. Matthaiopoulos's men finally rallied at Kozani where each regiment was reduced from three to two battalions. So nervous were the Greeks, that when Turkish peasants attacked engineer battalion outposts north-west of Kozani on 8 November it triggered another widespread panic and flight. The situation was restored during the afternoon with the arrival of the Larisa Detachment, reinforced on the night of 8/9 November by Gennades' Evzones, with Gennades immediately assuming command.

Unaware that the Ottoman forces had withdrawn to Bitola, but having secured Salonika, Constantine decided to move north. He reorganised his forces on 11 November into Right Group under Kallares with II and VII Divisions plus Konstantinopoulos's Evzones, which was to hold Salonika. He led the Centre Group with I, III, IV and VI Divisions and the Cavalry Brigade northwards while his western flank was covered by Gennades' Left

Group.[49] He now had Venizelos's support, for on 12 November the Premier had urged Constantine to join a combined offensive towards Bitola, but ominously he also wanted reinforcements for Epirus. When Venizelos learned of Bitola's fall he ordered Constantine to return three divisions to Salonika, with one destined for Epirus, which left the Crown Prince two and the Cavalry Brigade to pursue retreating Ottoman forces which now posed a threat to Greek control of Epirus.

Following its defeat at Bitola on 18 November, the Vardar Army was now trapped in the mountains of western Macedonia where it was joined by the remainder of the Western Army. There were two Ottoman groups; 16,000 men of V Corps with Riza Pasha's Western Army headquarters and 23,600 men of Zeki Pasha's Vardar Army with the remnants of VI and VII Corps, but many men had abandoned their weapons. The troops set out for Berat in south-eastern Albania, Riza Pasha reaching Bilisht on 20 November, while Zeki Pasha marched south of Lakes Ohrid and Prespa to reach Korce four days later. He absorbed Yanya Corps on 29 November.

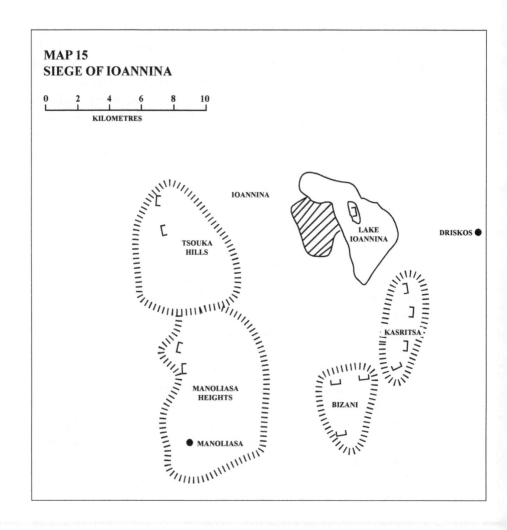

MAP 15
SIEGE OF IOANNINA

0   2   4   6   8   10
KILOMETRES

IOANNINA

TSOUKA
HILLS

LAKE
IOANNINA

DRISKOS

KASRITSA

MANOLIASA
HEIGHTS

BIZANI

MANOLIASA

Constantine advanced westwards towards Lake Ostrovo with VI Division in the centre, III Division on the right and IV Division on the left as V Division was ordered to renew its offensive towards Sorovits. Ottoman forces briefly held them east of Lake Ostrovo, but on 18 November Komnenos took the town of Ostrovo as Moschopoulos worked his way around the southern shores of the lake. Greek cavalry rode to Florina, which fell on 23 November, together with twenty-two guns and much matériel. Constantine set up his headquarters in Florina and rested his forces around Banitsa, the troops having marched 145 km in eleven days.

The arrival of Vardar Army at Korce showed that the Ottoman Empire was losing the war, and this led Muslim Albanians and the Christian minority briefly to make common cause by convening an Albanian Independence Congress under Ismail Kemal Bey. The declaration of independence was signed by the Congress on 24 November and proclaimed four days later in Tirane, gaining rapid recognition from both Italy and Austria. But the Serbs and Greeks ignored Albanian pleas to cease hostilities.[50] With justified concern about the allies' intentions, the Albanians had little option but to pledge continued support for the Ottoman forces. Riza Pasha noted Albania's independence on 29 November, but he still planned to continue on to Berat as he was aware that the armistice with Serbia and Bulgaria did not extend to the Greeks.

Only ten days earlier, Constantine had sent a Turk across the lines with letter offering terms to Riza Pasha, but the messenger was arrested and the missive was never delivered. Constantine was reluctant to commit large forces into eastern Albania, where Athens had no interests, and his only concern was to secure the newly acquired territory from any potential Ottoman counter-offensive. On 20 November, he went to Bitola to define with Crown Prince Aleksandar new operational areas, but he exceeded his remit when he proposed that the Serbs should cede Bitola to the Greeks in return for a Greek naval squadron being dispatched to Durres to support the Serbs. The Serbs rejected the proposal and it was clear they intended to hold the city, although they pledged not to probe down the Vardar and the *status quo* was accepted by both governments.[51]

Athens also pondered a landing at Gallipoli, although this foundered on the need both to reinforce the siege of Ioannina and to counter Zeki Pasha, whose intentions were uncertain. Intelligence suggested that he was on the defensive, but on 28 November, Constantine's chief-of-staff proposed watching Korce and the prince approved this before he transferred his headquarters to Salonika on 4 December. The competent Damianos was given command of the sector, his forces having taken Kastoria on 24 November, and there he settled into winter quarters. His orders were to hold a line south from Lake Prespa along the Albanian border and to prevent any Ottoman attack, but he was not to advance westward. He had operational control of part of the Kozani-based V Division and the Florina-based VI Division while IV Division secured communications between Florina and Salonika.

But the implementation of the Turco-Serbian armistice changed these plans. Potentially this agreement allowed Ottoman forces to concentrate against the Greeks in western Macedonia, and Cavit Pasha's VI Corps at Bilisht probed Greek defences. Damianos decided to strike westwards against Cavit Pasha and won Athens' approval on 14 December.

Komnenos's VI Division promptly worked its way around Cavit Pasha's open right to take the Bilisht Pass by dusk on 15 December. This opened the way for an advance upon Korce, which fell on 20 December, the defenders retreating northwards to establish a new line west of Lake Prespa. The Greeks then returned to winter quarters and the snowed-in front remained quiet for the rest of the winter. Soon after, IV and VI Divisions returned to Salonika, sailing for Epirus on 25 December and 8 January respectively.[52]

The Epirus campaign began as a Greek sideshow only to become the altar of national prestige that sucked in resources during the winter of 1912/13. The region's defender was the Ioannina-born Esat Pasha, an extremely capable former divisional commander promoted to corps command at the last minute. He would later distinguish himself further during the 1915 Dardanelles campaign.

His Yanya Corps had a nominal twelve active battalions in Brigadier General Cevat Pasha's 23rd Division and ten reserve battalions in Colonel Celal's Yanya Division. But he had to transfer resources to Tahsin Pasha, including machine-gun detachments and 1,100 draught animals, which left him with 890 to draw carts and guns, so he had to leave four batteries in Ioannina. His active division had only 2,100 trained infantry, while reserve battalions had only 300, but Ioannina's fortifications, under his brother Lieutenant Colonel Mehmet Vehip Kaci Pasha, were extremely strong and had been recently modernised. Esat Pasha decided to shield Ioannina and sent both divisions to block the southern approaches by holding Louros on the Preveza road, and the Pente Pigadia Pass on the Ioannina road.

Numerically inferior, Sapountzakis decided upon a dynamic defence and, despite torrential rain, sent the regimental-size Arta garrison across the frontier just before noon on 19 October. He also put an Evzoni battalion into the southern end of the Pente Pigadia Pass and then requested 10,000 reinforcements.[53] When he learned of the incursion, Esat Pasha, on the night of 19/20 October, decided to squash the Evezones. His 23rd Division would attack in the west while the Yanyar Division struck from the north, both formations reaching the pass on the morning of 20 October. But Esat Pasha did not believe in pushing his subordinates and they refused to attack because the conditions were so muddy. In addition, their communications were under attack by Albanian Christians, which gave the Greeks time to put another battalion into the pass and take the commanding ground.[54]

Only on the morning of 22 October did the Ottoman attack begin, and it was quickly halted. The following morning, the Yanya Division recovered the situation and drove the Greeks back 2 km to give Esat Pasha control of the pass and inflict 250 casualties. But it was not until dusk that the 23rd Division attacked the Greek centre, in the heights west of the pass, which was soon held, preventing Esat Pasha from exploiting his success. The setback convinced Athens that Sapountzakis did indeed need reinforcements, so 2,000 men of the Independent Cretan Regiment together with Cretan paramilitaries departed Piraeus on the night of 24/25 October and arrived a few days later. By now any threat Esat Pasha might have posed had evaporated, the defeats on Tahsin Pasha to the east having left him exposed, and on 24 October he ordered a withdrawal to Ioannina. The Greeks were understandably cautious in their pursuit, and it was not until the 26th that they took the town of Filippiada.

Meanwhile, Greek paramilitary forces had exploited the situation to isolate Preveza. This was held by a weak regular battalion, reservists and fortress troops, a total of 1,160 men, and while their defences had held off the Greeks during the siege of 1897, that had been when the garrison had five battalions. The arrival of a Greek battalion group put the issue beyond doubt, and this attacked at noon on 2 November with field and naval artillery fire support. The garrison, which had 80-mm Broadwell guns, retreated into the port and the following day negotiated a surrender through foreign consulates. At the cost of sixty-five casualties, the Greeks gained an undamaged port through which supplies and reinforcements could be shipped.

Even as Preveza was invested, Sapountzakis's mission was changed. Venizelos informed him on 29 October that he was now to take the whole Epirus region. Two days later, with his Cretan reinforcements, Sapountzakis began to move north and Esat Pasha decided once again to stop them just north of Pente Pegadia with his 23rd Division in the west and the Yanya Division in the east. On 3 November, the Greeks took Pente Pegadia, but Ottoman observers believed the enemy to be disorganised, Esat Pasha deciding to seize the initiative with an attack the following day, although this was stopped by noon. After a day-long hiatus, the Greeks attacked the Yanya Division and, although Esat Pasha reinforced it with Cevat Pasha's men, Sapountzakis was beginning to turn his left by 8 November. Torrential rain and thick fog thwarted Greek ambitions, and when Esat Pasha ordered a further withdrawal on 10 November, Sapountzakis, who had suffered some 250 casualties including twenty-six dead, was content to follow.

The Ottoman commander may have been influenced by news of a growing threat from the east. A Greek force of 350 Evzones from Constantine's army and a similar number of Cretan paramilitaries had struck towards Metsovo, some 20 km east of Ioannina, on 9 November. The town fell four days later, despite a robust defence by gendarmerie and frontier force troops, the Greeks being reinforced on 26 November by the Italian Legion. This was a force of 800 Italian volunteers under General Ricciotti Garibaldi, son of Italy's famed liberator, and many wore red shirts to emulate his father's troops.[55]

A brief pause descended upon the Epirus front as Sapountzakis awaited further reinforcements, but unlike the Serbian and Bulgarian fronts there was no armistice. Athens wished to bring Epirus under its control before the Great Powers assigned it to a newly independent Albania, and the Ottoman military presence could guarantee this. The widespread Greek opposition to an armistice, which included King George, was also due to the fluid situation with regard to the Aegean islands.[56] Athens therefore demanded as a condition of an armistice permission for its fleet to sail into the Straits, anticipating, correctly, this was unacceptable to Constantinople.

With Athens now anxious to see the rapid capture of Ioannina, reinforcements flowed to both sides. Sapountzakis was promised one of Constantine's divisions, and Kallares's II Division (minus 7th Infantry in the Aegean) began disembarking at Preveza from 29 November. Greek command of the sea allowed Cretan paramilitaries to land at Sarande and march inland to join Sapountzakis by 25 November, but they were unable to extend their hold further north. Meanwhile, Riza Pasha dispatched the Vardar Army's 19th and 21st Divisions, although these were little more than weak brigade groups with fewer than 7,500 men and ten guns.

Esat Pasha returned to his strategy of dynamic defence, his first reinforcements striking Metsovo on 8 December to push the allied force back 5 km to the town's gates where the attackers were held. Garibaldi proposed disbanding the Italian Legion because of casualties, but while many returned home, a cadre of some 300 remained. Late in January, 4,000 Greek troops (based upon 4th Infantry and some sailors and Territorials) crossed the Pindos Mountains to secure Metsovo, these troops becoming the core of the Metsovo Joint Brigade under Colonel Ioannes Papakyriazes. This formation, with six battalions and eight guns, replaced the paramilitaries whose bands were dissolved by General HQ on 20 January. Ostensibly this was because there were adequate numbers of regular troops, but actually it was due to the paramilitaries' poor discipline.

Four days later, Sapountzakis returned to the offensive, which was personally led by his chief-of-staff Lieutenant Colonel Demetrios Ioannou. The Greeks attacked on 12 December from three sides, with II Division as the western spearhead, and this formation, at a cost of 200 casualties, pushed the Ottoman forces into the Ioannina defences, Yanya Fortified Area by the following day.

Ioannina is on an elliptically shaped plateau some 40 km long and 22 km wide, 500 metres above sea level. In the winter the region suffers severe cold and heavy snows which usually block the northern roads and is also subject to dense fogs.[57]

The city lies on a narrow plain between the western shore of Lake Ioannina and a range of hills extending south-eastwards through the Tsouka Hills (Megale Tsouka) to the Manoliasa Heights (Manoliasa Tepe). Some 3 km east of the Manoliasa Heights lay the main road to Ioannina which ran along the lower slopes of Bizani, a dagger-shaped, flat-topped hill dominating the southern approaches to the city. The road into Ioannina from the east goes through the Driskos Heights and along the shore overlooked by Kasritsa, a low, steep-sided, oblong hill. Around the city were seventeen positions, including one on a lake island, the majority of these being open-topped concrete or stone emplacements, the most important of which was linked by a buried telephone system. They were armed with eighty-six older 87–90-mm pieces augmented on the eve of war by sixteen heavy guns, including a dozen 150-mm howitzers. The key fortification was Bizani, consisting of four positions with some thirty guns augmented by bunkers, trenches and barbed wire.[58]

Ioannina was a curious siege because most of the city's inhabitants were Greek and it was never completely invested, which allowed the Albanian peasants in the surrounding countryside to provide a steady stream of supplies. At the start, even with II Division, the siege force had some 25,000 troops supported by only field and mountain artillery, although it received four Krupp 120-mm guns late in December. By contrast, Esat Pasha had four divisions (19th, 21st, 23rd and Yanya) with 35,000 men who were initially well stocked with ammunition.

Despite the difficulties, Sapountzakis was keen to take the city quickly and targeted the Manoliasa Heights from where artillery fire could be directed upon Bizani. Kallares's

II Division attacked on the morning of 14 December, and by the afternoon had driven back the reserve battalions holding the heights. But the following morning a 21st Division counter-attack retook the hill and, aided by two newly created provisional divisions, further counter-attacks helped the defenders to tighten their grip. By 22 December, they had cleared the Greeks off the high ground and shielded Bizani, although at great cost, and the fierce fighting had left the Yanya Corps with fewer than 26,600 men. The Greeks' massed artillery fired to great effect, but the absence of heavy guns prevented them from inflicting significant damage on the defences, which doomed any attempt to storm Bizani. Yet an undaunted Sapountzakis tried on 16 December, with predictable failure, and by mid-December the siege had reached an impasse. A feature of the defence was the use of up to three divisional-sized task forces (Provisional Divisions) which Esat Pasha created from elements of his active divisions. Their prompt and frequent counter-attacks quickly regained lost ground and captured much equipment including two guns, an omen of the German counter-attack tactics five years later.

Sapountzakis now sent Athens alarming reports which claimed that the situation was critical, requesting further reinforcement and urging the government to sign an armistice. But an armistice was unthinkable to Athens while Ioannina remained in Ottoman hands. Greek troops were operating in a remote region served by rough roads over rugged terrain, and the bitter winter conditions saw many soldiers suffering both hunger and frostbite. Albanian guerrillas harassed their communications and, on 12 January, achieved their greatest success by wrecking the port of Sarande, which was the besiegers' main source of supplies.

On the night of 21/22 December, Athens decided to send substantial reinforcements (IV and VI Divisions) to the Epirus front. Venizelos proposed giving the Epirus Army to Constantine, who had wished to remain in Salonika and departed for Epirus reluctantly only at the Cabinet's insistence. The 22,300 reinforcements, led by IV Division (whose commander had been Constantine's choice to command the Epirus Army) began to arrive from 22 December but were not in the siege lines until 23 January, while a month later the understrength II Division finally received its 7th Infantry. The II Division commander Kallares now became Epirus Army chief-of-staff and was replaced by his divisional artillery commander Colonel Leonidas Paraskevopoulos, while former chief-of-staff Ioannou was given command of a four-battalion Evzone Group. This was part of a large-scale reorganisation which saw the Epirus Division created from formations of the Epirus Army and the Cretan Regiment under V Division commander Matthaiopoulos. The new formation, together with IV Division, formed a detachment under the latter's commander Major-General Moschopoulos, command of IV Division passing to Colonel Demetrios Antoniades. The reinforcements brought the Epirus Army strength to 40,000 men and ninety-three guns including a dozen heavy (105-mm, 120-mm, 150-mm) pieces. Also sent were six aeroplanes which operated at 1,600–2,300 metres (5,200–7,500 feet) and on occasion dropped grenades on the city. Once the novelty of seeing the aeroplanes wore off, the defenders fired on them with their rifles and forced down one flown by a Russian pilot who was uninjured.[59]

Sapountzakis considered the best way to exploit Athens' largesse while his heavy artillery began to bombard Bizani from 4 January. After a personal reconnaissance, Moschopoulos proposed securing the Manoliasa Heights in order to bring flanking fire on the fortifications, but this sensible idea was dismissed by the Epirus Army commander. Instead, on 13 January, he ordered a frontal assault by II Division in the centre, together with the Epirus and VI Divisions on the right, but political as well as meteorological storm clouds were gathering around his headquarters. Government representatives felt not only that the army lacked a comprehensive operational plan but also that there was friction between Sapountzakis and the divisional commanders. Indeed, on 6 January, Moschopoulos, who was very much in Constantine's confidence, telegraphed his former commander about Sapountzakis's command style and warned that Ioannina would fall only after a co-ordinated assault along the whole front.

On 17 January, Athens officially replaced Sapountzakis with Constantine and assigned acting command to Moschopoulos. But with the assault only days away, this was not a good time to change horses and the supremely confident Sapountzakis requested, and was granted, permission to execute the attack. Napoleon once said a good general needs luck, but this deserted Sapountzakis, for on the morning of 19 January two soldiers drove across the lines in a motor car. In fear that his plans would be compromised, Moschopoulos ordered the assault the next day, although he had little faith in its success.

His pessimism was more than justified. Greek artillery largely neutralised enemy batteries, but Antoniades failed to wait for the bombardment and instead sent IV Division on the left against Manoliasa. It gained little ground and suffered 357 casualties, while Bizani's fire stopped II Division's delayed attack in the centre. Komnenos's VI Division tried to bypass Kasritsa from the south as Epirus Division struck westwards towards Bizani, but both were unsuccessful. The Ottoman forces were well dug in and held the eastern attack by late afternoon, but Moschopoulos, more in hope than expectation, continued it the following day. The defenders' guns were running short of ammunition, but the besieged were saved by torrential rain which largely washed out the battlefield. Obstinately, the Greek attack was to continue, but dense mist thwarted all attempts to co-ordinate attacks, although Komnenos and Matthaiopoulos in the east drove back the defenders to the peak of Bizani. This was the last success, for now driving rain and snow as well as plummeting temperatures forced the abandonment of the assault, which had cost the attackers 1,200 casualties. The failure, as much as the weather, sapped Greek morale.

Sapountzakis was convinced that he had come close to success in the east, but on 23 January he was relieved by Constantine and given command of the east as the Epirus Division was redesignated VIII Division, while Moschopoulos returned to IV Division. The Greeks now had twelve heavy guns with eleven field and six mountain batteries but only 150 rounds per gun (12,000 rounds in total) and Constantine immediately began to build up ammunition dumps so that within a month there were 600 rounds per gun (totalling 48,000 rounds).

Heavy snow and dense fog brought a welcome respite to both sides, allowing Constantine time to restock his supply depots and to consider how best to take Ioannina.

1 Lieutenant General Abdullah Pasha was commander of the Ottoman Eastern Army in Thrace and was soundly defeated at Kirkkilesse and Luleburgaz.

2 The brand new Italian-built Hellenic Navy armoured cruiser *Averoff* virtually fought a one-ship war against the Ottoman battle fleet under the command of the dynamic Rear Admiral Pavlos Kountoriotis

3 The Ottoman battleship *Haireddin Barbarosse* was the backbone of the battle fleet together with her Brandenburg class sister ship *Torgud Reis*. Yet such were the low standards of maintenance of her new owners that within two years they lacked range finders, ammunition hoists and suffered major problems including the inability of the watertight doors to close!

4 The Bulgarian Army had 18 batteries of 120mm howitzers. One of these batteries is shown drawn up before moving off on campaign.

5 In all the Balkans Armies many field artillery batteries retained slow-firing weapons such as these Bulgarian 75mm Krupp guns.

6 Each side deployed para military forces with the largest group in Macedonia, parts of which were claimed by almost every country except Montenegro. These are Bulgarian guerrillas who would later form a division of the regular Bulgarian Army and fight in Gallipoli.

7 Bulgarian 120mm Schneider Quick Firers shelling Edirne. Unlike the earlier weapons they did not have to be re-laid every time they were fired and could rain down shells with unprecedented accuracy. This ability shaped the battlefields of the First World War.

8 Triumphant Bulgarian troops stand outside Fort Ayvazbaba one of the newest positions defending Edirne.

9 A meeting of dragons! The fire-breathing Lieutenant General Mikhail Savov (seated) was Tsar Ferdinand's principal military advisor and would be the driving force behind the Second Balkans War. He is visiting the headquarters of 3rd Army under Lieutenant General Dimitriev Radko (right) a charismatic leader who would serve the Imperial Russian Army in the Great War and be at the helm during two of its worst defeats. The Bolsheviks executed him!

10 Although posed, this picture gives a good idea of a Greek Schneider-Creusot Mle 1906 75mm Quick Firer field gun in action. These weapons could fire 15 rounds a minute and an experienced crew could double this for a short period. A mountain gun based on this weapon was designed for the Greek Army by Major General Panagiotis Danglis who would be Crown prince Constantine's chief of staff (Hellenic War Museum).

Izzet Pascha
Chef des Generalstabes der Armee

Above left: 11 Lieutenant General Ahmet Izzet Pasha was Chief of the Ottoman General Staff but the outbreak of the First Balkans War saw him in the Yemen suppressing a revolt. He would play an important role in the recovery of the Ottoman Army in late 1912.

Above right: 12 Ottoman III Corps commander Brigadier General Mahmut Muhtar Pasha was the only field commander to distinguish himself during the First Balkans War. His career was cut short when he was injured during the fighting in the Catalca Lines.

13 Tsar Ferdinand of Bulgaria would be the driving force for both Balkans Wars. He was a complex person with passions including the army and botany.

14 Almost all the Ottoman Army artillery came from Krupp with whom the Empire placed the company's biggest order, although it is uncertain whether or not payment was completed. While there were many Quick Firers all too many of the Ottoman guns were like this old 80mm gun which lacked recuperating equipment.

Above left: 15 King Nikola of Montenegro and his kingdom were the second greatest losers in the Balkans conflicts. He went to war hoping both the expand his kingdom and strengthen his position in a joint kingdom with Serbia. While he did expand Montenegro, Great Power pressure prevented him retaining Shkoder and undermined his political ambitions and when Yugoslavia was created it was under the rival Serbian King Petar Karadjordjevic. Nikola went into exile in France where he died in 1921.

Above right: 16 Serbian Premier Nikola Pasic would steer the country to victory both in the Balkans Wars and after the First World War. He was a major player in creating the Balkans League building upon Milovanovich's work.

17 Bulgarian commanders assembled on a hill during manoeuvres. This was the traditional way armies were led and most armies during the Balkans Wars were commanded in this way with orders distributed by aides on horseback. But with expanding armies and wider battlefields command had increasingly to be conducted from communications hubs using telephones and telegraphs.

18 Troops make their way through mountains. Much of the fighting was conducted in mountains where there were neither roads nor railways and movement was along paths of beaten earth easily blocked by snow or made hazardous by icy or mud (Hellenic War Museum).

19 Although of poor quality this appears to be one of the few genuine photographs taken on the battlefield and shows Greek infantry in action (Hellenic War Museum).

20 While railways provided movement at the Operational and Strategic Level at the Tactical, and often Operational level, animal power was the key. Here a horse-drawn Greek cart pauses on a stony road (Hellenic War Museum)

21 Vets check the hoofs of Greek cavalry horses. The declining value of cavalry was confirmed during the Balkans Wars and was aggravated by poor handling of cavalry units. European generals universally sought to retain the cavalry arm even when it repeatedly failed them (Hellenic War Museum).

22 King George (left) and Greek Army commander Crown Prince Constantine enter Salonika in triumph. Less than five months later the King would be gunned down while strolling through the city (Hellenic War Museum).

23 Bulgarian Maxim M.1908 machine-guns are dug in opposite the Catalca Lines. The machinegun proved useful but the paucity of weapons, averaging one per battalion, and confusion over their role as defensive or offensive weapons reduced their impact on the battlefield. In greater concentrations in the hands of major armies they would soon prove valuable in restricting battlefield movement.

24 The Hellenic Navy deployed two Maurice Farman seaplanes to Moudros and in March 1913 Lieutenant Michael Moutousis, and Ensign Aristeides Moraitinis flew over the Ottoman fleet on a reconnaissance mission and dropped small bombs without effect. From these beginnings came the naval air battles of the Second World War (Hellenic War Museum)

25 The Greek *Delfin* would make Europe's first submarine attack upon the Ottoman cruiser *Medjidieh* on December 22. The torpedo missed and the submarine grounded on the return trip and was out of action for the rest of the war (Hellenic War Museum).

26 Lieutenant Commander Stefanos Paparrigopoulos commander of the Delfin and the first of hundreds of submariners who would engage enemy warships and merchantmen (Hellenic Maritime Museum).

27 Mules are loaded onto a Greek ship shipping Serbian troops to the Siege of Shkoder. The Greek merchant marine played a largely ignored role in the First Balkans War providing the allies with reliable strategic movement (Hellenic War Museum).

28 A shortage of artillery meant that the Greek Army had to augment their Quick Firers with these older 80mm weapons during the Siege of Ioannina (Hellenic War Museum).

29 During the opening stages of the Battle of Kumanovo many Serbian troops were in camps like this when the Ottoman offensive began. The second echelon divisions remained there during most of the first day because neither the 1st Army commander, Crown Prince Aleksandar nor his staff recognised the seriousness of the situation.

30 Ottoman trenches in the Catalca Lines overlooking the no-man's land valley between the Ottoman and Bulgarian forces. Attackers had to cross this open ground to reach the trenches in front of which were barbed wire entanglements.

31 Thousands of Ottoman troops, like these, were taken prisoner during the conflict. Many were shipped to the Peloponnes for the duration of the First Balkans War.

32 Ottoman troops frantically strengthen the defences of the Catalca Line before the arrival of the Bulgarians. The natural strength of the defences was augmented by digging positions in depth making them impregnable. Defence in depth became an increasing feature on the Western Front from 1916 and, when properly prepared, could stop even the strongest attack notably at Arras in March 1918.

33 Bulgarian troops assemble outside Edirne before moving into their jump-off positions. Notice the officer on the left is carrying a sword. The great coats were not only to keep the men warm but also to cover barbed wire.

34 A Bulgarian heavy artillery crew prepare to dig out and move their gun while one of the oxen pulling it looks on. With most roads being unmetalled they were quickly turned into mud by rain slowing movement to a snail's pace.

35 The same gun has been freed from the slime and is slowly pulled by four oxen. Oxen were the preferred means of transporting heavy vehicles. There were few motor vehicles in any of the armies and lacking robust suspension systems they rarely lasted long on Balkans roads.

36 This is one of the few apparently genuine combat photographs of the Balkans Wars and shows a Bulgarian regiment moving up behind the firing line before charging enemy positions. The photograph is believed to have been taken during the battle of Luleburgaz.

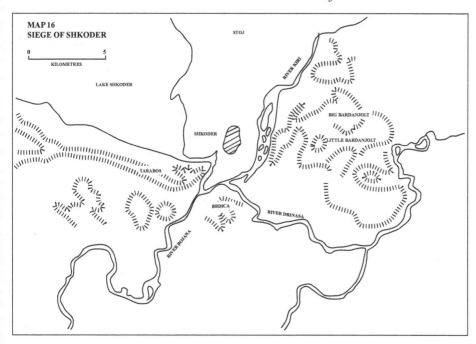

The deteriorating political position in Macedonia and growing tensions with the Bulgarians meant that Athens was reluctant to strip Constantine's Army of Thessaly. Yet the desire to secure Epirus remained strong, and the Metsovo Brigade was reinforced by I Division regiments. Venizelos's discussions with Danev in London had failed to produce agreement over Salonika, while the Ambassadors' Conference in the same city steadily defined the borders of an Albanian state that might well acquire Ioannina. Venizelos came to Epirus to brief Constantine on 19 February and increased pressure upon him to take Ioannina as quickly as possible.

Three days later, Constantine ordered a co-ordinated assault along the whole front, which would include a diversion by IV Division towards the Manoliasa Heights, but the plan was opposed by Moschopoulos who believed the key to Ioannina's defence was in the west. It took him six days to persuade Constantine to switch the main axis there, and the other attacks were now to be either support or diversionary operations in order to stretch the defenders to breaking point. Constantine now had 41,400 men with ninety-three guns and thirty-four as an artillery reserve under his direct command.

The weather now easing, the preliminary bombardment began on 1 March, although the main assault was not launched until four days later. Constantine intended to launch a major diversion on the south-eastern defences while the main assault was made in the south-west and Bizani came under a concentrated bombardment. The reinforced IV Division (twenty battalions and twenty-six guns) would strike in the west while a regimental-size attack was launched in the centre by II Division. On the Greek right, VIII Division struck Bizani from the west, and on its northern flank VI Division attacked

Kasritsa. The defenders had some 26,500 men with the 2nd Provisional Division on the Tsouka Hills, the reinforced 23rd Division on their right holding the Manoliasa heights and Bizani, and 3rd Provisional Division east of Bizani with Yanya Division in reserve.

The assault troops assembled in a severe snowstorm on 3 March, the preliminary bombardment beginning the following morning with the Greeks firing 200 rounds per gun. However, the Ottoman gunners conserved their ammunition, for they were now down to ten rounds per gun. While the Greek objective was Bizani, the initial infantry assault was on the Manoliasa Heights where part of IV Division was to drive north towards Ioannina to clear the western heights. This would outflank Bizani, which II Division would then strike from the south while VI and VIII Divisions attacked from the east. The offensive began in clear weather on 5 March and within two hours Moschopoulos took the Manoliasa and Tsouka Heights and then Dourouti. By mid-afternoon the defenders' gunners had fired off almost all their ammunition and the Ottoman defences were collapsing, while by dusk Bizani and Kasritsa faced isolation.

At Bizani, where Greek artillery had inflicted heavy damage, including the destruction of six guns, the defenders surrendered at dawn the following day. On the plain their comrades either fled northwards or surrendered to the advancing Greeks, Esat Pasha himself joining the flight north to Shkoder and reaching Turkey after the war to a hero's welcome. During the morning of 7 March, the Greeks entered the town, whose remaining defenders surrendered just after noon, some 8,600 being captured together with much equipment including 108 guns. Total Ottoman losses were 11,400 including 2,800 dead, while the Greeks reportedly lost 280 in the final phase, bringing their total casualties to 1,800.

At a cost of 15,000 casualties, Athens had expanded Greece and denied the nascent Albanian state a major economic area and territorial anchor. The victory also eased the Greek strategic situation, for they could now concentrate their forces in the east against the Bulgarians and secure Salonika. As Constantine was crowned, most of the divisions were rapidly transferred eastward.

Southern Albania

By the time of the Turco-Serbian armistice on 6 December the Ottoman Empire held only a pocket of south-eastern Albania from Berat to Ioannina, with Serb control of northern Albania contested only by guerrillas. Yet despite growing support from the Great Powers for an independent Albania and their pressure for the withdrawal of Serbian and Montenegrin troops, the spring thaw led to new Serbian operations in southern Albania. In late March, Jankovic's troops advanced southwards towards Berat. Cavit Pasha's VI Corps vainly tried to hold them at Lushnje on 6 April, with Berat lost six days later.[60]

The Ottoman forces were also under pressure from the south as Constantine consolidated his hold on Ioannina and established a strong frontier all the way east to Lake Prespa. He drove down the southern Drin valley to take Gjirokaster on 16 March and Tepelene the following day. By now the Vardar Army had fewer than 10,200 infantry out of 24,000 men, and as it was compressed into a pocket of 80 km by 80 km it was in no position to offer sustained resistance. It was saved by pressure from the Great Powers which forced first Serbia and then Greece to halt their advances. The Serbs began to withdraw in mid-April, with Lushnje abandoned on 19 April to give the Ottoman forces some breathing space.

When the Treaty of London was signed on 30 May 1913 the situation eased completely and the Western Army prepared to evacuate Albania. It had begun assembling near Albania's ports in early May and soon signed an agreement with the Greeks to guarantee safe passage by sea. The first sick and wounded departed on 14 May in two Austrian ships, the first combat troops embarking at Vlore on 4 June, followed by the Western Army leadership on the 17th. The Western Army, comprising some sixty-six battalions with 29,755 men, brought out forty-four guns and forty-three machine guns, 3,600 draught animals and 20,000 spare rifles. Arriving from 22 June, they were re-formed into the new Second Army in Anatolia and by the outbreak of the First World War were ready to re-enter the fray.[61]

THE WESTERN FRONT (ALBANIA)

The defence of northern Albania against the Montenegrin Army was assigned on 18 September to Colonel Hasan Riza Bey with the 13,600-man Iskodra Corps supported by ninety-six guns. This had the active 21st and 24th Divisions, the reserve Elbasan and Iskodra Divisions and the brigade-strength Provisional Division created from four active battalions and some mountain batteries. But 21st Division then became Ipek Detachment, whose officers included an ambitious Albanian officer, Brigadier General Esad Pasha (Toptani). The Montenegrins assembled at Podgorica the 15,000-strong Zetska Corps with forty guns under Crown Prince Danilo who was to envelop Shkoder from the east. The Coastal Corps, with 8,000 men and thirty-four guns under Brigadier General Mitar Martinovic, was to advance down the coast from Bar.[62]

On 9 October, Danilo attacked Tuzi, defended by four battalions in the heights surrounding the town which he eventually succeeded in isolating. The 3,000-man garrison surrendered on 14 October, but the exhausted Montenegrins had to pause for four days. Martinovic had also crossed the border on 9 October, but two days later was stopped by a regimental-size counter-attack. Danilo renewed his advance on 18 October, and after a six-day march hoped to storm Shkoder without pause after he first took the key eastern height of Great Bardanjolt (Veliki Bardanjolt) and then rolled up the defences. Danilo secured a foothold on Great Bardanjolt on 29 October, but was driven back by a counter-attack from Little Bardanjolt (Malo Bardanjolt) under Elbasan Division commander Colonel Cemal, and on 4 November King Nikola temporarily ended the first assault upon Shkoder.

The tribal nature of the Montenegrin Army was all too apparent in these early clashes. The infantry simply massed in the open before charging wildly, and were usually slaughtered by enemy fire. The Montenegrins' shortage of guns meant that there was little attempt to neutralise enemy artillery, while the absence of an overall commander prevented even the semblance of co-ordination.

Supplies for the Montenegrin Army were largely carried by women, who had to walk with large loads for several days. As King Nikola's sister was Queen of Italy, there was considerable Italian assistance in the Montenegrin supply system, with labourers improving roads and bridges. Three steamers were organised to ferry supplies across Lake Shkoder unhindered by two armed Ottoman steamers.[63]

The Ottoman defence of the coastal plain was weakened when troops were sent to reinforce the city's defence, and Martinovic wished to exploit this in order to isolate Shkoder. Several times he begged the king's permission to attack, but the monarch's dynastic ambitions meant that he wished his son to win his spurs. When it became clear that Danilo had failed, Martinovic attacked on his own initiative at the beginning of November. On 13 November, he led the reinforced 2nd Brigade across the River Bojana to threaten Shkoder from the south and then launched a week of fruitless assaults that ended only when the Montenegrins were exhausted. Meanwhile, his 3rd Brigade advanced upon Shengjin, whose two battalions were unable to prevent the Montenegrins taking the town three days later to close the only road south from Shkoder. Martinovic's advance continued along the coast, where the defenders faced not only him but also Paunovic's Serbian Drinska II Division from the east, and the combined Slavic forces took Lezhe on 18 November.

King Nikola now ordered Brigadier General JankoVukotic to send Eastern Corps' 9th and 11th Brigades under the 4th 'Niksicka' Division commander, Colonel Milo Matanovic, westward to support Danilo. Vukotic selected the direct route over the mountains so as not to lose time, his men setting out on a pleasant and dry day. However, the weather changed on 12 November and they had to advance through snowstorms, the strongest men trying to clear a path through the drifts. At night, unable to build a fire, they huddled in the open like Antarctic penguins and 120 men suffered frostbite, eighty-two dying before reinforcements reached the city on 20 November.

Shkoder was a natural fortress on the south-eastern shore of Lake Shkoder, which shielded the western approaches. To the north lay a rolling plain known as Stoj, with the River Kiri on its eastern side, but here as elsewhere, fortified heights dominated all the landward approaches.[64]

Running along the southern shore of the lake is a long, razor-backed ridge known as Tarabos because the eastern peak, 570 metres high, resembles the fez or tarabos. To the east is the 155-metre Brdica, separated from Tarabos by the River Bojana, while the south-eastern approaches to the city follow the River Drinasa which joins the Kiri just south of the city. The east of the city, and the Kiri and Drinasa valleys, are dominated by the 316-metre mass of Great Bardanjolt with the 164-metre Little Bardanjolt to the south. Tarabos, Brdica and Bardanjolt all had small forts and permanent batteries positions which the garrison commander, Brigadier General Mahmud Hayret Pasha, augmented during that summer with trenches and barbed-wire entanglements covered by machine guns. It is reported that the defences included anti-personnel mines.[65] The forts themselves contained a couple of old 150-mm guns, twelve 120-mm mortars and forty-seven 37 to 87-mm guns, the latter specifically to defend the positions, while four 90-cm searchlights could deprive the attacking infantry of the shelter of darkness.

Montenegro lacked the resources for an effective investment and, despite the loss of Lezhe, Shkoder still received men and supplies from the south, increasing the garrison by mid-November to 29,000, including 5,000 Albanian paramilitaries. By contrast, the Montenegrins, despite the arrival of Vukotic's 5,500 together with volunteers from the Austrian Empire and Bosnia, had only 33,000 men. Out of pique, Martinovic remained passive and left Danilo to conduct most of the active operations, which allowed Hasan Riza to meet the threat in detail.

Although sceptical about the prospects of success, Nikola ordered an assault for 4 December but was then informed by some unidentified ambassadors that most of the Great Powers supported his claim to the city. They also informed him that while Austria opposed his claim, it was diplomatically isolated. This deceit encouraged him to believe that the city would fall into his hands through diplomacy, so he cancelled the assault. In the aftermath of the Catalca armistice a similar agreement was signed at Shkoder on 3 December, which allowed the city to remain in Ottoman hands while denying it formal access to provisions. However, the sketchy siege lines allowed the garrison to launch raids during December to scour the Albanian countryside for food.

The armistice remained a pious hope because the undisciplined Montenegrin troops began to attack Ottoman positions on their own volition, even the Serbs joining in during mid-December. Although all these attacks were repulsed, Constantinople reprimanded Hayret Pasha for allowing the situation to develop! For the Montenegrin besiegers the situation was becoming grim as winter set in because they were short of clothing, footwear and food and had only flimsy shelters. This led to a steady stream of the sick and injured, which eroded their strength.

The greatest setback to the defence came just after dusk on 30 January as garrison commander Hasan Riza was returning into his lines after negotiations with Albanian religious leaders. He was shot and mortally wounded by three men and died in the early morning, but the assassins and their motivation were never officially identified. It was widely believed that Esad Pasha, who promptly assumed command of the garrison, was at the heart of the plot in order to further his ambitions of leading the new Albanian state.[66]

This was Nikola's only good news. Events at the London Ambassadors' Conference made him realise that he had been duped and that the Great Powers did not support his claim to Shkoder. The Young Turks' coup on 23 January confirmed Ottoman support for Albanian independence, and the armistice was scheduled to conclude on 3 February. The king again decided to take the city at bayonet point with Danilo's Zetska Corps and then present the Great Powers with a *fait accompli*.

The corps, now with eight brigades (thirty-six battalions), would strike from the north at Great Bardanjolt while Martinovic and the Serbs conducted diversions. Danilo's main attack would come in the hills on his left, led by Matanovic's 4th 'Niksicka' Division, reinforced with two *ad hoc* brigades, and supported by sixty guns including a dozen Serbian. This would take first Great Bardanjolt and then Little Bardanjolt and finally the city, while Danilo's 2nd 'Podgoricka' and 3rd 'Niksicka' Divisions, with the 4th Division's

10th Brigade, would stage a diversion on the Stoj. Martinovic, Vukotic and Serbia's delegate, and former Ibar Army chief-of-staff Lieutenant Colonel Dusan Popovic all tried in vain to persuade the monarch to attack from the south using Martinovic's troops and the Serbs, but he obstinately refused.

The attack was scheduled to begin on 7 February, but Drinska II jumped the gun and struck two days early over marshy ground and around the Brdica Heights in a surprise assault that gained some ground. However, the defenders quickly recovered and ended all further progress, although futile attacks continued until 9 February, by which time the Serbs had suffered 1,800 casualties including 430 taken prisoner.

The main attack on 7 February, which faced six mutually supporting strongpoints held by the Provisional and 24th Divisions, started badly. A shortage of wire-cutters made it difficult to cut passages through the entanglements, but eventually the Montenegrins managed to get through the wire. In some places they even reached the enemy trenches, but losses were heavy and the men were too exhausted to attack on the following day. When the assault was renewed on 9 February there was another depressing failure because the brigade operations were not co-ordinated, until the 11th Brigade commander, Brigadier Radomir Vesovic, suggested that the whole division attack at midday. This advice was followed and the renewed assault pushed the defenders off Great Bardanjolt onto Little Bardanjolt. Many of them began to flee towards the city until Esad Pasha rallied them and led a counter-attack which regained Great Bardanjolt just as the assault seemed on the point of success. With the attackers demoralised, the assault petered out at the cost of 4,000 casualties (some to their own artillery), while the defenders suffered nearly 1,340. Not to be left out, Martinovic instead of demonstrating towards Tarabos, launched a full attack on 9 February with 6,500 men and twenty-four guns, but this too was defeated at the cost of 1,500 casualties.

Unable to break the deadlock with his own resources, Nikola went cap in hand to his Serbian allies for more men and matériel on 12 February. He won Belgrade's agreement three days later, but the Serbs now demanded total control of the siege and the Montenegrins had to accept this humiliation. Belgrade promoted the 1st Army chief-of-staff Petar Bojovic to the rank of general and gave him the Coastal Group (formed in Serbia on 19 February), but it was impossible to transport his 30,450 men, forty-one guns and four aircraft by road through the depths of winter. Instead they were railed down to Salonika between 18 February and 7 April for the Greeks to ship them to Shengjin, the first men arriving on 11 March. The convoy bringing the second echelon was attacked in harbour by the Ottoman Turkish cruiser *Hamidieh* on 18 March, which led to a duel with shipborne Serbian mountain gunners before the warship withdrew. Transport of the last echelon was cancelled in April in the face of growing opposition from the Great Powers to the Montenegrin occupation of Shkoder, but by then the Coastal Group could deploy 17,000 men, forty guns and four aeroplanes.

The Great Powers were considering the future of Shkoder, or Scutari as they generally called it, just as Bojovic began his preparations to end the siege.[67] The ambassadors meeting in London argued whether or not Shkoder should either be part of a new Albanian state, as Vienna desired, or part of Montenegro, which was advocated by St Petersburg. The Russians blinked first, and on 14 February conceded that Shkoder would be incorporated in Albania, although, as a sop to Serbia, Vienna agreed on 20 March that it should receive some territory in Kosovo. This concession was to secure the Austrian objective that Albania's northern border should include the River Bojana and Lake Shkoder, and that the Great Powers would force a Slavic evacuation of newly independent Albania's territory.

As his diplomatic support evaporated, Nikola urged the Serbs on 24 March to join his troops in one last desperate throw of the dice at Shkoder. The Serbs by now were growing war-weary but faced a dilemma. Although they did not wish to abandon their allies, they needed to strengthen their diplomatic position on Macedonia as relations with the Bulgarians grew more strained. With Bojovic's men still marching up from Shengjin, the Serbs urged Nikola to await their arrival and refused to join any premature assault. Then, on 28 March, the Great Powers presented a collective demand to Montenegro to end the Shkoder siege. Nikola frantically prepared to strike on 31 March but, on the 29th, Serbia banned its troops from joining the assault, although they were willing to provide artillery support for their allies.

This time a desperate Nikola listened to military advice and agreed to strike from the south using 4,000 men of Martinovic's 1st 'Cetinjska' Division against both Tarabos and Brdica aided by 140 guns, including the Serbian heavy artillery. The main assault would be by the four-battalion central column, including a detachment of 150 older men. They were to clear mines and passages through the wire and devised a simple slogan, 'We must reach the wire, that is all that matters.'[68] Shkoder's garrison was now down to 12,500 infantry supported by eighty-five guns, with Tarabos held by battalions of the 24th Division.

The bombardment began on the morning of 31 March, and in the early afternoon the infantry assault, led by the grey beards, was launched. The attackers penetrated the Ottoman positions but were unable to break through, and by the end of the day had suffered some 620 casualties, while the defenders lost some 275. The assault was renewed, and repulsed, the following day as a naval blockade by the Great Powers was imposed upon the Montenegrin coast in order to increase diplomatic pressure. This had little effect upon Montenegro, which had neither ships nor foreign trade, but it provided Belgrade with the excuse to abandon the siege, Pasic informing the army leadership, 'The fate of Scutari is decided.' Serbian troops were not formally recalled until 10 April, and they left artillery when they departed so that the Montenegrins could continue the siege.

The defenders were now running short of both food and ammunition, with up to forty people a day dying of starvation, and on 20 April Esad Pasha reopened negotiations for the city's surrender. Negotiations some weeks earlier had foundered on Nikola's refusal to permit the garrison to march out with their arms and personal possessions. Now, in what Hall has described a 'a real scoundrels' bargain', Ottoman troops were permitted to leave the city with most of their weapons, except heavy guns. In return, King Nikola agreed to provide diplomatic and financial support for Esad Pasha's efforts to become the monarch of an independent Albania. Many of the defenders simply marched to the ports and awaited passage home.[69]

Austria immediately demanded that the Great Powers enforce Nikola's acquiescence to their demands and underlined this with a partial mobilisation. Recognising that he could not hold Shkoder in the face of such international pressure, Nikola decided on 5 May to bend before the wind and surrender the city, which had cost more than 9,400 casualties including 2,800 dead. Barely a fortnight after taking the city which had cost so much, his men marched out and were replaced by bluejackets from the international fleet who remained in control until November. The surrender dashed Nikola's hopes of co-leadership of the expanded Serbian state, and the money he received as a loan, or more properly a bribe, was no compensation for his permanent loss of prestige.

The thwarting of Serbian territorial ambitions in Albania doomed the Great Powers' attempts to dampen the regional powder keg. Belgrade was now determined that as compensation it would hold as much of the Macedonian territory as possible, even if it meant war with Bulgaria. For Montenegro, the fiasco at Shkoder had demonstrated the little state's weaknesses and doomed it to be the junior partner in any future south Slavic state. By contrast, although the siege of Ioannina might be the one serious blemish on Greece's new-founded military reputation, its hold upon Epirus and southern Macedonia, including the key city of Salonika, was not seriously disputed by the Great Powers. However, Sofia still seethed at the way the prize of Salonika had been snatched from its grasp. Its sense of entitlement to both the city and the contested Macedonian territory steadily grew during the spring and early summer, to bode ill for peace in the Balkans.

CHAPTER 5

The Naval and Diplomatic Struggles

The land battles overshadowed the naval campaigns which would feature a few clashes between ironclads, numerous small-unit actions and some amphibious operations.[1] Naval activity would prove surprisingly influential during the First Balkan War, with success or failure depending upon the way the region's major naval powers exploited British assistance.

Although the Ottoman Empire was still in a state of war with Italy, a separate decree of mobilisation had to be issued to the Ottoman Navy on 12 October.[2] The fleet was organised into three major task groups in the Straits to meet any strategic contingency: Admiral Tahir Mehmet Bey's Bosphorus fleet with the two Brandenburgs, six destroyers and four torpedo boats; Admiral Tevfik Bey's Dardanelles fleet with two rebuilt ironclads, the *Messudieh* and *Assar-i Tewfik* and a torpedo boat; while half-a-dozen destroyers and torpedo boats were at the Imperial Shipyard (Tersane-i Amire) in the Golden Horn. The armoured cruisers *Hamidieh* and *Medjidieh* were in the Black Sea, while detachments of minor surface combatants, including the rebuilt Red Sea Squadron, totalling ten torpedo boats and gunboats together with some despatch vessels, were scattered around the empire.

In the Black Sea the Ottoman Navy reigned unchallenged, moving troops and supplies along the north Anatolian coast and from the Rumanian port of Constanta. At the outbreak of war, the Porte chartered the SS *Marmara* (2,472 grt), *Guzel Girit* (1,232 grt), *Kizilirmak* (1,945 grt), *Akdeniz* (5,062 grt) and *Mithat Pasha* (2,255 grt) to ship arms, ammunition, coal and horses from Constanta, although by early 1913 this had declined to a weekly run by the *Kizilirmak*, often with a destroyer escort.

Bulgaria's minuscule maritime forces under Lieutenant Colonel Rusi Ludogorov were based upon six modern French-built torpedo boats, although there was also a Danube Flotilla with two steamers, a yacht and some small craft. Coastal defence, mostly around Varna, consisted of four fixed 150-mm howitzers and fifty-seven smaller-calibre weapons augmented by four mobile batteries with two 240-mm and four 100-mm guns and two smaller pieces as well as minefields. Two of the 100-mm gun were removed from a torpedo gunboat acting as a training ship.

To keep the Bulgarians off balance, and to prevent their torpedo boats interdicting the sea lanes, the Bosphorus fleet used the Brandenburgs, the cruisers and four S.165-class destroyers to engage coastal defence batteries around Varna from 19 October onwards. However, the cruisers suffered engine problems, which halved the speed of *Hamidieh*. The ironclads withdrew after 24 October, leaving the cruisers and the torpedo gunboat *Berk-i Satvet* to support the destroyers *Berkefshan* and *Yar-Hisar* as they maintained a distant blockade and broke the boredom by occasionally shelling installations.[3]

The Bulgarians monitored Ottoman maritime traffic and, despite the constant enemy naval presence, on 21 November the torpedo boats were ordered to intercept two steamers reported to be leaving Constanta. During the evening of 21/22 November, Captain Dimitary Dobrev in *Letyashti* led *Drazki*, *Smeli* and *Strogi* out of Varna through the minefields. Just after midnight they spotted a large ship, the *Hamidieh*, which was searching for two reported blockade runners 32 nautical miles (59 km) from Varna. Shielded by a moonless night *Letyashti* led the attack, discharging its three 18-inch (457-mm) torpedoes at distances of 500–600 metres. Her torpedoes missed, as did those of *Smeli* and *Strogi*, the former being damaged by a 150-mm shell, but the *Drazki* closed to 100 metres and hit the cruiser's starboard side. The squadron then withdrew, pursued by the *Berkefshan* and reached Varna safely the following morning with only one man wounded.

The cruiser also withdrew with a 10 square metre hole on the waterline, but was saved because she had a well-trained crew, her forward bulkheads held, all her pumps worked (unusually for an Ottoman warship) and there was a very calm sea. With thirty-eight casualties, including eight dead, she reached port with her bow awash but was repaired within months. The attack was followed by an easing of the Ottoman blockade, largely because the fleet now had to support the Catalca Line. The only significant action in these waters was in February when the old Ottoman ironclad *Assar-i Tewfik* was sent to support a raid upon Podima (78 km west of Constantinople). But as she approached on 8 February, she was stranded on an uncharted sandbank and abandoned by 11 February.

From mid-November the Ottoman fleet focused upon gunfire support missions, having earlier supported the vain defence of Tekirdag in the Sea of Marmara. They then aided the defence of the Catalca Line, the backbone being the Brandenburgs, while three transports were available to supply the defenders. In the first Bulgarian assault (on 17 November) the *Torgud Reis* supported III Corps from the Black Sea with 8-inch and 12-inch guns, while the *Barbarosse*, together with the older ironclad *Messudieh* and five smaller vessels, supported I Corps from the Sea of Marmara. The fire, which was directed by land observers correcting with flags, was spectacular but not particularly accurate, yet had a tremendous effect upon the morale of both sides. During the Ottoman offensive on 8 February, two torpedo boats landed volunteers behind enemy lines in a diversionary operation which saw half the troops lost. The final action was during the Bulgarian offensive of 20 March 1913, when the Brandenburgs, the torpedo gunboat *Berk-i Satvet*, the destroyer *Yar-Hisar* and the torpedo boat *Demir-Hisar* poured shells into the enemy positions during the afternoon. While impressive, naval fire support was never the deciding factor, but proved a useful tool in holding the Catalca Line.[4]

When the Bulgarians advanced through Thrace, tension rose in Constantinople where the Porte feared that he would be unable to stop a Muslim attack upon the Christian population. To guarantee protection of the Christians, the Ottoman government on 4 November requested naval support from the Great Powers. They responded quickly and within a fortnight seventeen warships from eight nations, including eight ironclads, were anchored off the Golden Horn under the command of the French Rear Admiral Dartige du Fournet. On 18 November, 3,000 bluejackets were landed and remained ashore until the end of the month, but Muslim morale rose with Ottoman success in the Catalca Line and the crisis faded. The sailors re-embarked, although for a couple of weeks the international squadron cruised the Sea of Marmara.[5]

However, the echo of this event would resound loudly in the early months of the Great War. The German Navy had only three gunboats in the eastern Mediterranean when the Balkan War broke out, so a Mediterranean Squadron was created under Rear Admiral Konrad Trummler with the new battlecruiser *Goeben* and the light cruiser *Breslau*. The battlecruiser reached Constantinople on 15 November and a fortnight later provided diplomatic asylum for former Interior Minister Halil Bey just as the Porte tried to buy the warship. Plans for the squadron to return to Germany were overtaken by the Shkoder Crisis, with *Breslau* joining the allied blockade and being replaced by the light cruisers *Strassburg* and *Dresden*, which remained on station until the end of the Second Balkan War. The *Goeben* and *Breslau* continued to operate together on a semi-permanent attachment, and Trummler was relieved in October 1913 by Rear Admiral Wilhelm Souchon, who cruised the Mediterranean until the outbreak of the Great War. Souchon avoided Royal Navy attempts to intercept him and escaped to Constantinople, where his presence was an important factor in bringing the Ottoman Empire into the conflict on Germany's side.[6]

The Ottoman Navy was also involved in the Sarkoy amphibious operation and assigned twenty steamers (two former Greek) to transport X Provisional Corps in two echelons (three of them would then bring part of the second echelon) and two to the third echelon. Small ferries were also acquired to provide early examples of roll-on, roll-off vessels for transporting heavy equipment. Bad weather and other problems (see Chapter 3) delayed the landing until the morning of 8 February, and the gunfire support group made up of the two Brandenburgs, the cruiser *Hamidieh* and the torpedo gunboat *Berk-i Satvet*, was delayed.[7]

When the troops did disembark they discovered, as did the British at Dieppe in August 1942, that it was difficult to take a defended port. Deprived of its facilities, the Ottoman troops were unable to unload heavy equipment which would have helped a rapid expansion of the beachhead. The decision to evacuate was made just after noon on 10 February and the beachhead was skilfully collapsed, covered by the Brandenburgs in the east and the other ships in the west. In supporting the Sarkoy amphibious operation in early February 1913, the Turkish Navy expended 1,119 shells, 857 by the battleships, which like cruisers usually relied upon their secondary armament (88–120 mm).

By contrast, the Greeks were far more successful with their amphibious operations, which saw little expenditure of ammunition. The Hellenic Navy was divided between Rear Admiral Pavlos Kountouriotis's Aegean fleet and Captain Ioannis Damianos's Ionian Sea Squadron, with the bulk of the force assigned to the former.

Kountouriotis, aged 57, was from the island of Hydra and his grandfather had been a prime minister. The future admiral joined the navy, participated in the brief Greco-Turkish War of 1897 and was a dedicated monarchist who acted as King George's aide from 1908 to 1911 before returning to active duty and the command of the *Averoff* in succession to Damianos. In the Great War he would support Venizelos's pro-Allied stance, yet afterwards he became Regent and, later still, the first president of Greece's second republic. He was re-elected and died in office in 1929. Damianos was the younger brother of III Division commander General Konstantinos Damianos, a former Minister of the Marine and the first commander of the *Averoff*. He had been criticised by Admiral Tufnell and relieved of his command after an eventful first cruise in which the ship ran aground off Plymouth in 1911 and the lower deck mutinied. Damianos never forgave either Kountouriotis or Tufnell.[8]

The bulk of the fleet was under Kountouriotis and included all three Hydras, the *Averoff*, ten destroyers (four each from British and French yards and the others from Germany) and the Aetos- and Keravnos-class 'scouts'. There were five 27-year-old German-built torpedo boats, the submarine *Delfin* and three large auxiliaries—the troop carrier *Sfaktiria*, the minelayer *Ares* and the torpedo depot ship *Kanaris*—as well as a hospital ship and two water-distilling vessels. Damianos had nine gunboats, three of which were former spar-torpedo boats. The Hellenic Navy would also exploit the nation's substantial merchant marine to create a Merchant Squadron, later under Damianos, consisting of six armed merchant cruisers and three auxiliaries to support the Aegean fleet.[9]

Kountouriotis departed on 18 October, having been informed:

> The primary objective of the Hellenic Fleet must at all events be for it to become master of the Aegean Sea and to sever maritime communications between Asia Minor and European Turkey…[10]

From experience in 1897, Athens was confident that the Ottoman fleet would not sortie from the Dardanelles to challenge them for the Aegean but as insurance, the Greeks planned to seize islands off the Dardanelles. Since 1900, Limnos, 32 nautical miles (60 km) from the Dardanelles with its excellent anchorage in the Gulf of Moudros, had been a prime objective and Kountouriotis was a strong advocate of its seizure, but Athens approved only after receiving tacit British agreement.[11] Once Kountouriotis secured the island he would seize others in the northern Aegean, both to impede the Ottoman fleet and blockade the coast of Asia Minor. He then aimed to take the remaining islands off Anatolia, although these were known to be strongly garrisoned since the Turco-Italian War.

For Limnos the Greek assault force consisted of two companies of 20th Infantry, with some 500 men in the SS *Penios* from the Ionian Sea Squadron.[12] Most of the fleet arrived off Limnos on the afternoon of 19 October and Kountouriotis immediately began to negotiate the surrender of the thirty-five-man garrison, although the *Penios* did not arrive until the following morning. With the defenders reluctant to comply, he sailed to Moudros Bay, landed the troops from the *Penios* the following morning and by 22 October had completed the unopposed occupation of the island. A week later, the military detachment was relieved by a 600-man naval detachment which brought in four 100-mm coastal defence guns and established a radio station. The army detachment was to have been transported to Macedonia, but Kountouriotis temporarily retained them after he was instructed to occupy more islands off the Dardanelles.

Bluejackets in the *Kanaris* on 31 October occupied first Agios Eustratios and then the small island of Strati a few miles south of Limnos. On the same day, the soldiers in the SS *Pelops*, escorted by the battleships *Hydra* and *Spetsai*, as well as the destroyers *Thyella* and *Lonchi*, took Thasos unopposed and the men were then sent to nearby Salonika. There were also unopposed landings by bluejackets on 31 October from the battleship *Psara* at Samothraki and by the *Psara*, the *Averoff* and the destroyer *Nafkratouisa* at Imroz.

November saw the Hellenic Navy tighten its grip on the Aegean, with the *Averoff* taking Bozcaada just off the Dardanelles on 7 November to become a forward base for the destroyers. Kountouriotis also anticipated orders for landings on Khios and Samos and began to take jump-off points; on 4 November the scout *Ierax* took the island of Psara off Khios, while on 17 November Ikaria, 10 nautical miles (18.5 km) south-west of Samos, was taken by the destroyer *Thyella*.[13] Athens recognised that taking the larger islands of Lesvos, Khios and Samos would not be so easy, as they were all garrisoned by the Smyrna-based 6th Division with one battalion on Lesvos and two each on Khios and Samos. Their capture required a large contribution from the army, which at that time was fully committed on the mainland. As the Porte sought an armistice during November the Venizelos government remained determined to take the islands before such an agreement closed the window of opportunity.

Venizelos put the case to Constantine, who now felt that the situation was secure enough to allocate a regiment and a battery from II Division in Salonika. The navy hastily put together a 250-man detachment from surplus personnel in Athens and shipped them to Limnos where they embarked in the *Pelops*. After they were joined by another detachment of 1,350 sailors and two guns from the Athos Peninsula together with the Limnos garrison, the task force departed for Lesvos on 17 November. The previous day a hastily raised *ad hoc* infantry battalion of 1,034 men departed Athens for the same objective in the steamers SS *Ismini* and *Kaloutas*. The transports were escorted by the Hydras, the *Averoff* and the destroyers *Aspis, Ierax, Niki, Thyella* and *Velos* together with the *Kanaris*. They were supported by the newly organised Light Cruiser Squadron under Damianos, who had been transferred from the Ionian Sea and flew his flag in the armed merchant cruiser *Esperia*, with the converted liners *Arkadia* and *Makedonia* supported by the two Keravnos and the SS *Patris*.

The Greeks entered Mitilini, the main port of Lesvos, on the morning of 20 November and Kountouriotis again demanded that the Ottoman defenders surrender. When they prevaricated, he landed his troops and the 1,500 men of the Turkish battalion (from 18th Infantry) withdrew into the centre of the island. At this point Kountouriotis was ordered to Salonika to escort a convoy that would carry Bulgarian troops along the Aegean coast from Salonika. He took the fleet with him, leaving the Light Cruiser Squadron and two destroyers at Mitilini. Meanwhile, the bluejackets established a beachhead around the port but remained on the defensive. Part of the force did embark in the *Makedonia* on 22 November in an attempt to take Lesvos's second largest town, Plomari, on the south coast, but storms prevented the ship reaching its objective and it diverted to Khios.

Athens remained concerned about Lesvos, and to secure the island a new battlegroup was created under Colonel Apollodoros Syrmakezes with a battalion of VII Division, 94 bluejackets from Salonika and two infantry companies with a mountain battery brought in from Greece. These began to arrive from 28 November and by the afternoon of 1 December Syrmakezes had a total of 3,175 men (including 300 bluejackets whom he used as police) with eight light guns. The following day, these troops began to advance slowly inland and encountered stubborn resistance, but on 18 December the defenders sought terms and surrendered by noon the following day, the occupation having cost the Greeks ninety casualties, 10 per cent of which were fatal.

Khios was a harder nut to crack, for it was defended by two battalions of 18th Infantry reinforced by two 75-mm mountain guns and a gendarmerie, a total of 1,800 men. The island's capture required a larger commitment from the Greek Army, which assigned the task to Colonel Nikolaos Delagrammatikas, commander of II Division's 7th Infantry, with two of his own battalions and one from the division's 1st Infantry augmented by a battery. The infantry embarked at Salonika on 18 November in the *Patris* and *Sappho* and departed the following day, escorted by Damianos's Scout Squadron and the armed merchant cruisers *Makedonia* and *Esperia*, while the artillery departed from Piraeus in the SS *Erietta*.

The two forces sailed into the port of Khios on the morning of 21 November and Damianos summoned the Ottomans to surrender. When they refused, he landed his troops outside the port during the afternoon. The landing was fiercely opposed, but during the evening the defenders withdrew into the island's mountainous interior where they continued to resist vigorously. Athens was now frantic to occupy the island before any armistice took effect, but, as Delagrammatikas informed them, the enemy defences were too strong and on 1 December he was ordered to cease offensive operations.

He was given two more battalions, together with more artillery, and on 18 December was ordered to renew the assault the following day. It was quickly suspended when the Ottoman forces sought terms, but when they prevaricated it was renewed with naval gunfire support on 20 December. This demoralised the defenders, who were encircled and surrendered on 3 January, after the Greeks had suffered 200 casualties. Delagrammatikas's troops were withdrawn a week later and transferred to the Epirus front but left a garrison company which was soon augmented by a bluejacket detachment and a locally raised battalion.

Samos, officially an autonomous principality, remained Athens' last objective in enemy hands, and its proximity to the Italian-occupied Dodecanese made the Greeks cautious. The island was defended by a battalion of 16th Infantry reinforced by the 6th Rifle Battalion, but the Greeks dispatched only two companies (320 men) in the SS *Thessalia* escorted by the battleship *Spetsai* and destroyers *Niki* and *Velos*. They landed in Vathy harbour on 13 March and almost immediately the Ottoman garrison withdrew to the mainland to give the Greeks complete control by 16 March.

The occupation of the islands strengthened the Hellenic Navy's blockade of the western Anatolian coast and the Dardanelles which was supported by the armed merchant cruisers. At first the blockade operated from Moudros Bay before moving to Bozcaada, using half a dozen destroyers to patrol 5 nautical miles (9 km) off the entrance to the Dardanelles and, augmented by torpedo boats, down the Anatolian coast to Smyrna.[14] The Greeks were kept busy because the Great Powers insisted on the Straits remaining open for commerce by non-combatants, with a daily average of some sixty steamers (4,000 grt) using the passage. Surprisingly, Greek steamers were allowed to use the Straits until 19 November to transport grain to neutral countries.[15] The blockade's greatest success was on 9 November when the Smyrna-based Ottoman armed merchant cruiser *Trabzon* ran through the channel east of Lesvos and encountered the torpedo boat *NF 14* off Ayvalik where it was torpedoed and sunk.[16]

There was never any question of forcing the Straits, because the Greeks, unlike an Anglo-French fleet three years later, recognised that they faced unacceptable losses if they challenged the formidable defences around the Dardanelles. These had been strengthened during the Turco-Italian War, and by 1912 the Chanak Fortified Area had thirteen forts (seven on the European side) with a total of eighty-seven guns (forty-four on the European side) including six 355-mm, eight 280-mm, nine 260-mm, twenty-seven 240-mm and sixteen 210-mm, while at Bolayir there were three batteries with eighteen guns, including three 150-mm, all augmented by torpedo batteries. The defenders may also have relaid the minefields they had deployed during the Turco-Italian War.[17]

Content to remain behind this shield, the Ottoman fleet was reluctant to engage the enemy because of the poor condition of its ships due to a chronic lack of maintenance. Kountouriotis was undoubtedly grateful but he had his own problems, chiefly the adverse effect of Tufnell's relentless training programme which had consumed war stores and coal, leaving the Hellenic Navy on short supplies when the war broke out.[18] It was only during the second half of November that these stores were replaced, but the most pressing concern was ammunition for the *Averoff*'s Armstrong-made 9.2-inch (230-mm) and 7.5-inch (190-mm) main armament. The ship's magazines were filled when she visited Britain in May 1912, but when the war broke out London's neutrality prevented them being restocked. The solution was provided by arms dealer Basil Zaharoff whose contacts allowed him, probably with judicious financial investment, to acquire two shiploads of ammunition. The first was loaded in the *Pelops* to restock the *Averoff* on 30 November, and her second voyage provided sufficient ammunition for the remainder of the war.[19]

The Porte's frustration with the inaction led to Tahir Bey's removal on 7 December and his replacement with the more dynamic Rear Admiral Ramiz Naman Bey, while competent, energetic officers assumed command of the tactical formations. Naman Bey pondered the prospects for decisive action to break the blockade, but while he had a marginal numerical superiority of four battleships to three, two of his ships—*Messudieh* and *Assar-i Tewfik*—were mutton dressed as lamb, upgraded 40-year-old ships with nominal top speeds of 12 knots. By contrast, the Brandenburgs, which were of similar age to the Hydras, could nominally make about 17 knots and their six turret-mounted 11-inch (280-mm) guns gave them an advantage over their opponents whose three 10.8-inch (275-mm) guns were in barbettes and could bring only one or two to bear. These advantages were offset by the Ottoman ships' poor mechanical condition as well as the unreliable arrangements to provide coal, stores or ammunition. When the armistice with Bulgaria was signed on 3 December, the Ottoman fleet focused upon the Aegean, and the Brandenburgs with the two cruisers sailed southwards through the Sea of Marmara.

The thorn in the Ottomans' side was the *Averoff* with its high speed of 23.5 knots and its four turreted 9.2-inch (230-mm) guns. Naman Bey sought both to remove her from the chessboard and to undermine the blockade with a war of attrition against the destroyers. He planned to conduct this by trapping the destroyers, but boiler trouble in the French-built Yar-Hisar-class destroyers thwarted the first effort on 12 December. Two days later, following a false report that the *Averoff* was stranded, the trap was again set, but when it was sprung the result did not meet Naman Bey's expectations. The Greek destroyers *Sfendoni* and *Lonchi* encountered a Turkish destroyer off the Dardanelles and began to pursue her, but she was soon shielded by the coastal defence guns. The armoured cruiser *Medjidieh* then appeared and the three ships exchanged fire before the Greek destroyers' sister ships, *Thyella* and *Nafkratouisa* joined the battle while the *Velos*, *Doxa* and *Nea Genea* rushed up from Bozcaada. Against these odds the Ottoman commander decided discretion was the better part of valour and withdrew into the Dardanelles.[20]

But from 11 December, reports reached the Greeks that the enemy was clearing its decks for action. Kountouriotis in *Averoff* led the three Hydras and the four scouts out of Moudros on the afternoon of the 14th to relieve the destroyers, which returned to Bozcaada. On the morning of 16 December the prowling ironclads received reports that the cruiser *Medjidieh* and eight destroyers were in the mouth of the Dardanelles. Kountouriotis in the *Averoff* made towards them but, it soon became clear that the cruiser and her charges were the bait. Half an hour later, the Ottoman battleships appeared in line abreast and left the cruiser task group to shelter under the coastal defence batteries. The sea was smooth and the weather bright and clear as the two squadrons closed and Kountouriotis was determined to seek a decisive fleet action. He radioed Bozcaada to summon not only the destroyers but also the submarine, but none would participate in the action and he was unable to use their deadly torpedoes. The Ottoman ships formed line-of-battle and cruised northwards at 6 knots, while the Greeks in two parallel lines, one of ironclads and the other of scouts, also turned and ran at 8 knots on a converging course from the enemy's port side.[21]

The Turks opened fire at just over 5 nautical miles (9.6 km) but their shells fell short, while the Greeks closed to 3.7 nautical miles (6.8 km) before returning fire, but only at a range of 2.5 nautical miles (4.6 km) did they begin to hit their targets. Kountouriotis, frustrated by the slow pace of the Hydras, now signalled that he would act independently and raced ahead at top speed to head off the enemy, whose line he crossed before he closed to 1.75 nautical miles (3.2 km). This move caught the Ottoman capital ships in a crossfire which struck hard at the *Barbarosse* and jammed the aft turret, damaged the boilers and set ablaze one of the coal bunkers. The *Barbarosse* now led the Ottoman line about and they pounded back to the Dardanelles pursued by the Greek battleships, which were now making 11 knots. They were unable to exploit the situation because no more than two guns each could come to bear on the retreating enemy. After an hour and a half, as the coastal defences opened fire, the Greeks abandoned the chase, the absence of torpedoes for the scouts being keenly felt. In the indecisive 150-minute action known as the Battle of Elli there were fifty-nine Ottoman casualties (eighteen dead), the majority in the battleships, while the relatively unscathed Greeks incurred only eight casualties, one fatal. The *Averoff* suffered fifteen hits from smaller-calibre weapons, the *Spetsai* being hit four times and the *Hydra* once, although her steering gear broke down during the action.

After this failure the Ottoman Navy was again reorganised and the 1st Destroyer Division's energetic commander Lieutenant Commander Rauf Bey was given a free hand in the Dardanelles.[22] A major supporter of reform, Rauf Bey would play an important role in Turkish politics and was to be the ambassador to London during the Second World War. Within two days he went onto the offensive and used his destroyers, supported by the *Medjidieh* and the torpedo gunboat *Berk-i Satvet*, in inconclusive bids to trap the Greek destroyers between an Imbros-bound task group and another waiting at the mouth of the Dardanelles.

The most notable event on this day was the first modern submarine attack by the *Delfin* upon the *Medjidieh*. After her arrival in Piraeus, the submarine spent a fortnight working up before Stefanos Paparrigopoulos sailed to Limnos in late October. There she was plagued by mechanical problems and it was not until 20 November that she departed on the first patrol. These patrols were made in daylight, with the boat retiring to the Greek destroyer base at Bozcaada every night.

Paparrigopoulos's encounter with the *Medjidieh* on 22 December saw the submarine launch a torpedo at 800 metres only for it to broach the surface and miss. When the *Delfin* returned to Bozcaada she ran aground and was saved from stranding only by dropping all her lead ballast which could not be replaced, so she was unable to dive again. She returned to Piraeus and played no further role in operations, an anticlimactic end to a historic patrol.

The Ottoman general staff were keen to retake Bozcaada and a combined operation was planned for 4 January, with the fleet landing the Yenihan Reserve Regiment. The fleet was ready but the troops failed to arrive, Naman Bey then proposing to shell Imroz to attract enemy warships. The plan was agreed, the cruisers departing with a destroyer escort on 10 January and encountering Greek destroyers which were outnumbered and fled. They returned when reinforced and the Ottoman ships fled in their turn to the Dardanelles, this scenario being repeated the following day.

Undaunted, the Turkish Admiralty remained determined to break the blockade and Rauf Bey was given the *Hamidieh* with orders to raid enemy merchant shipping in the Aegean. It was hoped this would entice the *Averoff* away from the Dardanelles and allow the Ottoman battle fleet to finish off the remaining Greek ironclads.[23] The cruiser's officers considered this a suicide mission and wrote their wills before departure.[24] The first part of the plan went well, the *Hamidieh* slipping out undetected during the night of 14/15 January to bombard the island of Syros before putting twenty-three 120-mm and five 114-mm shells into the armed merchant cruiser *Makedonia* (6,333 grt) which sank ablaze but was later raised and repaired.

The sinking of the *Makedonia* caused panic in Athens and on 20 January a defensive minefield was laid off Piraeus while the Admiralty ordered Kountouriotis to pursue the cruiser. He turned a blind eye to the signal and continued to watch the Dardanelles like a cat at a mouse hole, while Rauf Bey sailed like a modern Flying Dutchman. He was handicapped by the short range and unreliability of his radio communications with Constantinople and sometimes had to use the telegraph facilities of friendly ports. His most serious problem was the lack of coal, for while his bunkers could take 750 tons his stocks steadily dwindled. When he called at ports he was lucky to get even half of this; indeed, the British authorities permitted him only 200 tons when he arrived at Port Said on 19 January. He then sailed down the Suez Canal into the Red Sea, where there were neither Greek warships nor merchantmen, remaining there until 6 February.[25]

The Ottoman mice peeked out on the evening of 17/18 January when their light forces conducted another probe towards Bozcaada. The following morning the Turkish fleet, the two Brandenburgs and *Messudieh* together with the *Medjidieh* and five destroyers, sortied towards Limnos but were quickly spotted by Greek destroyers, which radioed the information to Kountouriotis in Moudros Bay.[26] Within ninety minutes the Hellenic ironclads had departed and, led by *Averoff*, sailed south to meet the enemy some 12 nautical miles (22 km) south-east of Limnos. However, as the Greeks closed with them, the Ottoman cruiser and the destroyers promptly turned back to the Dardanelles. The ironclads began to exchange fire shortly before midday at 4.5 nautical miles (8.4 km), with the Turks achieving an excellent firing rate although with little accuracy. The Greeks turned towards the enemy to reduce the range and after fifteen minutes the *Messudieh* also turned away, having suffered badly from the combined fire of the *Hydra* and the *Psara*, which knocked out one of her turrets.

Kountouriotis again tried to exploit his cruiser's superior speed and manoeuvrability to head off the enemy battle line, but he was too far astern and consoled himself by inflicting as much damage as possible in the chase. Just before midday the *Averoff* (or possibly one of the Hydras) hit the middle turret of the *Barbarosse* and as smoke, steam and fumes entered the engine and boiler rooms her speed was reduced to 5 knots. By now the Ottoman task force had almost reached sanctuary and after 150 minutes the Hellenic fleet again turned away, having inflicted 145 casualties including 41 dead. The *Barbarosse*, *Torgud Reis* and *Messudieh* were all badly damaged, the latter taking water, while the Greeks suffered minimal damage and casualties. They would hold the Aegean without further serious challenge, although there were inconclusive engagements after Ottoman destroyer sorties in March and April.

Kountouriotis displayed considerable leadership during the war and was certainly the most distinguished naval commander on either side. But he was hamstrung by the low speed and poor design of his battleships. Indeed, both sides urgently sought more modern capital ships. One feature of the engagements was the failure of both sides to follow the Japanese, or even Bulgarian, example and use torpedoes more extensively. Neither side sent torpedo craft against the enemy battle line—indeed, the Ottoman forces do not appear to have discharged a single torpedo—and while the Hellenic Navy did have some individual successes, its torpedo craft relied more upon their guns. The absence of torpedoes in the Greek scouts' tubes, as well as the poor mechanical condition of the Ottoman ships, provides part of the explanation, but the admirals seemed to display a noticeable reluctance to commit their torpedo craft into battle.

Before peace returned, the contested waters would see another first in naval history. In the New Year the Greeks converted two Maurice Farman biplanes into floatplanes and based them in Moudros. The Greeks and Bulgarians considered plans to land in Gallipoli and although these plans were stillborn, the Hellenic Navy needed to know the location of the Ottoman fleet. On 5 February 1913, Lieutenant Michael Moutousis, who had flown missions over Epirus, together with Ensign Aristeides Moraitinis conducted a reconnaissance over the Sea of Marmara. Their seaplane, christened *Nautilus*, made a 140-minute, 97-nautical mile (180-km) flight over the Nagara naval base and noted which ships were present. Moraitinis sketched some of the Dardanelles defences before dropping four small bombs without effect, the mission ending when the aircraft landed beside the destroyer *Velos* and was towed to Bozcaada.[27]

While the Aegean fleet concentrated upon its strategic mission of containing the Ottoman Navy and shielding maritime communications, it also performed an operational-level role along the northern coast where the Hellenic Navy drew first blood. The Ottoman naval presence in Salonika under Commodore Aziz Mahmut Bey consisted of the 42-year-old former casement ironclad *Feth-i Bulend*, whose armament and ninety crew members were removed during the Turco-Italian War to augment the coastal defences, which included a field of fifty mines. The ironclad, launched in 1870 and rebuilt in 1907, was now an accommodation hulk described by the British consul, Mr Harry Lamb, as 'a mass of old iron'.[28] Four tugs were lightly armed as patrol boats, one also acting as a minelayer, while the despatch vessel *Fouat* was reclassified as a hospital ship.

On the night of 31 October/1 November, as the Greek Army struck the last defences before Salonika, Lieutenant Nikolaos Votsis quietly sailed his 27-year-old torpedo boat *NF 11* into Salonika harbour and at a range of 135 metres launched four torpedoes at the *Feth-i Bulend*.[29] Three missed the target (one hit a pier) but one struck the ironclad almost amidships on the starboard side and she sank rapidly. Six of the crew (including the imam) died and the attack caused the crew of the *Fouat* to abandon ship in panic. In the confusion, Votsis escaped and was hailed a hero for his daring action.[30]

During late October the Greek Army made rapid progress towards Salonika and with its fall imminent, the Ottoman armed tugs were hastily transferred to the French register. To safeguard their interests and prevent urban unrest, the Great Powers had sent six warships, half of them ironclads, to preserve order in Salonika, and most were at anchor in the harbour when Votsis struck.[31] On 9 November, two Greek auxiliaries entered

Salonika and fired upon one of the former Ottoman tugs, which led to a French protest and the closure of the harbour by the Great Powers. But on 11 November, the Greek armed merchant cruiser *Sfaktiria* managed to enter and within twenty-four hours she was followed by the royal yacht *Amphitrite* with Queen Olga on board, and twenty-two Greek warships and merchantmen.[32] A fortnight later, the 'French' tugs sailed to the Dardanelles and promptly returned to the Ottoman register, while the Greeks refused to recognise the *Fouat* as a hospital ship and seized her.

As the Greek Army entered the port, the navy occupied the Chalkidiki Peninsula which reaches like a hand into the Aegean. The peninsula is home to the famed Mount Athos monastery, and to secure this deeply symbolic place Constantine ordered VII Division to send a battalion of 20th Infantry by sea. However, fears that the Bulgarians might arrive first at Mount Athos led the army to seek naval assistance. On 14 November, Kountouriotis in *Averoff*, together with the scouts *Panther* and *Ierax* and the destroyer *Thyella*, departed Limnos and 240 bluejackets secured the monastery. The battalion of the 20th Infantry in the SS *Aiolis* then occupied the westernmost promontory and shortly afterwards assumed responsibility for the peninsula. The occupation was completed on 15 November when the *Thyella* landed forty bluejackets at Daphne in Athos.[33]

In the Ionian Sea Damianos's squadron was largely involved in transporting men and supplies for the Army of Epirus.[34] It also conducted a blockade of the Albanian coast, initially with two gunboats at Vlore, which was bombarded on 3 December, but then extended to Durres on 27 February. The only Ottoman naval presence was at Preveza, where the torpedo boats *Tocad* and *Antalia* had been scuttled during the Turco-Italian War to leave the defence with two harbour-defence gunboats and seven 120 to 210-mm coastal defence guns.[35]

Apparently unaware that the warships had sunk, Damianos decided to pull the Ottoman fangs. The former spar-torpedo boats *Alfa* and *Delta* sailed into the harbour on the night that Greece declared war, the defenders promptly scuttling their remaining two harbour defence craft. The sunken Ottoman torpedo boats were later raised and commissioned in the Hellenic Navy as RHS *Nikopolis* and *Tatoi*.[36]

The navy helped the army advance by leap-frogging parties along the coast, beginning on 5 November with 200 Cretan paramilitaries from Corfu who were landed at Himare. The need to extend Greek control became more urgent as the Albanians grew closer to independence, and on 2 December it was decided to reinforce the Himare garrison with two companies. The II Division's 1st Infantry with two battalions, which had arrived in Preveza on 30 November, became the spearhead and sailed north to Sarande, to land unopposed with naval gunfire support on 7 December. They were reinforced from 10 December by two rifle companies and a battery of pack artillery originally intended for Khios. An Ottoman riposte stopped the Greeks from expanding the bridgehead which was now abandoned, having cost fifty casualties, the men being taken first to Corfu before they rejoined II Division. A new attempt was made on 16 March by the Acheron Detachment of Lieutenant Colonel Epites, carried in ten steamers escorted by the battleship *Psara*, the armed merchant cruiser *Mykali*, the scout *Aetos* and the destroyer

Lonchi, and the Ottoman defenders promptly abandoned the port. In addition to these missions, the Ionian Sea Squadron also conducted demonstrations off the coast during the final assault upon Ioannina.

The Greek merchant marine proved an extremely valuable operational- and strategic-level tool in a region lacking railways and metalled roads, and during the war transported a total of 83,400 Greek and Allied troops.[37] Initially these were operational-level movements, which began on 28 October when some 5,000 men of VII Division were shipped along the coast to support the advance upon Giannitsa. Then seventeen Greek steamers were provided to transport 10,200 men of the 1st Brigade/7th Bulgarian Division from Salonika to Dedeagac to assist an advance to isolate the Gallipoli Peninsula. The convoy, escorted by the *Mykali* with the *Kanaris* acting as the command vessel and the battle fleet as distant escort, departed Salonika on 27 November. It arrived the following day and was disembarked with great efficiency.[38]

Shipping played a key role in the decision at the end of 1912 to reinforce the Army of the Epirus, the navy assembling nineteen steamers to move some 17,700 men of Constantine's IV and VI Divisions from Salonika to Preveza. On 22 December, IV Division departed and arrived on the 30th, while VI Division required only eighteen ships to move it in the first week of January, followed by II Division with 10,000 men. The reinforcements were augmented by Delagrammatikas's 7th Infantry battlegroup with 4,500 men from Khios, which disembarked on 8 January. With the successful conclusion of the campaign, these 32,000 men were shipped back to Salonika from 14 March under naval escort to meet the growing Bulgarian menace in Macedonia.

The Greeks also transported a large body of Serbian troops into Ionian waters with dramatic results. Belgrade wanted to transport its 30,500-strong Coastal Group to support their Montenegrin allies at Shkoder and planned to hire sixty-five Greek steamers to move the troops in one 'lift'.[39] But Pasic balked at the daily bill of £2,500 (£244,200 at present-day values) and it was also recognised that Shengjin's facilities were inadequate to disembark such a large force. Belgrade compromised and decided to move the troops in smaller convoys.

The first echelon was railed to Salonika, embarked and sailed to Shengjin with a naval escort of the battleship *Psara*, the scout *Aetos* and the destroyers *Aspis* and *Lonchi* because the Ottoman cruiser *Hamidieh* was at large. The first convoy arrived on 1 March at Shengjin, where the limited facilities meant that most ships had to beach to unload their passengers and cargo into small boats. The second convoy, in eight steamers, reached the port on 12 March with the same escorts which then withdrew as the troops began to disembark. But shortly after they departed, the *Hamidieh* arrived off Shengjin.

Rauf Bey had returned to the eastern Mediterranean and then limped between coaling stations where he received just enough fuel to reach the next destination. On 6 March, he received both coal and ammunition and was ordered to sail for the Adriatic to supply the Ottoman troops in Albania. He had been promised a coaling ship, and as he approached the port he encountered the Greek SS *Leros* (2,020 grt) which was sailing in ballast. She stopped her, learned of the convoy's presence and decided to attack. To save ammunition she rammed and sank the merchantman and then arrived off the harbour where she was spotted by the destroyer *Lonchi*, which frantically radioed the news to the nearby armed merchant cruiser *Athina*.

The message was not received and the destroyer hastily withdrew to find the *Athina* leaving the Ottoman cruiser to fire some 150 rounds at the merchantmen. The SS *Trifilia* (1,336 grt) and *Chisomali Sifnaiou* (2,415 grt) were both badly damaged, and the *Elpis* (1,481 grt) and *Verveniotis* (2,397 grt) slightly damaged, the first ship losing four dead, while 119 Serbian troops also died. Fortunately, the Serbs' mountain guns had not been unloaded from the *Trifilia* and, with great enterprise, the troops got three into action, firing ninety-eight rounds at the cruiser, which withdrew. When the next Serbian echelon departed it was escorted by the battleship *Psara* and torpedo boats *Nikopolis* and *Aigli* to arrive without incident on 31 March, by which time international pressure over Shkoder made a fourth echelon unnecessary.[40]

Rauf Bey was unable to exploit his success, for he was down to 250 tons of coal, barely enough to reach Alexandria. As he fled, the Ionian Squadron's four Acheloos-class gunboats, with more courage than sense, hunted her in the Straits of Otranto. Indeed, the *Acheloos* sighted her but was driven off. The cruiser then patrolled the eastern Mediterranean and off Crete took her only prize, the sailing ship *Ispandis* with a cargo of bricks. Kountouriotis dispatched the battleship *Hydra*, the scout *Panther* and the destroyers *Keravnos* and *Doxa* to the eastern Mediterranean to hunt the cruiser, but the ironclad was too slow and the destroyers were never able to catch sight of the enemy. Rauf Bey now feared he would be trapped and decided discretion was the better part of valour, so returned to the Suez Canal on 8 April. He sailed back into the Red Sea while the *Hydra* and her escorts, accompanied by a collier, prowled off Port Said until the peace treaty was signed. The cruiser did not re-enter the canal until 24 August and returned home to a hero's welcome, but while she had caused much alarm in Athens she had failed either to draw away a substantial part of the Hellenic Navy or to interdict Greek maritime traffic.

It was in the Adriatic that the Great Powers used naval might to help drive King Nikola out of Shkoder.[41] They had decreed on 22 March that Shkoder would become part of the new Albania, ignoring the objections of the Montenegrins, who obstinately continued to besiege it. This defiance led the Great Powers to decide on 29 March to stage an international naval demonstration.

Vienna had done so independently from 19 March, deploying four ironclads, a protected cruiser and some destroyers to demonstrate Austria's opposition to a Slavic port on the Adriatic. Conrad would claim that the blockade, from the Dalmatian border to south of Durres, was to stop the shelling of civilian areas of Shkoder and to allow the civilian population to depart. In addition, Austria and Italy dispatched steamers with humanitarian aid which arrived the day after Shkoder fell, although fears that the Montenegrins might steal the largesse meant it was not delivered until 10 May, after they had departed.

For the international naval demonstration Russia delegated France to represent her interest. Austria dispatched the pre-dreadnoughts *Erzherzog Franz Ferdinand*, *Radetzky* and *Zrinyi*, the protected cruiser *Aspern* and the destroyers *Ulan, Scharfschütze* and *Dinara* all under Rear-Admiral Maximilian Njegovan, which arrived first on 2 April. In the following three days they were joined by the Italian pre-dreadnought *Ammiraglio di St Bon* and armoured cruiser *Francesco Ferruccio*, the German cruiser *Breslau*, the British pre-dreadnought *King Edward VII* (flying the flag of Vice Admiral Cecil Burney) and the protected cruiser *Dartmouth* as well as the French armoured cruiser *Edgar Quinet*.

Burney, aged 54 and a former commander of the Atlantic fleet, was unanimously selected to command the squadron on 5 April. He immediately telegraphed a demand on behalf of the Great Powers that Montenegro should immediately end its siege of Shkoder. King Nikola rejected this the following day and claimed the demand compromised the Great Powers' claims of neutrality. Burney immediately took steps to prevent the Greeks bringing in Serbian troops to reinforce the siege. HMS *Dartmouth* was dispatched to Corfu to warn off the Hellenic Navy and on the morning of 10 April the blockade went into effect, being joined by the Austrian minesweeper *Salamander* while the *Edgar Quinet* was replaced by another armoured cruiser, the *Ernest Renan*. The blockade benefited not only from ships but also from Austrian-operated and French-built Donnet-Lévêque floatplanes flown from their battleships to extend surveillance coverage. It was extended by 21 April, but a convoy of three Greek steamers escorted by the gunboat *Pinio* was allowed to carry Serbian troops away from Albania to Salonika after the fall of Shkoder. On 23 April, the continued Montenegrin presence in Shkoder led Burney to extend the blockade to Durres and three days later he was ordered to draft plans for Allied bluejackets to enforce law and order in Shkoder. In the meantime he supervised the withdrawal of Serbian troops while international pressure forced Nikola to order the evacuation of Shkoder.

On 9 May, the city's Montenegrin governor, Petar Palamenac, agreed to hand over the town to Burney five days later, but in anticipation of this a new task group was assembled with the armoured cruisers *Sankt Georg* (Austria), *Giuseppe Garibaldi* and *Varese* (Italy), the destroyers *Angler* and *Foam* (Britain), the torpedo boat *Iride* and monitor *Margherta* (Italy), four steamers with humanitarian aid and hospital ships from Greece and Russia. From these ships 1,000 bluejackets (300 British, 200 each from Austria, France and Italy, together with 100 Germans) were landed together with the first humanitarian aid on the morning of 14 May, with the blockade lifted that afternoon as Burney's council began to administer the town until a local administration was created. To further ensure security, Austria, France, Britain and Italy now dispatched troops to the city.

Burney's council was disbanded, in accordance with a Foreign Ministry decision, on 15 October and its duties were taken over by the Valona Control Commission. The foreign troops remained and were still there when the First World War broke out, the German naval detachment being incorporated into an Austrian infantry regiment. The French were the last foreign troops to leave Shkoder, but first they had to fight alongside their Serbian and Montenegrin allies, so it was not until January 1916 that they reached home.

During the Second Balkan War, the Hellenic Navy played only a minor part, although one of Bulgaria's provocative acts at the beginning of June was to shell the *Averoff* as she sailed along the coast to Salonika. The fleet was used largely to occupy ports along the

Macedonian and Thracian coasts—Kavala on 9 July by the destroyer *Doxa*, and on 25 July, Dedeagac by the battleship *Spetsai* and destroyer *Aspis*, although the Scout Squadron provided fire support to VII Division from the Gulf of Orfanou during the Battle of Kilkis-Lahanas.[42]

The Diplomatic Struggle between the Balkan Wars

The Balkan League's decision to go to war flew in the face of the wishes of the Great Powers and was partly a side-effect of the bitter diplomatic struggle between Austria and Russia for control of the Balkans.[43] This struggle rapidly threatened to lead to war between the two as St Petersburg cheered on Bulgaria and Serbia. Then the former's success acted like cold water dashed in the face as the Russians realised that their clients might ultimately control the Straits. In response to the deepening crisis, during September the Austrian Army had retained some conscripts in the Bosnia garrison and expanded some units with new recruits. The Governor-General, Oskar Potiorek, pressed for the reinforcement of the province's XV and XVI Corps and although this was agreed in principle on 4 October, War Minister General Moritz von Auffenberg persuaded Archduke Franz Joseph to delay its implementation.

However, when the Balkan League mobilised on 30 September, St Petersburg announced a 'trial mobilisation' exercise in the four military districts on the Austrian border, while the retention of conscripts who were due to complete their service raised fears of a European war.[44] By mid-October, Russia had 220,000 men in the Warsaw District alone, half the size of the Austrian active army, although there were severe shortages of artillery, ammunition and horses. The Russians also brought in the new conscript class, while 50,000 reservists were sent 'for exercises' in the Warsaw District, and by October St Petersburg had increased its peacetime army from 1.2 million to 1.6 million. Even the cautious von Auffenberg spoke of war with Russia within a year, but Austria did not respond until late October when it became clear that the Ottoman forces were crumbling.

The first step, on 28 October, saw the 40,000 Bosnia garrison reinforced by 16,400 men, while the Chief of the General Staff, General Blasius Schemua, pressed for a pre-emptive strike against Serbia, even if this meant war with Russia. He was supported by his predecessor Conrad, now an army commander, together with Franz Ferdinand and the new Foreign Minister Leopold Berchtold. The massive Russian military presence temporarily cooled the hot-heads, but with the Serbs set to gain a foothold on the Adriatic, Berchtold tried to persuade the Great Powers that this was an issue upon which Austria would go to war. On 19 November, Franz Joseph, von Auffenberg and Berchtold agreed to reinforce I, VI, X and XI Corps on the Russian border and raise their strength from 57,000 to 97,000. The Emperor was concerned about Berlin's reaction, but Germany raised no objections, and the following day the garrison on Serbia's border was also raised to 72,000.

Initially neither Tsar Nicholas nor Foreign Minister Sergei Sazonov tried to restrain Belgrade. Nicholas agreed in principle on 21 November to partial mobilisation of the Warsaw District, the whole of the Kiev District, and preliminary action in the Odessa District, but he deferred action for fear of the German reaction. A few days later, the Russians began to rein in the Serbs over the Adriatic port issue.

Austria and Russia were restrained by the other Great Powers, and especially their key allies Germany and France, who panicked over fears that the Balkan crisis might spark an Austro-Russian war.[45] Germany and France were honour-bound under the terms of their respective alliances to fight alongside their ally, but neither was confident that they could win a European war. Consequently, they informed their allies that, in the event of a war developing over the Balkan conflict, they would renege on their commitments. This so shocked Vienna and St Petersburg that both began to concentrate upon diplomatic solutions to the mutual tension. However, the financial cost of the crisis to Austria was £10.7 million (£11.7 billion at present-day values), which convinced many Austrian policymakers that it would be almost as cheap to go to war than to endure a similar crisis.

There was thus a collective sigh of relief in European chancelleries when the Catalca Line armistice was arranged, for this was regarded as the first step to a peace conference. Negotiations to expand the armistice began on 25 November with the Bulgarians, who were also speaking for their Serbian and Montenegrin allies, represented by Generals Fichev and Savov together with Danev. The Greeks sent their own delegation, led by ambassador Panas, which arrived on 28 November, while the Ottoman delegation was led by Nazim Pasha.

The Balkan League demanded that the armistice be extended throughout the European part of the Ottoman Empire and that the armies would remain in their positions, with Edirne, Ioannina and Shkoder still invested and denied food. The Porte agreed to lift the blockade of Bulgaria and to allow the Bulgarians use of the railway running past Edirne to feed their men in the east. The Greeks did not believe the Bulgarians would unilaterally sign such an agreement, and to strengthen their position they set conditions which were clearly unacceptable to the Porte. These included the immediate transfer of Ioannina to Greece, free passage of Greek merchantmen and warships through the Straits, and authority over all foreign ships in the Aegean.

The Porte rejected these terms, but the Greeks were then shocked to learn that the Bulgarians signed an armistice on 3 December and were also representing both Serbia and Montenegro. Athens consoled itself that its hands were not tied by the agreement and that it remained free both to take Epirus and to maintain the naval blockade. The Bulgarians themselves were dissatisfied, for they had hoped the armistice would give them Edirne, and their determination to take the city dashed hopes of diplomatically exploiting their Thracian victories.

The Great Powers tried to reassert their authority through the framework of the Berlin Treaty to prevent the Balkan War escalating into a European conflict. The first diplomatic effort from 17 December was officially described as the 'Reunion of the Ambassadors of the Six Great Powers, signatories of the Treaty of Berlin'. Almost a century earlier the Congress of Vienna had established a similar framework to resolve European disputes in order to avoid war and had generally succeeded, but the continental-wide will to achieve this was now weakening. Under the chairmanship of British Foreign Secretary Sir Edward Grey, the ambassadors considered three prime issues: Albania; Serbian access to the sea; and control of the Aegean islands. But other issues were raised, including adjustment to the Bulgarian-Rumania border as well as control of both the Straits and the Sanjak.

Early in December, Austria again began to lurch towards war with Serbia when it further increased the Bosnia garrison to some 100,000 men just as Conrad returned as Chief of the General Staff, while von Auffenberg was replaced by the 'hawk' General Alexander Krobatin. Franz Ferdinand also became more militant and supported Conrad's call for a strike against Serbia. The 'hawks' and 'doves' met at Schönbrunn on 11 December, and the Emperor, who had no confidence in Berlin, came down on the side of the 'doves'. Franz Ferdinand soon changed sides and by 4 January Berchtold secured support for a diplomatic solution which was backed by Berlin. But Vienna retained the military option and, having called up 60,000 men, now had 100,000 troops facing Serbia, while there remained 130,000 in Galicia (I, X and XI Corps).

As Berchtold informed one of his officials, 'I could easily provoke a war in 24 hours, but I do not want to do that,' so Vienna, like the other chancelleries, responded favourably to Grey's proposal for a conference. Its dual purpose was to oversee the peace negotiations and to protect the Great Powers' interests, but it also sought to resolve the deeper differences between Austria, Italy and Russia, all of whom had interests in the region.

However, the Albanian declaration of independence and demand for guaranteed borders sparked another crisis, for this seemed set to thwart Serbian and Greek ambitions. One reason why the Albanians created Kemal Bey's provisional government was to prevent their nascent country being devoured by the Balkan League, whose troops occupied so much of their territory. The Albanians especially wanted the port of Durres, which they regarded as vital to their national interests because it lay in the centre of their nascent state.[46]

The Serbian seizure of Adriatic ports infuriated the Austrians, who believed that they were acting in proxy for Russia. They interpreted Belgrade's action as a move to create a Russian naval base both to thwart Vienna's ambitions in the western Balkans and to threaten Austria's maritime outlets at Trieste and Fiume. The Italians made common cause with the Austrians as they also feared a Serbian/Russian presence on the Adriatic. Vienna's policy to thwart Serb ambitions was to espouse the creation of a viable Albanian state to absorb the maximum number of Albanians currently subjects of the Ottoman Empire, including the towns of Dakovica, Prizren and Shkoder. Matters were brought to a head when the Austrian consul in Prizren was arrested by Serbian troops, and although he was soon released there were fears for his safety and even reports that he had been murdered.

Vienna's only concern was with Albania's northern frontier. Like all the Great Powers, it had little interest in the southern frontier, which was remote from their centres of interest. This opened the way to Athens' claims for Epirus, for although it lacked the patronage of the Great Powers it faced no significant opposition, apart from a ban on occupying

Vlore by Austria and Italy. Certainly, the London conference raised no serious objection to Greek demands for Epirus and Ioannina, provided its troops could take them. The Great Powers also did not oppose the Greek blockade of the Albanian coast, although this trapped the Albanian Provisional Government in Vlore. Serbia obstinately pressed its case for an Adriatic port in the teeth of Austrian and Italian opposition. Indeed, Pasic stated that his country could not renounce this requirement. He anticipated Russian diplomatic support, but this proved half-hearted, while Bulgaria loyally stood by its pre-war agreements and also supported the Serbian claim. Self-interest may also have played a role in the Bulgarian position because support for a Serbian Adriatic port denied Belgrade an excuse to retain those parts of Macedonia that Sofia regarded as its own.

On 20 December, the ambassadors recognised the existence of an independent Albania, which included Durres, but the new state's frontiers proved harder to define in the welter of claim and counter-claim. Vienna and Rome sought a large country to contain Serbia-Montenegro and to deny the Serbs access to the sea, while the Russians wanted a smaller Albania and supported the Serb claim for an Adriatic port. The Albanian view was largely ignored, and the talks continued into the spring of 1913 as Austria and Italy demanded that Shkoder be part of Albania and Russia opposed them. On 26 January, the Russians changed tack and said that if Shkoder became part of Albania then ethnically Albanian Dakovica should go to Serbia, and here the issue stuck until Vienna conceded it at the end of March.

This easing of tensions followed a successful secret mission to St Petersburg in early February 1913 by Prince Gottfried zu Hohenlohe-Schillingfürst, a personal friend of the Tsar. The Shkoder Crisis proved a temporary obstacle, but Austria's agreement to concede Dakovica to Serbia removed Russian opposition to an Albanian Shkoder and led St Petersburg to convince Belgrade to accept this decision. Shortly afterwards, Austria and Russia began to reduce their forces in Galicia in confidence-building moves, although there were further scares in May and October.

It was against this background that the ambassadors conferred in London to ensure their Balkan interests, while a parallel meeting of the combatants took place from 16 December at St James's Palace to draft a peace treaty. The St James's Palace negotiations involved the Ottoman ambassador to Paris (Mustafa Reshid Pasha), the former premiers of Bulgaria (Danev), Montenegro (Lazar Mijuskovic) and Serbia (Stojan Novakovic), and the Greek Premier Venizelos. He and Geshov arranged to attend the conference in a move that the Greeks hoped would resolve territorial claims, but Geshov did not attend, which left Venizelos the only acting premier at the conference. Reshid Pasha objected to his presence because Athens was not a signatory of the armistice agreement and had continued military operations. However, a week's diplomatic pressure led him to take a more pragmatic perspective and the talks resumed on Christmas Eve. The Bulgarians, in turn, opposed Rumania's attendance, but the British desired Bucharest's presence although discussions on the Bulgarian-Rumanian border were excluded from the agenda.

Macedonia was the paramount question for all the Balkan League partners. The Bulgarians recognised that their agreement to arbitration on the disputed territory meant they would not achieve all their goals and they sought as compensation a substantial portion of Thrace, including Edirne. Their diplomacy was not helped by Danev's abrasive personality, which quickly irritated almost everyone, while by contrast Venizelos skilfully won support for Greek interests.

The Ottoman strategy was to gain time to give its forces time to recover, and the Porte played off the Balkan League delegates against each other to split the united front. Reshid Pasha recognised that the western reaches of the empire (Macedonia and Albania) were untenable and was willing to concede them. But he was determined to resist Bulgarian demands for Edirne, and one member of the Ottoman delegation informed Danev that it was 'a window into our harem'. For the Ottomans, Edirne was not only a vital shield for Constantinople but it had also been their first European capital and the site of the sixteenth-century mosque of Sultan Selim II. Danev's strident demands showed that the issue was an obsession which no Bulgarian government could concede, and he would later claim that it was the sole obstacle to a peace agreement. If it had been conceded, he claimed, then Greece would have been isolated and a peace treaty signed early in the New Year.

The Porte also wished to regain the four islands at the mouth of the Dardanelles (Imroz, Limnos, Samothraki and Tenedos) to shield Constantinople, which it regarded as vital to the empire's strategic interests. On New Year's Day 1913, Reshid Pasha presented his final position, which reluctantly conceded all territory west of Thrace, including Shkoder and Ioannina, but he insisted that Thrace and the Aegean islands should remain part of the Ottoman Empire. This was unacceptable to Bulgaria and Greece and, with no further compromise, the talks were suspended on 6 January.

The combatants' failure to reach agreement saw the Great Powers start to twist arms. On 17 January, the ambassadors demanded from the Porte an end to hostilities and acceptance of the Balkan League's terms. Constantinople did not officially respond, although the Ottoman Cabinet meeting later in the day did decide to accept the terms. This decision was overwhelmingly endorsed by the Grand Council (comprising civil, military, judicial and religious leaders) when it met on 22 January, just as Russia warned that it would not remain neutral if hostilities were resumed. Yet the Cabinet's decision was the last straw for the ever more nationalist CUP, which had wide support among the younger officers. They had long loathed Grand Vizier Kamil Pasha and Nazim Pasha, whom they regarded as ineffectual, and three CUP members—Colonel Cemal Pasha (Inspector of Lines of Communications), Lieutenant Colonel Enver Pasha (X Corps' chief-of-staff, the corps being in Constantinople at the time) and former Interior Minister Talat Pasha—plotted a coup which became known as the Raid on the Sublime Porte.

On the afternoon of 23 January, they broke into the council chambers just as the ministers were about to approve the Great Powers' demands. Enver Pasha and Talat Pasha forced Kamil Pasha to resign at gunpoint, while other members went through the building and encountered Nazim Pasha with his aide. A gun battle broke out, resulting in Nazim and his aide being killed, leaving both the government and armed forces without leaders. The Sultan quickly rubber-stamped the coup and Enver's 'recommendations' for new leaders: the respected former War Minister Mahmud Shevket Pasha as Grand Vizier, Talat Pasha as Interior Minister, Ahmet Izzet Pasha as War Minister and Cemal Pasha as commander of the Eastern Army on the Catalca Line. Afterwards Enver returned to X Corps, having probably received tacit support from corps commander Hursit Pasha.

The new government was instructed to hold Edirne at all costs but compromised on 30 January by offering to partition the city along the River Meric, giving Bulgaria the right bank. This was not workable, as the Greeks and Bulgarians discovered in Salonika, and the difficulties of a joint administration would also become apparent in Berlin and Vienna after the Second World War. The Porte also agreed to allow the Great Powers to determine the fate of the Aegean islands, but both proposals were rejected by the Balkan League which allowed the armistice to end on 3 February. However, winter severely restricted operations, which bought more time for discussion.

The unsuccessful Ottoman offensives of March, together with the fall of both Edirne and Ioannina, removed most of the immediate obstacles to peace, and on 7 April the Porte proposed a new armistice. Following a meeting at Catalca railway station on 13 April, terms were agreed for a ten-day, renewable agreement to take effect the following day. A separate approach to Athens saw a meeting on 15 April at which the draft of a peace treaty was agreed on, although fighting continued along the Montenegrin front around Shkoder.

The final push for peace was at the London Ambassadors' Conference where the Great Powers jostled to strengthen their interests by ensuring that their clients secured as much of the territory they claimed as possible. With relations between Sofia, Athens and Belgrade deteriorating, preparations were being made for a new conflict once the way had been cleared by the diplomats. Sofia, wanting to regroup its forces in Thrace to face its former allies in the west, urgently required a treaty, while its former allies deliberately procrastinated to give their own forces time to prepare.

Eventually pressure from the Great Powers brought Athens and Belgrade to heel and the Treaty of London was signed on 30 May 1913, bringing a formal end to the First Balkan War which had cost the armies alone nearly 395,000 casualties, excluding the sick (see Table 2)—minute compared with the holocaust to come, but a terrible burden for small nations. At the time many thought the treaty had averted the horrors of a European conflict and it received the rapturous applause matched a quarter of a century later by the Munich Treaty of 1938. However, the more astute observers recognised that the agreement merely delayed another conflict for a few months.[47]

Table 2   Casualties of the First Balkan War (excluding sick)

Country	Dead	Wounded	Missing	Total (rounded out)
Bulgaria	8,840	36,877	4,926	50,600
Serbia	5,000	34,000	???	39,000
Greece	3,461	22,022	1,883	27,360
Montenegro	2,500	5,000	???	7,500
Ottoman	50,000	100,000	120,000	270,000

Figures based upon official returns, Carnegie, Erickson and Vachkov

At Grey's suggestion, the Ottoman Empire surrendered all territory west of a straight line linking the Aegean and Black Sea ports of Enez and Midye, although this new frontier lacked any form of defendable point and left the Porte dependent upon the Catalca Line to shield Constantinople. The empire also abandoned all claim to Crete and the Aegean islands, except Tenedos and Imroz, which Constantinople needed to protect the approaches to the Bosphorus. Their fate, and Albania's borders, would be decided by the Great Powers, who promptly gave the remaining Aegean islands, except the Italian-held Dodecanese, to Greece. However, they decided to leave the key issue of Macedonia in the hands of the Balkan League, although Russia would be the arbitrator. This left St Petersburg on the horns of a dilemma, for the arbitration was bound to offend either Bulgaria or Serbia. The recognition of Albania was a diplomatic triumph for the Vienna-Rome partnership and a disaster for St Petersburg. Albanian joy was tempered by the discovery that there was no support for their demand that the largely Albanian region of Kosovo should become part of the new country.

During the summer of 1913, Albanian tribes with Austrian, Bulgarian and Ottoman support invaded Kosovo but were quickly contained and driven back by Serbian troops. The Serbian Army then advanced into Albanian territory just as the Great Powers began to define the new country's frontiers, a task completed by August, although their decisions excluded many ethnic Albanian areas. The new state remained anathema to Belgrade whose troops remained inside its borders until they were again forced to withdraw in the face of an Austrian ultimatum on 18 October.[48]

A further complication for the Great Powers, and one potentially more dangerous to Bulgaria, was its border dispute with Rumania, a member of the Triple Alliance whose benevolent neutrality towards the Ottoman Empire had intensely irritated Sofia. Rumania was the strongest regional power and regarded its forces as the 'gendarmes of the Balkans', but this position was now challenged by Bulgaria's military success. Prime Minister Titu Maiorescu was under tremendous public pressure to abandon neutrality in the Balkan War, but remained both Premier and Foreign Minister when a coalition government was created in October 1912. His coalition partner, Take Ionescu, who claimed good relations with the Bulgarians, was authorised on 29 October to open negotiations with Geshov about conceding part of southern Dobrogea. This was an area of fertile land between the bend in the Danube and the Black Sea that was split between Bulgaria and Rumania at the Berlin Congress. Control of this region by Bucharest would enrich Rumania's economy as well as securing control of the mouth of the Danube.

Sofia was unwilling to lose so valuable a prize, although there were elements in the government, including Tsar Ferdinand and Geshov, willing to concede the port of Silistra on the border. After Bucharest rattled its sabre and Russia put pressure upon Sofia to open negotiations, Danev and Maiorescu met in Bucharest on 9 December. The Rumanians repeatedly offered Bulgaria an alliance in return for the disputed territory, but Bulgaria was still preening itself after its Thracian victories and would make only minor concessions. Eventually, Bucharest ended the negotiations and caused personal offence to Danev by accusing him, probably accurately, of arrogance.

Bulgarian optimism was bolstered by the Varna Agreement, but Serbia's failure to secure an Adriatic port undermined this guarantee. Sofia's best hope was that the 1902 agreement with Russia would restrain Rumania, although it had been repudiated by Sazonov when Bulgaria attacked the Ottoman Empire despite St Petersburg's objections. Danev obstinately stuck to his guns, even in the face of Rumanian threats to mobilise. The Rumanians had begun to discuss the possibility of war from 25 January, but King Carol and Maiorescu feared military intervention from both Serbia and Russia. The other Great Powers also strongly warned Rumania against military intervention, but disputes between Germany and Austria, which wished to use Bulgaria as leverage against Serbia, undermined this threat. Bucharest cleared the decks on 5 February by resolving a dispute with Austria over Transylvania and now awaited the outcome of the London conferences.[49]

With Bulgaria's relations with their allies deteriorating and its forces still pinned down on the Catalca Line and Edirne, Sofia's hands were tied. It was under pressure to make concessions by the Great Powers, including Russia, who feared a European war, and Sazonov supported the secession of Silistra to maintain the peace. The Bulgarians bought some time through offers of minor border changes, as well as good old diplomatic evasion, but Maiorescu and Ionescu now decided to claim the whole of southern Dobrogea. Isolated, and with the Ottoman front again in flames, the cornered Bulgarians bowed to the inevitable and on 24 February agreed to submit the dispute to arbitration by the St Petersburg Ambassadors' Conference, and two days later Bucharest also signalled agreement.

The conference offered St Petersburg an opportunity to preserve Russian interests in Bulgaria, and in a moment of wild optimism the prospect swung before Sazonov's eyes, like a string in front of a kitten, of detaching Bucharest from the Triple Alliance. However, these hopes were soon dashed, for the Triple Alliance was determined to maintain Rumanian loyalty at the expense of Bulgarian interests. On 8 May, to the fury of Sofia, the ambassadors assigned Silistra to Rumania with the implication that Bulgaria would be awarded substantial Ottoman territory as compensation.

Surprisingly, Geshov was pleased, for he hoped that it heralded Russian support in the dispute with Serbia, but many Bulgarian politicians were unhappy and doubted St Petersburg's good intentions. Rumanian politicians were equally unhappy because they felt they should have received the whole of south Dobrogea, but Maiorescu carried the day. He was also aware that Bulgaria's allies were plotting against the country and had been offered an alliance by Serbia in April. On 4 June, he strongly hinted to the Great Powers that Rumania might take the remaining territory at bayonet point, and indeed his government informed Bulgaria on 28 June that it would not remain neutral in the event of a new Balkan War.

The Balkan League Splits

As the diplomatic minuet continued, the Balkan League fractured beyond repair over the issue of Macedonia, the greatest friction being between Bulgaria and Serbia. Both desired the largest piece of the pie, and the importance of the region increased as both parties sought compensation for thwarted territorial ambitions elsewhere.[50]

The Great Powers had doomed Serbia's hopes of extending the nation to the Adriatic, so the disputed Macedonian territory was now even more important to Belgrade. Many had never accepted the March 1912 agreement because they regarded the region as part of Serbia's historical legacy, and there remained strong opposition, especially in the army, to arbitration. Yet the Serbs also faced an unpleasant truth, for many of Macedonia's inhabitants were ethnically Bulgarian and proudly nationalist after successful Bulgarian educational efforts from the end of the nineteenth century. They did not regard the new occupiers as liberators and, as Serbian troops advanced into Macedonia, they became determined. As one Serbian journalist wrote, 'What falls under Serbia, remains Serbian; what falls under Bulgaria, is assimilated.' This boded ill for regions under Serbian occupation which were claimed by Bulgaria.[51]

On 13 January, the Serbs formally requested a revision of the March 1912 treaty and repeated this in February when Pasic outlined to Geshov the Serbian case for additional Macedonian territory. He argued that Bulgaria had already acquired most of Thrace but failed to meet the terms of the pre-war military convention despite Serbian aid at Edirne. Geshov airily responded that he was not responsible for the Serbian failure to gain an Adriatic port and that the changing military situation had caused his country's failure to meet its military obligations. He offered financial recompense for the Serb presence at Edirne, but this was rejected by Pasic. The Serbian ambassador then demanded 200,000 troops to meet the potential threat from Austria, but Geshov, who had received promises of German and Austrian diplomatic support, naturally refused.[52] The Serbian complaints about the lack of Bulgarian military support in Macedonia were disingenuous because in the aftermath of their victory at Kumanovo their forces were adequate to control the Vardar valley. Indeed, the absence of Bulgarian troops made it easier for the Serbs to tighten their grip in Macedonia.

Pasic now began to strengthen Serbia's position with an offer to concede some of the disputed territory as he strengthened his country's relations with the Russians. As insurance, he now also began to assemble troops on the Bulgarian border, although he denied this when challenged by the Bulgarian ambassador. Sofia knew that the Serbs were tightening their control in Macedonia, even in areas allocated to Sofia in 1912, for they closed Bulgarian schools, arrested Bulgarian administrators and even harassed Bulgarian priests. Only the belief in Russian advice and support stayed Bulgaria's hand, for Geshov was willing to await the Tsar's arbitration. A more sceptical Danev also sought insurance and demanded that St Petersburg should first confirm the Russo-Bulgarian treaty of 1902.

Bulgaria still hankered for the San Stefano borders, yet its diplomatic response saw divisions within the leadership between the 'doves' Fichev and Geshov and the 'hawks'

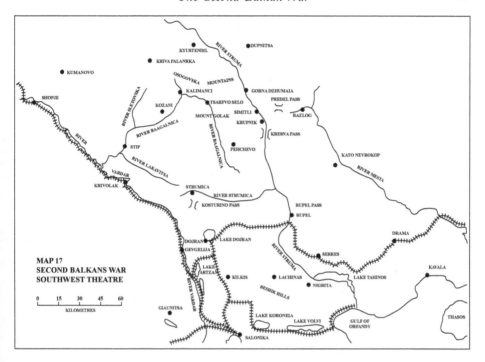

MAP 17
SECOND BALKANS WAR
SOUTHWEST THEATRE

Ferdinand, Savov and Danev. Geshov was angry when some of the government supported Austrian efforts to thwart Serbian access to the sea, and again when Danev persuaded the government to accept the Great Powers' demands for an independent Albania. This followed discussions with Berchtold, who promised to support Bulgarian claims for Edirne. Geshov's policy was to concede Salonika to Greece and Silistra to Rumania in order to secure favourable Russian arbitration over Macedonia. He had many opponents, although on 15 January he succeeded in gaining the signatures of Savov, Ivanov, Kutinchev, Dimitriev, Fichev and Kovacev on a document confirming that Bulgaria could not fight a war on two fronts.

Salonika remained the bone of contention with Greece, although this dispute in Sofia's view was the lesser of two evils. While both countries had administered Salonika since 9 November, Greece was determined that its flag alone would fly over the city. Venizelos's proposal for dividing southern Macedonia, with Athens retaining Salonika, Kavala and Serres and a common frontier with Serbia, was dismissed by Geshov who pointedly commented on the different sizes of the two armies. His counter-offer of dividing the territory based upon the proportion of forces committed was in turn rejected by the Greeks. At the beginning of the war the two sides had agreed that the administration of the area west of the Vardar would be in Greek hands and the Bulgarians would be responsible for the area to the east. Now the Greeks began to encroach into Bulgarian territory and established their own administrations, while there were also numerous clashes between the troops. The situation was complicated by the Serbian presence in Macedonia north of Gevgelija where each side had its own governor.

King George had favoured conciliation but his son demanded a more assertive policy, and both sides were more interested in securing their territorial claims than in resolving differences. Venizelos and Danev met three times, the former repeating his proposal to renounce claims to southern Macedonia, including Drama, Kavala and Serres, in Bulgaria's favour provided Athens retained Salonika. Danev claimed he had no authority to negotiate the issue, although he warned Sofia that the fate of Salonika might have to be resolved by force. In fact Bulgaria had decided not to surrender Salonika in the belief of its military superiority, which ignored the possibility that Serbia might also be involved in a conflict. Certainly, Bulgaria missed a splendid opportunity in London to ease tensions with Greece by conceding Salonika.

As Sofia sought ever more inventive ways to justify its claims, to the exasperation of its allies, Greece and Serbia turned to each other. During the winter, Sofia was outraged at Serbian persecution of Bulgarian activities in northern Macedonia. From March, Bulgarian and Greek forces frequently clashed and although both sides agreed to a joint commission to investigate incidents, this could not be impartial. The Greeks and Serbians began to draw closer and during a parade in Salonika at the beginning of March officers from both armies wore each other's caps and proclaimed brotherhood between the two nations.

Serbia's increased persecution of Bulgarians during April raised tensions, although the Bulgarians themselves persecuted minorities in their occupied territories. Ferdinand wrongly suspected the existence of a military alliance between Serbia and Greece, but correctly forecast war. There was a war scare in Sofia in mid-April when the embarkation in Greek ships of Serbian troops from Shkoder for transport to Salonika was interpreted as the first move of a joint offensive. The Serbians were actually being transported home via Salonika, but the reports caused panic in Sofia, with the Foreign Ministry and works of art being evacuated. As relations with Serbia deteriorated, Sofia now reconsidered its diplomatic options as Geshov sought to abandon the principle of proportionality in favour of arbitration. A faction led by Danev rejected this in favour of imposing Bulgarian demands, especially over Salonika, at bayonet point. Geshov prevailed and, on 25 April, Bulgaria requested formal Russian arbitration under the March 1912 treaty to secure its Macedonian claims.

Geshov hoped to secure a peaceful settlement with the Serbs and to isolate Greece, which would then be vulnerable to military pressure. He was also confident, even after the Silistra decision, that his country's special relationship with St Petersburg would help to secure the support from the Great Powers that he needed. But the Russians recognised that no matter what they decided, they would lose one friend in the region, and they prevaricated. In early May, for example, Sazonov insisted that arbitration included the Greeks, a proposal which he knew Danev had already rejected.

Russia's loss of influence was demonstrated by the support for an independent Albania at the London Ambassadors' Conference despite St Petersburg's opposition. Ominously, in April 1913, Serbia's Pasic hinted to St Petersburg that his country would not adhere to the March 1912 agreement. 'The Serbian government will not allow Bulgaria to extend between Serbia and Greece and to connect with Albania, even if it loses the sympathy of the whole world.' He warned that his country would go to war if the Great Powers restricted Bulgarian Macedonia to the eastern bank of the River Vardar. St Petersburg chose to ignore these statements, although Sazonov could have invoked the arbitration clause in the treaty to control or to influence events.

However, by then it was too late, for Venizelos informed the Cabinet in March that a *de facto* state of war with Bulgaria existed north-east of Salonika. All recognised that Athens lacked the resources to win a military trial of strength on its own. But Serbian military support would compensate for Bulgarian military superiority and could help secure not only Greek gains in Macedonia but also the balance of power within the Balkans. The Cabinet agreed that negotiations could begin on an alliance with Serbia and these made rapid progress during April.

The foundations had been laid several months earlier. At a meeting between Crown Prince Aleksandar and Prince Nicholas (Commander of Salonika) in January, the Serb proposed the Serbian-Greek border should run from Ohrid to Bitola to Stip. About the same time, Venizelos met Pasic in Belgrade and they agreed to postpone negotiations on their common border until after a peace treaty with the Ottoman Empire. The decision by Venizelos to seek an agreement with the Serbs was confirmed after a visit to Sofia, where his hosts ignored his proposals for a diplomatic settlement.

On 5 May, Serbia and Greece signed a draft agreement in which they divided Macedonia west of the River Vardar on a boundary based upon the military status quo. They agreed that the new frontier would be held through joint diplomatic and military action if Sofia objected. There was a fifty-year guarantee of unrestricted transport between Skopje and Salonika, as well as customs-free import and export of Serbian goods through Salonika. Albania would be divided into two spheres of influence, although this might bring Serbia into conflict with Vienna. A military convention was signed on 14 May and confirmed on 1 June in the Treaty of Salonika, just two days after the Treaty of London formally ended the First Balkan War. The agreement was a provocative act in itself but, at Serbia's request, its military elements excluded a pre-emptive war.

While the negotiations continued in April the two partners separately approached Bucharest, but the sympathetic Rumanians refused to make any commitments. This was to exploit the situation for their own ends but also because the Rumanians were unsure of the Russian response and did not intend to offend their powerful northern neighbour. Belgrade and Athens separately contacted their former enemy Constantinople to investigate the prospects of joint action against Bulgaria, but the Porte was equally non-committal. Nevertheless, the skilled diplomatic preparation of Athens and Belgrade helped to ensure Sofia's isolation in the subsequent conflict.

Bulgaria's great gain from the Treaty of London was the freedom to move its troops westward into Macedonia where their bayonets might hold their desired territory. Indeed, Sofia's diplomacy was always driven by the belief in its military power. But this assumed both that Rumania would remain neutral and that the Great Powers would guarantee the security of the new Ottoman frontier. The most significant casualty of the Treaty of London was Geshov, who saw all his attempts at concession thwarted and the Balkan

League disintegrate. On 21 May, he belatedly tried to win his way into Venizelos's good graces when he agreed that the military status quo would be the basis of the new border and conceded Greek control of southern Macedonia. Days later came news of the Greco-Serbian alliance, and Geshov made one last desperate attempt to avoid a war with Serbia by meeting Pasic at the frontier town of Tsaribrod on 1 June as the Treaty of Salonika was confirmed. The meeting was fruitless and Geshov returned to Sofia to resign, while Pasic returned to Belgrade convinced that there would soon be another war.

CHAPTER 6

The Second Balkan War

Background to War

The Bulgarians felt that the Treaty of London robbed them of their just rewards, for they had suffered the heaviest casualties and spearheaded the destruction of the Ottoman Army. The national sense of injustice was aggravated by delays in the division of Macedonia, where Sofia's Serbian and Greek allies now controlled much of the territory which it had anticipated would fly the Bulgarian flag. Consequently, after the treaty was signed Geshov retired, ostensibly on health grounds but really because he recognised that he could not prevent a disastrous new war caused by the country's sense of outrage.[1]

The 'hawks' were flying high, led by Ferdinand and Savov, the latter only too willing to feed the Tsar's bellicose fantasies. Fichev recognised Savov's growing baneful influence and on 12 June he too resigned on health grounds, but this was not accepted for six months and he remained in the army. Three days later, Bulgaria had a new government under the Russophile hardliner Danev, who rejected Serbian efforts to renegotiate the 1912 treaty and blindly pinned his faith on Russian arbitration to secure the lion's share of Macedonia. He blithely ignored Tsar Nicholas's anger about Bulgarian procrastination over the Russian-arbitrated agreement on Silistra, and Danev's unswerving belief in the righteousness of Bulgaria's course blinded him both to the constraints on Sofia and to the shallowness of Berchtold's assurances of Austrian support. But Danev had some cause for optimism, for he knew Sazonov was increasingly exasperated by Serbian belligerence and had warned Belgrade that the Bulgarians would beat them in a clash of arms. This he wished to avoid, for fear that a weak Serbia would strengthen Austria's position in the Balkans.

While Danev sought a diplomatic resolution, Savov increasingly advocated a military one, arguing that his army was superior to those of its enemies. But he warned that this superiority was becoming eroded by inactivity which left the men demoralised. In fact the war-weary troops increasingly desired to return home, for they felt betrayed by their allies and saw little point in fighting for territory which had brought them no benefit. With few military duties, they devoted their energies to politics and began to question the politicians' effectiveness on the Macedonian issue. Savov believed that the best way to counter the demoralisation would be a war against Bulgaria's Balkan League allies, and the army leadership were confident that they would win.

Savov also believed that in the great ball of European diplomacy, military success over the combined armies of Serbia and Greece would allow Bulgaria to take its pick of the partners within the great alliances. However, Finance Minister Teodorov was more cautious and urged the government to isolate Greece by persuading it to accept international arbitration over the Macedonian border. With greater acumen than most of his countrymen, he realised that if Bulgaria's forces struck Serbia and Greece, they would be unable to meet any new threat from Rumania and Turkey. He was supported by the country's representative at Greek General HQ, Major-General Hristofor Hesapchiev, who also urged greater conciliation with Greece in order to isolate Belgrade which he confidently believed would not fight Sofia alone. The Great Powers sought to defuse the situation and urged 25 per cent demobilisation, but mutual distrust meant that all sides rejected this suggestion.

It was recognition of Serbian and Greek military weakness, compared with Bulgaria, that meant their leaders sought a diplomatic rather than a military solution and kept their armies on a tight rein. Pasic faced increasing parliamentary demands to reject both concessions and Russian arbitration, with the pressure so great that he twice offered his resignation in June, only for King Petar to refuse. Venizelos proposed international arbitration as the army grew restive, but as insurance he sought alliances not only with Rumania but also with his country's traditional enemy, the Ottoman Empire! Pasic and Geshov met on 1 June and agreed to attend a conference at St Petersburg, but the Bulgarian then refused to attend a preliminary meeting of premiers in Salonika to discuss the agenda and then resigned.

While Vienna might view a renewal of the Balkan conflict with some equanimity, St Petersburg could see thirty-five years of diplomatic effort unravelling after its apparent triumph a year earlier in brokering the Balkan League. This had now disintegrated and it was clear that Russian influence in the region would be compromised, and that whatever it decided either Bulgaria or Serbia would be driven into its enemies' arms.

Sofia had considerable ties with Russia, where many of its citizens had completed higher education, and these had been strengthened by the 1902 military agreement and the guarantees for the 1912 treaty. During the First Balkan War, St Petersburg had provided military equipment and allowed its officers to join the Bulgarian Army, and for these reasons Danev remained confident of Russian support. He ignored Russian concerns about the proximity of Bulgarian forces to Constantinople and the potential for friction. By contrast, Serbia was smaller but far from the Straits, held most of the disputed Macedonian territory, and possession was nine-tenths of the law. Moreover, Bucharest was making noises about intervention on its side and Russian intelligence could not have been unaware of Greco-Serbian attempts to secure an alliance with it.

In a desperate effort to keep his country's Slavic allies from internecine warfare and to win back national prestige, Tsar Nicholas on 8 June sent messages to his fellow monarchs with an offer to arbitrate under the 1912 treaty. The Bulgarians procrastinated, and an irritated Savov on 16 June urged the government to make a decision for either peace or war. Five days later, Danev informed the Ministerial Council that the Serbs would accept

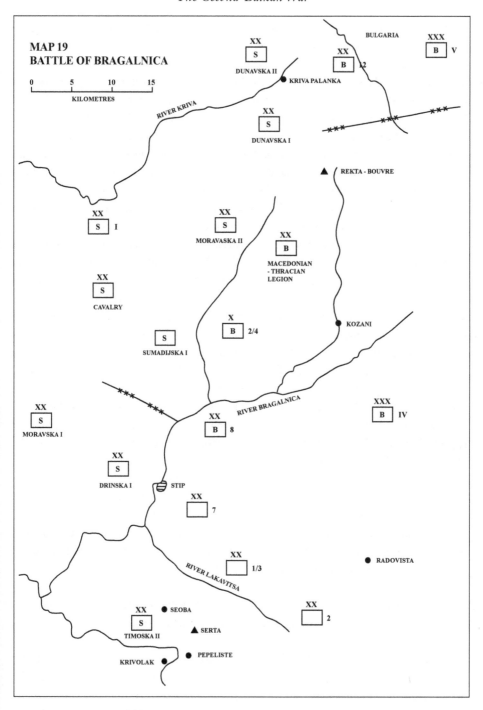

MAP 19
BATTLE OF BRAGALNICA

0   5   10   15
KILOMETRES

RIVER KRIVA

BULGARIA

XXX
B V

XX
B 12

KRIVA PALANKA

XX
S
DUNAVSKA II

XX
S
DUNAVSKA I

▲ REKTA - BOUVRE

XX
S I

XX
S
MORAVASKA II

XX
B
MACEDONIAN
- THRACIAN
LEGION

XX
S
CAVALRY

X
B 2/4

S
SUMADIJSKA I

● KOZANI

RIVER BRAGALNICA

XXX
B IV

XX
S
MORAVSKA I

XX
B 8

XX
S
DRINSKA I

STIP

XX
7

XX
1/3
RIVER LAKAVITSA

● RADOVISTA

XX
S
TIMOSKA II

● SEOBA

▲ SERTA

XX
2

KRIVOLAK ●

● PEPELISTE

neither joint occupation nor joint government in Macedonia. He warned that if Belgrade refused to accept Russian arbitration then war was inevitable.

The Bulgarian Crown Council then met in Varna, attended by Ferdinand, Danev, Savov and Teodorov, and it was decided to give the Russians a seven-day deadline to announce the result of the arbitration. But when Danev made the demand, a furious Sazonov told him on 24 June, 'Do not expect anything from us and forget the existence of any of our agreements from 1902 to the present.' This was serious, for Sofia believed that the 1902 agreement would restrain Rumania from military intervention. Eventually, the Bulgarians and Serbians did agree to accept Tsar Nicholas's offer and in late June, after Sazonov had calmed down, both Danev and Pasic prepared to depart for St Petersburg, the former sailing from Varna.

However, hopes for a peaceful solution would be dashed by the fire-breathing Savov, who was determined to exploit the situation on the Serbian front where an uneasy peace was punctuated by sniping and raids. The general staff had drafted an ambitious plan for a full offensive against the Serbs which aimed both to gain all the disputed Macedonian territory claimed by Sofia (for details see below) and to wreck the Serbian Army. Realising that he would never persuade the government to accept this plan, Savov became mesmerised by the concept of a 'limited' offensive to regain the disputed Macedonian territory east of the Vardar.

Following the decision to accept Russian arbitration, Savov pressed Tsar Ferdinand for authority to launch this 'limited' offensive which, he claimed, would also restore army morale. Whether or not he mentioned that he intended to take Salonika if this land-grab succeeded is uncertain. Undoubtedly, the proposals revealed Savov's naively blinkered attitude which ignored the diplomatic and strategic repercussions. The fact that Ferdinand approved them on 28 June, apparently without consulting the government, confirms the old adage that 'fools seldom differ'.

The following afternoon, Savov informed his army commanders of the Tsar's decision and ordered Kovachev's 4th and Ivanov's 2nd Armies to strike without a formal declaration of war. The objectives were to raise the troops' morale, to make the enemy more 'conciliatory' and to ensure that Russian arbitration provided a 'favourable' solution which the Great Powers would confirm in a new peace agreement. Savov's exultant mood was expressed in a new burst of optimism:

> Salonika will be captured within nine hours and Belgrade within five days. The Greeks are an army of peddlers and traders and the Serbs were soundly defeated back in 1885.[2]

Yet the decision displayed an incredible diplomatic naivety and ignored numerous diplomatic gestures indicative of Bulgaria's isolation. One included the ominous appointment by St Petersburg of Rumania's King Carol as an honorary marshal in the Imperial Russian Army to show disapproval for Bulgarian policy. To 'strengthen' their hand, Savov and Ferdinand decided to delay Danev's departure from Varna and cut the railway line.[3]

As Hall comments with commendable understatement, the Bulgarian idea of fighting to improve a negotiating position was, at best, ill-advised, for it allowed their enemies to exploit their bungling on the battlefield and at the negotiating table. If Sofia had been willing to abandon claims to Macedonia, it would have retained a substantially expanded nation, including eastern Thrace and the Aegean coast from the Struma to the Gallipoli Peninsula, and would have remained in a position to threaten Constantinople. It would have been the dominant military power in the region.[4]

Yet even its leaders recognised that the Bulgarian Army had not recovered from its victories in Thrace.[5] Ottoman booty had replaced most of the matériel losses and allowed both the Cavalry Division and Macedonian-Thracian Legion to receive Quick Firers, while heavy ordnance strengthened the defences of fortresses. But ammunition stocks were still low following the prodigious expenditure of the previous months. There also remained shortages of war matériel, and even after the army expanded, it had only 378,998 rifles, compared with 343,428 at the outbreak of the first conflict.

Manpower was the crucial problem, not only because of the scale of losses during the First Balkan War but also because they had an adverse effect upon its capability. Inevitably, the losses had included a disproportionate number of junior officers and non-commissioned officers, the army's glue, which left it with only half the numbers it needed—7,900 against an establishment of 15,500. Their replacements were of a lower quality, which affected army morale that had already been eroded by months of inaction. The newly conquered territory provided only 60,000 men aged 20–26, but these were little more than untrained cannon-fodder, so army strength remained at 500,500. Even with the new drafts, Bulgaria could deploy only 360,000 men, compared with 376,300 in October 1912.[6]

Once the Treaty of London was signed in May, Sofia gambled upon the neutrality of Rumania and the Ottoman Empire to transfer most of its troops in Thrace to the west. Kutinchev's 1st Army and Dimitriev's 3rd Army were withdrawn from the Catalca Line and moved to north-west Bulgaria: Kutinchev moved into the line from Vidin to Berkovitsa supported by the Cavalry Division on his right, while Dimitriev was on his left and shielded Sofia. Dimitriev provided a division for General Stefan Toshev's newly organised 5th Army as it assembled around Kyustendil and received another two formations to bring the total forces in the new front's northern sector to 114 battalions and eighty-one batteries. South of them was Kovachev's 4th Army, which had arrived from the Gallipoli Peninsula to face the Serbs and held a bow-shaped position centred on Stip along the east bank of the River Sletovska, with 100 battalions and sixty-three batteries. Ivanov's 2nd Army faced the Greeks along a line from Kavala on the Aegean Sea to Lake Dojran, holding this with sixty-two battalions and forty-four batteries.

There were no troops on the Rumanian frontier, while the frontier with the Ottoman Empire was anchored by the fortresses at Shumen and Edirne and held by the Eastern Thrace Occupation Army under Major-General Stoyu Bradistilov, with eight battalions and three batteries. Major-General Valko Velchev, Military Governor of Thrace, had five battalions, mostly around Edirne. Sofia's reserve consisted solely of the sixteen battalions and six batteries of the 6th 'Bdinska' Division, with 27,100 men and thirty-six guns. The Bulgarians had the dual advantages of unitary command and internal lines of communication, which allowed them to integrate planning, to retain the initiative and to defeat their enemies in detail.

Serbia too had suffered badly in the war, and out of a total army of 348,000 would put only 261,000 men and 230 guns in the field, compared with 319,000 nine months earlier. Belgrade ordered Putnik to make no overtly aggressive moves, and this fed Savov's belief in an easy victory because the Serbs remained passive when the Bulgarians openly assembled opposite them. Putnik faced complex strategic demands, for he had to hold the existing border with Bulgaria as well as the disputed Macedonian territory and simultaneously conduct a counter-insurgency campaign against the Albanians. He realised that he must surrender the strategic initiative to the Bulgarians, but he was also mindful of the aphorism 'he who tries to hold everything holds nothing'. He gambled and left the defence of the Bulgarian border largely to Ban III units, and in response to the government's concerns he gave priority to the defence of the newly acquired Macedonian territory.

Colonel Vukoman Arachich commanded the weak Timok Army, which had thirty-one battalions and twelve batteries (40,000 men) to hold the line from the confluence of the Danube and Timok to Sveti Nikole, while on his right was Stepanovic's 2nd Army with thirty-six battalions and twenty-six batteries (46,000 men). Their mission was to defend the original Serbo-Bulgarian border, while the occupied territories in Macedonia were held by Aleksandar's 1st Army north-east of Skopje, with sixty battalions and thirty-eight batteries (105,000 men and 153 guns), and Jankovic's 3rd Army around Veles, with forty-six battalions and twenty-four batteries (70,000 men, and ninety-six guns). Another forty-one battalions and five batteries, mostly second- or third-line units, with 75,000 men, conducted counter-insurgency operations against the Albanians which deprived Putnik of a potential strategic reserve. Although Montenegrin King Nikola had no quarrel with the Bulgarians, he decided as a goodwill gesture to his Serbian neighbours to send Vukotic with the 12,800-man, four-brigade Dechanski Division which was attached to Jankovic.

In Putnik's eyes, Greece was the key to a successful strategic-level defence. Pasic asked him whether or not war with Bulgaria could be won either by Serbia alone or acting in concert with Greece. He responded that with the former the outcome was uncertain, but with the latter victory was certain.[7] He was anxious to collaborate with his allies, although the military elements of the alliance agreement were confined to generalities, but Athens proved less accommodating. When he realised a Bulgarian attack was imminent he asked the Greeks to assemble three divisions around Gevgelija, on the boundary of the two armies, ready to strike the flank of a Bulgarian offensive from Strumica and Bregalnica. However, Athens was more concerned with holding Salonika, and refused.[8]

The Greeks, who were also recovering from the First Balkan War, had made their own preparations. They re-formed the paramilitary volunteer scout battalions on 6 June, and these provided 'absolutely reliable information' of an imminent attack upon Salonika.[9] At the beginning of the year the city was shielded by only three divisions (I, V and VII) but from March, reinforcements from Epirus sailed into Salonika: VI Division in late March, IV Division a fortnight later, II Division in mid-April, III Division in early May and VIII Division in early July. Within the theatre the Greeks formed X Division in March and re-formed the Cavalry Brigade in late April, while eight independent battalions were created, five going to IV and

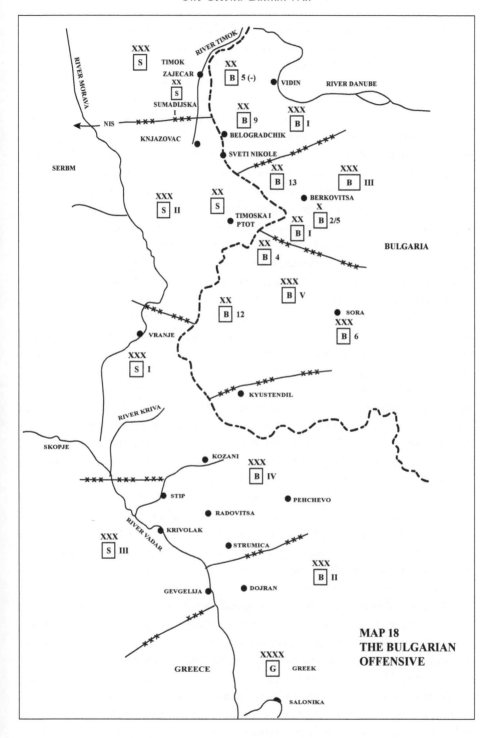

MAP 18
THE BULGARIAN
OFFENSIVE

X Divisions and the remainder to Fortress Thessalonica created on 14 June.

As the heart of Greek strategy, Salonika was now shielded by eighty-two battalions and forty-two batteries of Constantine's 109,000-man Macedonia Army. It was organised into eight divisions and a cavalry brigade supported by a divisional-size garrison formed on 1 June at Salonika, but this was an unwieldy force for one man to control and *ad hoc* command arrangements needed to be implemented. Another 24,900 men (seventeen battalions and three batteries) remained in the Army of Epirus, now under Constantine's former chief-of-staff Danglis, to secure Greek territorial claims, with nineteen battalions and three batteries.

The Bulgarians originally planned to strike their former allies with all five armies in a strategy to shield their capital, which was only 55 km away from the border with Serbia. The recent Greek advances had brought their forces 120 km south-west of the capital, but its defence was aided by the mountainous terrain of eastern Macedonia, eastern Serbia and western Bulgaria. This confined any would-be aggressor to poor roads over the passes and along river valleys, although these were not insurmountable obstacles. There was therefore a very real prospect that the Bulgarians might have to fight in the streets of their own capital.

The Bulgarian general staff's ambitious plan had involved an advance by the 1st and 3rd Armies to the Nis–Morava line in order to penetrate the south Morava valley, while the 4th and 5th Armies enveloped the main Serbian forces in eastern Macedonia through an advance westward from the Kriva Palanka–Bregalnica–Stip line. However, this scheme would stretch the Bulgarian Army over a 500-km front of mountainous terrain. Given the Serbian Army's passive response, Savov decided on 28 June to reduce the original plan to a brief land-grab attack by Kovachev's 4th and Ivanov's 2nd Armies in Macedonia against the Serbs and Greeks respectively. Kovachev would secure the disputed Macedonian territory east of the Vardar, with his right covered by Toshev's 5th Army. The 4th Army would strike across the River Sletovska from Stip, advance on Skopje, pin down the Serbian 1st Army and possibly help to envelop the Serbian 3rd Army. Meanwhile, Ivanov would strike into southern Macedonia towards Gevgelija, which linked the Serbian right with the Greeks, and Salonika. If Kovachev was successful then Ivanov would be reinforced by two or three brigades and would then take Salonika.

The Allies, already confident of Rumanian intervention during the conflict, in their Salonika military agreement of 1 June had envisaged three scenarios. If Bulgaria focused upon either Serbia or Greece then the other would come to their aid, but if Bulgaria declared war on both the allies they would quickly launch a combined offensive along the whole front. The Serbs were aware of Bulgarian concentrations along their mutual border and recognised them as omens of an offensive. Belgrade put its forces on alert from 8 June and ordered them to contain any attack until it ran out of momentum, when the Serbian offensive would then begin. The Serbian troops were also specifically warned to alert for Bulgarian night attacks. Yet war still did not seem inevitable, and on the morning of 29 June, Greek and Serbian military headquarters apparently believed that St Petersburg's forthcoming arbitration would avert conflict.[10]

The stunning news of the Bulgarian attack that night was given to Danev while he was still on the train to Varna. He hastily returned to Sofia, and on the morning of 30 June, looking pale and confused, he summoned the Cabinet to inform them that their army had provoked a border conflict. The Cabinet was understandably stunned, but still did

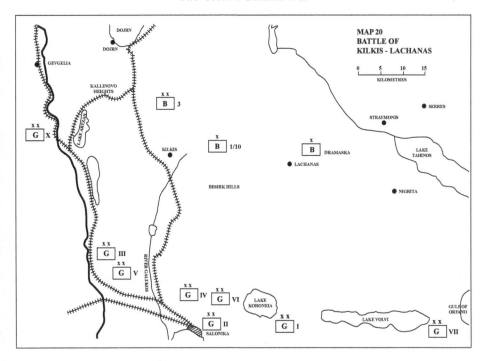

MAP 20
BATTLE OF
KILKIS - LACHANAS

not recognise the scale of the army's duplicity or anticipate that it would lead to all-out war. As the Serbs and Greeks publicly presented themselves as the victims of Bulgarian aggression, Danev made frantic efforts to stop operations and sent desperate messages to Athens and Belgrade of his country's peaceful intentions.

On 1 July, he ordered Savov to end the offensive but, when the general obeyed, Ferdinand countermanded the order and demanded that his troops continue their attack. When Savov still opted to obey the government's orders, partly because of the offensive's obvious failure, Ferdinand dismissed him on 3 July. He just beat the government to the punch, for the politicians were incensed that Savov had failed to secure their authority for the army's actions. The government desperately demanded that the troops should return to their original positions and tried to convince its former allies that there had been a mistake. Understandably, neither trusted Sofia, and on 5/6 July they declared war on Bulgaria. Savov was replaced by the 3rd Army commander the Russophile General Dimitriev (who was replaced at the 3rd Army by Lieutenant General Racho Petrov) as a sign to St Petersburg that Sofia still hoped for Russian diplomatic intervention. But there were no Slavic fraternal feelings from the east as the ferocious war St Petersburg had feared now broke out.

Serbian Front

Kovachev's 4th Army struck on schedule across the Sletovska and Bregalnica along the boundary of the Serbian 1st and 3rd Armies.[11] Aleksandar guarded the approaches to Ovce

Polje and held the line between Kriva Lanka and the confluence of the Sletovska and the Bregalnica. The Sletovska front was held by Nedic's Moravaska II and Sumadijska I under Colonel Bozhidar Terzich, the latter supported by Prince Arsen's Cavalry Division some 5 km behind it. To the south, Jankovic held a salient that extended south to Gevgelija, the town garrisoned by two Ban III battalions. The Bulgarians had a bridgehead at the confluence of the rivers facing Drinska I, now under Colonel Stevan Hatzich, while Milutinovic's Timoska II held the right along the River Lakavitsa, another tributary of the Bregalnica. In reserve, to cover Veles, was Gojkovic's Moravska I.

Kovachev had Major-General Nikola Genev's Macedonian-Thracian Legion on his right facing Nedic and the 2nd Brigade/4th Division opposite Sumadijska I. The main blow would be launched from around Stip against Hatzich's Drinska I by Todorov's 7th 'Rilska' Division supported by Major-General Dimitar Kirkov's 8th 'Tundzhavska' Division, while his left was covered by Colonel Dimitar Geshev's 2nd 'Trakiyska' Infantry Division reinforced by 1st Brigade/3rd Division. Surprise and weight of numbers gave the Bulgarians the initiative, and they slowly pushed Hatzich back some 5 km. But threats to his flank were contained by the arrival of Gojkovic's Moravska I, which left Jankovic's line intact although badly dented. Milutinovic's Timoska II also repulsed attacks, but Jankovic was worried about the viability of the whole line north of the Bregalnica and sought Putnik's permission to withdraw to better positions.

The Serbian leadership in Belgrade pondered events during the afternoon of 30 June. Putnik, who had learned earlier in the day that the enemy was advancing upon Gevgelija (which fell on the night of 29/30 June), again urged Constantine to send three divisions to maintain contact with the Serbs. It was only during the conference that Putnik discovered that the Bulgarians had also attacked the Greeks, and he reluctantly concluded that his men would have to hold on until a Greek success relieved pressure.

Most of the conference participants agreed with Jankovic about a withdrawal north of the Bregalnica, but a minority, led by Putnik's deputy General Zivojin Misic, insisted that the line be held. The absence of any strategic reserve was a major handicap, and Putnik initially considered using part of Aleksandar's army to reinforce Jankovic but recognised this would take too long. Instead he ordered Aleksandar's right, together with Timoska II, to attack towards Kozani in order to isolate the Bulgarians, while his left remained on the defensive. Jankovic was ordered to stop the enemy advance with counter-attacks which were also to regain lost ground and to stop the enemy advance. To the north, Aleksandar had a better day as his men held their positions supported by fierce artillery fire, and potentially he was well placed for a counter-offensive, although the Macedonian-Thracian Legion pushed Moravaska II off the important 1775-metre Retke-Boukve.

By now the Bulgarian offensive had descended into farce as Danev and Ferdinand scuffled for control of the army. As they did so, Bulgarian officers came forward into the Serb lines under flags of truce, usually claiming that the offensive was 'due to a fatal misunderstanding and that it would be necessary to stop shedding fraternal blood'. Similar claims were made by Bulgarian negotiators who visited both the Serbian and Greek headquarters in an attempt to seek a truce, but they were received with scepticism. The

Greeks and Serbs claimed that they were not authorised to accept an armistice because Bulgaria had made no formal declaration of war, and they fought on with growing success. The confusion within the Bulgarian high command was demonstrated on Kovachev's right, where Toshev sought permission on 30 June to stage his own attack but was initially denied. The attack was approved the following day but had barely begun when he was ordered to halt, thereby dashing all hopes of relieving the pressure on the 4th Army.

The Serbian counter-offensive proved successful, Jankovic's left first holding the enemy before joining Aleksandar to drive the Bulgarians across the Sletovska. This was despite the poor co-ordination of 1st Army operations, whose staff appeared to have learned nothing from Kumanovo. During the day Serbian artillery caught the Bulgarians either in the open or in shallow trenches and foxholes, inflicting such heavy losses that Genev and Todorov's divisions were incapable of offensive operations and were poorly placed for defensive ones. The only setback was on Jankovic's right where Geshev's 'Trakiyska' Division managed to get around the flank of Timoska II to isolate it from the rest of the 3rd Army. The Serbs here were forced to withdraw 2 km to positions anchored on Seoba and the 228-metre Serta hill closer to the Vardar.

Encouraged by Aleksandar's success, at noon on 1 July Putnik ordered him to continue his advance upon Kozani. Meanwhile, Kovachev, whose centre had failed, decided to exploit the success of his left and drive Milutinovic's Timoska II across the Vardar. He would then transfer regiments from his left to his right to begin a new advance, but this would take a day and he was running out of time. Milutinovic's men stubbornly contested every centimetre of ground, but by 4 July they were on the banks of the Vardar at Pepeliste and had suffered 3,510 casualties, which doubled when cholera broke out. Jankovic was especially concerned about this threat, and he appears to have infected Putnik with his fears. The pressure eased only when the Greeks took Dojran on the evening of 5 July and forced the Bulgarians to withdraw to Strumica.

While the Bulgarians put pressure upon the Serbian left, the Serbs were pushing back the Bulgarian right, Nedic retaking Retke-Boukve on the evening of 4 July. The advance upon Kozani threatened Kovachev's wrecked forces with encirclement, and he began a rapid retreat up the Bregalnica valley. To cover him, Toshev launched an offensive with some success south-west of Kyustendil against Aleksandar's left (Dunavska I and II), but the 5th Army was compromised by Kovachev's retreat. On 6 July, Toshev fell back to the old Bulgarian border to defend both Kyustendil and the south-western approaches to Sofia.

The Bulgarians abandoned Kozani on the night of 6/7 July, but Aleksandar and his men were too exhausted to maintain pressure and the enemy broke contact. The Serbs had inflicted 25,000 casualties and suffered 16,600, including 3,000 dead, but they had captured thirty-two guns including a dozen old Krupp pieces.[12] The scale of losses led 2nd Serbian Army commander Stepanovic to order his subordinates to conserve their precious manpower and use it only for the most important operations. It was a measure of the physical and moral exhaustion on both sides that there were informal truces between some troops without their officers' approval.

Putnik failed to exploit a nominal opportunity to isolate Kovachev or the Bulgarian 2nd Army as it retreated up the Struma. He remained more concerned with the fate of

Milutinovic's troops and exploited Aleksandar's contracting lines to withdraw Terzich's Sumadijska I and place it on Jankovic's right. Although these measures were later condemned as 'inept directives and half-measures' which allowed Kovachev to escape, the reality was that transport problems meant that the Serbian forces could never move fast enough to isolate the retreating enemy.[13] Putnik was also concerned about the Bulgarian offensive in the north which had taken Knjazevac, and by the continued Bulgarian presence at Stip. He ordered Jankovic to take the town, but the 3rd Army commander paused and demanded reinforcements.

By the time they arrived and Stip had fallen, Kovachev had recovered sufficiently by 11 July to establish a new defensive position straddling the former Bulgarian-Ottoman border in the Osogovska Mountains between Kyustendil and Tsarevo Selo. Two days later, Savov established an army group headquarters to co-ordinate 4th and 5th Army operations in the south-west. The key was to hold Tsarevo Selo which barred the way up a broad valley through the mountains, and the Bulgarian line was anchored just south of the town on the 1,551-metre Mount Golak. Aleksandar advanced north of the Bregalnica and, led by Nedic, attempted a breakthrough on 14/15 July but was stopped.

In heavy rain Vukotic's Montenegrin division struck on 18 July, but the defenders stubbornly held their positions and their artillery proved extremely effective in blasting the attackers, who lost any gains to prompt counter-attacks with the bayonet. Before these counter-attacks the defenders would entice the enemy close to their positions by deliberately reducing their fire, although this exposed them to Serbian hand grenades. South of the Bregalnica, Jankovic's advance was led by Moravaska I but failed to storm Mount Golak on 20/22 July, and by the armistice the Serbian Army had been halted at a cost of 7,300 casualties, including 700 dead.[14]

Bulgarian morale rose because the men felt that they were protecting their homes from foreign invaders. By thwarting the Serbs, Savov secured the rear of the hard-pressed Bulgarian 2nd Army and bought time for the transfer of the 1st Army to the Greek front. The assault on the new Bulgarian line cost the Serbs another 24,000 casualties, including 2,600 dead, and the Montenegrins nearly 680. Bulgarian casualty figures are unknown but were probably less, and they believed that they had prevented a Serbian invasion from the south, although this was never Putnik's intention.

Bulgarian Northern Offensive

While the fighting raged in Macedonia, to the north Kutinchev's 1st Army and Dimitriev's 3rd Army cooled their heels in north-western Bulgaria with seventy-six battalions and forty-nine batteries (100,600 men and 228 guns), but their defensive role was changed radically on 4 July.[15] With the collapse of the southern front an active defence was urgently required, and Kutinchev's 1st Army (56,700 men and 108 guns) was now to strike the Timok Army (holding the River Timok sector) and advance upon Knjazevac. Once it had taken the town it was to be divided, with part driving north to Zajecar and the other south towards the rail and road centre of Pirot. Meanwhile, the 3rd Army (43,900 men and 120 guns) would also attack towards Pirot in the hope that the two armies would envelop the 2nd Serbian Army around Nis. Arachich's Timok Army had only Marinovic's Sumadijska II Division, together with a divisional-strength garrison at Zajecar, a total of 40,000 men and sixty-eight guns, while Stepanovic's 2nd Army had responsibility for the defences around Pirot, held by the reinforced Timoska I Division under Colonel Vladimir Kondich.

Kutinchev exploited his numerical superiority to push back Arachich, and after heavy fighting that cost 1,100 casualties he took Knjazevac on 7 July. But the following day the deteriorating situation elsewhere on the front, together with the Rumanian invasion from the north, brought the order for him to retreat to the frontier. There was a brief lull which saw Kutinchev and his staff withdrawn on 17 July and sent to the southern front, leaving the 26,000-strong 9th 'Plevenska' Division as the core of resistance on the northern flank.

The sudden retreat shortened the Bulgarian lines of communication, eased the flow of supplies and should have strengthened the defenders, but it also completed the demoralisation of the 'Plevenska' Division. The 2nd Brigade mutinied and was then enveloped at the town of Ferdinand by the Rumanians, to whom it surrendered on 18 July. The rest of the division managed to reach Sofia to form Samokov Detachment, which later fought in the Battle of Kresna Gorge. The remainder of the army tried to hold the mountain passes, but Stepanovic's 2nd Army were still able to break through and take Belogradchik on 18 July, and there it met the Rumanian 1st Army on its march to Sofia.

Stepanovic then advanced into north-western Bulgaria, his progress eased by the transfer of Bulgarian troops to Macedonia, and with the capture of Rakovitsa the Serbs isolated the fortified Danube town of Vidin. Its defences had eighty-five obsolete guns augmented by seven Gatlings, but only eight guns were less than forty years old and they had little ammunition. The garrison under General Krastyu Marinov consisted of 1,200 fortress troops in seven rifle companies augmented by 4,500 militia, police and volunteers. Given the task of taking the defences, Arachich committed up to sixteen battalions with fifty-four guns, only twenty-four of which were Quick Firers. He began to bombard the town from 29 July, but a half-hearted infantry assault was driven off and an armistice came into effect two days later before the attack could be renewed.

To the south there was a last-minute command change in the 3rd Army, Dimitriev being promoted to Deputy Commander-in-Chief on 3 July and replaced by General Racho Petrov. Petrov's mission was to pin down as many of the enemy as possible, and based upon plans drawn up by Dimitriev he split his forces into two. The Right Group (13th Infantry Division and 1st Brigade/1st Division) was to strike Pirot, while the Left Group (or Tran Detachment), with the 2nd Brigade/1st Division, 2nd Brigade/5th Division, the Cavalry Division and 5th Division's 46th Infantry, was to advance upon Vranje. Once again, the Bulgarian leadership had divided its advance, with the gap covered by a single battalion battlegroup which included two batteries.

On 7 July, the Right Group set off and in six days pushed the Serbs back into their defences around Pirot and then took positions in the surrounding heights. But on that day, with the Rumanian advance threatening the weakened 1st Army, Sofia hastily ordered a withdrawal eastward which made the attack upon Pirot redundant. Nevertheless, Petrov's troops maintained the pressure on Pirot until 23 July before withdrawing. They began to dig in to protect the north-western approaches to Sofia, barely 50 km away, and held these lines unchallenged until the end of the war.

The Left Group had been the first to advance, on 5 July, but bad weather, including fog, as well as poor roads, slowed progress while Stepanovic's troops resisted fiercely. The same day, the 5th 'Dunavska' Division commander, Hristov, assumed command of operations around Pirot. He was ordered to cut communications between Nis and Vranje, but several days of fighting left his men poised to take the town despite being exhausted. To meet the threat an alarmed Putnik withdrew troops from opposite the 4th Bulgarian Army, their arrival easing the pressure on Pirot but ruining any chance of enveloping the retreating Bulgarian forces. In the event, the move was unnecessary because the Rumanian invasion forced the Bulgarians back to their own borders from which they fiercely resisted all Serbian advances.

Greek Front

Despite Savov's bombastic and disparaging claims, Salonika could not be taken from the despised Greeks. Ivanov's 2nd Army had only 75,075 men and 175 guns but faced a numerically superior force of 109,000 men and 176 guns.[16] Qualitatively, he was also outclassed, for more than a quarter of his men (20,000) were, at best, semi-trained new recruits, while their only supply line was the coastal railway running through Serres to their main supply base at Dojran.

Worse still, Savov could not deploy his whole army: the 11th Infantry Division had to hold the coast from Kavala almost to the Struma, while Colonel Ivanov's Serska Brigade garrisoned Serres. Facing Salonika were Major-General Ivan Sarafov's 3rd 'Balkanska' Division which anchored the army right from Dojran to Kilkis, with the 1st Brigade/10th Division (Colonel Petev) on the 663-metre summit at Lahanas. The Dramska Brigade (Colonel Petrov) held the western bank of the Struma and Lake Tahinos, to give the 2nd Army only thirty-one battalions with just under 41,400 men and eighty-nine guns to face a numerically superior Greek force.

Since October, Ivanov had strengthened his positions in the 300- to 760-metre Beshik Hills which run north-west to south-east of Salonika. Anchored on the villages of Kilkis and Lahanas, these defences were naturally strong and provided excellent observation of the rolling, open valleys. Ivanov planned to strengthen this position and await enemy attacks and reinforcements until the Greeks were exhausted, and then assault Salonika. His attacks on 30 June were upon the extremities of the front, to take Gevgelija, which cut the main railway down the Vardar, and extend his hold along the coast. In the centre the Bulgarians confined themselves to pushing in the Greek outposts and then awaited Constantine's response.

King Constantine sailed into Salonika in the royal yacht *Amphitrite* on 30 June, and after a briefing he completed his preparations. His X Division (Colonel Leonidas Paraskevopoulos) was deployed on the western bank of the Vardar some 20 km south-west of Dojran, while the rest of his regiments held an 80-km line between the river and the Gulf of Orfanou, the defence eased by Lake Koroneia and Lake Volvi which reduced the actual line by 30 km.[17] Between the rivers Vardar and Gallikos were III Division (Damianos) and V Division (Gennades), while IV Division (Moschopoulos) and VI Division (Delagrammatikas) held the line from the Gallikos to Lake Koroneia. Between the two lakes was I Division (Manousogiannakis), while the last part of the main line of resistance, between Lake Volvi and the Gulf, was VII Division (Colonel Napoleon Sotiles). In reserve at Salonika was II Division (Kallares), while Lieutenant Colonel Konstantinos Zacharakopoulos's Cavalry Brigade was behind III and V Divisions.

Athens' response to the Bulgarian provocation was surprisingly conciliatory. Venizelos was willing to accept an apology, but then the Bulgarians began to claim that it was their former allies who had provoked the new conflict. Worse still, Danev, still out of touch with the situation, failed to apologise for the Bulgarian attack. On the morning of 1 July, the Greek Cabinet considered Constantine's request for authority either to recapture lost ground or to conduct a counter-offensive. Having pondered the matter for only three hours, they informed the monarch that he was authorised to conduct a full counter-offensive. The Bulgarian military presence in Salonika was a problem and, since April, Constantine had assigned II Division the task of solving it. However, fearing this would wreck the port, the Cabinet ordered him only to contain the Bulgarians.

The following morning, Constantine ordered his centre to scale the heights while his flanks probed forward. In the centre Manousogiannakis and Delagrammatikas were to advance towards Lahanas; Damianos, Gennades and Moschopoulos would strike towards Kilkis; Kallares would support either of these two main thrusts. On the flanks, Paraskevopoulos, with the cavalry, was to take the Kallinovo heights north of Lake Artzan ready to strike towards Dojran. Sotiles was to advance towards Nigrita, and could, at his own discretion, continue on to Strymoniko to take the bridge over the Struma.

Although numerically superior, the Greeks faced a formidable task against strong defences on 2 July, and some troops had to march 30 km to reach them. The IV and V Divisions, supported by II Division and 100 guns, advanced upon Kilkis, which was held by a brigade (eight battalions) of the 'Balkanska' Division, while VI and I Divisions advanced upon Lahanas. The defenders ranged their artillery, only two-thirds of which were Quick Firers, but the Greek infantry dashed between gaps in the limited cover and forced the enemy gunners to cease fire in order to adjust their range. Once the infantry reached cover, Greek field guns came up and provided new covering fire until the regiments could move forward again. In some places the cover was inadequate and enemy guns inflicted heavy casualties, but the attackers steadily advanced northwards. They eventually reached the main line of resistance where they took six guns but their losses were heavy: VI Division suffered 530 casualties, and V Division 1,275.

The following afternoon, VI Division reached Nigrita, which the Bulgarians torched and abandoned, while I Division assaulted the defences around Lahanas, although VI Division was unable to provide support, still being a kilometre away. The attack upon Kilkis failed to penetrate the defences and at best secured jump-off positions, but at great cost. The only good news was the recapture of Gevgelija and the bridge over the Vardar from the other 'Balkanska' Brigade by X Division, but the Cavalry Brigade on its right proved so timid that Constantine reprimanded Zacharakopoulos.

Irritated by the general lack of progress in the Beshik Hills, Constantine demanded that II, III, V and VI Divisions storm Kilkis that night, but because the orders arrived late they had no time to co-ordinate the attack. The only serious effort was by Kallares, who with little artillery support began to outflank the enemy left despite fierce counter-attacks, which inflicted heavy losses but failed to drive him back. This threat sucked in defenders, and during the morning the other Greek divisions began to fight their way into the defences around the village. Despite the arrival of the Serres Brigade, the Greeks began to envelop Kilkis, Damianos in the west and Kallares in the east, and these forced out the Bulgarians during the morning, although the Greeks were too exhausted to pursue them.

Manousogiannakis and Delagrammatikas pulled a regiment each out of the line to support the Kilkis attack, but then had to reorganise when this mission became redundant. After an hour's fighting they stormed Lahanas in mid-afternoon and took sixteen guns as the defenders fled north. The two divisions then pursued the enemy to the heights overlooking the Struma and made camp. To the east, Sotiles displayed a lamentable want of initiative when he crept forward only in mid-morning and made no attempt to isolate the retreating Bulgarians. The battle cost the Greeks more than 8,800 casualties, including ten battalion and regimental commanders, V Division suffering the greatest losses with more than 2,100 casualties. But the victory saw the Greeks take 2,500 prisoners and nineteen guns together with much equipment, and they inflicted 6,970 casualties. It was Bulgaria's worse defeat of the Second Balkan War and would cost the country virtually all of Aegean Macedonia. The only saving grace was Ivanov's success in keeping his army intact.

The Greek Offensive

On the morning of 5 July, as the Greek centre (I, II, IV and VI Divisions) rested, the flanks pushed northwards as X and III Divisions marched towards Dojran. That night the I Division commander Manousogiannakis was made commander of his own Corps Group with I, VI and VII Divisions to pursue the enemy across the Struma.[18]

On 6 July, the Greek left took Dojran, although the Bulgarians exploited the lack of co-ordination between the divisions to inflict 860 casualties (106 dead) upon X Division. During the evening, Manousogiannakis was ordered to destroy the retreating enemy and to seize the Rupel Pass. Meanwhile, Ivanov pulled back his right just he was reinforced by the Bulgarian strategic reserve, Tenev's 6th 'Bdinska' Division, to hold the Dojran–Strumica road together with 2nd Brigade/3rd 'Balkanska' Division. Sarafov's 'Balkanska' 2nd Brigade and 1st Brigade/10th Division were ordered to hold the Rupel Pass, while the 11th Division remained on the coast between the Struma and the Mesta. Manousogiannakis exploited his numerical superiority and took Strumica on 9 July before outflanking the Rupel Pass defences, but the 4th Bulgarian Army escaped. The same day III and X Divisions advanced into the Strumica valley and overcame strong opposition to take the Kosturino Pass, crossing the Struma over the wrecked road and rail bridges on 10 July.

This was also the day that Venizelos informed the army that Rumania would declare war upon Bulgaria the following day and that Sofia was already seeking an armistice with the Greeks and Bulgarians. Simultaneously, Putnik asked the Greeks to advance to the fortified town of Dupnitsa and Constantine was ordered to continue his pursuit. However, Manousogiannakis was deprived of VII Division, which secured the army's right, and was now divided: part was sent towards the Mesta valley, while the remainder was to take Serres and Drama. At noon on 10 July, the latter force crossed the Struma and advanced upon Serres which was in flames, having been fired by the enemy.

To ease command and control of the northern advance, Constantine split Manousogiannakis's command into two, the Left and Right Groups, with the ever-reliable Damianos leading the former which had III and X Divisions; the latter was under the monarch's personal command, with I, II, IV, V and VI Divisions together with the dubious support of the Cavalry Brigade. Damianos was to cover the left flank while Constantine led the remainder up the Struma to Gorna Dzhumaia, and on 15 July he pushed into the upper Bregalnica valley. He was briefly stopped until combined Serbo-Greek pressure forced the Bulgarians to withdraw two days later. On 18 July, the Serbs asked for Damianos's men to threaten Tsarevo Selo from the south to assist their assault on Mount Golak. The autonomous VII Division was now ordered to protect the right of the main advance by an advance north-east towards Kato Nevrekop.

This advance was led by a regimental battlegroup which first took Drama on 14 July, and then Kato Nevrekop itself on 19 July, together with twenty-four guns. To protect the main advance upon Gorna Dzhumaia, VII Division was then ordered on 18 July to continue northwards to Razlog, but Athens now recognised that the expansion of Greek control into eastern Macedonia and western Thrace required more men. On 6 July, it decided to ship Matthaiopoulos's VIII Division (the former Epirus Army) from Epirus to Kavala where it debarked in mid-July and almost immediately had a regiment transferred to VII Division. On 24 July, it began to advance along the coast to take Xanthi two days later and Gumulcine the following day.

With the Bulgarians everywhere in retreat, the Greeks now decided to remove the tiny Bulgarian military presence in Salonika, the III/14th Macedonian. The Salonika-based Bulgarian representative to the Greek general staff, General Hesapchiev, had been given advance warning of his army's plans for an offensive and hastily departed the city on 30 June. Savov recognised that the battalion was exposed, and in April he ordered it to abandon the city and join Ivanov's main force. Unfortunately, the government vetoed the order for fear it would undermine Sofia's claims to the city and the surrounding region. It was a suicide mission for the battalion because there were only 1,250 troops (later augmented by eighty paramilitaries) with 200 rounds of ammunition per man, and they faced not only part of II Division but also some 300 Cretan police.

On 30 June, Kallares demanded that the Bulgarians surrender their weapons and leave the city within an hour. The battalion commander refused, his men fighting gallantly and using bayonets when their ammunition ran out. But the issue was never in doubt, and by the end of 1 July the Bulgarians had suffered some 340 casualties (237 dead), while the

Greek figure was about sixty, including twenty-two dead. For Sofia it was a futile loss of life sacrificed upon the altar of political ambition.

Kresna Pass

Constantine's Group continued its advance up the Struma towards Gorna Dzhumaia, reaching the southern entrance to the Kresna Pass on 21 July, where Ivanov tried to make a stand with 3rd 'Balkanska' Division, the rest of 10th Division bought in from eastern Thrace as well as Dramska and Serska Brigades. He faced I Division on the road, with II Division on its left, while VI Division advanced along the wooded mountain slopes on its right.[19]

It was II Division which unlocked the pass by fighting its way over the heights to the west by 24 July, as I Division, covered by VI Division, advanced up the pass to take the northern entrance. This allowed VII Division on VI Division's right to swing westward from Razlog, which it seized on 19 July as part of a move to take first the Predel Pass and then Simitli. But the following day, 25 July, the Greek advance everywhere encountered fierce resistance and progress was at great cost until, during the afternoon, VII Division sent a regiment up the Predel Pass, which it took during a three-hour battle in heavy rain.

The following morning, this division attacked Simitli, supported by I Division from the south, and after close-quarter fighting the Bulgarians abandoned the village, which the Greeks occupied in the morning. At this point Constantine reorganised his forces for the final push upon Gorna Dzhumaia. He gave Manousogiannakis command of the Right Group (I, II, V, VI and VII Divisions) and paired I and V Divisions under the latter's commander, Gennades. He was ordered east of the Struma to maintain contact with Damianos, while VII Division was ordered to make a night march northwards.

Yet Central Group was over-extended and at the end of a very long supply line reached back to Salonika. The newly won pass ran through a narrow gorge and the rock-strewn road had been partially damaged, while the defenders had also destroyed many bridges. It was difficult to bring forward artillery and the infantry had begun to run short of both ammunition and food, yet Constantine was determined to advance. He contacted the Serbs on 11 July and believed, wrongly, that they would maintain pressure upon the enemy and weaken the defences in front of him.

Damianos on the left had kept pace with the main force from 19 July and pushed down the Bregalnica with III Division on his left and X Division on his right (it took Pehchevo on 19 July) and supported Constantine's IV Division, which was transferred to him on 22 July. With the Serbian 3rd Army held on Mount Golak, Damianos now decided to use III Division to take the mountain while X and IV Divisions advanced upon Tsarevo Selo. The attack began on 23 July, but made little progress against stubborn resistance from 6th 'Bdinska' Divisions supported by 1st Brigade/10th Division. At midday on 24 July, Damianos was forced to pull back the exposed X Division, and while IV Division made some progress, its mountain batteries ran out of ammunition.

Venizelos informed Constantine that both Russia and Austria were putting pressure on both sides to accept an armistice and that Rumania had accepted. He left the decision with the King, who accelerated operations that evening and insisted that the offensive should continue until a peace treaty had been pencilled. Constantine still continued to underestimate his own problems, believing not only that Bulgarian morale was plummeting but also that they were incapable of serious resistance. In fact Bulgarian preparations for a counter-offensive were well advanced, using troops from the Serbian front which were already assembling opposite the Greeks.

The Bulgarian plan may have been driven by Savov's attempt to regain his reputation, his army group being reinforced by the 2nd Army on 27 July. Two days earlier, Kutinchev's 1st Army had arrived from north-west Bulgaria and, after Savov dismissed Ivanov following a dispute, Kutinchev took over the 2nd Army. Success over the Serbs at Tsarevo Selo allowed the 4th Army to transfer Geshev's 'Trakiyska' Division to the south where it joined Tenev's reinforced 'Bdinska' Division. Kutinchev now had numerical superiority, 110 battalions and forty batteries (122,748 men) against eighty-four Greek battalions and thirty-seven batteries, and he decided to envelop the enemy while the 4th Army kept the Serbs at arm's length. Geshev and Tenev would launch the main blow in the west and advance towards Pehchevo-Breznitsa, to prevent a Greek withdrawal to Pehchevo-Strumica. In the centre Sarafov's reinforced 3rd 'Balkanska' Division, together with the Dramska and Serska Brigades, would pin down the enemy. In the east the Samokov and West Rodop Detachments were to retake Razlog, advance through the Predel Pass to Simitli and Krupnik, and then on to the Struma to isolate the Greeks.

Initially unaware of this threat, Constantine renewed his advance northwards on 27 July, making steady progress until he gradually became aware of the enemy concentrations opposite Damianos. Despite this, he ordered Damianos to continue his advance and failed to request a diversionary attack from the Serbian 3rd Army. The following night the Bulgarians launched their counter-offensive and pinned down the centre of the Right Group. The attacks upon the Greek right succeeded during the afternoon and drove out VII Division from Razlog to the Predel Pass, while only the prompt action of Gennades prevented the envelopment of VI Division. The main Bulgarian blow fell upon Damianos, whose III Division was pushed back to Pehchevo and carried with it the exposed X Division. To relieve the pressure on the left, Moschopoulos was given command of II and IV Divisions and ordered to counter-attack.

The Greek Army was now in a salient 24 km long and 40 km wide, and the sudden reversal of fortune led Constantine to claim the situation was critical, for which he blamed the passive Serbs. He telegraphed Venizelos:

My army is physically and morally exhausted. In the light of these conditions I can no longer refuse the armistice or suspension of hostilities. Endeavour to find some way of securing a suspension of hostilities.

The situation, while serious, looked worse on paper than in reality. The rugged terrain was easy to defend, although it was difficult to supply the forward troops, but it also prevented the attackers from co-ordinating their operations. The Bulgarians also had supply problems, especially on their right, after an advance of 15–18 km in three days. On 29 July, Bulgarian pressure upon the flanks increased with the loss of the Predel Pass, but Moschopoulos prepared a riposte. The Serbs reported that their 3rd Army had begun diversionary attacks, although these were easily held by the 4th Army's 'Rilska' Division, and Belgrade may have sought to undermine Greek ambitions on Macedonian territory.

That night, Damianos beat off attacks launched with strong artillery support and on the morning of 30 July Moschopoulos's attack not only pinned down the Bulgarians but also gained some ground despite heavy losses from enemy artillery. In the east VII Division recaptured the Predel Pass with a frontal assault which pushed back the enemy 2.5 km at the cost of nearly 1,330 casualties, including 250 dead. The Greeks had briefly contained the threat, but whether or not they would continue to do so became a moot point, for on 31 July the armistice came into effect after Constantine's ill-judged ambition had cost the Greek Army up to 10,000 casualties. The victory boosted Bulgarian morale but in compensation the Greek offensive claimed to have taken 5,330 prisoners, eighty-four guns and 7,900 rifles, although the Bulgarians later stated that they had lost only seventy-three guns to them.[20]

THE NEUTRALS' OFFENSIVES

The Rumanian Offensive

It was the Rumanians who decided the outcome of the Second Balkan War as Bucharest exploited a unique opportunity to secure southern Dobrogea while Bulgaria was almost totally committed in Macedonia. Rumanian mobilisation began on 5 July, and within ten days 417,700 men with 247 battalions and 180 batteries, including twenty-five heavy, were assembled. Nearly 350,900 would be committed, a force almost as big as the Bulgarian active army ten months earlier.[21] Bucharest declared war on 10 July, and its main thrust would be by II and III Corps under Major-Generals Grigore Crainiceanu and Iarca Alexandru respectively, shielded in the west by Major-General Dumitru Costescu's I Corps. The last would mask the Bulgarian 1st Army while the other corps would slice through northern Bulgaria and allow Major-General Ioan Culcer's V Corps to occupy southern Dobrogea.[22]

Nominally under Crown Prince Ferdinand, the Rumanian Army was actually commanded by the chief-of-staff, Major-General Alexandru Averescu, who came to prominence by brutally crushing a peasant revolt in 1907. As a young man he had studied at a seminary and had then planned to become an engineer before deciding to join the gendarmerie. He served with Rumanian troops during the Russo-Turkish War, although frostbite injuries delayed his entry into the army. His military education was at home as well as in Italy, and he was rapidly promoted to become chief-of-staff in November 1911.[23]

Culcer, with 9th, 10th and 3rd Reserve Divisions augmented by 31st Reserve Brigade, struck from Medgidia and with 72,300 men and 128 guns quickly occupied southern Dobrogea. His cavalry then briefly advanced towards Varna to thwart any anticipated

Bulgarian riposte, and when it became clear that none would be forthcoming, it withdrew to Dobrogea.

For four anxious days the Bulgarians waited to see what would follow, all too aware of the ominous Rumanian build-up across the Danube. On the night of 14/15 July, the dreaded news arrived that the Rumanians were crossing the mighty river: I Corps at Oryakhovo, one end of the ferry service to Bechet; II Corps at Gigen, opposite Corabia; and III Corps at Nikopol; which left only IV Corps to defend Bucharest. The crossings were made over five pontoon bridges thrown across the river by Rumanian engineers in seven hours, allowing their troops to range deep into Bulgaria.

Costescu, supported by General Bogdan's 1st Cavalry Division, was anxious to isolate the 1st Bulgarian Army, unaware that it was being stripped to meet threats from the south. He advanced to the town of Ferdinand which fell on 18 July and allowed Bogdan to achieve the cavalry's sole success. They forced the surrender of the demoralised 'Plevenska' brigade, whose men were disarmed and then allowed to go home. With little opposition, Costescu rapidly approached Sofia and took Vratsa on 20 July, before halting about 12 km from the capital on 23 July while his aeroplanes dropped leaflets on the city. This advance took the Rumanians deep into the rear of the 3rd Bulgarian Army facing the Serbs, who linked up with their new allies at Belogradchik on 25 July to isolate Vidin.

Meanwhile, II Rumanian Corps advanced south-westwards down the River Iskur while III Corps made for Pleven as the 2nd Rumanian Cavalry Division ranged southward and came within 10 km of Plovdiv. Even Major-General Alexandru Lambrino's IV Corps joined the campaign, taking Staro Selo against minimal resistance as the Rumanian operation became less an offensive and more an occupation.[24] Only three fortifications faced the Rumanians: Sofia, with eighty-four guns including forty-four heavy (120–150 mm) and a couple of Gatlings; Shumen, the main fortress in the east of the country some 80 km west of Varna, with seventy-six guns including thirty-six heavy (120–150 mm); and Vidin. But they were reeds too slender to prevent the total occupation of the country. The only obstacle to the Rumanians was 'King Cholera' which scythed their ranks to fell 9,050 men, of whom 1,960 died, there being virtually no deaths to enemy action.[25]

Ottoman Invasion

Constantinople also exploited the Balkan League's internecine warfare to rub salt in Bulgaria's wounds by regaining lost territory and prestige. The anger of many members of the Liberal Union and the CUP over concessions in the Treaty of London led to the assassination of Mahmud Shevket Pasha on 11 June as he drove from the Ministry of War to the Porte. The CUP, led by Cemal Pasha, Talat Pasha and Enver Pasha, used the event to tighten its grip on power and then discovered a Liberal Union conspiracy which led it to drive many of its members into exile. The new Grand Vizier was an Ottoman prince of Egyptian heritage, Mehmet Sait Halim Pasha, who appointed general staff chief Ahmet Izzet Pasha as War Minister on 18 June.

During the spring, the Bulgarians had stripped Thrace of troops for their Macedonian adventure, leaving token forces on the Ottoman front. Bradistilov's Eastern Thrace Occupation Army had a reinforced brigade on the Gallipoli Peninsula, while most of Velchev's troops were in Edirne, although a single cavalry regiment covered the Enez–Midye Line. With the outbreak of the Second Balkan War on 30 June, the Ottoman government quickly recognised that it too had a unique opportunity, and Ahmet Izzet began to plan an advance west of the Enez–Midye Line by the Catalca and Gallipoli armies.

On the evening of 11 July, Ahmet Izzet went to the Catalca Army headquarters, which became his field headquarters, and informed the local Bulgarian commander that he intended a peaceful advance up to the Enez–Midye Line. The Ottoman armies received their orders the following day just as Constantinople declared war.[26] They had overwhelming numerical superiority: Catalca Army (I, II, III, IV Provisional and X Corps) had twenty divisions, while Brigadier General Fahri's Gallipoli Army (I Provisional, II Provisional and III Provisional Corps) had eight, a total of 250,000 battle-hardened troops.

Their advance began cautiously on 13 July but faced no opposition, and within four days the Ottoman troops were only 3 km from the Enez–Midye Line as the Bulgarians fell back to Edirne. Ahmet Izzet remained in constant communication with Constantinople in order to react to any diplomatic development, augmenting his telegraph and telephone lines with a back-up fleet of motor-cycle couriers. Now aware that there was no substantial Bulgarian force in front of him, on 18 July he attended a cabinet meeting convened by Halim Pasha to discuss the situation. A further advance to Edirne was authorised the next day.

The advance was scheduled for 22 July, but on the afternoon of the 20th one of the Catalca Army's cavalry brigades learned that Bulgarian infantry were retreating and advanced 6 km beyond the Enez–Midye Line to take Luleburgaz railway station. The following day, the other cavalry brigade also crossed the line on its own initiative as Enver Pasha contacted Velchev, whose Edirne garrison had only 4,000 troops who were interested only in saving their skins. Enver swiftly made arrangements to occupy the city, and on the morning of 22 July the main Ottoman force crossed the Enez–Midye Line as Enver learned that his cavalry patrols were just entering Edirne. He rushed forward to accept the city's surrender, while at almost the same moment Kirkkilisse was also recaptured. The Bulgarian occupation of Edirne had lasted 118 days following a siege of 147 days, and now all the Bulgarian sacrifices vanished on a summer's day. Nine months earlier, the Bulgarians had been almost at Constantinople's gates but now Ottoman forces were invading their territory.[27]

The Ottoman forces continued to advance westwards, crossing the original Bulgarian frontier on 25 July. The Bulgarians hastily sent infantry eastwards and resistance to the Turks increased, but on 2 August Izzet Pasha halted his advance, disbanded the Gallipoli Army and assigned Edirne's defence to one of its corps. The Turks had taken fifty-two guns and two machine guns but, like the Rumanians, suffered scant loss to enemy fire, although here too cholera claimed another 4,000 victims. Immediately after Edirne fell in March 1913, the German Embassy was asked to send an experienced German officer to supervise the construction of fortifications around Constantinople. The clear need for military reform saw the dispatch by the end of the year of a mission under General Otto Liman von Sanders.[28]

The Diplomatic Resolution

With his foreign policy in tatters due to Ferdinand and Savov, and with neither political nor military action from Russia, Danev was helpless.[29] On 10 July, his government proposed a meeting in St Petersburg to discuss an armistice, but Pasic was lukewarm to the idea and it was opposed by Venizelos. The snub led to the resignation of Danev and his government on 13 July and it was replaced four days later by a government headed by the more pragmatic Russophobe Vasil Radoslavov. He recognised that the defensive successes, notably at Kresna Pass, would not alter the strategic situation because the Rumanians and Ottomans were now in Bulgaria, and actually feared a Bulgarian victory in the Kresna Pass because it might stiffen Serbian, Greek and Rumanian resolve, although it did provide an opportunity to salvage something from the wreck in south-east Macedonia. When Pasic invited him on 19 July to send a delegation to Nis for talks about an end to hostilities he accepted with alacrity.

The Serbs and Greeks were now engaged on a Macedonia land-grab and did not wish to create any obstacles. In the absence of progress at the conference table, Ferdinand on 22 July successfully appealed to King Carol, through the Italian ambassador to Bucharest, to halt the Rumanian advance on Sofia. This would be the first move in the new Bulgarian government's turn towards the Triple Alliance, with which it would grow closer during the next few years.

The Great Powers now intervened to end the war by putting pressure upon both Serbia and Rumania, and even Austria's 'hawks' surprisingly decided not to intervene during the second conflict.[30] The combatants agreed to a Rumanian proposal that peace talks be held in Bucharest, to which all the delegations at Nis departed on 24 July. They reassembled six days later, the Greeks led by Venizelos, the Serbs by Pasic and the Montenegrins by Prime Minister Vukotic. The hosts were headed by Titu Maiorescu, while Bulgaria's new finance minister Dimitur Tonchev led his country's delegation. There was no Ottoman presence, for the Rumanians claimed that the matters under discussion affected only themselves and the former Balkan League. This decision inconvenienced only the Bulgarians, who were now the sole combatants with the Ottoman Empire.

Under pressure from the Great Powers, the war-weary delegates were quick to agree an armistice, which came into effect the following day. They then began to address weightier matters of territory. Tonchev led the Bulgarian delegation because Radoslavov recognised that he was no diplomat and also did not wish to be personally associated with the inevitable surrender of territory. Tonchev's hopes of dividing his enemies were dashed, for they maintained a surprisingly united front which forced him to settle the issues piecemeal. He started with the Rumanians and confirmed a decision made by Sofia on 19 July to surrender all of south Dobrogea, and in response Bucharest moderated its allies' claims.

The sticking point in the talks with Serbia and Greece was, of course, Macedonia. Bulgaria desired a frontier along the River Vardar, while Serbia sought Macedonia up to the Struma valley, or almost all the territory claimed by Bulgaria. Belgrade came under pressure to moderate its demands from Russia, which was seeking to regain lost political ground, and Austria, which wished as usual to strengthen its influence. The Serbians insisted that they would hold territory up to the Vardar valley, but Pacic did concede the town of Stip 'in honour of General Fichev', a member of the Bulgarian delegation.

There was bad news from the Greeks. Venizelos, who at the end of June had offered Bulgaria the small port of Kavala, as well as Serres and Drama, now told Fichev that these concessions had been withdrawn on the grounds that the winner takes all. Sofia had wanted this port to serve the newly captured territory across the Rhodope Mountains, which was the heart of eastern Macedonia's tobacco-producing region. The Great Powers were split on the issue, with traditional rivals united in support of each side: Russia and Austria with the Bulgarians; France and Germany with the Greeks, partly because King Constantine was the Kaiser's brother-in-law. The latter pairing triumphed and Bulgaria was left only with 'undeveloped' Dedeagac as an outlet on the Aegean.

The Montenegrin delegation had no disputes with Bulgaria but wanted to demonstrate solidarity with the Serbs and to benefit from Belgrade's share of the spoils, in particular the Sanjak of Novi Pazar. The tactic proved successful, Serbia conceding most of the Sanjak in a separate agreement between the two states signed in Belgrade on 7 November.

By 8 August, the negotiations were complete and the Treaty of Bucharest was signed two days later. Macedonia was divided into three, with the lion's share going to Serbia, including, as Belgrade desired, the Vardar valley, together with the disputed Macedonian territories. Greece received most of the region upon the Aegean coast, which left Bulgaria with only the south-eastern corner. The treaty gave Serbia and Greece more territory than they could ever have expected a year earlier and also temporarily weakened Bulgaria. Serbia was now the strongest power in the region after Rumania and enjoyed exclusive Russian patronage.

Rumania's stab in the back gave them the whole of south Dobrogea and also established the country as the arbitrators of the Balkan Peninsula. The conference was a catastrophe for Bulgaria, for although it retained considerable territory won in the first conflict, especially in western Thrace, it lost almost all of Macedonia, which was its *raison d'être* for entering the struggle. Salt was rubbed in the wound, for the Aegean port it received as a nominal outlet to the sea was worthless because the country lacked the financial resources to exploit it. Yet the Bulgarians did not regard the Treaty of Bucharest as binding, and Tonchev observed, 'Either the Powers will change it, or we ourselves will destroy it.'

The Second Balkan War aggravated tensions between Rumania and Austria, which had proved one of Bulgaria's few friends. Rumania caused bickering between Austria and

Germany because Vienna had refused to help Bucharest to secure a diplomatic solution on Dobrogea, and Berlin correctly feared that this lukewarm support would cause Rumania to leave the Triple Alliance. By 30 November 1913, Count Ottokar Czernin, Austria's new ambassador to Bucharest, concluded that the alliance between the two countries was 'a scrap of paper with no content' and during early 1914 Rumania steadily moved into the Franco-Russian camp.

There remained only for Sofia to sue for peace with the Ottomans as St Petersburg made half-hearted attempts during August to regain Edirne for Bulgaria. It received no support from the other Great Powers and did not dare push the issue unilaterally for fear of further undermining Bulgaria's Russophiles. Negotiations opened in Constantinople on 6 September between a Bulgarian delegation consisting of Savov and the diplomats Andrei Toshev and Grigor Nachovich, the Ottoman Foreign Minister, Mehmed Talat Bey, being assisted by Naval Minister Mahmud Pasha and Halil Bey.

The Bulgarians hoped at least to salvage Kirkkilisse from the wreck, but as Mahmud Pasha bluntly informed them, 'What we have taken is ours.' The Porte increased the pressure through the proclamation of a provisional government of western Thrace at Gumulcine, and the Bulgarians had no other choice but to sign the Treaty of Constantinople on 30 September, the provisional government immediately disappearing like the morning mist. Bulgarian troops reoccupied the land south of the Rhodope Mountains in October, although the loss of so much of captured Thrace did not prove a problem because most of the population were not Bulgarians. Radoslavov tried to strengthen relations with the Ottoman Empire with a view to an alliance, the ultimate aim being to regain Macedonia from Serbia and Greece. The Porte rejected the proposal, but it did lead to the beginning of a *rapprochement* which strengthened as both countries spun into the orbit of the Triple Alliance, and by 1915 they were allies.

As for the Ottoman Empire, it had regained a modicum of prestige by retaking Edirne and simultaneously strengthened the security of Constantinople. However, it remained nominally at war with Greece until the Treaty of Athens on 14 November. The agreement failed to settle the question of the Aegean islands, where Greek-occupied Bozcaada and Imroz were potential springboards into the Dardanelles, while the Italian occupation of the Dodecanese was a further complication, and there was no improvement in relations, with both close to war during the spring of 1914. The Great Powers continued to seek a mutually satisfactory solution until July 1914, when the outbreak of the Great War turned their minds to other things.

The state of war between the Ottomans and Serbians ended when a second Treaty of Constantinople was signed on 14 March 1914 to reaffirm the London Agreement. The Montenegrins, who had started the First Balkan War, were not invited to sign and their country's autonomy would cease when it was merged with Serbia to create Vienna's nightmare of a major Slavic state on its borders. Within five years, this new state was scavenging the carcass of the Austro-Hungarian Empire.

The Second Balkan War extended the territories of all the Ottoman Empire's enemies to a greater or lesser extent and cost the combatants more than the first conflict, with some 142,000 casualties including nearly 23,600 dead (Table 3) compared with 124,400 casualties (19,800 dead), although deaths from disease, notably cholera, were higher in the first conflict. Not only had the combatants suffered appalling casualties but they had also bankrupted themselves, which made them loath to rush into the great European conflict that followed (Table 4).

Table 3   Casualties of the Second Balkan War (excluding sick)

Country	Dead	Wounded	Missing	Total (rounded out)
Bulgaria	7,583	42,911	9,694	60,200
Serbia	9,000	36,000	U/K	45,000
Greece	5,851	23,847	188	29,900
Montenegro	1,000	2,000	U/K	3,000
Rumania	150	1,500	118	1,750

Figures based upon official returns, Carnegie and Vachkov

Table 4   The financial cost of the Second Balkan War

Country	Francs	Sterling	
		Contemporary	Present-day
Bulgaria	824,782,012	32.99 million	3.2 billion
Greece	317,816,101	12.7 million	1.24 billion
Montenegro	100,631,100	4.02 million	393 million
Serbia	574,815, 500	22.99 million	2.24 billion

Figures based upon Carnegie study

MILITARY LESSONS

The Balkan Wars provided many military lessons with both established and emerging technologies, although some of those lessons, such as the development of electronic warfare, would mature only a generation later. However, Europe's armies had little chance to absorb the lessons because, barely a year later, they were involved in the major conflict everyone had dreaded. The generals especially had no time to comprehend the implications as quick-firing artillery, and especially heavy guns, became universal.

Artillery could now fire with a speed and accuracy never before encountered, to create within moments a barrier of flame and steel through which no body of troops could pass. This would be vividly illustrated during the early days of the Great War, during the Battle of the Frontiers, when a German brigade outflanked French infantry but found its way barred by an artillery regiment with soixante-quinzes. The brigade commander ordered his men to charge down the guns, and many times in the past against slow-firing cannon such tactics had succeeded, although often at great cost. In this case, however, the brigade was torn apart, leaving the commander bewailing the fate of 'my beautiful brigade'.

Most armies focused upon the value of quick-firing field guns in offensive operations and went to war in the belief that it would involve the usual battles of manoeuvre. But against trench systems, field guns proved of limited value due to their light shells, and armies discovered that they needed heavy artillery both to wreck such systems and for counter-battery fire to neutralise the defenders' guns. An interesting comment came from France's General Frédéric-Georges Herr after the Battle of Kumanovo:

> He said that he had not before realised the importance of heavy guns to an army in the field, their long range and superior shell power enabling them to achieve results impossible to field guns.[31]

Artillery, and especially heavy howitzers, would become the arbiter of battlefield success in the Great War, with clashes becoming essentially artillery contests. This was especially noticeable at the Battle of Verdun in which Herr would play a key role before becoming Inspector of Artillery in the French Army. Upon returning to France he advocated in the *Revue d'Artillerie* assigning batteries of light field howitzers to every corps and, in April 1913, the French Army placed orders for 220 modern 105-mm howitzers. Herr's visit to the Serbian Army was ostensibly unofficial, but an official delegation was with the Bulgarians at Edirne. One member was Captain Georges Bellinger, a fortress artillery gunner who would have been expected to take a similar view to Herr, but his article in the *Revue d'Artillerie* in November 1913 argued that heavy artillery played little part in the Balkan battles.

By contrast, the Germans were already deploying larger numbers of 105-mm, 150-mm and 210 mm howitzers in the field than any other power. But this was less in recognition of lessons learned in recent conflicts and more a combination of manufacturers' marketing and the need to engage fortifications. There was also the need to neutralise the French 75-mm Quick Firer with heavier firepower to support battlefield manoeuvrability, but the use of heavy artillery also underlined the growing importance of indirect fire which was confirmed during the Balkan Wars and would become vital as the importance of counter-battery fire grew.[32]

One feature obvious to all sides during the Balkan conflicts was the prodigious consumption of artillery ammunition, which would soon help to shape battles and campaigns during the Great War. Bulgarian guns consumed 254,000 rounds a month, while France's Henry Barby noted that the Serbs consumed 30,479 of their 200,000 shrapnel shells and 3,275 of their 40,000 howitzer rounds during the first Balkan conflict. He reported that during the second conflict a single battery of the Serbian Moravska I fired 7,173 shells between 18 and 29 July, and on 23 July a single battery fired 1,712.[33] Yet rather than place massive orders for shells, the European armies concluded, from observing the Balkan Wars, that the Quick Firers' greater accuracy made it possible to use the limited stocks more effectively. They would rely upon economy of fire until bitter experience against the trenches demonstrated the need for volume as well as accuracy.[34]

Infantry also had no time to absorb the lessons, because the Balkan Wars appeared to confirm that with adequate Quick Firer field artillery support, determined troops could still storm enemy entrenchments. Observers ignored the size of the problem, for infantry now had to fight their way forward through a rain of shells and torrents of machine-gun fire, with barbed-wire entanglements the final hurdle in front of the trenches. Armies would learn that success would depend upon close co-ordination between the arms, and that the infantryman required more than a rifle and bayonet. Even in the Balkan conflicts, trench warfare relied more upon the hand grenade than the bayonet, and the infantry would need even more firepower.

Machine guns were also given offensive roles, although the Balkan armies had relatively few, usually one per battalion, half the establishment of the armies of the Great Powers, who would soon recognise the value of these weapons in defence. But the machine gun's bulk restricted its mobility and in the Great War it would be augmented by what were called, at the time, automatic rifles, such as the Lewis gun, which could deliver bursts of direct fire to support infantry movement. Because the German Army anticipated engaging fortifications, its infantry were given a form of short-range artillery with grenade launchers (*Granatenwerfern*) and ultra short-range mortars (*Minenwerfern*), while Allied forces in the Great War would use rifle attachments to launch grenades and the Stokes mortar to reach deeper.

Traditional infantry formations also needed to be modified, with moves away from linear tactical formations in both offence and defence as well as greater reliance upon dispersion and firepower. Some of the combatants in the Balkan conflicts, unlike those of the Great Powers, appear to have responded to the need for junior leader initiative; they dispersed troops and adopted fire-and-movement tactics to advance. During the Great War the traditional skirmish lines would largely be abandoned in favour of sub-unit (platoon, section) columns, but as late as July 1918, the French were still holding their trenches with men almost shoulder to shoulder.

The Balkan conflicts also hinted at the need for closer co-operation between the various arms and services at all levels, and this would prove essential in the Great War. Similarly, a more flexible organisation at divisional level became apparent, and even the Bulgarians began to adopt triangular formations to provide easier command and control. The Balkan Wars also confirmed the increasing irrelevance of cavalry as the growth in firepower left the former 'queen of the battlefield' unable to shatter enemy lines. In the Balkans, cavalry even proved inadequate in the secondary roles of reconnaissance and pursuit. Yet the military leaders of the Great Powers ardently hoped against hope to restore the arm to its traditional role, like an elderly man pining over the lost love of his youth.

The Balkan Wars saw armies and navies use the latest technologies that provided hints of their value in the Great War. The aeroplane was used for reconnaissance and occasionally helped the generals, while a few bombs were also dropped, but it remained a fragile tool that was vulnerable to both wind and weather. Ground fire forced aeroplanes to fly so high that they could distinguish little on the ground; indeed, by September 1914, many armies considered abandoning them completely. The aeroplane was saved as trench systems covered almost the whole battlefield, to make it the prime means of tactical-level reconnaissance, together with the observation balloon, and the sole means of operational- and strategic-level reconnaissance, to emphasise still further the redundancy of horsed cavalry.

The aeroplane's potential in naval warfare was also demonstrated by the Greek Navy, both for reconnaissance and through the attack by Moutousis upon Turkish warships. Barely two years later, a British bomber torpedoed and sank a Turkish transport in the Sea of Marmara, while those same waters saw the impact of the submarine when British and Australian boats interdicted Turkish maritime traffic. The threat from the submarine would quickly grow to the point that within four years a German submarine blockade would bring Britain to the verge of starvation. A generation later, submarines and air power would shape naval warfare and decide the fate of the Japanese Empire.

As wars raged in the Balkans, the armed forces of the Great Powers completed their re-equipment with the latest technologies, including Quick Firer artillery, to feed their confidence by 1914. This slipped off the safety catch and turned the Great Powers' diplomatic minuet increasingly into a war dance as all the features for a perfect diplomatic and strategic storm grew. Germany in particular became convinced that it would need to lance the strategic boil by going to war as soon as possible. In 1913, it began a further expansion of the army, the effects of which spread across Europe like ripples in a pond and caused other armies to expand.[35] A year later, Berlin perceived the opening of a window of opportunity: the Belgians were weak and the French planned a major expansion of their army but funding was uncertain and it could not be implemented quickly. In the meantime, France was inferior to Germany in heavy artillery, while Russia was also weak, although it too planned to expand its army and strengthen its artillery.[36]

By 1914, the Balkan Wars had created a situation in which Europe was like an unstable mountainside where an avalanche could be started when the smallest pebble was dislodged. Serbia's success placed it in the key position as Russia's prime client in the Balkans and the main barrier to Austria's regional ambitions, and it now became the focus of the century-long traditional struggle between the two empires.

In June 1914, Archduke Franz Ferdinand, since 1913 the Inspector General of the Austrian Army, decided to visit Bosnia-Herzegovina. This was both to observe major manoeuvres in the empire's newest territory and to provide an opportunity for the public honouring of his beloved wife Sophie, who was officially snubbed in Vienna because she was not of aristocratic birth. He and General Franz Conrad von Hoetzendorf both advocated war with Serbia to pave the way for the empire to annex the kingdom.[37] Conrad now recognised that any attack upon Serbia would bring in Russia and, despite failing to get German assurances of military support in the east, he became obsessed with settling accounts with Serbia. Because of this obsession he dismissed potential Russian reactions, although St Petersburg was now determined to regain lost prestige in the Balkans through support of the region's new Slavic power, even at the risk of war.

The news of his visit attracted the interest of a Bosnian anarchist secret society which was supported by the Serbian Army Intelligence Department under Colonel Dragutin Dimitrijevic or 'Apis', and which had supplied them with pistols and bombs. 'Apis' wanted to strain relations with Austria further as part of an internal power struggle with Pasic, who knew that after the Second Balkan War his country was in no condition to enter another conflict. Although the Austrian authorities feared some form of incident, they failed to take significant security precautions. Indeed, even 'Apis' was not optimistic about the Bosnians' prospects for success.

His pessimism seemed justified. When the royal couple, who were celebrating their fourteenth wedding anniversary, were being driven through Sarajevo on 28 June, a Bosnian threw a grenade at them, but it rolled off the vehicle before exploding and slightly injuring the Archduchess. The spectators and officers accompanying the couple were less lucky, and many were taken to hospital. The royal party paused for a few minutes, but two other would-be assassins nearby failed to act and the Archduke decided to visit one of the wounded officers. The chauffeur obeyed and had turned the motor car towards Franz Josef Street when General Oskar Potiorek, who had accompanied the royal party, ordered him to continue along the riverside Appel Quay. The confused chauffeur stopped and by ill fortune the vehicle was only a few steps from one of the Bosnian anarchists, Gavrilo Princip, who was dejectedly walking home, having witnessed the failure of the assassination attempt. Seeing his opportunity, Princip pulled out his Browning semi-automatic pistol and stepped forward to fire shots that went around the world and started the race to war.

First Balkan War Order of Battle, October 1912

OTTOMAN FORCES

Eastern Army: Lieutenant General Abdullah Pasha

Army troops
Independent Cavalry Division
　　　　1st Brigade: 1st, 2nd Cavalry
　　　　2nd Brigade: 3rd, 4th Cavalry
　　　　4th Brigade: 9th, 11th Cavalry
　　　　1st, 2nd Horse Artillery Battalions
Light Cavalry Brigade: 1st, 2nd Light Cavalry
Edirne Fortified Area: Major-General Shukru Pasha
　　　　4th Rifles
　　　　12th Cavalry
　　　　6th, 7th, 8th, 9th, 10th Heavy Artillery
10th Infantry Division
　　　　28th, 29th, 30th Infantry
　　　　10th Rifle Battalion
　　　　10th Artillery

11th Infantry Division
>32nd, 33rd Infantry, Bursa Reserve Infantry
>
>11th Rifle Battalion
>
>11th Artillery

Edirne Reserve Division
>Dedeagac, Edirne, Kosukavak Reserve Infantry

Gumulcine Reserve Division
>Gumulcine, Iskece, Sultanyeri Reserve Infantry

Babaeski Reserve Division
>Babaeski, Corlu, Kesan, Kirklareli Reserve Infantry
>
>Horse Artillery Battalion

Kircaali Detachment: Brigadier General Mehmet Yaver Pasha

Kircaali Reserve Division
>II, III/36th Infantry, Egri Dere, Kircaali, Palas Reserve Infantry
>
>1st Mountain Artillery Battalion

Kircaali Home Guard Division
>I/36th Infantry, Palas, Kircaali, Kosukavak Home Guard Regiments

I Corps: Major-General Omer Yaver Pasha

Corps troops
>5th Cavalry
>
>1st Engineer Battalion

1st Provisional Division
>1st Rifles, 3rd Infantry, Izmir Reserve Infantry
>
>I/1st Artillery Battalion

2nd Infantry Division
>4th, 5th, 6th Infantry
>
>2nd Rifle Battalion
>
>2nd Artillery

3rd Infantry Division
>7th, 8th, 9th Infantry
>
>3rd Artillery

Usak Reserve Division
>Kasaba, Simav, Usak Reserve Infantry
>
>II/1st Artillery Battalion

II Corps: Major-General Shevket Turgut Pasha

Corps troops
>10th Cavalry
>
>2nd Engineer Battalion

4th Infantry Division
> 10th, 11th, III/12th Infantry
> 4th Rifle Battalion
> 4th Artillery Regiment

5th Infantry Division
> 13th, 14th, 15th Infantry
> 5th Artillery

6th Infantry Division
> 16th, III/17th, I/18th Infantry, Aydin, Nazili Reserve Infantry
> I/6th Artillery

Kastamonu Reserve Division
> Inebolu, Kasamonu, Sinop Reserve Infantry

III Corps: Brigadier General Mahmut Muhtar Pasha

Corps troops
> 2nd Cavalry
> 3rd Engineer Battalion

7th Infantry Division
> 3rd Mixed Rifles, 20th, 21st Infantry
> 7th Artillery
> 2nd Howitzer Battalion

8th Infantry Division
> 22nd, 23rd, 24th Infantry
> 8th Rifle Battalion
> I/8th Artillery
> 3rd Mountain Artillery Battalion

9th Infantry Division
> III/25th, 26th, 27th Infantry, Cankiri Reserve Infantry
> 1st, 2nd Ankara, 1st Ayas Reserve Battalions
> 9th Artillery
> III/3rd Artillery Battalion

Afyonkarahisar Reserve Division
> Afyonkarahisar, Aksehir Reserve Infantry

IV Provisional Corps: Major-General Ahmet Abuk Pasha

Corps troops
> 7th Cavalry

12th Infantry Division
> 35th Infantry, Bandirma, Kermastan Reserve Infantry
> 12th Artillery

Izmit Reserve Division
        Bilecik, Eskisehir, Izmit Reserve Infantry
        II/11th Artillery
Canakkale Reserve Division
        Biga, Canakkale, Pazar, Reserve Infantry
        2nd Mountain Artillery Battalion

XVI Provisional Corps: Brigadier General Mehmet Hakki Pasha

Corps troops
        1st Cavalry
Denizli Reserve Division
        Civril, Denizli, Isparta Reserve Infantry

XVII Provisional Corps: Brigadier General Curuksulu Mahmut Pasha

Konya Reserve Division
        Karaman, Konya, Seidisehir Reserve Infantry
Kayseri Reserve Division
        Develi, Kayseri, Nevsehir Reserve Infantry

XVIII Provisional Corps: Brigadier General Hamdi Pasha

Eregli Reserve Division
        Bartin, Bolu, Eregli Reserve Infantry
Samsun Reserve Division
        Giresun, Samsun, Unye Reserve Infantry
Izmir Reserve Division
        Akhisar, Soma Reserve Infantry

Western Army: Lieutenant General Ali Riza Pasha

Iskodra and Ipek Forces Command: Brigadier General Mahmud Hayret Pasha
Ipek Command
        1st, I/2nd Infantry, 31st, III/55th, 59th, 61st, 62nd, 63rd Infantry
        21st Rifle Battalion
        Akova, Gosina, Ipek, Kolasin, Tergovista, Yakova Reserve Battalions
        10th Mountain Artillery Battalion
Iskodra Fortified Area
        Debre Reserve Infantry
        13th Heavy Artillery

Iskodra Provisional Corps: Colonel Hasan Riza
24th Infantry Division
        70th, 71st, 72nd Infantry
        24th Rifle Battalion
        24th Artillery
Provisional Infantry Division
        III/50th, I/51st, 53rd, 54th Infantry
        Drac, Kavaya, Tiran Reserve Battalions
        8th Mountain Artillery Battalion
Elbasan Reserve Division
        Berat, Drac, Elbasan, Tiran Reserve Infantry

Yanya Independent Corps: Brigadier General Esat Pasha
23rd Infantry Division
        67th, 68th, 69th Infantry
        23rd Rifle Battalion
        II/23rd Artillery
Yanya Reserve Division
        Avlonya, Ergeri, Yanya Reserve Infantry
Yanya Fortified Area
        11th Heavy Artillery

VIII Provisional Corps: Brigadier General Hasan Tahsin Pasha

Corps troops
        14th Cavalry
22nd Infantry Division
        64th, 65th, 66th Infantry
        22nd Rifle Battalion
        I/22nd Artillery
Naslic Reserve Division
        Gorice, Naslic, Kozana Reserve Infantry
        II/22nd Artillery
Drama Reserve Division
        Drama, Kavala Reserve Infantry

Selanik (Salonika) Area Command

Selanik Reserve Division
        Kelemeriye, Vardar, Vodina Reserve Infantry
        Kesindire, Sanayi Reserve Battalions

Ustruma Corps: Major-General Ali Nadir Pasha

Corps troops
      25th Cavalry
14th Infantry Division
      40th, 42nd Infantry
      14th Rifle Battalion
      14th Artillery
Serez Reserve Division
      Avrathisar, Serez, Ustrumca Reserve Infantry
      6th Mountain Artillery Battalion
Nevrekop Detachment
      41st Infantry, Nevrekop Reserve Infantry

Vardar Army: Lieutenant General Helpi Zeki Pasha

Army troops
Independent Cavalry Division
      7th Brigade: 13th, 16th Cavalry
      8th Brigade: 15th, 16th Cavalry
      3rd Horse Artillery Battalion
Firzovik Detachment: Brigadier General Mehmet Pasha
      20th Infantry Division
      Pristine, Vulcetrin Reserve Infantry
      20th Rifle Battalion
      II/20th Artillery
      18th Cavalry
      II/13th Artillery
Taslica Detachment: Colonel Halit Munir
      58th, 60th Infantry, Mitrovica Reserve Infantry
      Mitrovica, Taslica Reserve Battalions

V Corps: Major-General Kara Sait Pasha

Corps troops
      26th Cavalry
      5th Rifles
      5th Engineer Battalion
13th Infantry Division
      37th, 38th, 39th Infantry
      13th Rifle Battalion
      I/13th Artillery

15th Infantry Division
> 43rd, 44th, 45th Infantry
>
> 15th Rifle Battalion
>
> 15th Artillery

16th Infantry Division
> 46th, 47th, 48th Infantry
>
> 16th Rifle Battalion
>
> 16th Artillery

Istip Reserve Division
> Istip, Kocana, Koprulu Reserve Infantry
>
> 7th Mountain Artillery Battalion

VI Corps: Major-General Cavit Pasha

Corps troops
> 25th Cavalry
>
> 6th Rifles
>
> 5th Howitzer Battalion
>
> 6th Engineer Battalion

17th Infantry Division
> 49th, II/50th, 51st Infantry
>
> 17th Rifle Battalion
>
> 17th Artillery Battalion

18th Infantry Division
> 52nd, I/54th Infantry
>
> 18th Rifle Battalion
>
> 8th Mountain Artillery Battalion

Manastir Reserve Division
> Manastir, Pirlepe Reserve Infantry

VII Corps: Major-General Fethi Pasha

Corps troops
> 17th Cavalry
>
> 7th Rifles
>
> 4th Howitzer Battalion
>
> 7th Engineer Battalion

19th Infantry Division
> 55th, 56th, 57th Infantry
>
> 19th Rifle Battalion
>
> 19th Artillery

Uskup Reserve Division
> Kalkandelen, Presova, Uskup Reserve Infantry
> I/21st Artillery

Pristine Reserve Division
> Geyland, Gore, Priren Reserve Infantry
> I/20th Artillery
> 3rd Mountain Artillery Battalion

BULGARIAN ARMY

1st Army: Lieutenant General Vasil Kutinchev

Army Troops
> 9th Cavalry

1st 'Sofiyska' Division
> 1st Brigade: 1st, 6th Infantry
> 2nd Brigade: 37th, 38th Infantry
> 4th Quick Fire Field Artillery
> 4th Field Artillery
> 1st Pioneer Battalion

3rd 'Balkanska' Division
> 1st Brigade: 11th, 24th Infantry
> 2nd Brigade: 29th, 32nd Infantry
> 3rd Brigade: 41st, 42nd Infantry
> 6th Quick Fire Field Artillery
> 6th Field Artillery
> 3rd Pioneer Battalion

10th 'Sborna' Division
> 1st Brigade: 16th, 25th Infantry
> 2nd Brigade: 47th, 48th Infantry
> 10th Field Artillery (Mixed)
> 10th Pioneer Battalion

2nd Army: Lieutenant General Nikola Ivanov

Army troops
> Life Guard Cavalry
> 2nd Quick Fire Howitzer Battalion

Haskovo Detachment
> 2nd Brigade/2nd 'Trakiyska' Division: 28th, 40th Infantry
> 3rd Field Artillery
> Mixed Cavalry Brigade: 3rd, 6th Cavalry

8th 'Tundzhanska' Division
>> 1st Brigade: 10th, 30th Infantry
>> 2nd Brigade: 12th, 23rd Infantry
>> 3rd Brigade: 51st, 52nd Infantry
>> 8th Quick Fire Field Artillery
>> 8th Field Artillery
>> 8th Pioneer Battalion

9th 'Plevenska' Division
>> 1st Brigade: 4th, 17th Infantry
>> 2nd Brigade: 33rd, 34th Infantry
>> 3rd Brigade: 53rd, 54th Infantry
>> 9th Quick Fire Field Artillery
>> 9th Field Artillery
>> 9th Pioneer Battalion

3rd Army: Lieutenant General Radko Dimitriev

Army troops
>> 8th Cavalry
>> 3rd Quick Fire Howitzer Battalion
>> I/1st Quick Fire Mountain Artillery
>> IV/1st Mountain Artillery

Cavalry Division
>> 1st Brigade: 1st, 2nd Cavalry
>> II/35th Infantry
>> 2nd Brigade: 4th, 7th ,10th Cavalry

4th 'Preslavska' Division
Commander MG. Kliment Boyadzhiev
>> 1st Brigade: 7th, 19th Infantry
>> 2nd Brigade: 8th, 31st Infantry
>> 3rd Brigade: 43rd, 44th Infantry
>> 5th Quick Fire Field Artillery
>> 5th Field Artillery
>> 4th Pioneer Battalion

5th 'Dunavska' Division
>> 1st Brigade: 2nd, 5th, I/24th Infantry
>> 2nd Brigade: 18th, 20th Infantry
>> 3rd Brigade: 45th, 46th Infantry
>> 1st Quick Fire Field Artillery
>> 1st Field Artillery
>> 5th Pioneer Battalion

6th 'Bdinska' Division
       1st Brigade: 3rd, 15th Infantry
       2nd Brigade: 35th, 36th Infantry
       2nd Quick Fire Field Artillery
       6th Pioneer Battalion

Rodop Detachment

2nd 'Trakiyska' Division
       1st Brigade: 9th, 21st Infantry
       3rd Brigade: 27th, 39th Infantry
       III/3rd Quick Fire Field Artillery
       II, III/1st Quick Fire Mountain Artillery
       3rd Mountain Artillery
       2nd Pioneer Battalion

Independent

Macedonian-Thracian Legion
       1st Brigade: 1st, 2nd, 3rd, 4th Battalions
       2nd Brigade: 5th, 6th, 7th, 8th Battalions
       3rd Brigade: 9th, 10th, 11th, 12th Battalions

SERBIAN ARMY

1st Army: Crown Prince Aleksandar Drinska I Division
       4th, 5th, 6th, 17th Ban I Infantry
       Drinski Ban I Cavalry
       Drinski Artillery
Dunavska I Division
       7th, 8th, 9th, 18th Ban I Infantry
       Dunavski Ban I Cavalry
       Dunavski Artillery
Dunavska II Division
       7th, 8th, 9th Ban II Infantry, 4th Special Infantry
       Dunavski Ban II Cavalry
       IV/Dunavski Artillery
Moravska I Division
       1st, 2nd, 3rd, 16th Ban I Infantry
       Moravski Ban I Artillery

Timoska II Division
  - 13th, 14th, 15th Ban II Infantry
  - Timoski Ban II Cavalry
  - IV/Timoski Artillery
Cavalry Division
  - 1st Brigade: 1st, 2nd Cavalry
  - 2nd Brigade: 3rd, 4th Cavalry
  - Cavalry Artillery Group
2nd Army: Major-General Stepa Stepanovic
Timoska I Division
  - 13th, 14th, 15th, 20th Ban I Infantry
  - Timoski Cavalry
  - Timoski Artillery
Bulgarian 7th 'Rilska' Division
  - 1st Brigade: 13th, 26th Infantry
  - 2nd Brigade: 14th, 20th Infantry
  - 3rd Brigade: 49th, 50th Infantry
  - 5th Cavalry
  - 7th Quick Fire Field Artillery
  - 7th Field Artillery
  - 2nd Quick Fire Mountain Artillery
  - 7th Pioneer Battalion

3rd Army: Major-General Bozidar Jankovic

Army troops
  - 1st, 2nd Mountain Artillery Groups
Sumadijska I Division
  - 10th, 11th, 12th, 19th Ban I Infantry
  - Sumadijski Ban I Cavalry
  - Sumadisjski Artillery
Moravska II Division
  - 1st, 2nd, 3rd Ban II Infantry
  - IV/Moravski Artillery
Drinska II Division
  - 5th, 6th Ban II Infantry
  - Drinski Ban II Cavalry
  - IV/Drinski Artillery
Moravska I Brigade
  - 1st, 2nd Special Infantry

Army of the Ibar: Major-General Michailov Zivkovich

Sumadijska II Division
        10th, 11th, 12th Ban II, 5th Special Infantry
        Sumadijski Ban II Cavalry
        IV/Suadijski Artillery
Javor Brigade
        4th Ban I, 3rd Special Infantry
MONTENEGRIN ARMY

Coastal Corps: Brigadier General Mitar Martinovic
1st 'Cetinjska' Division

1st 'Katunska' Brigade: Cetinjski, Cevsko-Bijelicko, Cucki, Komansko-Zagaracki, Njegusko-
    Ceklicki, Pjesivacki Battalions
2nd 'Rijecko-Ljesanska' Brigade: Donji-Ceklinski, Gornjo-Ceklinski, Ljesanski, Ljubotinski Battalions
3rd 'Primorska-Crmnicka' Brigade: Barski, Donjo-Crmnicki, Gornjo-Crmnicki, Krajinski,
    Mrkojevicki, Seljacko, Ulcinjski Battalions

Zeta Corps: Lieutenant General Prince Danilo

2nd 'Podgoricka' Division

4th 'Zetska' Brigade : Bratonozicki, Donjo-Kucko, Gornjo-Kucko, Podgoricki, Zatrijevacki, Zetski
    Battalions
5th 'Spuzka' Brigade: Ljeskopolski, Piperski, Spuzki Battalions
6th 'Brdska' Brigade: Brajovicko-Martinicki, Grmski , Pavkovicki, Petrusinski, Vraze Battalions

3rd 'Niksicka' Division
7th 'Niksicka' Brigade: Goljirski, Lukovski, Niksicki, Trebjeski, Zupski Battalions
8th 'Vucedolska' Brigade: Banjaski, Grahovski, Oputno-Rudinski, Rudinski-Trepacki Battalions

Eastern Corps: Brigadier General Janko Vukotic

4th 'Niksicka' Division
10th 'Kolasinska' Brigade: Donjo Moracki, Gornjo Moracki, Kolasinski, Lipovski, Poljski, Rovacki
    Battalions
11th 'Gornovasojevicka' Brigade: Andrijevicki, Kraljski, Ljevorecki, Polimski, Trepacki-Sekularski,
    Veljicki Battalions

9th 'Durmitorska' Independent Brigade: Drobnjacki, Planine Pivski, Uskocki, Zupa-Pivska Battalions
Donjovasojevicka Serbian Volunteer Brigade

GREEK ARMY

Army of Thessaly: Crown Prince Constantine
I Division
        2nd, 4th, 5th Infantry
        I, II/1st Field Artillery
II Division
        1st, 3rd, 7th Infantry
        I, II/2nd Field Artillery
III Division
        6th, 10th, 12th Infantry
        I, II/3rd Field Artillery
        III Mountain Artillery Battalion
IV Division
        8th, 9th, 11th Infantry
        I, II/4th Field Artillery
        I Mountain Artillery Battalion
V Division
        16th, 22nd, 23rd Infantry
        III/1st Field Artillery
        IV Mountain Artillery Battalion
VI Division
        1st Evzones, 17th, 18th Infantry
        III/3rd Field Artillery
VII Division
        19th, 20th, 21st Infantry
        II/3rd Field Artillery
Cavalry Brigade
        1st, 3rd Cavalry
        I, II/4th Field Artillery
        I Horse Artillery Group
Gennades Detachment
        1st, 4th Evzones Battalions
Konstantinopoulos Detachment
        2nd, 6th Evzone Battalions

Army of Epirus: Lieutenant General Konstantinos Sapountzakis
Epirus Division
        15th Infantry
        3rd Independent, 3rd, 7th, 10th Evzone Battalions
        III/4th Field Artillery
        II Mountain Artillery Battalion

Second Balkan War Order of Battle, June 1913

BULGARIAN ARMY

1st Army: Lieutenant General Vasil Kutinchev

Army troops
        Independent Infantry Brigade: 65th, 66th Infantry
        Vidinski Fortress Battalion
5th 'Dunavska' Infantry Division
        1st Brigade: 2nd, 5th Infantry
        2nd Brigade: 18th, 20th Infantry
        1st Quick Fire Field Artillery
        1st Field Artillery
9th 'Plevenska' Infantry Division
        1st Brigade: 4th, 17th Infantry
        2nd Brigade: 33rd, 34th Infantry
        9th Quick Fire Field Artillery

2nd Army: Lieutenant General Nikola Ivanov

Army troops
        10th Cavalry
        2nd Quick Fire Howitzer Battalion
        Dedeagac Garrison: IV/16th Infantry
        Salonika Garrison: III/14th Infantry
3rd 'Balkanska' Infantry Division
        2nd Brigade: 29th, 32nd Infantry
        3rd Brigade: 41st, 42nd Infantry Regiment
        6th Quick Fire Field Artillery
        6th Field Artillery
11th Infantry Division
        55th, 56th, 57th Infantry Regiment
        11th Field Artillery
1st Brigade/10th Division: 16th, 25th Infantry
Serska Brigade: 67th, 68th Infantry
Dramska Brigade: 69th, 70th Infantry

3rd Army: Lieutenant General Radko Dimitriev

Army troops

        3rd Cavalry Regiment

        I/1st Quick Fire Artillery

        1st, 3rd Howitzer Battalions

        Sofiyski, Shumenski Fortress Artillery Battalions

1st 'Sofiyska' Infantry Division

        1st Brigade: 1st, 6th Infantry

        2nd Brigade: 37th, 38th Infantry

        4th Quick Fire Field Artillery

        4th Field Artillery

13th Infantry Division

        62nd, 63rd, 64th Infantry

        13th Field Artillery

3rd Brigade/5th 'Dunavska' Division: 46th Infantry

Cavalry Division

        1st Brigade: 1st, Life Guard Cavalry

        2nd Brigade: 2nd, 7th Cavalry

4th Army: Major-General Stiliyan Kovachev

Army troops

        5th Cavalry

        3rd Quick Fire Howitzer Battalion

2nd 'Trakiyska' Infantry Division

        1st Brigade: 9th, 21st Infantry

        2nd Brigade: 27th, 28th Infantry

        3rd Brigade: 39th, 40th Infantry

        3rd Quick Fire Field Artillery

        3rd Mountain Artillery

7th 'Rilska' Infantry Division

        1st Brigade: 13th, 26th Infantry

        2nd Brigade: 14th, 22nd Infantry

        3rd Brigade: 49th, 50th Infantry

        7th Quick Fire Field Artillery

        9th Field Artillery

8th 'Tundzhavska' Infantry Division

        1st Brigade: 10th, 30th Infantry

        2nd Brigade: 12th, 23rd Infantry

        3rd Brigade: 51st, 52nd Infantry

        8th Field Artillery

1st Brigade/3rd 'Balkanska' Division: 11th, 24th Infantry

2nd Brigade/4th 'Preslavska' Division: 8th, 31st Infantry

Macedonian-Thracian Legion

        1st Brigade: 1st, 2nd, 3rd, 4th, 13th Infantry Battalions

        2nd Brigade: 5th, 6th, 7th, 8th, 14th Infantry Battalions

        3rd Brigade: 9th, 10th, 11th, 12th, 15th Infantry Battalions

5th Army: Major-General Stefan Toshev

Army troops

        6th Cavalry Regiment

        45th Infantry

        Army Artillery

        II/1st, I/3rd Quick Fire Mountain Artillery

        IV/3rd Mountain Artillery

        1st Quick Fire Howitzer Battalion

4th 'Preslavska' Infantry Division

        1st Brigade: 7th, 19th Infantry

        3rd Brigade: 43rd, 44th Infantry

        5th Quick Fire Field Artillery

        5th Field Artillery

12th Infantry Division

        59th, 60th, 61st Infantry

        12th Field Artillery

Odrinska Brigade

        71st, 72nd Infantry

High Command Reserve

6th 'Bdinska' Infantry Division

        1st Brigade: 3rd, 36th Infantry

        2nd Brigade: 15th, 36th Infantry

        2nd Quick Fire Field Artillery

Eastern Thrace Occupation Army: Major-General Stoyu Bradistilov

2nd Brigade/10th Division: 47th, 48th Infantry

I/2nd Field Artillery

Gallipoli: I/39th Infantry

        9th Cavalry

Military Governor of Thrace
> IV/43rd, IV/44th, 58th Infantry
> 8th Cavalry

SERBIAN ARMY

1st Army: Crown Prince Aleksandar
Dunavska II Division
> 7th, 8th, 9th Ban II, 4th Special Infantry
> Dunavski Ban II Cavalry
> Dunavski Ban II Artillery

Dunavska I Division
> 7th, 8th, 9th, 18th Ban I Infantry
> Dunavski Ban I Cavalry
> Dunavski Ban I Artillery

Moravska II Division
> 1st, 2nd, 3rd Ban I Infantry
> Moravski Ban II Cavalry
> IV/Moravski Artillery

Sumadijska I Division
> 10th, 11th, 12th, 19th Ban I Infantry
> Sumadijski Ban I Cavalry
> Sumadisjski Artillery

Cavalry Division
> 1st Brigade: 1st, 2nd Cavalry
> 2nd Brigade: 3th, 4th Cavalry
> Cavalry Artillery Group

2nd Army: Major-General Stepa Stepanovic

Army troops
> 14th, 15th Ban I Infantry
> 1st, 3rd, 14th Ban III Infantry

Pirot Fortress
> 4th Fortress Artillery Group
> Heavy Howitzer Regiment
> Mixed Fortress Artillery Battalion

Timoska I Division
> 13th, 20th Ban I, 4th, 6th Ban III Infantry
> Timoski Ban I Cavalry
> I, III/Timoski Artillery

3rd Army: Major-General Bozidar Jankovic

Army troops
> Drinski, Moravski Ban I Cavalry
> I/14th Ban II Infantry
> I/5th Ban III Infantry

Moravska I Division
> 1st, 2nd, 3rd, 16th Ban I Infantry
> Moravski Artillery

Drinska I Division
> 4th, 5th, 6th, 17th Ban I Infantry
> Drinski Ban I Artillery
> 3rd Mountain Artillery Battalion

Timoska II Division
> 13th, 14th, 15th Ban II Infantry
> Timoski Ban II Cavalry
> IV/Timoski Artillery

Army of the Timok: Colonel Vukoman Arachich

1st Mixed, 2nd, 8th, 13th Ban III Infantry
Zajecharski Quick Fire Artillery Battalion
Zajecharski Howitzer Battalion
Sumadijska II Division
> 10th, 12th Infantry Regiment II
> Sumadijski II Cavalry Battalion
> IV/Sumadijski Artillery

General Headquarters Reserve

Montenegrin Division
> 1st, 2nd, 3rd, 4th Brigades
Volunteers Brigade

Garrisons
Albanian border
Drinska II Division
> 4th, 5th, 6th Ban II Infantry
> Drinski Ban II Cavalry
> IV/Drinski Artillery

Moravska I Brigade: 1st, 2nd Special Infantry
        2 Cavalry Squadron/Moravski Cavalry Regiment I
Kosovo Military District
        3rd, 5th, 6th Special Infantry
Vardar Military District
        11th Ban II, 10th, 11th, 12th Ban III Infantry

GREEK ARMY

Army of Macedonia: King Constantine

Army troops
Cavalry Brigade: 1st, 2nd Cavalry
Thessaloniki Fortress Command
        26th, 27th, 28th, 29th Infantry
        1st Fortress Artillery Battalion
I Division
        2nd, 4th, 5th Infantry
        1st Field Artillery
        I Mountain Artillery Battalion
II Division
        1st, 3rd, 7th Infantry
        2nd Field Artillery
III Division
        6th, 10th, 12th Infantry
        3rd Field Artillery
IV Division
        8th, 9th, 11th Infantry
        4th Field Artillery
V Division
        16th, 22nd, 23rd Infantry
        Alpha Field Artillery Battalion
VI Division
        1st Evzones Regiment (8th, 9th Evzones Battalions, 3rd Cretans Battalion)
        17th, 18th Infantry
        Beta Field Artillery Battalion
VII Division
        19th, 20th, 21st Infantry
        1st, 2nd Field Artillery Battalions
        III Mountain Artillery Battalion

VIII Division

        1st Evzones, 14th, 15th Infantry

        Krupp Field Artillery Battalion

X Division

        3rd, 4th, 5th Evzones

        II Mountain Artillery Battalion

Epirus Group: Major-General Panagiotes Danglis

IX Division

        24th, 25th, 26th Infantry

RUMANIAN ARMY

I Corps: Major-General Dumitru Costescu

1st Cavalry Division

        1st Cavalry Brigade: 2nd, 3rd Rosiori

        2nd Cavalry Brigade: 4th, 9th Rosiori

        3rd Cavalry Brigade: 7th, 8th Rosiori

        1st Horse Artillery

1st Division

        1st Infantry Brigade: 17th, 18th Infantry

        2nd Infantry Brigade: 1st, 31st Infantry

        1st Rifle Battalion

        1st Artillery Brigade: 1st, 5th Field Artillery

2nd Division

        3rd Infantry Brigade: 2nd, 26th Infantry

        4th Infantry Brigade: 3rd, 19th Infantry

        2nd Rifle Battalion

        2nd Artillery Brigade: 9th, 13th Field Artillery

1st Reserve Division

        21st Reserve Brigade: 41st, 57th Reserve Infantry

        22nd Reserve Brigade: 42nd, 43rd Reserve Infantry

        1st Reserve Rifle Battalion

        2nd Calarasi

        1st Reserve Artillery

II Corps: Major-General Grigore Crainiceanu
3rd Division
       5th Infantry Brigade: 4th, 28th Infantry
       6th Infantry Brigade: 22nd, 30th Infantry
       3rd Rifle Battalion
       3rd Artillery Brigade: 6th, 15th Field Artillery
4th Division
       7th Infantry Brigade: 5th, 20th Infantry
       8th Infantry Brigade: 6th, 21st Infantry
       4th Rifle Battalion
       4th Artillery Brigade: 2nd, 10th Field Artillery

III Corps: Major-General Iarca Alexandru
2nd Cavalry Division
       4th Cavalry Brigade: 1st, 3rd Calarasi
       5th Cavalry Brigade: 9th Calarasi, 11th Rosiori
       2nd Horse Artillery
6th Cavalry Brigade: 5th, 6th Rosiori
5th Division
       9th Infantry Brigade: 7th, 32nd Infantry
       10th Infantry Brigade: 8th, 23rd Infantry
       5th Rifle Battalion
       5th Artillery Brigade: 3rd, 7th Field Artillery
6th Division
       11th Infantry Brigade: 9th, 10th Infantry
       12th Infantry Brigade: 11th, 24th Infantry
       6th Rifle Battalion
       6th Artillery Brigade: 11th, 16th Field Artillery
2nd Reserve Division
       23rd Reserve Brigade: 44th, 46th Reserve Infantry
       24th Reserve Brigade: 60th, 62nd Reserve Infantry
       2nd Reserve Rifle Battalion
       2nd Reserve Artillery

IV Corps: Major-General Alexandru Lambrino
7th Division
       13th Infantry Brigade: 12th, 25th Infantry
       14th Infantry Brigade: 13th, 14th Infantry
       7th Rifle Battalion
       7th Artillery Brigade: 4th, 8th Field Artillery

8th Division

        15th Infantry Brigade: 15th, 27th Infantry

        16th Infantry Brigade: 16th, 29th Infantry

        8th Rifle Battalion

        8th Artillery Brigade: 12th, 17th Field Artillery

7th Cavalry Brigade: 2nd Calarasi, 1st Rosiori

V Corps: Major-General Ioan Culcer

9th Division

        17th Infantry Brigade: 33rd, 34th Infantry

        18th Infantry Brigade: 35th, 36th Infantry

        9th Rifle Battalion

        9th Artillery Brigade: 13th, 18th Field Artillery

10th Division

        19th Infantry Brigade: 23rd, 39th Infantry

        20th Infantry Brigade: 38th, 40th Infantry

        10th Rifle Battalion

        10th Artillery Brigade: 3rd, 20th Field Artillery

3rd Reserve Division

        25th Reserve Brigade: 47th, 48th Reserve Infantry

        36th Reserve Brigade: 50th, 51st Reserve Infantry

        3rd Reserve Rifle Battalion

        3rd Reserve Artillery

31st Reserve Brigade: 26th, 59th Reserve Infantry

OTTOMAN ARMY

Catalca Army: Lieutenant General Ahmet Izzet Pasha

Army troops

Ankara, Amasya, Selimiye, Yozgat Reserve Divisions

Independent, 1st Ashiret Cavalry Brigades

Heavy Artillery Regiment

I Corps

2nd, 28th Infantry Divisions

Fatih Reserve Division

II Corps

3rd, 5th, 12th Infantry Divisions
10th Cavalry

III Corps

7th, 8th, 9th Infantry Divisions
8th Cavalry

IV Provisional Corps

29th Infantry Division
Aydin, Eregli, Kayseri Reserve Divisions
2nd Cavalry

X Corps

4th, 31st Infantry Divisions
Mamuretulaziz Reserve Division

Gallipoli Army: Major-General Fahri Pasha

Army troops
2nd Ashiret Cavalry Brigade

I Provisional Corps

30th, 32nd Infantry Divisions
Provisional Infantry Division

II Provisional Corps

27th Infantry Division
Afyon, Samsun Reserve Divisions

III Provisional Corps

Canakkale, Edremit Reserve Divisions

Endnotes

Chapter 1

1. For the background to the Balkan Wars see Albertini, Bobroff, Bridge (*Great Britain* and *Sadowa*), Cornwall, R. J. Crampton, Kent, Lieven, Quataert, Ragsdale, Rossos, Taylor, Thaden and Williamson, also Carnegie pp. 28-49. For contemporary views see Crawfurd Price pp. 29-49 and Rankin pp. 140-147, while Le Queux provides an interesting snapshot of the Balkans and national viewpoints on the verge of war.
2. *Bab-i Ali*, the term used to describe the Turkish government.
3. Glenny pp. 71-72, 75, 98.
4. *Op. cit.*, pp. 91-92. The Austro-Hungarian Empire faced similar problems but created a pan-empiric political framework, although nationalist passions undermined even this structure.
5. Within three years of the Crimean War, France and Britain were involved in a naval arms race.
6. Gerolymatos pp. 149, 196.
7. Glenny pp. 89-90.
8. For Russian policy to the Balkans before 1877 see Gerolymatos pp. 197-199.
9. Glenny p. 125.
10. For economic problems see Gerolymatos pp. 199-200; Glenny pp. 86-90. The Great Powers took control of the empire's finances in 1881.
11. Glenny pp. 95-97.
12. Gerolymatos pp. 199-200; Glenny pp. 102-111.
13. Gerolymatos p. 37.
14. Glenny pp. 125-127, 255-256.
15. For the diplomatic background see Gerolymatos pp. 200-202; Glenny pp. 124-131.
16. Gerolymatos pp. 202-203; Glenny pp. 131-132.
17. For the Russo-Turkish War see Gerolymatos pp. 203-204; Glenny pp. 133-134; Horsetzky pp. 461-470; Langensiepen and Güleryüz pp. 5-7.
18. Statistics for Macedonia varied. *Encyclopaedia Britannica* estimated it at 1.15 million Bulgarians, 500,000 Turks, 250,000 Greek, 120,000 Albanians, 93,000 Vlach, 75,000 Jews and 50,000 Roma. But the Turkish 1906 census showed 423,000 Muslims (Turks and Albanians) or 44.70 per cent, 259,000 Greek (27.4 per cent), 178,000 Bulgarian (18.81 per cent), 13,150 Serbs (1.39 per cent) and 73,000 others (7.72 per cent) = 946,150.
19. Cassevetti p. 310.
20. Gerolymatos pp. 204-206; Glenny pp. 134-136. Earlier, in 1864, Greece acquired the British Ionian island protectorate of Corfu.
21. For the occupation see Gerolymatos pp. 38-39, 124, 208; Glenny pp. 76, 160-163, 268-276; Horsetzky pp. 480-482.

22. Despot p. 13.
23. Despot pp. 10-11; Gerolymatos p. 130, 197, 207-208.
24. Quoted Hall p. 3. See Glenny pp. 168-174.
25. For the Serbo-Bulgarian War see Gerolymatos p. 208; Glenny pp. 175-178; Horsetzky pp. 483-487; Tarnstrom pp. 270-271, 452-454.
26. Gerolymatos p. 20.
27. For Bulgaria see Richard Crampton and under Ferdinand see Glenny pp 189-191.
28. For the Greco-Turkish War of 1897 see Erickson pp. 14-15; Horsetzky pp. 488-493; Langensiepen and Güleryüz pp. 7-9; Tarnstrom pp. 46-48, 190-191.
29. For Crete see Glenny pp. 193-195; Schurman pp. 42-48.
30. Glenny pp. 115-116.
31. Despot pp. 13-14, 17-20; Gerolymatos pp. 188-190. During the Balkan Wars both sides would make extensive use of paramilitary forces.
32. Gerolymatos pp. 190-192; Glenny pp. 154-160, 191-193. Ironically, Ferdinand feared assassination by the Macedonians for much of his life.
33. Despot pp. 14-16; Gerolymatos pp. 192-193; Glenny pp. 195-205.
34. Gerolymatos pp. 193-194; Glenny p. 206-208.
35. Stevenson pp. 64-65.
36. *Op. cit.*, pp. 38-39.
37. Despot p. 35. Note that in 1913 the exchange rate was 25 Francs = £1.00. The US dollar was worth 50 old British pence (about 20 per cent of £1).
38. Despot p. 36.
39. Glenny pp. 209-210.
40. For Serbia see Glenny pp. 163-168.
41. Gerolymatos pp. 32-33.
42. Gerolymatos p. 209; Glenny pp. 220, 223-225, 281-283; Stevenson pp. 82-83, 123-124. The 95 million franc order was for sixty field and twenty-five mountain batteries.
43. Gerolymatos p. 209.
44. Despot p. 21; Glenny pp. 212-216. See also Ahmad.
45. For the First Moroccan Crisis see Stevenson pp. 67-76.
46. Until 1934, Turks did not have family names and were known by their personal name or names and then by an honorary title such as Pasha or Bey. For a long time they did not regard themselves as 'Turks'; the elite regarded themselves as Ottomans, while the peasants were regarded as Anatolians.
47. Despot pp. 22-28; Glenny pp. 216-219.
48. For the annexation see Schmitt; Despot pp. 23-24, 33; Glenny pp. 255-256, 281-302; Herrmann pp. 113-138; Stevenson pp. 64, 112-122.
49. For the Russian and Austrian Armies 1905-10 see Herrmann pp. 60-63, 72, 92-94, 97-100, 115-124; Stevenson pp. 76-86, 124-131, 136-159.
50. For Austrian policy to the Balkans see Helmreich pp. 165-192.
51. Glenny p. 292.
52. Herrmann pp. 131-136.
53. Glenny pp. 295-296.
54. For Russia's Balkan policy see Helmreich pp. 146-164.
55. Glenny pp. 227-228.
56. For the Albanian rising see Crawfurd Price pp. 29-33. For background see Swire.
57. In 1910, Ferdinand fell out with Austria's Franz Ferdinand over the location of his carriage in a train carrying them both to the funeral of King Edward VII.
58. For the Italo-Turkish War 1911-12 see Stephenson's new book as well as Beehler; Langensiepen and Güleryüz pp. 15-16; Stevenson pp. 225-229; Tarnstrom pp. 48-56.
59. For the crises after 1911 see Erickson pp. 245-246; Helmreich pp. 90-102.

60. For negotiations and drafting of the Balkan League see Despot pp. 37-48; Gerolymatos pp. 209-210; Glenny pp. 226-227; Hall pp. 11-13; Helmreich pp. 3-89; Opacic in Kiraly and Djordjevic pp. 85-97—hereafter Opacic; Schurman pp. 34-42; Vojvodic in Kiraly and Djordjevic pp. 240-251—hereafter Vojvodic.
61. Spalajkovic would later become ambassador in St Petersburg.
62. He would be the architect of post-First World War Yugoslavia. Although anti-Austrian, he reportedly owed his life to intervention by Vienna when he was accused of an attempt to kill the former king a decade earlier.
63. For the weakening of Bulgaria's contribution to the Macedonian campaign see Opacic pp. 88-90.
64. Despot p. 42.
65. Venizelos won a third election in March 1912 to strengthen his domestic position.
66. The treaty was scheduled for signing on 30 May, but this was a Tuesday and considered unlucky by the Orthodox so the signing was brought forward. For the negotiations see Papadrianos pp. 183-186 in the International Symposium of Military History 'Moudros 92' (Proceedings)—hereafter Acta.
67. For the international reaction see Despot pp. 52-53; Gerolymatos pp. 210-211; Helmreich pp. 231-248; Stevenson pp. 180-195, 231-366.
68. Despot p. 55.
69. UK National Archives (UKNA) FO 195/2436 'The Balkan Wars'.
70. Cassevetti p. 28.
71. They are identified in Langensiepen and Güleryüz Appendix 13.
72. Despot p. 53. UKNA FO 195/2436. The French SS *Danube* had discharged 810 tons of war matériel from 14 September, including fifty-two guns and 89 tons of ammunition or 4,240 rounds.
73. Erickson p. 237; Hall p. 56; Helmreich pp. 138-141.

Chapter 2

1. Spears p. 272 and fn.
2. One British Expeditionary Force regiment took its regimental mascot on campaign in 1914 and when it died, buried it with full military honours.
3. For European armaments, armament programmes and the strategic balance before the First World War see Herrmann, Stevenson, Stoker and Grant.
4. Herrmann pp. 8-9.
5. The British Royal Small Arms Factory in Enfield was reorganised from 1853 to exploit these American techniques and would be a major supplier of rifles to both sides in the American Civil War.
6. For the effect of a shrapnel shell see Buxton p. 35.
7. A valuable work on artillery development in this period, albeit from an Anglocentric viewpoint, is in Rogers pp. 53-111.
8. Most were water-cooled and fed by a 250-round canvass belt, but the French Hotchkiss and St Étienne machine guns were gas-operated and air-cooled, the former fed with 12-round metal strips. Large orders for Maxims were not received until the turn of the century. Herrmann pp. 20-21; Stevenson p. 17.
9. See Sater and Herwig's article 'The Art of the Deal' in Stoker and Grant p. 60. Larger-calibre guns on both land and sea retained separate propellant charges and projectiles for ease of handling.
10. Herrmann pp. 17-18; Stevenson pp. 17-18. Alfred Dreyfus was accused of attempting to sell the mechanism's secrets to the Germans.
11. French sales of Quick Firers helped to halve Krupp's artillery sales between 1890 and 1914. Many contemporary commentators regarded the First Balkan War as a victory of Schneider guns over Krupp's. Stevenson pp. 23, 243.
12. Herrmann p. 19.

13. Rogers p. 132.
14. The German Army adopted the famed Feldgrau only in 1912 in place of its blue uniform, yet still retained the leather Pickelhaube helmet. Herrmann pp. 70-73.
15. For the German Army see Herrmann p. 90.
16. When the Siegfried Stellung was built in 1916, a seventeen-man squad could lay 800 square metres of barbed-wire entanglements in a day. Professor Holger H. Herwig, *The First World War: Germany and Austria-Hungary 1914-1918*, Arnold Publishing, London, 1997 p. 251.
17. Herrmann pp. 81, 87; Rankin p. 299. Photographic and other evidence shows that dense waves were used by Russian troops in 1914 and even by the German Army during the counter-offensive at Cambrai in 1917. During the latter stages of the First World War infantry 'waves' tended to be in squad columns behind a skirmisher screen aiming to infiltrate defences.
18. For Grandmaison's influence upon the Bulgarian Army see Howell p. 57. For the Russo-Japanese War see Warner and Warner.
19. Herrmann p. 73.
20. *Op. cit.*, pp. 22-29, 79-80, 85.
21. Gudmundson p. 24; Herrmann p. 47.
22. Herrmann pp. 10, 90-92; Stevenson p. 217.
23. For machine-gun development and tactics in the First World War see Hutchison pp. 48-118. See also Herrmann pp. 68-70.
24. Herrmann p. 73.
25. The rocky roads shredded the tyres of German trucks when they invaded Yugoslavia and Greece in April-May 1941. This prevented Fliegerkorps VIII's motor transport driving northwards after the occupation of Greece, while the limited capacity of the rail line into Greece meant that the vehicles could not be brought back by train, so all the vehicles had to be left behind just before Operation 'Barbarossa' in June 1941.
26. For the Serbian Army see Ratkovic in Kiraly and Djordjevic pp. 146-157—hereafter Ratkovic. Buxton pp. 11-12, 28; Gibbs and Grant pp. 82-83, 87; Rankin p. 447.
27. Ratkovic pp. 151-152.
28. During the Second World War members of the Special Operations Executive noted that Greek guerrillas insisted that women carry the heavy and bulky dynamos used for the radios because they were too heavy for mules!
29. Most Balkan peasants believed in vampires.
30. See Stoilov in Kiraly and Djordjevic pp. 35-62—hereafter Stoilov. In the German Army in 1911 while only 42.5 per cent of the population were rural dwellers they provided more than 64 per cent of the reservists. Stevenson p. 47.
31. Despot pp. 28-29.
32. Stoilov pp. 40-41.
33. The US Army in the First World War had a similar problem, with the result that its operations swiftly lost momentum.
34. Stoilov p. 36.
35. Crawfurd Price p. 54; Despot p. 66; Gibbs and Grant pp. 15-16; Rankin p. 3.
36. For the Ottoman Army see Ashmead-Bartlett pp. 50-76; Despot pp. 55-62; Erickson pp. 15-33, 51-61; Hall pp. 19-18; Jowett pp. 10-11, 23-24, 33-35, 37, 40; Ryabinin pp. 132-140; Tarnstrom pp. 48-50, 56-57; Vachkov pp. 42-47.
37. Goltz would again become an adviser in 1914 and would die of typhoid in Baghdad in 1916. By a bizarre twist of fate, the British army commander who occupied the same house a year later died of the same disease. See Erickson pp. 25-26.
38. For German military presence in Turkey see Trumpener in Kiraly and Djordjevic pp. 346-355—hereafter Trumpener.
39. The 42nd Division was destroyed in Libya in 1912 before it could be reorganised.

40. Both the Martini-Henry and Snider-Enfield were breech-loading rifles but the former had a lever-actuated ejection and loading mechanism while the latter lacked an ejector so the spent cartridge had to be extracted either by hand or by turning the rifle upside down and shaking it.

41. The Ottoman contract in 1905 was Krupp's largest. For arms sales to the Balkans see Jonathan A. Grant, 'The Arms Trade in Eastern Europe' in Stoker and Grant.

42. For the Bulgarian Army see British General Staff: Military Notes on the Balkan States August 1915—hereafter Military Notes; Despot pp. 62-68; Erickson pp. 67-69; Hall pp. 16-17; Jowett pp. 11-12, 23-24, 33-35, 37-38, 40-41; Ryabinin pp. 140-143; Stoilov pp. 35-49; Tarnstrom pp. 271-273; Vachkov pp. 15-27.

43. Glenny pp. 219-220.

44. For the Serbian Army see Despot pp. 68-73; Erickson pp. 69-70; Glenny pp. 123-124; Hall p. 18; Jowett pp. 17-18, 23-24, 33-35, 38, 41; Military Notes; Rakocevic in Kiraly and Djordjevic pp. 112-125—hereafter Rakocevic; Ratkovic pp. 146-157; Ryabinin pp. 144-147; Stevenson pp. 132-133; Tarnstrom pp. 454-456; Vachkov pp. 34-39. *Kingdom of Serbia and Montenegro in Wars 1912-1918* website—hereafter Kingdom: First Balkan War—Introduction.

45. For the Greek Army see Cassevetti pp. 69-73; Despot pp. 77-79; Erickson pp. 70, 72; Hall p. 17; Hellenic Army Directorate in Kiraly and Djordjevic pp. 99-111—hereafter HAD; *Hellenic Army General Staff, Army History Directorate, A Concise History of the Balkan Wars 1912-1913* pp. 11-15 paras 14-18—hereafter Hellenic Army; Jowett pp. 13-16, 23-24, 33-35, 38, 41; Military Notes; Ryabinin pp. 143-144; Tarnstrom pp. 191-193; Vachkov pp. 27-34. For the French military mission see Laroche pp. 178-182 in Acta.

46. Gerolymatos pp. 187-188.

47. For the Montenegrin Army see Despot pp. 73-76; Durisic in Kiraly and Djordjevic pp. 126-139—hereafter Durisic; Erickson pp. 69, 72; Hall pp. 18, 55; Jowett pp. 18-19, 23-24, 33-35, 39, 41; Military Notes; Rakocevic pp. 112-125; Ryabinin p. 144; Stevenson pp. 131-132; Tarnstrom pp. 470; Vachkov pp. 39-42. Kingdom: First Balkan War—Introduction.

48. Durisic p. 127.

49. For the Rumanian Army see Jowett pp. 20, 24, 34-35, 39; Military Notes; Petrescu pp. 35-41; Tarnstrom pp. 324-326.

50. For irregulars see Erickson p. 137; Jowett pp. 5, 12-13,15-16, 20-22, Plates H1-3.

51. Despot p. 66; Gerolymatos p. 194; Stoilov pp. 36-37. The force had 27,585 men by the end of the war.

52. For Ottoman planning see Erickson pp. 61-67, Appendix B; Hall pp. 19-20.

53. For the Balkan Pact planning see Erickson pp. 70-72; Hall pp. 14-15; Stoilov pp. 37-39. Kingdom: First Balkan War—Introduction.

54. Hall p. 17.

55. For naval ordnance development, again from an Anglocentric viewpoint, see Rogers pp. 136-145; Stevenson pp. 16-17.

56. The Hellenic Navy had some of these ships in its Ionian Sea Squadron, although they had been converted to patrol boats by 1912.

57. Whitehead torpedoes were first used in the Russo-Turkish War of 1877-78 when a Turkish steamship was sunk. One of the last successes of early Whitehead torpedoes was on 9 April 1940 when weapons fired from a fort in Oslofjord inflicted fatal damage on the German heavy cruiser *Blücher*.

58. For the Hellenic and Turkish navies see Jane 1912 pp. 440-444, 445-454; Jane 1913 pp. 409-415, 416-424.

59. Cassevetti p. 29.

60. Chesneau and Kolesnik pp. 388-394; Gray pp. 387-394; Hall pp. 18-19.

61. Langensiepen and Güleryüz pp. 14-15; Higham in Acta p. 110. Also see Rooney's article on the British naval mission.

62. For the modernisation of the Ottoman fleet see Langensiepen and Güleryüz pp. 9-13. See also Güleryüz's *Torpedoboats & Destroyers*.
63. For the purchase of German warships see Langensiepen and Güleryüz pp. 16-18.
64. She was sunk by battlecruisers during the Battle of the Dogger Bank in 1915.
65. Langensiepen and Güleryüz pp. 16-17; Grove in Acta p. 101 fn. 4 comments that the Brandenburgs were not real pre-dreadnoughts either in armament or protection, for their slow-firing main armament was incapable of hitting anything except at close range or through luck.
66. Langensiepen and Güleryüz pp. 15-16.
67. Beehler pp. 67-69, 72-74, 87, 89-90.
68. Langensiepen and Güleryüz pp. 17, 19-20.
69. For the Greek Navy background see Fotakis pp. 5-24.
70. Chesneau and Kolesnik pp. 387-388; Gray pp. 382-387; Hall pp. 17-18. Although officially the *Georgios Averoff*, the cruiser is simply called *Averoff* by *Jane's Fighting Ships*.
71. Fotakis pp. 25-29, 32-35.
72. Cassevetti pp. 32-34.
73. Cassevetti pp. 34, 42; Fotakis pp. 32-35; Robinson in Hythe *Brassey's Naval Annual* p. 158.
74. Kessler in Acta p. 64.
75. The destroyers, also called the Theria or 'Wild Beast' class, had five boilers, one of which was oil-fired, and they were supported by Greece's first tanker, the SS *Ioannis Koutsis*, which would herald the nation's dominance in the late twentieth-century tanker market.
76. Kessler in Acta pp. 64-65.
77. Chesneau and Kolesnik p. 415; Gray pp. 411-412; Hall p. 17.
78. Chesneau and Kolesnik p. 419; Gray pp. 421-423. For the Rumanian Navy see article in Acta pp. 88-90.
79. Erickson p. 211.
80. The ships and their details are stated in Langensiepen and Güleryüz Appendix 12. However, Langensiepen and Güleryüz p. 19 state that the figure was thirty-three steamers, some sailing vessels and thirty-eight tugs, and this figure is repeated in Erickson on p. 131.
81. For the expansion of the Greek merchant marine see Cassevetti p. 32, Chase, Papathanassopoulos in Vacalopoulos et al. pp. 177-187.
82. Robinson in Hythe *Brassey's Naval Annual* p. 158. For the Greek merchant marine see Paloubis Chapter 5.
83. Italian aircraft and dirigibles were used against tribesmen in Libya in 1911-13.
84. For the air arms see Erickson Appendix A; Green's article 'Wings of Hellas' in *Flying Review*; Hall pp. 17-19; Jowett pp. 35-36; Vachkov pp. 58-62. Pusher aircraft had the engine in the rear of the fuselage, 'pushing' the aeroplane through the sky.

Chapter 3

1. Ashmead-Bartlett pp. 50, 58.
2. For Bulgarian and Turkish plans and preparations see Erickson pp. 77-81; Gibbs and Grant pp. 46-47; Hall pp. 22-25; Hellenic Army p. 92 para. 128; Howell pp. 1-47; Kutschbach pp. 105; Pastukhov pp. 238-239; Rankin pp. 148-149; Ryabinin pp. 148-152, 158-160.
3. For the chaos on Turkish trains see Gibbs and Grant pp. 152-154.
4. Ashmead-Bartlett p. 92.
5. For shortages or horses and oxen see Erickson p. 85.
6. Ashmead-Bartlett p. 78.
7. Stoilov p. 39.
8. See Despot p. 82; Rankin p. 150. After the Second Balkan War he was again dismissed and later went to live in France, where he died in 1928.

9. Pastukhov pp. 239-240. Dimitriev's armies held key positions during the Gorlice-Tarnow Offensive in 1915 and the Battle of Riga in 1917.
10. Ivanov resigned his commission after the Balkan Wars and never rejoined the colours.
11. Stoilov p. 49.
12. Rankin pp. 148-149.
13. Carnegie pp. 71-77, 109-124; Gibbs and Grant pp. 88-90.
14. Gibbs and Grant pp. 93-96.
15. For the battle of Kirkkilisse see Despot p. 83; Erickson pp. 86-100; Hall pp. 26-28; Hellenic Army pp. 92-93 para. 128; Hochwächter pp. 13-30; Howell pp. 47-84; Immanuel, *Guerre* Vols 2-4 pp. 37-50; Kutschbach pp. 106; Pastukhov pp. 241-245; Rankin pp. 151-152, 155-157; Rogers pp. 150-153; Ryabinin pp. 162-171; Yonov pp. 64-69 in Kiraly and Djordjevic— hereafter Yonov.
16. Details on the Bulgarian Artillery website—The forts of Lozengrad.
17. Bulgarian and Serbian forward observers were proficient in the use of telephones for direct or indirect fire. By contrast, Ottoman gunners always deployed in the open on forward slopes or occasionally just behind the crests of hills. Rogers p. 147.
18. Pastukhov p 246.
19. Hall pp. 27-28.
20. For the Battle of Luleburgaz see Ashmead-Bartlett pp. 139-167; Erickson pp. 101-122: Hall pp. 28-32; Hellenic Army pp. 92-93 para. 128; Howell pp. 85-138; Immanuel, *Guerre* Vols 2-3 pp. 51-70; Kutschbach pp. 106-107; Pastukhov pp. 250-251; Rankin pp. 275-276; Rogers pp. 153-154; Ryabinin pp. 172-184.
21. Ryabinin p. 174.
22. Howell p. 98.
23. Ashmead-Bartlett p. 92.
24. Pastukhov p. 251.
25. Ashmead-Bartlett p. 169.
26. Ashmead-Bartlett pp. 171-181, 213-214, 230; Erickson p. 121; Gibbs and Grant pp. 177-211; Rankin p. 277.
27. Ashmead-Bartlett pp. 250-251, 255, 260-262; Gibbs and Grant pp. 212-224.
28. For the Catalca Line campaigns see Ashmead-Bartlett pp. 267-273, 276-277; Despot p. 90; Erickson pp. 122-138, 272-274, 285-290; Gibbs and Grant pp. 232-234; Hall pp. 33-38, 90-91; Hellenic Army pp. 92-93 para. 128; Immanuel, *Guerre* Vols 2-3 pp. 71-98; Kutschbach pp. 107-108; Pastukhov pp. 254-258; Rankin pp. 453-454; Ryabinin pp. 184-194; Yonov pp. 73-75. Turkey in the First World War website: Balkan Wars Part II Balkan States against the Ottoman.
29. Erickson p. 122.
30. For details of the Catalca Line see Ashmead-Bartlett p. 268; Pastukhov pp. 252-253; Ryabinin p. 187; The Catalca position on the Bulgarian Artillery website.
31. During the last decades of the nineteenth century, Brialmont also designed fortifications for Bucharest, Sofia and the Dardanelles. A detailed report on the line in July 1900 is in UKNA ADM 121/70 'British Mediterranean Fleet'.
32. The Catalca Fortified Area was redesignated Catalca Defensive Position on 12 November. Erickson pp. 126-127.
33. Ryabinin p. 186.
34. Some reports suggest that this ordnance included the fifty-two Serbian 75-mm QFs seized at Salonika.
35. Despot p. 90.
36. Hall pp. 34-35.
37. *Op. cit.*, p. 36.
38. *Ibid.*, p. 36.

39. *Ibid.*, p. 43.

40. Trumpener p. 350.

41. By contrast, thanks to good field hygiene the armies on the Western Front between 1914 and 1918 were in relatively rude health until Spanish influenza swept through their ranks in 1918.

42. For the siege of Edirne see Despot p. 122; Erickson pp. 138-146; Gibbs and Grant pp. 97-111; Hall pp. 38-42, 86-90; Hellenic Army p. 93 para. 130; Immanuel, *Guerre* Vols 2-3 pp. 99-113, Vol. 4 pp. 43-61; Kutschbach pp. 88-95; Opacic pp. 92-93; Pastukhov pp. 270-279; Rankin pp. 442, 446-450; Ryabinin pp. 172, 194, 196; Yonov pp. 77-80. Websites of Syed Tanvir Wasti and Kingdom: First Balkan War—Edirne; Turkey in the First World War website: Balkan Wars Part II Balkan States against the Ottoman.

43. Hall pp. 38-39.

44. For details of the defences of Edirne see The Fortress of Odin entry on the Bulgarian Artillery website.

45. Erickson p. 275.

46. Rankin p. 447.

47. Hall p. 90.

48. For the campaign in western Thrace and the Rhodope Mountains see Crawfurd Price pp. 168-184; Erickson pp. 146-153; Hall pp. 42-43; Hellenic Army p. 93 para. 131; Ryabinin pp. 196-197; Yonov p. 75.

49. Armstrong p. 135.

50. For the Gallipoli campaigns see Erickson pp. 124, 127, 136-137, 153-157, 251-274, 282-284; Hall pp. 80-83; Hellenic Army p. 93 para. 129; Immanuel, *Guerre* Vols 2-3 pp. 99-113, Vol. 4 pp. 21-42; Pastukhov pp. 268-269; Rankin pp. 442-444; Ryabinin pp. 197-198; Yonov pp. 76-77.

51. Erickson p. 127. He identified three divisions, Canakkale, Trabzon and Afyon, but the first was the Gallipoli Reserve Division. The last was from the Catalca Army.

52. For the background see Hellenic Army p. 66 para. 93, pp. 69, 78 paras 96 & 106, pp. 104-105 para. 145. The British had also considered this idea, with a report prepared on 27 January 1896 by Colonel Herbert Chermside 'Feasibility of a Naval Force unexpectedly seizing the European side of the entrance of the Dardanelles', UKNA ADM 121/70.

53. Enver Pasha would lead Turkey into the First World War on the side of the Central Powers. Mustafa Kemal refused to allow him to fight alongside him against the Greeks after the First World War, having broken contact with him personally and the CUP in 1914. Enver Pasha would die fighting Communist forces in August 1922.

54. Erickson p. 258; Hall pp. 81-82.

55. Roll-on, roll-off (or ro-ro) is now an integral requirement in major amphibious warfare vessels.

Chapter 4

1. V Corps, for example, had fewer than 21,000 men against an establishment of 52,000. Erickson Table 5.2.

2. For Turkish Army preparations see Crawfurd Price pp. 51-55; Erickson pp. 163-171; Hall pp. 22, 24, 45; Ryabinin pp. 154-155, 199-202.

3. Skoko in Kiraly and Djordjevic pp. 20-21—hereafter Skoko.

4. For the occupation of the Sanjak and Kosovo see Aleksic-Pejkovic in Kiraly and Djordjevic pp. 171-173—hereafter Aleksic-Pejkovic; Despot pp. 93-94; Durisic pp. 127-134; Erickson pp. 201-204; Hall pp. 45-46, 53-56, 58-59; Hellenic Army pp. 90-91 paras 126, 127; Kutschbach p. 83; Pastukhov p. 297; Ryabinin pp. 210, 212; Skoko pp. 20-21. Kingdom: First Balkan War—Kumanovo, Raska and Albania.

5. Skoko pp. 17-18.

6. *Op. cit.*

7. Ratkovic p. 150.

8. Skoko pp. 17-18.
9. For Austro-Serbian relations during the First Balkan War see Vojvodic pp. 252-254. To put pressure upon Serbia, 200,000 troops were concentrated along its borders, while 190,000 were concentrated in Bosnia-Herzegovina, including XIII, XV & XVI Army Corps. Williamson p. 273.
10. Skoko pp. 21-22.
11. For the Serbian advance to the sea see Aleksic-Pejkovic pp. 171-173; Erickson pp. 196-199, 204-207; Hall pp. 52, 54-55, 85-86; Hellenic Army pp. 90-91 para. 126; Opacic p. 92; Rankin pp. 251, 253; Ryabinin p. 224; Skoko pp. 23-24. Kingdom: First Balkan War—Albania.
12. For the Battle of Kumanovo see Barby, *Victoire Serbes* pp. 49-78: Crawfurd Price pp. 67-76; Erickson pp. 179-181, 199-201; Hall pp. 45-49, 52-53; Hellenic Army pp. 89-90, 94 paras 122-123, 132; Immanuel, *Guerre* Vols 2-3 pp. 115-131; Kutschbach pp. 31-44, 66-76; Opacic pp. 90-91; Pastukhov pp. 286-289; Rankin pp. 158-159, 243; Ratkovic pp. 155-156; Ryabinin pp. 152-154, 202-209; Skoko pp. 17-23. Kingdom: First Balkan War—Kumanovo.
13. He would be assassinated by a Bulgarian IMRO member in Marseilles in 1934.
14. Skoko pp. 17-18.
15. Opacic p. 91; Skoko p. 21.
16. Ratkovic pp. 151-152.
17. The VI Corps commander is often referred to as Djavid Pasha.
18. Pastukhov p. 289.
19. Erickson p. 181. The latest study, by Despot pp. 95-96 fn. 370, gives Serbian casualties at 4,492 (1,200 dead and missing) and Ottoman casualties at 6,000, including 1,200 dead and 2,500 captured.
20. For the Battle of Prilep see Barby, *Victoire Serbes* pp. 109-117; Crawfurd Price pp. 152-154; Erickson pp. 184-187; Hall pp. 49-50; Hellenic Army p. 90 para. 124; Kutschbach pp. 44-49; Pastukhov pp. 291-292; Ryabinin pp. 209, 216-218. Kingdom: First Balkan War—Bitola.
21. UKNA FO 195/2437 p. 210.
22. Opacic pp. 91-92.
23. For the Battle of Bitola see Barby, *Victoire Serbes* pp. 119-149; Crawfurd Price pp. 149, 158-162; Erickson pp. 187-195; Hall pp. 50-52, 60-61; Hellenic Army p. 90 para. 125; Immanuel, *Guerre* Vols 2-3 pp. 131-141; Kutschbach pp. 50-66; Pastukhov p. 293; Ryabinin pp. 218-219. Kingdom: First Balkan War—Bitola.
24. He was replaced by Brigadier General Galip Pasha. Erickson p. 194.
25. For preparations see Cassevetti pp. 69-73, 75-77; Erickson pp. 211-214; Hall pp. 59, 62; Hellenic Army pp. 15-18 paras 19-21.
26. Cassevetti pp. 75-76.
27. He also was a founder of the modern Olympic movement at this time.
28. Cassevetti p. 77.
29. *Op. cit.*, p. 76. Danglis, who improved the French 75-mm mountain gun as the Schneider-Canet-Danglis, is also written Dangles.
30. Sapountzakis's name is also transliterated as Sapundzaki, Zapundzakis and Zapundsakis. This transliteration is from Hellenic Army.
31. For the Battle of Sarantaporo see Cassevetti pp. 78-84; Crawfurd-Price pp. 58-66; Erickson pp. 214-2198; HAD pp. 101-102; Hall pp. 59-60; Hellenic Army pp. 20-42 paras 28-56; Immanuel, *Guerre* Vols 2-3 p. 141; Pastukhov pp. 303-304; Rankin pp. 337-340; Ryabinin pp. 212-213.
32. Greek artillery was poorly trained in indirect fire and preferred to deploy within sight of the enemy. Rogers p. 147.
33. Cassevetti p. 82.
34. Constantine was later restored in 1920, but was again forced to abdicate in the aftermath of the disastrous Greco-Turkish War of 1919-22.
35. Cassevetti pp. 93-94.

36. The lake and surrounding area were drained from 1928 to 1932.
37. For the Battle of Giannitsa see Cassevetti pp. 86-93; Crawfurd-Price pp. 90-95; Erickson pp. 220-223; HAD pp. 101-102; Hellenic Army pp. 42-49 paras 56-65; Ryabinin p. 220.
38. Constantine's aeroplanes achieved little because they were usually grounded by bad weather and lacked airstrips. Cassevetti p. 124.
39. Rankin p. 341.
40. For the occupation of Salonika see Cassevetti pp. 95-97, 99-115; Crawfurd Price pp. 58-66, 86-103; Despot pp. 100-101, 106; Erickson pp. 219-226; Glenny pp. 179-187; HAD p. 102; Hall pp. 60-62; Hellenic Army pp. 49-61, 94-98 paras 66-82, 133-138; Pastukhov p. 304; Ryabinin pp. 223-224. For the development and importance of the port see Tsiuvandou.
41. It was the birthplace of Mustafa Kemal.
42. Trumpener p. 354. The former emperor remained under house arrest until his death in September 1918.
43. Some sources state that the main armament consisted of 210-mm weapons.
44. Hall p. 62.
45. Jowett pp. 15-16.
46. Kyril, who became Prince Regent when Boris died in 1943, was shot by Bulgaria's Communist rulers in February 1945.
47. Crawfurd Price pp. 227-230; Rankin pp. 382-384.
48. For operations in western Macedonia see Cassevetti pp. 115-126; Crawfurd-Price pp. 163-167; Erickson pp. 187, 196-199; HAD pp. 102-103; Hall pp. 60-62, 83; Hellenic Army pp. 61-68 paras 83-121; Ryabinin pp. 213.
49. Colonel Napoleon Stiles was given command of VII Division.
50. For the situation in Albania after the proclamation of independence see Aleksic-Pejkovic pp. 177-181.
51. Relations between the Greeks and the Serbs on the fringes of their territories remained tense. See Rankin p. 373.
52. Hellenic Army p. 104 para. 144.
53. For the advance into Epirus see Cassevetti pp. 128-140, 146; Erickson pp. 226-237; HAD pp. 104-105; Hall pp. 63-64; Hellenic Army pp. 118-139 paras 160-200; Immanuel, *Guerre* Vols 2-3 pp. 158-163; Rankin pp. 374-380; Ryabinin p. 215.
54. The Greeks in Epirus had to deal with both pro- and anti-Greek Albanians. Rankin p. 373.
55. A similar Italian volunteer force fought alongside the Greeks in 1897, and some of the survivors of this struggle now returned to Greece. The survivors of the second force returned home at the end of the First Balkan War. Jowett pp. 16-17.
56. For King George's view see Crawfurd Price p. 224.
57. For the siege of Ioannina see Cassevetti pp. 141-155; Erickson pp. 293-298, 300-304; Hall pp. 63-64, 83-85; Hellenic Army pp. 139-156, 158-159 paras 200-227, 231, 232; Immanuel, *Guerre* Vols 2-3 pp. 63-79, Vol. 4 pp. 63-79.
58. For details of the fortifications see Weeks pp. 264-266. Axis History Forum: The end of the Ottoman Empire Yanya/Yanina/Ioannina fortifications, posts from 31 March 2013.
59. For air operations in Epirus see Cassevetti pp. 156-157.
60. For operations in southern Albania see Erickson pp. 313-314; Hall pp. 85-86; Hellenic Army pp. 156-158 paras 228-230.
61. Erickson pp. 318-321.
62. For Montenegrin operations see Barby, *Victoire Serbes* pp. 169-183; Despot pp. 101-103, 122-124; Durisic pp. 126-130, 134; Erickson pp. 236-239; Hall pp. 55-57; Hellenic Army p. 91 para. 127; Immanuel, *Guerre* Vols 2-3 pp. 152-158; Kutschbach pp. 76-83; Rankin pp. 163-167, 243.
63. Rankin pp. 173,178, 184, 187-188.
64. For the siege of Shkoder see Durisic pp. 134-139; Erickson pp. 304-313; Hall pp. 55-56, 85-86, 91-95; Hellenic Army p. 91 para. 127; Immanuel, *Guerre* Vols 2-3 pp. 163-174, Vol. 4

pp. 81-89; Kutschbach pp. 84-88; Pastukhov pp. 297-300; Rankin pp. 170-172, 174, 177, 180-182, 184-186, 188, 191-195, 198-200, 209, 219-220, 222, 224-225; Kingdom: First Balkan War—Montenegro.

65. Rankin p. 191.
66. The assassin is reported to have been one of Esad Pasha's men, Osman Bali, who was executed by Albanian Communists after the Second World War.
67. For what was called 'The Scutari Crisis' see Aleksic-Pejkovic pp. 174-176, 182-191. For a contemporary view see Rankin pp. 196-239.
68. Durisic p. 138.
69. Erickson p. 320; Hall p. 94.

Chapter 5

1. For the war at sea see Cassevetti pp. 26-58; Crawfurd Price pp. 79-85; Hall pp. 62, 64-67, 92-93; Hellenic Army pp. 96-97, 105-115, 134-135, 143-144, 158-159; Robinson's report in Hythe *Brassey's Naval Annual* 1914 pp. 150-168; Immanuel, *Guerre* Vols 2-3 pp. 175-183, Vol. 4 pp. 93-100; Wilson pp. 274-281. Acta, notably Dimitrakopoulos pp. 51-60 and Higham pp. 107-111.
2. Robinson in Hythe *Brassey's Naval Annual* p. 151.
3. For operations in the Black Sea see Langensiepen and Güleryüz pp. 20-21; Robinson in Hythe *Brassey's Naval Annual* pp. 161-162; Wilson pp. 276-277; Petrov in Acta pp. 136-141.
4. Langensiepen and Güleryüz p. 25; Erickson p. 133; Hall pp. 36, 65-66; Robinson in Hythe *Brassey's Naval Annual* pp. 161-162.
5. Hall p. 33; Robinson in Hythe *Brassey's Naval Annual* pp. 166-167. The ships included the battleships *Emanuele Filiberto* and *Benedetto Brin* (Italian), *Panteleimon* and *Rostislav* (Russian), the battlecruiser *Goeben* (German), the armoured cruisers *Hampshire* (British), *Leon Gambetta* and *Victor Hugo* (French) and the protected or light cruisers *Admiral Aspern* and *Admiral Spaun* (Austrian), *Weymouth* (British), *Vineta* (German), *Coatit* (Italian), *Gelderland* (Netherlands), *Elisabeta* (Rumanian), *Reina Regente* (Spanish) and *Kagul* (Russian). UKNA Balkan War: Mediterranean Telegrams November and December 1912, ADM 116/1189. For the French Navy during the First Balkan War see Kessler in Acta pp. 63-73. For the British Navy see Grove in Acta pp. 97-100. For the US Navy see Hagan in Acta pp. 118-131.
6. Trumpener pp. 355-357.
7. For the Sarkoy landing see Erickson pp. 259-271; Hall pp. 80-82; Langensiepen and Güleryüz p. 25.
8. Fotakis p. 34.
9. The Merchant, later Light Cruiser, Squadron consisted of the SS *Arkadia, Athina, Esperia, Makedonia, Mykali, Pelops, Sapfo, Sfaktiria* and *Themistoklis* and would be the key element in the blockade. Gray p. 387.
10. Hellenic Army pp. 105-106 para. 147.
11. Fotakis pp. 47-48.
12. For the capture of the islands see Cassevetti pp. 39-40, 42-45; Erickson pp. 157-159; Hellenic Army pp. 107-115 paras 148-150; Robinson in Hythe *Brassey's Naval Annual* p. 160.
13. The grandfather of the *Ierax*'s commander came from the island of Psara.
14. For the blockade see Robinson in Hythe *Brassey's Naval Annual* p. 159; Schurman pp. 51-52.
15. Beehler p. 69. UKNA FO 195/2437 'The Balkan Wars'.
16. Fast Boats Command History. Hellenic Navy website (www) hellenicnavy.gr.
17. Details from website Naval Operations in the Dardanelles 1915. Although these figures relate to the Gallipoli campaign of 1915, the author notes that there had been no significant changes since the Balkan War. See also Beehler pp. 43-49, who appears generally to confirm these details. The 5th Heavy Artillery Regiment manned four forts at the entrance to the

Dardanelles, while the 3rd and 4th Heavy Artillery Regiments manned ten more forts on either side of the waterway. Erickson pp. 154-155. See also Beehler p. 45.

18. Fotakis p. 46.
19. The *Pelops* had earlier carried troops to Thasos and would participate in the occupation of Lesvos.
20. For Ottoman operations in the Aegean see Langensiepen and Güleryüz pp. 21-25, Appendix 17. Turkey in the First World War website: Balkan Wars Part II Balkan States against the Ottoman.
21. For the Battle of Elli see Cassevetti pp. 47-52; Langensiepen and Güleryüz pp. 21-22; Hall pp. 64-65; Robinson in Hythe *Brassey's Naval Annual* pp. 161-163; Wilson pp. 276-278. See also Stathakis p. 95 in Acta. Three decades later the *Averoff* was again the flagship of the Free Hellenic Navy commanded by Kountouriotis's son Theodoros.
22. He took the name Rauf Orbay in 1930.
23. For the cruise of the *Hamidieh* see Cassevetti pp. 52-55, 57-58; Güleryüz, *Cruisers* pp. 6-25; Hall pp. 92-93; Langensiepen and Güleryüz pp. 25-27; Robinson in Hythe *Brassey's Naval Annual* pp. 165-166; Wilson pp. 279-280.
24. Fotakis p. 51.
25. Athens protested that allowing the cruiser to re-coal in Port Said violated British neutrality, but London pointed out that Egypt was nominally still part of the Ottoman Empire. The Egyptians secretly provided him another 150 tons.
26. For the Battle of Lemnos see Langensiepen and Güleryüz pp. 22-24; Cassevetti pp. 56-57; Robinson in Hythe *Brassey's Naval Annual* pp. 161-165; Wilson pp. 276-279.
27. Cassevetti p. 58; Wilson pp. 280-281. Green's article 'Wings of Hellas' in *Flying Review*. See also Skoutelis in Acta pp. 45-47.
28. UKNA Balkan War FO 195/2436 pp. 307-309.
29. The torpedo boat received new engines in 1908 but could make only 10 knots.
30. For this and subsequent incidents in Salonika see Cassevetti pp. 40-42; Erickson p. 223; Hall p. 61; Langensiepen and Güleryüz pp. 19-20, 138, 168; Robinson in Hythe *Brassey's Naval Annual* pp. 159-160; Wilson p. 276. Cassevetti and Robinson quote Votsis's report.
31. The ships included the battleship *Ammiraglio di St Bon* (Italy), the armoured cruisers *Kaiserin und Konigin Maria Theresia* (Austria) and *Bruix* (France) and the protected cruisers *Medea* and *Yarmouth* (Britain) and *Oleg* (Russia). UKNA Balkan War: Mediterranean Telegrams November and December 1912, ADM 116/1189.
32. Cassevetti pp. 108-109.
33. For these operations see Cassevetti pp. 42-43; Hellenic Army pp. 96-97 para. 135.
34. Damianos was relieved by Commander Konstantinos Georgantas flying his flag in the gunboat RHS *Alpheos*.
35. The *Antalia* is described in some sources as a gunboat, but as a torpedo boat in *Jane's Fighting Ships*.
36. For naval operations in the Ionian Sea and Adriatic see Cassevetti p. 37; Hall p. 62; Hellenic Army pp. 118-119, 130-131, 134-135, 153, 156 paras 161, 185,191-192, 224, 228; Rankin p. 373; Wilson p. 275.
37. See Cassevetti pp. 32, 46; Hall pp. 65, 92-93; Hellenic Army pp. 98, 143-144, 158-159 paras 139, 207-208, 232; Langensiepen and Güleryüz pp. 15, 156, 192; Robinson in Hythe *Brassey's Naval Annual* pp. 160-161. The Greeks also transported more than 38,000 prisoners of war to camps in Greece.
38. The original plan was for the whole division to be shipped in fifty-one vessels, but this probably proved too expensive for Sofia. In February, five Greek steamers carried supplies for the Bulgarian Army in Gallipoli from the Austro-Hungarian port of Fiume. Constantinople ordered the cruiser *Hamidieh* to intercept the convoy but she never received the signal.

39. For the background see Kingdom: First Balkan War—Montenegro. Also Axis History Forum: End of the Ottoman Empire, Serbs at siege of Scutari, posts from April 2013.
40. I am greatly indebted to Admiral Paloubis for his help in understanding this incident; also Axis History Forum: End of the Ottoman Empire, Greek merchant ships at Shengjin/San Giovanni de Medea, posts from 20 August 2013.
41. For the Shkoder (Scutari) Crisis see Tibor Balla's article 'The military participation of the Austro-Hungarian Monarchy in the settlement of the Scutari crisis'. Also Hall p. 94; Helmreich pp. 310-325; Rankin pp. 235-238; Robinson in Hythe *Brassey's Naval Annual* p. 166; Stevenson pp. 266-271; Vojvodic pp. 254-256.
42. HAD p. 109; Hellenic Army p. 179 para. 270.
43. For the diplomatic background see Despot pp. 112-120, 131-135, 137-139; Erickson pp. 243-248, 317-318; Hall pp. 69-74, 77-79, 97, 101-102; Hellenic Army pp. 98-100 para. 140; Helmreich pp. 249-309, 326-340; Rankin pp. 416-437; Stevenson pp. 232-275.
44. For the Austro-Russian crisis 1912-13 see Williamson in Kiraly and Djordjevic pp. 273-293—hereafter Williamson. Also Herrmann, pp. 178-180, 194-197; Kiraly and Djordjevic pp. 260-285—hereafter Ekmecic; Rankin pp. 456-458; Stevenson pp. 234-243, 254, 256-266.
45. Herrmann pp. 150-161.
46. For a contemporary view of Albania and the crisis see Rankin pp. 389-404.
47. For a contemporary view of the London peace conference see Rankin pp. 405-415, 439-441, 444, 459-467, 495-522.
48. Despot pp. 164-167.
49. On 30 November, General Conrad arranged a mutual defence agreement between Bucharest and Vienna against Russia. In February 1913, Austria sold Rumania 60,000 rifles. Stevenson p. 244; Williamson p. 292.
50. For the break-up of the Balkan League see Cassevetti pp. 314-318; Crawfurd Price pp. 185-218, 231-242; Despot pp. 107, 111-112, 119-120, 124-131, 135-136; Hall pp. 74-77, 98-102; Hellenic Army pp. 164-168, 170-173, 175-176 paras 246-255, 258-261, 265-266; Helmreich pp. 341-367; Opacic pp. 94-96; Skoko p. 25.
51. All sides treated the civilian population of the 'wrong' ethnic group brutally, as reported by Carnegie pp. 78-92, 95-108, 135-147.
52. During the First Balkan War, Austria delivered 50,000 rifles to Bulgaria which it regarded as a potential ally against the Serbs. Stevenson p. 243.

Chapter 6

1. For the background to the new war see Carnegie pp. 49-69; Despot pp. 139, 143-147, 150; Erickson p. 321; Hall pp. 102-106, 110-111; Helmreich pp. 368-379; Schurman pp. 64-86, 94-106. For an interesting opinion on national viewpoints before and during the Second Balkan War see Pélissier's *Dix mois de guerre dans les Balkans*, Cassevetti pp. 309-314 and Rankin pp. 478-494, 523-530-531.
2. Skoko pp. 25-26. The texts and details of the orders were later captured and printed in Cassevetti pp. 319-320; Crawfurd Price pp. 265-270.
3. Despot p. 150.
4. Hall p. 105.
5. For military preparations see Cassevetti pp. 316-223; Ekmecic pp. 274-275; Hall pp. 107-111; Hellenic Army pp. 169-170, 177-178, paras 256-257, 267-268; Kutschbach pp. 104-106; Skoko pp. 26-28. Bulgarian Artillery website.
6. The new recruits were mostly assigned to the independent Serska, Dramska and Odrinska Brigades.
7. Skoko p. 25.
8. *Op. cit.*, p. 26.

9. Hellenic Army p. 178 para. 278.
10. Cassevetti pp. 318-319.
11. For the Battle of Bregalnica see Barby, *Brégalnitsa* pp. 73-98, 223-233, 251-259; Cassevetti pp. 327-328; Crawfurd Price pp. 248, 263; Despot pp. 151, 156; Hall pp. 105, 110-112, 114-117, 120-121; Kutschbach pp. 106-117; Pastukhov pp. 313-315; Skoko pp. 26-32; Yonov p. 80.
12. Published reports in 1914 by Bulgarian Army Inspector of Artillery, General Panteley Tzenov.
13. Cassevetti p. 328; Skoko pp. 30-31.
14. Barby, *Brégalnitsa* p. 243 notes that a Moravska I battery of 75-mm Quick Firers expended 7,173 rounds between 18 and 29 July.
15. For operations in the north see Barby, *Brégalnitsa* pp. 251-259; Hall pp. 116-117, 122-123; Kutschbach pp. 117-120; Skoko pp. 31-32.
16. For Kilkis-Lahanas see Cassevetti pp. 324-331; Crawfurd Price pp. 279-298; Despot p. 151; HAD pp. 106-109; Hall pp. 112-115; Hellenic Army pp. 177-188, 213 paras 267-274, 276-287, 338.
17. Since the battle Lake Koroneia has slowly been drained and by 2010 was almost dry.
18. For the Greek offensive see Cassevetti pp. 321-322, 328-330; Crawfurd Price pp. 275-278, 305-327; HAD pp. 107-109, 114-115; Hellenic Army pp. 179, 181, 188-196 paras 270, 272, 288-302; Pastukhov pp. 316-318.
19. For Kresna Pass see Cassevetti pp. 330-335; Crawfurd Price pp. 328-341; HAD p. 108; Hall pp. 112, 121-122, 127; Hellenic Army pp. 196-205, 214 paras 303-319, 340; Jowett p. 12; Yonov pp. 80-81.
20. Crawfurd Price p. 341. Published reports in 1914 by Bulgarian Army Inspector of Artillery, General Panteley Tzenov. This stated the losses were twenty Schneider 75-mm Quick Firers, forty-seven old 75 to 87-mm Krupp guns and six heavy guns (120-mm howitzers, 120-mm guns and 105-mm guns).
21. Petrescu pp. 35-41.
22. For Rumanian operations see Hall pp. 117-118; Petrescu pp. 58-65, 71-95.
23. He would become Premier three times between the wars.
24. The absence of opposition is highlighted by the fact that the Bulgarians lost only twenty guns to the Rumanians, mostly modern Schneiders. Published reports in 1914 by Bulgarian Army Inspector of Artillery, General Panteley Tzenov.
25. As Hall points out, Bulgaria would replay the invasion in September 1916 when Romania joined the alliance. Bulgarian troops seized southern Dobrogea and in conjunction with German and Austrian troops crossed the Danube at Svishtov to invade, defeat and occupy Romania. Hall p. 118.
26. For Ottoman operations see Ericsson pp. 322-328; Hall pp. 118-119; Pastukhov p. 320.
27. Hall p. 119.
28. Trumpener pp. 357.
29. For the diplomatic background to the end of the Second Balkan War see Despot pp. 157-163; Hall pp. 119-120, 123-129; Helmreich pp. 380-406; Stevenson pp. 352-357. For a contemporary view of the Treaty of Bucharest see Rankin pp. 537-541.
30. Stevenson p. 328.
31. Balkan War UKNA FO 195/2438. pp. 220-223.
32. Bailey pp. 220, 236.
33. Bailey p. 232; Barby, *Victoire Serbes* pp. 281-282 and *Brégalnitsa* p. 243.
34. Bailey pp. 226-227. A century later a somewhat similar view now prevails in artillery regiments the world over. However, here the emphasis is upon 'smart' munitions to replace weight of fire.
35. Herrmann pp. 180-198.
36. Stevenson pp. 298-329. For the strategic situation in 1914 see Stevenson pp. 329-408.
37. For Sarajevo see Glenny pp. 303-306. Franz Joseph described his heir as a 'rash fool'. Stevenson p. 48.

Bibliography

Books

Ahmad, Feroz: *The Young Turks* (Oxford: Clarendon Press, 1969).

Albertini, Luigi: *The Origins of the War of 1914 Vols 1-2* (Oxford University Press, 1952).

Anderson, Major David S.: *The Apple of Discord: Macedonia, the Balkan League, and the Military Topography of the First Balkan War* (Fort Leavenworth, Kansas: School of Advanced Military Studies, United States Army Command and General Staff College, 1993).

Armstrong, Hamilton Fish: *The New Balkans* (London: Harper & Brothers, 1926).

Ashmead-Bartlett, Ellis & Ashmead-Bartlett, Seabury: *With the Turks in Thrace* (New York: George H. Doran Co., 1913).

Bailey, Major-General Jonathan B. A.: *Field Artillery and Firepower* (Annapolis: Naval Institute Press, 2004).

Barby, Henry: *La Guerre Serbo-Bulgare: Brégalnitsa* (Paris: Bernard Grasset, 1914).

Barby, Henry: *La Guerre des Balkane: La Victoire Serbes* (Paris: Bernard Grasset, 1914).

Beehler, Commodore W. H.: *The History of the Italian-Turkish War September 29, 1911 to October 18, 1912* (Annapolis: US Naval Institute, 1913).

Bobroff, Ronald: *Roads to Glory: Late Imperial Russia and The Turkish Straits* (London: I. B. Tauris, 2006).

Bridge, F. R.: *Great Britain and Austria-Hungary 1906-1914: A Diplomatic History* (London: Weidenfeld & Nicolson, 1972).

Bridge, F. R.: *From Sadowa to Sarajevo: The Foreign Policy of Austria-Hungary, 1866-1914* (London: Routledge & Kegan Paul, 1972).

Buxton, Noel: *With the Bulgarian Staff* (New York: The Macmillan Company, 1913).

Carnegie Endowment for International Peace: *Report of the International Commission To Inquire into the Causes and Conduct of the Balkan Wars* (Washington DC: Endowment for International Peace, 1914).

Cassevetti, D. J.: *Hellas and the Balkan Wars* (London: T. Fisher Unwin, 1914).

Chase, George H. (ed.): *Greece of Tomorrow* (New York: American Friends of Greece, 1943).

Chesneau, Roger and Kolesnik, Eugene M. (eds): *Conway's All the World's Fighting Ships*

1860-1905 (London: Conway Maritime Press, 1979).

Cornwall, Mark (ed.): *The Last Years of Austria-Hungary* (University of Exeter Press, 1990).

Crampton, Richard: *A Short History of Modern Bulgaria* (Cambridge University Press, 1987).

Crampton, R. J.: *The Hollow Detente: Anglo-German Relations in the Balkans 1911-1914* (London: George Prior, 1979).

Crawfurd Price, W. H.: *The Balkan Cockpit: The Political and Military Story of the Balkan War in Macedonia* (London: T. Werner Laurie, 1914).

Despot, Igor: *The Balkan Wars in the Eyes of the Warring Parties: Perceptions and Interpretations* (Bloomington, Indiana: iUniverse, 2012).

Erickson, Edward J.: *Defeat in Detail: The Ottoman Army in the Balkans 1912-1913* (Westport, Conn.: Praeger, 2003).

Fotakis, Zisis: *Greek Naval Strategy and Policy 1910-1919* (London: Routledge, 2005).

General Staff (British): *Military Notes on the Balkan States August 1915* (London: Imperial War Museum, 1996).

Gerolymatos, André: *The Balkan Wars: Conquest, Revolution and Retribution from the Ottoman Era to the Twentieth Century and Beyond* (New York: Basic Books, 2002).

Gibbs, Philip and Grant, Bernard: *The Balkan War: Adventures of War with Cross and Crescent* (Boston: Small, Maynard and Co., 1913).

Glenny, Misha: *The Balkans 1804-1999: Nationalism, War and the Great Powers* (London: Granata Books, 2000).

Gray, Randal (ed.): *Conway's All the World's Fighting Ships 1906-1921* (London: Conway Maritime Press, 1985).

Gudmundsson, Bruce I.: *On Artillery* (Westport, Conn.: Praeger, 1993).

Güleryüz, Ahmet: *Ottoman Navy's Cruisers* (Istanbul: Denizler Kitabevi, 2011).

Güleryüz, Ahmet: *The Ottoman Navy Torpedoboats & Destroyers* (Istanbul: Denizler Kitabevi, 2011).

Hall, Richard C.: *The Balkan Wars 1912-1913: Prelude to the First World War* (London: Routledge, 2000).

Hellenic Army General Staff, Army History Directorate: *A Concise History of the Balkan Wars 1912-1913* (Athens: Army History Directorate Publications, 1998).

International Commission of Military History, Hellenic Committee of Military History: *Acta— International Symposium of Military History 'Moudros 92—'Pavlos Melas 92'* (Athens: Hellenic Committee of Military History, 1992).

Helmreich, Ernst Christian: *The Diplomacy of the Balkan Wars 1912-1913* (New York: Russell & Russell, 1938).

Hentea, Calin (Tr. Cristina Bordianu): *Brief Romanian Military History* (Lanham, Maryland: The Scarecrow Press, 2007).

Herrmann, David G.: *The Arming of Europe and the Making of the First World War* (Princeton University Press, 1996).

Hochwächter, G. von: *Mit den Türken in der Front: Im Stabe Mahmud Muchtar Paschas* (Berlin:

Ernst Siegfried Mittler und Sohn, 1913).

Horsetzky, General A. von: *A Short History of the Chief Campaigns in Europe since 1792* (London: John Murray, 1909).

Howell, Major P.: *The Campaign in Thrace 1912* (London: Hugh Rees, 1912).

Hutchison, Lieutenant Colonel G. S.: *Machine Guns: Their History and Tactical Employment* (London: Macmillan & Co., 1938).

Hythe, Viscount (ed.): *The Naval Annual 1912 (Brassey's)* (Portsmouth: J. Griffin & Co., 1912).

Hythe, Viscount (ed.): *The Naval Annual 1913 (Brassey's)* (Portsmouth: J. Griffin & Co., 1913).

Hythe, Viscount and Leyland, John (eds): *The Naval Annual 1914 (Brassey's)* (London: William Clowes & Son, 1914).

Immanuel, Lieutenant Colonel Friedrich: *La Guerre des Balkans de 1912* (four volumes in one book) (Paris: Henri Charles-Lavauzelle, 1913. (Also *Der Balkankrieg 1912–1913*. Berlin: Ernst Siegfried Mittler und Sohn, 1913).

Jane, Fred T.: *Fighting Ships 1912* (London: Sampson Low, Marston & Co., 1912).

Jane, Fred T.: *Fighting Ships 1913* (London: Sampson Low, Marston & Co., 1913).

Jowett, Philip S.: *Armies of the Balkan Wars 1912-13: The priming charge for the Great War.* Men-at-Arms Series, Book 466 (Botley: Osprey Publishing, 2011).

Kent, Marian (ed.): *The Great Powers and the End of the Ottoman Empire* (London: Routledge, 1996).

Kiraly, Bela K. and Djordjevic, Dimitrije (eds): *East Central European Society and the Balkan Wars* (New York: Columbia University Press, 1987).

Kutschbach, Albin: *Der Serben im Balkankrieg 1912-1913 und im krieg gegen die Bulgaren Auf Grund amtlichen Materials des Generalkommandos der Serbian Armee* (Stuttgart: Franckh'sche Verlagshandlung, 1913).

Langensiepen, Bernd and Güleryüz, Ahmet: *The Ottoman Steam Navy 1828-1923* (Annapolis: Naval Institute Press, 1995).

Le Queux, W. T.: *The Balkan Trouble or an Observer in the Near East* (London: Eveleigh Nash, 1912).

Lieven, D. C. B.: *Russia and the Origins of the First World War* (Basingstoke: Macmillan, 1983).

Paloubis, Vice Admiral Ioannis: *Balkanikoi Polemoi: O Nautikos Agonas 1912-1913/Balkan Wars: The Naval Struggle 1912-1913.* Third Edition. (Piraeus: Hellenic Maritime Museum, 2012).

Pastukhov, N. I.: *Balkanskie Voiniy* (Moscow: Book Trade and Publishing Association, 1914).

Pavlowitch, Stevan K.: *A History of the Balkans 1804-1945* (London: Longman, 1999).

Pélissier, Jean: *Dix mois de guerre dans les Balkans: Octobre 1912-Août 1913* (Paris: Librairie Académique Perrin, 1914).

Petrescu, Corvin M.: *Istoricul Campaniei Militare din Anul 1913* (Bucharest: Tipografia Ion C. Vacarescu, 1914).

Quataert, Donald: *The Ottoman Empire 1700-1922* (Cambridge University Press, 2005).

Ragsdale, Hugh (ed.): *Imperial Russian Foreign Policy* (Cambridge University Press, 1993).

Rankin, Reginald: *The Inner History of the Balkan War* (London: Constable and Co., 1914).

Rogers, Colonel H. C. B.: *Artillery Through the Ages* (London: Seeley Service and Co., 1971).

Rossos, Andrew: *Russia and the Balkans: Inter-Balkan Rivalries and Russian Foreign Policy 1908-1914* (University of Toronto Press, 1981).

Ryabinin, Alexander A.: *Balkanskaya Voina* (St Petersburg: Terra Fantastica, 2003).

Schmitt, Bernadotte E.: *The Annexation of Bosnia 1908-1909* (Cambridge University Press, 1937).

Schurman, Jacob Gould: *The Balkan Wars 1912-1913* (London: Humphrey Milford, and Princeton University Press, 1914).

Spears, Major-General Sir Edward: *Liaison 1914: A narrative of the Great Retreat* (London: Eyre & Spottiswoode, 1968).

Stephenson, Charles: *A Box of Sand: The Italo-Ottoman War 1911-1912* (Tilehurst: Tattered Flag, 2013).

Stevenson, David: *Armaments and the Coming of the War: Europe 1904-1914* (Oxford: Clarendon Press, 1996).

Stoker Jr, Donald J. and Grant, Jonathan A. (eds): *Girding for Battle: The Arms Trade in a Global Perspective, 1815-1940* (Westport, Conn.: Praeger, 2003).

Swire, J.: *Albania: The Rise of a Kingdom* (New York: Arno Press, 1971).

Tarnstrom, Ronald: *Balkan Battles.* (Lindsborg, Kansas: Trogan Books, 1998).

Taylor, A. J. P.: *The Struggle for Mastery in Europe 1848-1918* (Oxford University Press, 1954).

Thaden, Edward C.: *Russia and the Balkan Alliance of 1912* (Philadelphia: Pennsylvania State University Press, 1965).

Vacalopoulos, Apostolos; Svolopoulos, Constantinos D.; Kiraly, Belak (eds): *Southeast European Maritime Commerce and Naval Policies from the Mid-Eighteenth Century to 1914* (New York: Columbia University Press, 1968).

Vachkov, Alexander: *The Balkan War 1912-1913* (Sofia: Angela Publishing, 2005).

Warner, Denis & Warner, Peggy: *The Tide at Sunrise: A History of the Russo-Japanese War 1904-1905* (London: Angus and Robertson, 1975).

Weeks, Allan: *Castles of Northwest Greece: From the early Byzantine Period to the Eve of the First World War.* Aetos Press, Huddersfield, 2013.

Williamson Jr, Samuel R..: *Austria-Hungary and the Origins of the First World War* (New York: St Martin's Press, 1991).

Wilson, H. W.: *Battleships in Action. Volume 1* (London: Conway Maritime Press, 1995) (first published in London by Sampson Low, Marston & Co., 1926).

Articles

Aleksic-Pejkovic, Ljiljana: 'Political and Diplomatic Importance of the Balkan Wars' in Kiraly and Djordjevic, pp. 371-383.

Balla, Tibor: 'The military participation of the Austro-Hungarian Monarchy in the settlement of the Scutari crisis' in AARMS, Vol. 4, No. 1 (2005) 93-110.

Cazanisteanu, Constantin: 'The Military Potential of Romanian, 1900-1914' in Kiraly and Djordjevic, pp. 141-145.

Dimitrakopoulos, Vice Admiral A.: 'The Contribution of the Hellenic Navy to the Allied Effort

During the First Balkan War' in International Symposium of Military History 'Moudros 92', pp 51-60.

Djurisic, Mitar: 'Operations of the Montenegrin Army During the First Balkan War' in Kiraly and Djordjevic, pp. 126-140.

Grant, Jonathan A.: 'The Arms Trade in Eastern Europe' in Stoker and Grant pp. 25-41.

Green, William: 'Wings of Hellas' in *Flying Review*, June 1969.

Grove, E.: 'The Rising Sea Power of Greece: British reactions to the achievements of the Greek Navy in the First Balkan War' in International Symposium of Military History 'Moudros 92', pp. 97-101.

Hagan, Professor Kenneth J.: 'The US Navy's Response to the Balkan War of 1912' in International Symposium of Military History 'Moudros 92', pp. 118-131.

Hall, Richard C.: 'The Next War: The Influence of the Russo-Japanese War in Southeastern Europe and the Balkan Wars of 1912-1913' in The Journal of Slavic Military Studies, Vol. 17 No. 3 (July-September 2004).

Hellenic Army History Directorate, Army General headquarters: 'Hellenic Army Operations During the Balkan Wars' in Kiraly and Djordjevic, pp. 99-111.

Higham, Professor Robin: 'The Royal Navy and the Balkan Wars 1880-1914' in International Symposium of Military History 'Moudros 92', pp. 107-111.

Kessler, Contre Amiral Jean: 'Les Aspects Maritimes de la Première Guerre Balkanique à Travers les Archives de la Marine Française' in International Symposium of Military History 'Moudros 92', pp. 63-72.

Laroche, Colonel Serge: 'La Mission Militaire Française en Grèce de 1911 à 1913' in International Symposium of Military History 'Moudros 92', pp. 178-182.

Opacic, Petar: 'Political Ramifications of Serbo-Bulgarian Military Co-operation in the First Balkan War' in Kiraly and Djordjevic. pp. 85-98.

Papadrianos, Professor I.: 'The Negotiations Between Greece and Serbia for the Conclusion of an Alliance Treaty in 1912' in International Symposium of Military History 'Moudros 92', pp. 183-186.

Papathanassopoulos, Constantinos: 'The State and the Greek Commercial Fleet During the Nineteenth Century' in *Southeast European Maritime Commerce and Naval Policies from the Mid-Eighteenth Century to 1914*, pp. 177-187.

Petrov, Dr Ljudmil: 'Kampfhandlungen der Bulgarischen Flotte im Schwarzen Meer während des Balkankrieges 1912-1913' in International Symposium of Military History 'Moudros 92', pp. 136-141.

Rakocevic, Novica: 'The Organization and Character of the Montenegrin Army in the First Balkan War' in Kiraly and Djordjevic, pp. 112-125.

Ratkovic, Borislav: 'Mobilization of the Serbian Army for the First Balkan War, October 1912' in Kiraly and Djordjevic, pp. 146-157.

Robinson, Chas. N.: 'The Balkan War: Operations of the Greek and Turkish Fleets' in *The Naval Annual 1912 (Brassey's)*, pp. 150-168.

Rooney, Chris B.: 'The International Significance of British Naval Missions to the Ottoman Empire 1908-1914' in *Middle Eastern Studies*, Vol. 34 No. 1 (January 1998).

Skoko, Savo: 'An Analysis of the Strategy of Vojvoda Putnik During the Balkan Wars' in Kiraly and Djordjevic, pp. 17-34.

Skoutelis, Lieutenant General P.: 'The Aviation During the First Balkan War' in International Symposium of Military History 'Moudros 92', pp. 39-49.

Stathakis, Rear Admiral N. A.: 'Naval Tactics and their Impact on Balkan Wars 1912-1913' in International Symposium of Military History 'Moudros 92', pp. 94-96.

Stoilov, Petar: 'The Bulgarian Army in the Balkan Wars' in Kiraly and Djordjevic, pp. 35-62.

Trumpener, Ulrich: 'German Military Involvement in the First Balkan War' in Kiraly and Djordjevic, pp. 346-361.

Tsiuvandou, Theano: 'The Commercial Development and Economic Importance of the Port of Thessalonika from the End of the Eighteenth Century to the End of World War I' in *Southeast European Maritime Commerce and Naval Policies from the Mid-Eighteenth century to 1914*, pp. 273-279.

Vojvodic, Mihailo: 'Serbia and the First Balkan War: Political and Diplomatic Aspects' in Kiraly and Djordjevic, pp. 240-258.

Williamson Jr., Samuel R.: 'Military Dimensions of Habsburg-Romanov Relations During the Era of the Balkan Wars' in Kiraly and Djordjevic, pp. 317-337.

Yonov, Momchil: 'Bulgarian Military Operations in the Balkan Wars' in Kiraly and Djordjevic, pp. 63-84.

Websites

Axis History Forum: The end of the Ottoman Empire 1908-1923: http://forum.axishistory.com

Bulgarian Artillery: www.bulgarianartillery.it

Copyright Association 'Amanet', Uzice www.prvibalkanskirat.rs—*kraljevine srbija i crna gora i ratovima 1912-1918* (Kingdom of Serbia and Montenegro in the wars of 1912-1918).

Hellenic Navy: Fast Boats Command History: www.hellenicnavy.gr

Military Books: http://militera.lib.ru

Naval Operations in the Dardanelles 1915 by Piotr Nykiel: www.navyingallipoli.com

Turkey in the First World War: Balkan Wars Part II Balkan States against the Ottoman: www.turkeyswar.com/balkan.html